My vegetable love :
635 KLA

42714

Klaus, Carl H.
Solon Public Library

W9-BNQ-220

My Vegetable Love

A

JOURNAL

OF A

GROWING

SEASON

CARL H. KLAUS

MY VEGETABLE LOVE

A Frances Tenenbaum Book
HOUGHTON MIFFLIN COMPANY
BOSTON · NEW YORK
1996

For information about permission to reproduce selections from
this book, write to Permissions, Houghton Mifflin Company,
215 Park Avenue South, New York, New York 10003.

For information about this and other Houghton Mifflin trade
and reference books and multimedia products, visit
The Bookstore at Houghton Mifflin on the World Wide Web
at http://www.hmco.com/trade/.

Library of Congress Cataloging-in-Publication Data
Klaus, Carl H.
My vegetable love : a journal of a growing
season / Carl H. Klaus.
ISBN 0-395-78587-1
1. Vegetable garden — Iowa — Iowa City — Anecdotes.
2. Gardeners — Iowa — Iowa City — Anecdotes.
3. Klaus, Carl H.   I. Title.
SB320.7.I8K58   1996   96-17836
635'.092 — dc20   CIP

Printed in the United States of America

Book design by Robert Overholtzer

QUM 10 9 8 7 6 5 4 3 2 1

TO KATE

Acknowledgments

I am grateful to the University of Iowa for a research leave that gave me time to envision this journal and begin the work of turning my days into a daybook. Once under way, I was buoyed by the generosity of several people who took the time to read a few weeks or months or a draft of the entire season. For their thoughtful reactions and suggestions, I'm grateful to Connie Brothers, Bill Bulger, Rebecca Childers, Paul Diehl, Trudy Dittmar, David Hamilton, Diane Horton, Dan Roche, Mary Swander, and Tom Simmons. My special thanks to Mary Hussmann for her careful reading of every draft; also to Natalie Bowen and Liz Duvall for their meticulous copy editing and to Clay Harper for his assistance with the title. For her singular guidance in shaping the journal and finding a good home for it, I'm very grateful to my agent, Elizabeth Kaplan. For her sage advice in refining it and bringing it so attractively into print, I am very grateful to my editor, Frances Tenenbaum.

Most of all, I am indebted to Kate Franks for keeping me accurate and grammatical every day from March through November, and for putting up with this daily intrusion in her life. Without her sufferance of it — and her support — I could not have written this book.

Contents

My vegetable love should grow
Vaster than empires and more slow . . .

But at my back I always hear
Time's winged chariot hurrying near . . .

— Andrew Marvell, "To His Coy Mistress"

INTRODUCTION

I t's high summer, and I'm out in the yard, gazing at the back vegetable bed, the sun-filled site of tomatoes, peppers, and eggplants. Gazing because it's the day I've been waiting for ever since the first hard frost of last year — the day when all these warm-weather plants are pumping out ripe fruit again, all at the same time. Tomato vines along the back row more than five feet up the seven-foot poles, their red and green fruit entwined with leaves from top to bottom, like della Robbia garlands in the garden. Three-foot-tall cubanelle and Italian pepper plants along the next row, branching out like fruit trees — tropical fruit trees — bullhorn peppers dangling from their branches. An eggplant at each end of the row, their purple-veined leaves and long purple fruit framing the yellow-green, dark green, and red peppers. Bell pepper plants in front, branches beginning to bend under the weight of their fruit. Cherry tomato plants at each end of the row in large clay pots. A monument to Mediterranean cooking.

Which reminds me that I'm not just gazing. I'm harvesting things for the first all-fresh ratatouille of the summer. "Vegetable stew," according to my wife Kate. "Remember, we're in Iowa, not France. And besides, I don't cook it to death like the French." Actually, she cooks it like the Italians, quickly, so the vegetables retain more of their distinct colors, textures, and tastes. Which reminds me that on the way in I'm supposed to stop at the big vegetable garden for a green zucchini, a yellow pattypan, and a couple of onions. Then at the herb bed by the gazebo for some basil, parsley, and thyme. By the time I reach the back porch off the kitchen, my oak basket will be as fit for a still life as a stew.

A strange moment. So filled like the basket with heat and sunlight and color that I think it could easily last for months on end. Tomatoes and peppers and eggplants galore. Red and green and purple and more. And all the others too — beans, chard, cucumbers, okra, pattypans, zucchini. All the stuff for gazpacho, gumbo, baba ghanouj, and God knows what else. Until I suddenly realize it's just about time to seed up some flats of lettuce to go in front of the peppers a month or so from now. Fall lettuce exactly where I planted the spring greens back in mid-March. My head is spinning, fast forward and reverse. A month from now, the first cool nights of September. Two months from now, the first hard frost. And not even my row covers can keep those warm-weather vegetables warm enough to keep going for more than three months at most. Three months of high-summer harvest for nine or ten months of planning, seeding, transplanting, and tending. Seven months of harvest for all the vegetables, from May to December.

So many days, so many hours devoted to bringing on so many vegetables all at once that my basket runneth over, like a horn of plenty, with more than we can possibly eat fresh or can or freeze or pickle or preserve. Why is it, I wonder, that I go through all the hassle, when Kate and I can easily walk a few blocks to the nearest supermarket, or a few blocks more to the local co-op, and get all the fresh produce we need, as we do during most of the winter and early spring? Whenever I ask that question, as I do several times each gardening season, I always come up with the same answers. The freshness. The taste. The variety. The exercise. The fresh air. The challenge. The environment. The past. All the present virtues, all valid, but none of which convey what I go through in the garden or why I go through it day after day, week after week, month after month, year after year.

So, in an effort to make sense of it, I decided one day in mid-December of 1994 that I'd take stock of my garden and my gardening every day during the growing season of 1995. And every day write a brief report of my activities. From the first outdoor planting in early spring to the last harvest in very late fall, when the gardening catalogues for 1996 are beginning to arrive and winter dreamtime is about to begin. A vegetable gardener's year. But I didn't want to confine myself so narrowly to the vegetable garden that I ignored all the conditions that influence a gardener and his plants. So my reports regularly take stock of the weather and the seasons and everything else in my immediate world, which includes Kate, our Welsh terrier Pip, our foundling cat Phoebe, and the other gardens, trees, and shrubs we've been tending on our three-quarter-acre lot for the past twenty-five years. Especially Kate's sixty-foot ornamental flower border, centered near the back of the yard, changing like a vivid backdrop with the changing seasons. Also the various wild animals that live on our land or that pass through it. Crows, deer, groundhogs, moles, possums, rabbits, raccoons, squirrels, and sparrows — all the creatures that trouble the heart of an ardent vegetable gardener. Also from time to time our neighbors, our neighborhood, the university where I teach, as well as other places and people I encounter or think about on my walks in the City of Iowa City, where I live.

In the garden of Eden, where Adam and Eve lived, the sun, I assume, shone every day, except for brief periods of refreshing and replenishing showers. The seasons did not exist. Temperatures were continuously moderate — neither so cold nor so hot as to be even slightly uncomfortable. The weather, you might say, was ideal. The only biblical reference to it describes "the Lord God walking in the garden in the cool of the day," shortly after the serpent had tempted Eve, and Eve had tempted Adam to eat of the forbidden fruit. Change, on the other hand, is at the heart of my garden — so much so that if it didn't change, it wouldn't be an actual garden but some mythic place, like the garden of Eden, where there were no seasons or seasonal changes to be observed.

Like any reports in this world, the ones that follow are only as reliable as the reporter, who in this case makes no special claim for himself, except that he took stock of things every day during the growing season of 1995.

MARCH

Radishes seeded in earlier than ever before, thanks to the exceptional warm-up this week. Cherry Belle, French Breakfast, German Giant, Hailstone White. I planted them in the sandy sun trap of a plot along the south side of my neighbor Jim's garage. Jim wasn't home, so I prepared the bed myself. In less than an hour, the seeds were in and topped with one of my spun-bond polyester row covers — long strips of gauzelike material, stretched over metal hoops, that give the vegetables four to six degrees of additional warmth. I've never planted anything outside this early, so I'm curious to see what will come of them. Then I put in the onion sets — a twenty-foot row of diminutive onion bulbs, centered along the front edge of my own large vegetable bed. Though the soil was still a bit cool just below the surface, I was sweating from the suddenly elevated temperatures in the mid-seventies. Almost a hundred degrees higher than the wind-chill factor a week ago, when the garden was still covered with snow. Winter one week, spring the next. The top of the topsoil already dry enough along the front stretch of the bed that I could easily draw my hoe through it to loosen things up a bit before I leveled the row, set up my string line, and pressed the little bulbs in about two inches apart. They went in so easily the earth seemed as if it was meant for them. And now in a month or so we can begin harvesting every other one for scallions, leaving the others to swell into fully mature onions. Meanwhile, I can look down from my attic study, where

I'm writing this report, and see the string line marking the row. And perhaps see their green tips breaking through the soil in a week or so. An extraordinary prospect, thanks to El Niño — that periodic warm-up of the ocean off the coast of Peru that seems to be responsible for weather disruptions around the world. It's a long way from Peru to Iowa, but like many things in this world, they're connected by the wind.

If I didn't have a department meeting in an hour, I'd still be outside, transplanting the lettuce seedlings I started in mid-February. But the time's so short I couldn't get them all planted comfortably and pleasurably. Twenty-five years ago, I'd still be in the garden, frantically working to get everything in as fast as I could, even if I showed up at the meeting sweating and out of breath. Even if my back ached and my knees were stiff for the next three days. Bodily decrepitude is wisdom, all right. Also the fact that one day sooner or later makes little difference, especially when the gardening season is two or three weeks ahead of schedule, as it is right now.

But then I notice Phoebe curled up in the window seat behind my computer — her coon-ringed tail wrapped around her reddish-brown body, her faintly speckled head nestled in between her tail and legs. Napping as peaceably as she has for almost twenty years. Just a year ago, she seemed so robust, I thought she'd keep going four or five more years. Now she's come up with a cancerous tumor, and I wonder how many weeks or months she has to live. I don't know how to reckon the passing of time anymore, except to note that it's passing, and a month or so from now when the green onions and radishes are ready Phoebe may already be gone. Some harvest. In this year of El Niño, nothing's quite in sync or in season. Not even the seasons.

FRIDAY *March 17*

St. Patrick's Day. Traditionally the day to plant potatoes — in memory of the potato famine that brought the Irish to this country. But my clayey soil's never been dry enough or warm enough six inches down to plant potatoes this early, not even this year. So I marked the day, instead, by planting the greens — arugula, buttercrunch, Carmona butterhead, endive, escarole, Simpson green leaf, purple oak leaf, romaine, and radicchio. A double row. Forty plants in all. Usually an exhausting task given my desire not only to get them comfortably situated and fed, but also to have them attractively arranged from one end of the row to the other. Butterheads at each end of the row gradually rising toward the tall romaines in the center. Ruffled leaves alternating with straight edges. Dark greens or reds alternating with light greens. A compulsive's delight. But the soil was so easy to work and the mid-sixties temperature so comfortable to work in that it took me only a couple of hours to plant the seedlings and protect them against cold and rabbits and deer with a polyester row cover.

Speaking of row covers, I removed all the layers from the spinach I started last fall, pulled away the straw mulch from the sides and top of the plants, and discovered that the entire row had survived all the severe cold snaps of January, February, and early March. So, in a few weeks, we'll be eating spinach from the garden, thanks to the insulating powers of straw, the cold-resistant powers of spun-bond polyester, and the toughness of spinach itself. But the two artichoke plants didn't fare anywhere near so well. Only a few freeze-dried tatters of them under the straw. Something there is that doesn't love an Iowa winter. On the other hand, the artichoke that wintered over in the Plexiglas-covered outside cellarway has been sunning itself on the terrace wall for the past two days. The herb plants have also come up from the cellarway and are taking the sun at the south end of the gazebo.

Spring, it seems, is undeniably in residence. Even though the vernal equinox has not yet taken place. Even though I've not yet planted my peas, the ritual with which I traditionally mark the beginning of my spring gardening. Given this Niñoesque state of affairs, I decided to get in the rhythm of things and began the day by starting my eggplant, pepper, and tomato seedlings. Then in further obedience to the season, I moved all the broccoli and cauliflower to the outside cellarway — newly sprouted just five days after being planted last Sunday. Maybe it was just the influence of the full moon. Or the miraculous power of St. Patrick. But all the signs seem to agree that spring is here — at least for the time being.

SATURDAY *March 18*

According to my personal gardening calendar, today must be the first day of spring. For this morning, the soil in the west side of my garden was workable enough that I could rake it out, draw my hoe through it, kneel down beside the furrow, and plant a double row of snow peas — usually the first thing I plant outside each spring. The sky was overcast during the entire process, so the sun never shone on my right cheek, as I like it to do when I'm planting peas. But it did come out briefly after lunch when I was admiring the finished project. And the temperature was in the low- to mid-fifties, typical of early spring.

Peas. Their seeds are so large that planting them seems like kid stuff compared to the smaller seeds of most other vegetables. But from start to finish, the process of planting and tending them is a labor of love that yields abundance and sweetness only to those who are willing to give them the ardent care they demand. During my first few years of growing peas, I discovered they can easily rot before they germinate if sown too deep in a clayey soil such as ours, especially during the cold and damp period of early spring. Or they can break their necks trying to get through the hardened surface that forms on a clayey soil after a spring rain. Peas are by no means so tough as they seem from the hardened exterior of their dried seeds. So I now plant them no more than one inch deep and cover them with lightweight compost. Before adding the compost, I dust them lightly with a powdered bacterium to help them draw nitrogen from the soil. And when the planting is done, I protect the entire double row with a polyester row cover to raise the inside temperature a few degrees, keep the soil from being pummeled during a hard rain, and prevent the sparrows from pecking at the sweet and tender seedlings when they emerge.

But that's only the beginning of the process. After the seedlings have grown a few inches tall, I build a vertical structure of twigs and brush that arches over the plants on both sides, so their vines can climb up it to a height of about three or four feet and remain erect even in winds of sixty or seventy miles an hour. Also so their blossoms and pods are exposed to the air and the sunlight, rather than falling over and rotting on the ground. I learned this structure from observing the garden of my old neighbor Herman, who evidently learned it from his ancestors in Germany before he emigrated to the United States. And as I discovered from an illustration in one of Kate's medieval books of hours, the twig and brush structure for supporting peas is at least five hundred years old. Domesticated peas themselves have been dated as far back as 9750 B.C. to a "spirit cave" on the border between Burma and Thailand.

So, in the slightly chill air of an overcast morning, I felt as if I were taking part in an enduring primeval ritual, befitting the advent of spring.

SUNDAY *March 19*

Spring yesterday, and today I'm already working on summer, starting a few more seedlings of the patio cherry tomato to follow the ones now developing in the outside cellarway. Also a few seeds of the Ecuadorian relleno pepper and Brandywine tomato that arrived yesterday in the mail. Nothing special about starting them in the house. I just wet down some seed starting mix, put it in plastic six-packs, seed it up, then put the six-packs in a covered plastic tray to keep things moist, and put the tray on a radiator to keep it warm. Germination usually takes place in a week or so.

But there was something about the picture of that Brandywine tomato on the seed packet that caught my eye, just as I'd been captivated by that picture when I first saw it in the catalogue several weeks ago. I guess it was the pinkish coloring of the skin and the faint green stripes on the shoulders that surprised me — so different from the uniformly red sheen of most tomatoes that one sees in the gardening catalogues. Not a glossily assertive modern-day tomato, jumping off the page, but an heirloom tomato that almost seemed to be fading out a bit, like the memory of my first fresh-picked garden tomato.

It was a hot summer that August in Cleveland. 1940 or '41. I and my older brother Marshall were out for a Sunday afternoon in the country at the farm of my cousin Art, a distant cousin, old enough to be one of my grandparents. The farm itself was more like a country estate, a large white clapboard showplace with a wide wraparound porch. A place that Art and his family used as much for business and entertaining as for a weekend retreat from their two-story apartment in Shaker Heights. I can't remember who all was there that Sunday. But I can remember Art, the gruff multi-millionaire, telling the resident caretaker to "get each of them a salt shaker and take them out to the tomato plants." And I can remember the caretaker telling me just to pull one of the tomatoes off the plant, take a little bite, shake a little salt on the exposed part of the tomato, take another bite, and so on. The warmth and juiciness and piquancy of those first few bites have been in my mind's mouth ever since. And ever since I started gardening, I've been trying to grow a tomato that would taste like the one I picked off the vine on that hot day in August with a salt shaker in my hand.

So, when I looked at that haunting picture of the Brandywine on this overcast, chilly morning, I thought it might be the way back to those fifty-year-old tomatoes of my childhood, especially because the Brandywine, an Amish heirloom, was preserved by a seed-saver who lived during the first half of this century. You can't go home again, I know, but an heirloom tomato may be able to get you a bit closer than a hybrid. I'll know better come August.

MONDAY *March 20*

Meanwhile, back here in March, the first rainstorm of the year finally arrived last night around midnight, complete with lightning and thunder, and more rain fell this morning. Enough to saturate the soil that had been drying out during the unusual warmth of last week. Also enough to cool and slow down all the prematurely budding trees, shrubs, vines, brambles, and perennials. The leonine side of March also blustered in with a northwest wind gusting up to thirty-five miles an hour. An uncomfortable day for people, a blessing for things in the garden.

But a near-freezing temperature scheduled for this evening had me shuttling all the tender herb plants from the gazebo back to the house. And the tomato seedlings from the cool of the outside cellarway back up to the warmth of the kitchen, then back down again, when Kate and I agreed they're sturdy enough to take it down there. Ever watchful and fretful, like nurses in a preemie ward, we continually check on our seedling trays. Are they germinating on time? Have new ones emerged? Are they shedding their seed husks in good order? Do they need their surfaces moistened or bottoms watered? And we're continually moving them back and forth between radiators or other warm spots at night to window sills during the day, or the terrace if it's warm enough and calm enough outside. Kate's already tending about two hundred flower seedlings for our yard and the neighborhood park, and before long she'll be up to about five hundred. So my hundred vegetable seedlings are a breeze.

Especially by comparison with the fifty graduate students I was tending last year at this time, when I was still directing our program in nonfiction writing. Students looking for advice about admission, or courses, or manuscripts, or theses, or financial aid, or jobs, or publishers, or agents, or doctors, or writing blocks. Back then, they came to see me or waited to see me almost every day of the week, as I was reminded recently by my colleague Carol, whose office is next to mine. "Aren't you delighted to be free of all that?" Well, yes, I couldn't deny that I was happy to be free of all that. To be working on my own writing. But upon reflection, I also had to admit there was a time, and not so long ago, when I was happy to be involved in all of that. To be of help, to have a good influence, to build an outstanding program. Why is it, I wonder, that I no longer care to do such things so much as I once did? Is it just fatigue? Or burnout? Or is it also selfishness? Or some irrepressible desire to withdraw? Or even to be estranged, as a way of preempting the inevitable estrangement to come? Now, at last, I think I'm beginning to understand why some of my retired colleagues seemed to behave so strangely in the years shortly before their retirement.

TUESDAY *March 21*

Though spring arrived for me last Saturday, when I planted the Oregon Giant snow peas, I could hardly ignore its arrival today, in keeping with the vernal equinox, the most ancient and reliable standard for determining the onset of spring. What better way to mark this season of rebirth than by dating it from the moment at which the earth's orbit around the sun begins to yield a greater amount of daylight than darkness, of warmth rather than chilliness, of growth rather than decay. And on all counts, this day fulfilled its promise — from a light frost and a clear sunrise to a mild afternoon in the mid-fifties with scattered clouds moving across the sun. And a few daffodil buds beginning to make their way above ground in Kate's perennial border, and a few tulip leaves beginning to break ground by the edge of the terrace.

But for me the most special gift of the day arrived first thing, when I went to the radiator in the living room to check the tray of eggplant, pepper, and tomato seeds I planted last Friday and discovered that almost all the Enchantment and Whopper tomatoes had emerged, their seed husks shucked and seed leaves fully unfurled, seeking the light. A few came up yesterday, but their husks were still clinging so tightly to their leaves that I was fretting to Kate about my potentially stifled newborns. "Just keep them misted with the spray bottle, and they'll take care of the rest. There's nothing else you can do, except to stop fussing over them." So, thanks to Kate and the mist and the plants themselves, our main crop of tomatoes is safely underway, just five days after the seeds were planted. If I didn't know any better, I'd say the vernal equinox itself had something to do with their swift emergence. But then I'd be hard put to explain why only one of the Big Beef tomatoes had emerged — a delay that can only be attributed to the fact that Big Beef's a later tomato and thus takes longer to germinate.

Every hybrid, it seems, has its own internal clock and thermometer that determine the number of days and the temperature it will take to germinate, mature, flower, bear fruit, and die. Within the span of those days and temperatures, individual variations will depend on soil and weather conditions. But the boundaries are firmly fixed by the genetic control of the hybridizers. I've often wondered about my own boundaries, but my parents died too early — from breast cancer and postoperative blood poisoning — to reveal anything about the genetic controls that have been bred into me. All I know is that my clock's still ticking and my thermometer's still rising on this equinoctial day of days. And for that I'm grateful to the sun and the soil and the vernal weather of my life.

WEDNESDAY *March 22*

The university's spring break started last Saturday, so for the first time in several years it's actually coordinated with the beginning of the season itself. The only problem is that the ground's still so wet and cold from the recent rain that I can't get into either of the vegetable gardens to plant any more seeds or seedlings. And the ones I planted at the height of last week's warmth are now cooling their heels under the row covers, as I discovered this morning when I went out to check on things and take a few snapshots for the records. The onion sets haven't yet begun to put up any green tips, the lettuces have grown just a bit, the radishes by Jim's garage are just breaking ground, and the snow peas haven't shown any signs of emerging. For all I know the peas may be on the verge of rotting, so I'm thinking about adding another row cover to heat things up a bit more and possibly bring them on a bit sooner. Ever fretful, ever fretful. And now, in keeping with my fretfulness and the overcast sky, I'm worrying about the rains predicted for later this evening. Yet just last week I was worrying about the dryness and the lack of rain. In the world of a compulsive gardener, there's always something to fret about. Maybe that's why Kate was musing yesterday about my fuss over the emergent tomato seedlings. "Sometimes I wonder what goes on inside that head of yours."

Maybe she'd not be so puzzled about the inside of my head if she were a vegetable gardener rather than a perennial gardener. Every spring I have to start my whole garden over from scratch, uncertain of what might happen with every vegetable at every point along the way, whereas she's sitting in the catbird seat, everything in her bed already well established and she just calmly waiting for all her things to emerge, each in its turn. But then again, I wouldn't trade places with her, given all the digging and dividing that has to be done every year in a perennial bed just to prevent overcrowding and to make room for new varieties. Whereas I can easily make wholesale changes in the selection and arrangement of things in my garden without any trouble at all.

Actually, I'm far less troubled about the spring vegetables right now than I am about the spring break. It's not that I have anything against it as such. Who in his right mind could possibly be at odds with a spring break? It's just that I don't really feel as if I'm having one. Because, when all is said and done, I don't think my work load this semester has been so heavy that I need a break from it. Just teaching one course, serving on one committee, directing a couple of theses, and writing these gardening reports. So light a load I sometimes feel as if I've been on a break all along. In fact, I didn't even know when the break was coming this semester, until someone asked me what I planned to be doing this week. Usually I can't wait for it to come, just to catch up with the mail and all my other professional obligations. I suppose that I oughtn't to be worrying about it, since I'm being paid a part-time rather than a full-time salary. And besides, the light load this semester can't begin to compensate for the overload of theses and committee assignments and administrative work I carried during the past two years of my phased-in retirement. I guess it's just that I'm having trouble making sense of this transitional season in my life, when I find myself so betwixt and between that I still can't decide whether I should put on another row cover or be happy with the temperatures just as they are.

THURSDAY *March 23*

The summer vegetables also have me feeling betwixt and between. The eggplants I started last Friday emerged today, their heads up and seed husks shed. The second batch of patio tomatoes I planted on Sunday were also up, the fabled Brandywines had broken ground, and most of the peppers I planted last Friday were emerging. Such quick germination all around should have been cause for celebration. But I was puzzling over the laggard and spotty germination of the Big Beef tomatoes, only three of the twelve seeds up thus far. In years past, I'd have fretted far longer than the few minutes I fussed over them this morning, even though I didn't need any more than the three already up, except perhaps for a few spares. This morning, instead, I felt impelled to order some of the dark Russian tomatoes that Kate's been talking about — the Black Prince and Black Krim. If I can't get all the certainty I'd like with the All-American award-winning, multiply-disease-resistant Big Beef hybrid tomato, then I might as well live with some of the uncertainty of those Russian heirloom tomatoes, so I can see if they really do have a "rich, earthy, almost smoky flavor" to go along with the "exotic" color of their skin and interior. Besides, anything that can survive all the uncertainties of Russian life and the harshness of Siberian weather must certainly have enough resistance to stand up against anything it might encounter in the soil and air of an Iowa summer. Or so I hope.

The hunger for certainty or at least a measure of control. Such irrepressible desires have probably been felt by most vegetable gardeners who have watched their tomato plants succumb to any of the numerous diseases that can suddenly make a plant go limp or its leaves gradually speckle, turn brown, curl up, and die. After it happened to me a couple of times, I started switching over to the disease resistant hybrids. But I still found myself having to use some organic fungicides to curtail the diseases. And the tomatoes themselves were never quite so piquant and meaty and juicy as the preresistant hybrids and heirlooms. Not even the hybrids with the "old-fashioned" taste. I guess that's when I realized that in gaining control over one thing I'd lost control over another. Somewhat like the experience of going on betablockers to control my blood pressure and then losing control of my ability to drink more than two or three glasses of wine. In each case, it seems, survival has come at the expense of something precious. Though I don't have much choice about my blood pressure, I do about my tomatoes. So, in my tomato bed, if not in my body, I'm planning a minor rebellion, a Russian revolution.

FRIDAY *March 24*

lear skies all the way from here to the East Coast. Perfect weather for flying to Washington, D.C. But before the flight, I have to water the newly sprouted eggplant, pepper, and tomato seedlings and put them on the south window sill in our bedroom. Also put a row cover on the onion sets and another over the lettuce seedlings to protect them from the nighttime freezes. And eyeball things in the yard to see what else is going on. The grass is greening, daffodils swelling, and blue squills opening. I feel a twinge about leaving on so vivid a spring day as this, even though there's nothing I can do in the wet, cold soil of the vegetable gardens. I also wish Kate were coming, for Washington is special to both of us from a train trip we took there fifteen years ago this month. A trip that included a visit to Mount Vernon and a tour of its gardens on just such a bright and brisk day as this. But this time, we agreed, our budget's too tight for both of us to go.

So I'm on my way alone to a meeting of college writing teachers, a convention I've been going to for almost thirty years. The first time I went, I was still a young member of the department, and the organization was still a relatively small group of about six hundred people, many of them devoted teachers from modest schools, who knew each other so well from their annual get-togethers that the meeting felt like a large family reunion. Now I'm on the verge of retirement, and the convention attracts three to four thousand people, many of them ambitious academicians in the heady fields of rhetorical theory, research on written composition, and studies in literacy — fields that have burgeoned in the wake of the longstanding literacy crisis the country first recognized about twenty years ago. I once tried my hand at dealing with that problem during the late seventies and early eighties, when I directed the Institute on Writing, a five-year project funded by the National Endowment for the Humanities and the University of Iowa to improve the teaching of writing at colleges and universities throughout the country. But in the ten years that have passed since my heart attack, I've turned my attention to the quieter precincts of the personal essay. So tomorrow, instead of stirring up two or three hundred people, as I did twenty years ago, with a fiery talk about reforming the graduate training of writing instructors, I'll be guiding a workshop in the personal essay for two or three other writing teachers. If I didn't know any better, I'd feel like an outsider here. But it takes all kinds to make a professional meeting. Besides, I'll also get to see two former graduate students, Doug and Laura, dine with my textbook collaborators, Nancy and Rebecca, and revel in the splendid food, fine wines, and amusing stories of my sometime editor Tom. Not what you'd call a busy or influential schedule of professional activities. But a rich harvest for me.

SATURDAY *March 25*

One of the best ways to attend a professional convention is not to go to any of the meetings, especially if it's taking place in Washington. And that's what I did this bright, brisk, windy morning with the help of Laura and her trusty map of the city. We started with breakfast at the Old Ebbitt Grill, a wood-paneled eatery serving traditional fare in a straightforward style befitting its name. And from there we progressed down Pennsylvania Avenue, taking in the Treasury Building, the White House, and the Old Executive Office Building. Then around the block — some block — to the back of the White House and a view of the Mall and the Washington Monument in the distance, surrounded by the fluttering of kites and the flights of migrating birds.

The sidewalks were also aswarm with tourists, gawking like us at the White House. "The wedding cake," as Kate calls it, was being circled by a steady stream of people, who didn't seem to be paying much attention to the amplified sounds of their tour guide resonating around the block. "Now you are about to see the historic . . ." Though I didn't see any of the historic interior, I did see enough of the exterior to notice that it needs some touching up here and there, judging from the grayish patches on both of the left-hand columns of the front portico. But the grounds seem to be in excellent shape and much further along than ours. The grass all greened up. A large vibrantly yellow forsythia bush, a large pink and white magnolia, and a large cream-white magnolia on each side of the lawn.

A neoclassically balanced layout that suddenly transported me back to the day like this some fifteen years ago when Kate and I were walking the carefully planted grounds of Mount Vernon. If that were the only moment of reverie, the morning would have been simple enough. But a bit later, inside the Corcoran Gallery, looking at a large nineteenth-century American oil of a turquoise lake backed by a range of snow-covered mountain peaks, I suddenly felt as if I were inside the Boston Museum of Fine Arts, where I'd been just a few years ago at this time with Kate, reveling in the romantic vistas of nineteenth-century American landscape painting. Actually, if I'd just been remembering the vistas that Kate and I had seen together, the morning would have been complicated enough. But I was also listening to Laura worry about the vistas of her life that seem to have led her away from the path she wants to follow. So I too was thinking about all the ways I had allowed my own professional life to be drawn away from the path I had originally intended to follow. And I was just on the verge of telling Laura not to make the same mistakes that I had, when it occurred to me that perhaps none of those directions had been misleading, that they might all be taking her somewhere else, the terrain of which would only be clear after she had arrived.

SUNDAY *March 26*

Three hours ago, I was sitting under an umbrella at La Tomate, a restaurant in Washington, having a late lunch with Don, a former graduate student who works in the city. Though the breeze on the Mall was still strong enough for the kite fliers, an aged man at the table next to ours quickly let us know that the air was warm enough to dine outside without an overcoat or jacket. "You don't need any of that heavy stuff you're wearing. Just take it off and enjoy yourselves." Now, as I write this, I'm sitting in O'Hare Airport in Chicago, and still don't need any of that heavy stuff. But outside I certainly would, for the temperature here is in the low forties.

So I'd much rather be back at that table with Don, especially because his story, and the advice of the grinning old man, had me thinking again about various ways of weathering life. Traveling light, like the old man? Or heavily accoutered like Don, who's the only person I've ever known with three separate master's degrees — one in business, one in literature, and one in nonfiction writing. He's a man of many caps and gowns. And at various times in his life, he's worn them all, separately and in combination. And usually with great success. He's taught business writing at two different schools. Been a speechwriter for presidents of some of the largest corporations in America, as well as for some of the most powerful figures in Washington. And written five books on investing. But for all the success, he's never seemed comfortable in any of his caps and gowns. Just last year, he tells me, his situation was so unsettled he was thinking of coming back to graduate school.

I wonder why he keeps moving around from one climate to another. Curiosity? Indecision? Short attention span? Disenchantment? I also wonder why I've never tried anything beyond my life in the academy. Cautiousness? Cowardice? Laziness? Contentment? I sometimes wish it were possible for me to answer such questions as simply as they can be asked. Like a multiple choice exam. Or, better still, like the seventy-seven-year-old cabby who was taking me to the airport after lunch, when I asked him why he had moved from New York City to Washington. "I grew up on the Lower East Side. Know what I mean? I wanted to better myself. Didn't want to be shining shoes all my life for the guys in the pool hall. The ones with the patent leather shoes. Remember those? So I came here and got a job laying bricks. And for forty years I made good money at it. Made enough to get my own cab. Know what I mean?" I knew what he meant, because he too was traveling light. Or seemed to be. Just him and his cab — no jacket, no hat, his sleeves rolled up, his white hair waving in the breeze.

MONDAY *March 27*

F lying home last night from Chicago to Cedar Rapids was like riding a bucking bronco all the way. The man sitting next to me had his hands gripped tightly to both of the arm rests all the way. And I kept trying to distract myself with thoughts of Kate and the garden. Suddenly, Washington seemed a thousand miles away. And it felt a thousand miles away when we landed. The skies heavily overcast. Temperature in the high thirties. And the wind gusting up to around thirty miles an hour. But it felt good to be back where I belong, with Kate, and mildly amusing on the way home from the airport to stop at the Tomato Pie, another restaurant named in honor of my favorite vegetable. And when we finally got home, it was also a pleasant surprise to see that the Big Beef tomatoes I'd been fretting about last Thursday had all emerged while I'd been away. If I didn't know any better, I'd say a watched seed never germinates. But I imagine the seed-lings were slow to break ground because I planted them a bit too deep.

Still, it's always a surprise to return home and notice how much has changed in one's absence, even in so short a time as two or three days. Last night, I noticed the Salsa peppers were finally beginning to emerge, the Ecuadorian relleno peppers had all broken ground, the seed leaves of the eggplants were almost twice as large, and many of the tomato seedlings were beginning to form their first pair of true leaves. And this morning, when I checked things outside, I was pleased to see the radishes at Jim's were all up, the entire row of onion sets had finally begun to show their green tips, the lettuce seedlings were forming new central leaves, and even the snow peas seemed on the verge of breaking ground, judging from the humped-up soil down the middle of both rows. Despite the chill air of the last few days, growth is irrepressible this time of year, especially under those row covers.

But even outside the covers, everything has been taking its course. The chives a bit taller, the grass a bit greener, the daffodil buds a bit yellower, the apple, cherry, and pear buds a bit larger. If all this can happen in just a few days, I wonder what things might look like if I were away for a week, or a month, or six months. Or forever. The thought is irrepressible, as it's been all the time I've been gone. And coming back, it seems, does not entirely dispel it. Nothing ever does, of course. But it does help just to be back again, with Kate again, in the place where I belong again, watching the world come to life again, with a bit of a nudge from my hand again. And again and again and again.

TUESDAY *March 28*

The one thing that doesn't need any nudging right now is Kate's sixty-foot perennial border, everything coming up just as it's supposed to do. Ferny, black-stemmed leaves of the feverfews. Spear-shaped leaves of the day lilies, magic lilies, and Siberian iris. Dark green rosettes of the coral bells. Silver-gray rosettes of the mulleins. Lacy-gray leaves of the yarrows. Hairy green crowns of the poppies. Mahogany tips of the peonies. No wonder she thinks "it's sexy" just to see all that foliage making its way above ground. So different from the rich brown hues of late fall and the faded colors of winter. So different too from everything to come, it's always a bit hard for me to believe the bed will actually make its way through five distinctly different bloom periods, even though most of the foliage comes up in March and April.

Twenty-five years ago, when we moved in here, I didn't know anything about perennial gardening, and only the most obvious things about bulb gardening. So it never occurred to me that someone might design a bed like Kate's, to bloom all spring, summer, and early fall, in a staggered series of coordinated colors, textures, structures, and heights. And Kate herself didn't begin with such a fully worked-out scheme. In the beginning, as I recall, we just planted a slew of yellow daffodils across the back lot. Then my colleague Fred, a master day lily gardener and breeder, gave her several flats of his divisions, and we rescued a mess of iris from the demolition of a temporary housing site on campus. And before I knew it, Kate was on her way to this bed for all seasons, each year culling out some things and giving them to the neighborhood park, or to our neighbor Jim, or to our gardening friend Rebecca, or to others around town, but each year cramming in more and more varieties, each year pushing the bed to bloom later and later, in more fully articulated bloom periods, with matching blooms distributed across the bed in carefully disguised balances and repeats during every one of the periods. First the yellow tulips, the white daffodils, and the blue Jacob's ladder coming on the next few weeks. Then so many more in each of the later bloom periods

I can hardly remember them all until they actually appear. And to think I once imagined myself engaged in a fancy juggling act just to go from spring to summer to fall vegetables. Oh yes, I too have my balances and my repeats — snow peas at one end matching shell peas at the other, broccoli at one end matching cauliflower at the other, and so on. But all the while I was proudly constructing my tidy little neoclassical balances, she was quietly but systematically creating a five-act play at the back of the yard. Still, I'd rather have it this way than both of us squabbling over the same plot.

WEDNESDAY *March 29*

For an hour or two this morning, when I was thinning and transplanting the young broccoli and cauliflower seedlings, the sun was shining and the eastern portion of the sky was mostly blue. So vivid and inviting outside after yesterday's gloomy pallor, I could hardly keep myself at the kitchen sink stuffing each of the seedlings into its own slot and filling them up with a wet transplanting mix. And two or three times, I couldn't resist the temptation to go outside in my pajamas and take stock of things in the back yard. Though the temperature then was only in the low forties, the air each time felt surprisingly warm, thanks to the sun. But a few hours later when I was getting ready to walk down to campus, the clouds had built up so heavily in the southeastern sky that I decided to put on all my winter gear — gloves, muffler, hood, and parka. Firsthand proof that along with everything else it brings, spring also marks the beginning of the time when the amount of cloud cover has an important hand in determining not only how light or dark the day will be, but also how warm or cool the air will be, blocking or releasing the warmth of the sun.

Uncertain skies. Uncertain weather. No wonder everything in the back yard is coming on so slowly, so deliberately, that it seems as if the buds or leaves could possibly even pull back, or turn in upon themselves, if we were about to have one of those fabled spring blizzards like the one of '74, when twelve inches of snow fell overnight during the second week of April. Reddish-green leaves of the raspberries just above the soil line. Crinkly reddish leaves of the rhubarb just above the soil line. Purple leaves of the bluebells just above the soil line. Black currants just open, red currants holding back. Lilacs just open, honeysuckle holding back. And the same with the trees. Bald cypress putting out a new head of needles. Maple buds outside our bedroom window swollen almost to the point of bursting, but still holding back, as if they'd heard about the lows in the low twenties predicted for the next few days. They haven't, of course, as Kate would be quick to remind me. But the chill in the air and the chill at their roots is enough to keep them self-contained. Early spring in a northern clime is no time for midsummer madness.

THURSDAY *March 30*

Though most things in the back yard seem to be on hold, the stuff under the row covers keeps coming on a bit more every day. The tips of the snow peas are now breaking ground, while just a couple of days ago I could only see the humped-up soil where I assumed they were germinating. The tops of the onion sets are now an inch above ground, while a couple of days ago they were just peeking through. The radishes are now starting to put out their first pair of true leaves. The lettuce seedlings are visibly larger and beginning to look like well-formed little heads, rather than so many waiflike little leaves. And the overwintered spinach is now only a few days away from being large enough to pick for the first homegrown salad of the spring.

A spring garden underway and about to bear its first crop a month and a half ahead of the usual time! Thanks in part to El Niño, thanks in part to my desire for an early spring garden, thanks in part to those mid-February and mid-March warm-ups, but thanks most of all to the spun-bond polyester row covers. Without them the spinach would never have made it through the winter. Without them the lettuce seedlings would be frozen, the onion sets dormant, the radishes ungerminated, and the pea seeds rotting. Looking at those flimsy, porous, semitransparent strips of cloth, it's hard to believe that each layer raises the temperature beneath it by four to six degrees. But I can feel the difference just by sticking my hand under the covers. So, with the two or three layers I'm using right now, those vegetables are growing in a climate of fifty to fifty-five degrees, rather than the forty-degree temperatures we've been having these days. And the same kind of increase takes place at night, so the tender young plants have never had to put up with freezing temperatures, even when nighttime lows have dipped into the low twenties.

The covers themselves are not much to look at. Ghostly white cloth stretched over metal hoops, weighted down with broken bricks. I'd much rather see the dark soil and the variegated green of the vegetables themselves. It's also a hassle to set up the row covers, especially on the windy days of early spring. And once they're in place, I can only see the vegetables by trying to look through the cloth on a sunny day or by lifting it up on cloudy days like this. Still it's a great comfort to know that the vegetables are protected not only from the cold, the heavy rains, and insects, but also from sparrows, squirrels, rabbits, raccoons, possums, groundhogs, and deer. Come to think of it, the row covers do as much for my peace of mind as for the vegetables themselves. With the covers in place, I no longer go to bed fretting about what I might find drowned or eaten or frozen or pecked or trampled the next morning. I dream instead of the spinach to come next week.

FRIDAY *March 31*

March is going out below normal — in the thirties, with a northwest wind and a heavily overcast sky. Not exactly a lion, but far from being a lamb. Definitely not weather for working outdoors. So I seeded up a little three-pack with the Russian heirloom tomatoes that arrived yesterday. And then spent some time revisiting the fruits of last fall's garden in a batch of snapshots I just got developed this week. Three of them caught my eye.

The first, a still life from mid-October of plum tomatoes, fingerling eggplants, pears, and an onion, arranged on a flat, circular wooden bowl. If it weren't for the pears, I could easily imagine a ratatouille-to-be. A summery dish in midfall. But my eye is drawn to the contrasting colors, shapes, and textures — the oval red tomatoes against the glossy dark purple fruit and pale green stems of the eggplant against the flat yellow of the pears and the faded brown skin of the onion. I remember how pleasurable it was to arrange them, spreading out the fingerlike eggplants in the shape of a fan, then stuffing the tomatoes in the space between them and the upper rim of the bowl, then tucking each of the three pears and the onion under the stems of the eggplants to form an inverted triangle within the circular bowl. Nature into art, to be savored months later.

The second, a portrait from late November of the largest head of lettuce I've ever grown — a reddish-green Carmona butter-head, about twenty inches in diameter, sitting on the butcher-block table in the center of our kitchen. A work of art in itself, like a gigantic flower, a multifoliate rose, its leafy petals unfurling outward from the center of its head. I first noticed it was growing larger than all the rest in early October and then secretly checked on its progress from time to time under the row covers, until one day Kate peeked under the covers and discovered it too. Thanks to Kate, I harvested it before the unexpected dip below zero that wiped out the rest of our late fall lettuce crop. Some secrets, after all, are made for public consumption.

The third, a display of beets from mid-December, freshly pulled and washed, their reddish-purple skins and stems glistening against the platter's dark brown glaze. Nature into art again. But before the month was over, Kate turned the beets into a master-piece of her own for a Christmas Eve feast — a Russian borscht made with her own beef broth, julienned beets, shredded cabbage, and chopped onion. Served hot with a chilled side dish of yogurt. And paired yin-yang-like with a puréed leek and potato soup, garnished with diced potatoes, diced ham, and minced scallions. Dark and light breads too. Fine art for a festive winter night that was warmer all around than this spring day.

A P R I L

Apri Fools' Day, but it certainly didn't feel like it this mild and sunny morning, as I told Kate at lunch. "That's because it's fooling you." I didn't know what she meant by that retort, but I didn't want to ask, lest it turn into an April Fool joke. Maybe she was just referring to the fact that by noontime it was turning cloudy and chill, and by late afternoon would become almost completely overcast, except for a few passing moments of sunlight. A mild deception from start to finish. Or maybe she was alluding to the possibility that the day was pulling a trick on me in some other way — a practical joke I'd discover only after the day was completely over. Or maybe she was just pulling my leg by making a remark she knew would get me to thinking about it like this.

Joke or otherwise, I should've spent the morning potting up all the tomato seedlings and the lettuce seedlings, but I didn't get any further than going to one of the local nurseries to pick up a bunch of deep plastic six-packs. Sometimes, after all, the gardener rebels, and this was one of those days. No gardening outside, no transplanting inside. Not even an inspection tour of the grounds. Let the veggies vegetate on their own.

The closest I got to gardening was on a late morning walk with Kate and Pip, when we stopped to admire a bank of squills fronted by a lawn full of crocuses, all blooming their heads off amid the unraked and rotting leaves of last fall. A rank bed of spring bulbs, planted some ten or fifteen years ago by an eccentric landlord, now long dead. A traveling dictionary salesman, turned Oriental rug merchant (from whom Kate and I once purchased a used rug), turned antique dealer, turned fabricator and landlord of apartments whose interior walls were cobbled together out of doors, windows, and other unlikely stuff. A whimsical haven all year long. A hangout for student artists and writers, and a target for city building inspectors. But a pleasing spectacle to behold in almost any season, especially in spring and summer, when the bulbs are in bloom.

Looking at those flowers this morning, I couldn't help thinking about the hundreds of early spring bulbs we planted under our front spruce trees a few years ago. I couldn't help wondering what would become of them, and of our place, ten or fifteen years after we were gone. Would they spread and multiply? Would others stop to admire them? Would others bother to tend them? Questions too painful to ponder, or even to voice, especially on April Fools' Day.

SUNDAY *April 2*

Kate was right about my being fooled by yesterday, for despite getting cloudier all afternoon, the sky was completely clear last night. A night of the new moon, as we noticed upon coming out of the American Legion Hall in Solon, a small town ten miles north of here where we went for an old-fashioned roast duck dinner with all the middle-European fixings — giblet dressing, dumplings, sauerkraut, rye bread, and gravy. A feast that sent us swooning back to our German roots, and our companions Ken and Marybeth back to their junior year abroad in Vienna. If anybody had told me our plates would be piled high with all that luscious food for seven dollars apiece, I'd have said it must be a joke.

Today certainly felt more like a prank than yesterday. And not because of the weather but because of our return to daylight saving time, thanks to which we lost an hour today. "Spring forward," as the local newspapers cheerily put it. So I set the clocks forward when I got up this morning, but I didn't feel at all cheery about it. I felt cheated from start to finish. A day with twenty-three hours rather than twenty-four. One hour less to garden in, or to write in, or to relax in. And I felt the loss so keenly at one moment that Kate must have noticed it showing on my face.

It was about two in the afternoon, and I'd just finished transplanting all the tomato seedlings into the larger and deeper six-packs where they'll spend the next month or two before I move them into the garden. And I was trying to decide whether there was enough time to go outside and plant a double row of shell peas — an attractive prospect on this mild and sunny day, especially because I heard it would soon be turning chillier. Just then Kate came into the kitchen and asked if I wanted to go for a walk with her and Pip. Suddenly, I found myself confronted with more things to do than there was time for, especially because I hadn't yet showered or shaved or had anything for lunch, thanks to our late morning breakfast, which was late only because of the time change.

My frustration at that moment must have shown so visibly on my face that Kate looked worried herself. "Is something wrong?" And all I could do was to splutter about the time, a splutter that sent her and Pip on an inspection tour of the back yard, and left me time enough to realize that the spring gardening season was still very early, that there would still be plenty of time to plant the shell peas tomorrow or the day after that or the day after that. But there might never be a better time to be with Kate, beholding all the lawns and hillsides blue with blooming squills.

MONDAY *April 3*

So chilly and overcast this morning that I went out first thing and put another row cover on the lettuce, the snow peas, and the radishes, to protect them against the severe frost predicted for the next two evenings. No chance of planting the shell peas today. So I decided to work indoors on the second crop of lettuce seedlings. But an hour or so later the sky was clear enough that when I stuck my head out the back door again, the air was palpably warmer. Warm enough to lure me away from the lettuce to the shell peas, especially after Kate reminded me that I could protect them with row covers.

Out in the garden somewhere, the dove was sounding its mourning notes, the notes that seem to have sounded down the years whenever I've been planting the spring peas. The sun was out, and a gentle breeze was wafting in from the south. All I needed to complete this pastoral scene was the companionship of Pip, whom I brought out to sit under the pear tree just a few feet from the garden. And he too responded to the spirit of the day, spreading his hindquarters out in a leonine posture, crossing his paws in front of him, and raising his head, as if to catch the sweetness in the air. Looking, as he always does, like a compact Airedale.

If I hadn't already announced the advent of spring on March 17, 18, and 21, I'd have declared this to be the day it definitely arrived, around ten in the morning, when I was kneeling in my garden, planting the Green Arrow peas, with the warmth of the sun on my right cheek. An experience too idyllic to be true, as I realized a couple of hours later when I stopped to check the lettuce under the row covers and discovered that eight of the forty had disappeared overnight — not even a trace of them visible above ground. The first assault on the garden, and no telltale evidence to identify the criminal. Spring had definitely arrived, bittersweet as ever. Temperature in the sixties. Garden under siege.

And the rest of the day proved bittersweet as well. Watching the shapely cumulus clouds arrive while replacing seedlings in the lettuce patch and then making them cutworm-proof, slug-proof, and rabbit-proof with an arsenal of organic weapons — Dipel, diatomaceous earth, and Hinder. Now, as I finish this report in late evening, the temperature has dropped thirty degrees, the wind is blowing forty miles an hour, and a low in the teens is predicted for tomorrow morning. Some day. Some spring. Like the return of winter.

TUESDAY *April 4*

The Arctic air mass blew in last night as predicted, producing a wind-chill factor this morning of twenty below — almost ninety degrees colder than yesterday afternoon when I was planting the peas. A near-record chill, and a shocking reversal that

I felt the minute I stuck my head out this morning. Harsh enough to make me fret about things under the row covers, but I resisted the temptation to check on them, lest I let in any of the cold I was trying to keep out. Harsh enough to make Kate worry about the fruit trees, and my colleague Alan worry about "the state's entire apple crop," and me worry enough about their worries to call the county extension service and one of the local nurseries, both of whom assured me that most local fruit trees were probably not at risk because they hadn't yet opened their leaves, much less begun to unfurl their buds. Harsh enough, though, to make me wonder what it might have felt like had the Arctic air not been "eased" and "modified," as the meteorologists put it, by the energy of the sun and the prevailing warmth.

Most of all I found myself thinking how inattentive and heedless I'd been yesterday afternoon when this extraordinary weather reversal began to take place. I'd heard, of course, that an Arctic cold snap was predicted for last night, but the prediction was difficult to believe, given midday temperatures in the high sixties. Even the appearance of those cumulus clouds didn't arouse any worry in me, they were so lovely to behold. Nor the occasionally chill air that arose when they passed in front of the sun. Nor even the palpable shift in the prevailing wind direction from southwest to northwest. Not until the wind was gusting up to forty miles an hour and the sky was almost completely overcast did I begin to take things seriously, scurrying around to move the sage and tarragon plants back inside and put additional row covers on the onions and spinach. But even then I was still beguiled by the warm air and still preoccupied with the unknown predator in my lettuce patch.

I couldn't, of course, have done anything to impede the movement of that air mass, nor could I have done anything more to protect things in the garden. Still, I couldn't help wondering about my inclination to acknowledge the weather prediction but downgrade its severity. It's getting colder, I thought, but it couldn't possibly get that cold. What is it, I wonder, that often makes me respond that way in the face of a sudden cold snap? Is it the suddenness of the reversal that I can't accept? The swift movement from warmth to bitter cold? Or the bitter cold itself? The knowledge that it's coming and nothing I can possibly do will make any difference? Whichever it is, I sure don't like to face such deadly cold. Who does?

WEDNESDAY *April 5*

The other thing I don't care to deal with is taxes. But it's that time of year, and it was clearly that kind of day when I got up this morning. Temperature in the mid-thirties, wind gusting up to forty miles an hour, wind-chill around zero. A day to stay inside and hunker down over the tax forms and the canceled checks and all the other accumulated receipts and records from a year in the life of Carl H. and Kate F. Klaus.

But before taking stock of the year, I decided to take a quick inventory of the vegetable garden to see how the row covers worked during yesterday's cold snap. Onions, peas, radishes, and spinach all in good health and even a bit further along than two days ago. Lettuce too, except for the newly transplanted seedlings, all of them limp, evidently not hardy enough from their time in the outside cellarway to take the severe cold. But Kate thinks their roots may have survived, so I'll wait a week or two and see if they start putting out new leaves. Inside, the Russian heirlooms broke ground the past two days, as if they'd been inspired by the Siberian weather.

Still, April is the cruelest month, breeding taxes out of the dead year, mixing memory and mathematics. I suppose I could make things easier for myself by turning them over to my lawyer or an accountant. But the last time I did that, about twenty years ago, all the calculations were botched. So I decided to do them myself, and now I find they help me take stock of my life, especially when I'm sorting through all the canceled checks and charge card receipts. It's like running the whole year on fast forward, from New Year's to Christmas in just a few hours, without having to worry about the weather or the garden or anything else like that. But now that I'm keeping a detailed record of the garden, I suddenly find myself curious about last year's total gardening costs, and discover that we spent $715.62 in all. Far more than I'd imagined. That, in turn, makes me intensely curious about what we got for all our money. But I didn't keep a tally of the beans and beets and broccoli and cauliflower and eggplants and lettuce and peas and peppers and spinach and tomatoes and zucchini, much less all the canned, frozen, jellied, and pickled produce. And even if I had, it wouldn't really tell me what we'd gotten for our money. Some things, after all, can't be tallied up or taken account of in the federal tax forms or in any other kind of ledger.

THURSDAY *April 6*

B ean counting again and not just for the Department of Internal Revenue, but also for the Departmental Salary Review Committee and the dean, as dictated yesterday in a memo from Ed, our department chair, informing me and my colleagues that we should turn in our "updated vitas . . . immediately." Also that we should submit "an additional page or two" that provides "an overview of your teaching, scholarship, and service during the last three years, with a focus on the past year." In other words, what have you done for us lately? Not an unreasonable request, especially if you believe in merit raises, as I do. I conduct a somewhat similar review of the vegetables every fall near the end of the gardening season, taking stock of what each variety has done for me lately. The ones that produce tastefully and abundantly get a favored position in next year's garden. The others are either confined to a limited space in the next garden or to the backlog of less successful seeds on hold in the refrigerator. Questionable cases are referred to Kate, my Chief Vegetable Review Consultant. In other words, I'm familiar with the so-called review process from many years of doing it to the vegetables and many years of having it done to me.

But this time around, there was something about the process that made me uneasy. At first, I thought it was the absurdity of the Departmental Salary Review Committee, the department chair, and the dean all taking the trouble to review me, just for the possibility of a one or two percent increase, which would probably be reduced so much by withholding taxes that it might do no more than buy me a new rake or hoe or soil thermometer. But then I realized my discomfort was occasioned by the fact that this would be the last time I'd ever be going through the process, since I'm retiring at the end of next year. No more vitas, no more overviews of my work. No further occasions to construct my professional life anew in a categorical listing of my academic accomplishments. It never occurred to me that I might be troubled by such a prospect, since I've always been inclined to regard vitas as necessary fictions at best and self-serving concoctions at worst. Yet there's no denying that however much I might scorn the merit-badge mentality embodied in a vita, it does to some extent constitute the record of one's professional life, as indicated by the word itself. But henceforth, it seems, my vita, my life, will be of no interest to anyone, except perhaps the Great Review Committee in the Sky — and the committee of one inside me. So perhaps that's what it means to retire, to be professionally accountable to no one but myself. The ultimate freedom for which I've always yearned, but also the ultimate indifference that makes me wonder whether it ever really mattered to anyone but me.

FRIDAY *April 7*

The only thing that really mattered to me today was getting the full-season onions planted, even though the overcast sky, the moist air, and the steady breeze made for an unpleasant day to be outside in the garden. Not the sort of thing I can take stock of in my vita, but it will show up in the size of the onions I get when they start to ripen off in midsummer. I also wanted to get them in before the thunderstorms predicted for tonight, so they'd benefit from the rain rather than being delayed by it. It's at times like this that I feel like a servant of the vegetables and a victim of their schedules. Sometimes, of course, I'm just a victim of my own compulsions, but when it comes to the onions, there's no putting things off if you want a good crop. So I gritted my teeth and went off to one of the local nurseries to buy some Walla Walla onion plants, the only variety of sweet onion that reliably develops a full-size bulb in a northern climate.

By the time I got back and was working at the kitchen counter, trimming up the tops and roots of the scallionlike onion plants, Kate, who's been under the weather with a worsening cold, had also gritted her teeth and decided to concoct a special version of her homemade tomato soup — a Creole style made from our own canned tomatoes with fresh chopped celery, peppers, and onions. Then our gardening friend Rebecca showed up to start working on the flower bed and lot lines. And she too had apparently gritted her teeth after an overnight stomach upset. Suddenly my onion ordeal seemed mild compared to the deeds of Kate and Rebecca. Actually, the onions turned out to be easier than usual, because this year at Kate's suggestion I decided to use the little bulblike sets for the red onions and the hot cooking onions. No trimming or fussing required. The only problem is that sets usually don't develop as quickly or as sizably as plants. So I'm eager to see whether the Dutch sets we ordered will produce the large bulbs predicted in the advertisements. I'm also eager for the predicted thunderstorms, since the top inch or two of soil has become quite dry from the below-normal moisture we've had the past two months. El Niño is still in the weather picture.

But the rain will come when it's ready to come, somewhat like Rebecca, who comes more or less when the spirit moves her. She called last night and she's here this morning. "I'm coming tomorrow. OK?" She's been coming for the past six years, ever since we hired her one spring to help get the place in order for a citywide garden tour. And she's one free spirit, so in tune with the plants she intuitively knows what they need. This afternoon, when I was kneeling over my string line, fussing my way through the onions, there she was in the background, in her dark blue beret and her jaunty blue top, moving swiftly and silently through the perennial bed and the borders, leaving them immaculate in her wake.

SATURDAY *April 8*

There's a time to sow and a time to reap, and today they came much closer than usual for this time of year. Just a few minutes apart, in fact, late in the afternoon when the sun came out for its one and only appearance of the day. So I took the occasion to plant the last row of Dutch onion sets and then picked the first crop of spinach from the stuff that wintered over under the row covers. I've never harvested anything from the garden in early April or anytime in April for that matter. Nor have I ever had a spinach salad that tasted so mild, some of its leaves so sweet and tender they reminded me of game fish caught in the chill waters of early spring.

Though it was a bit chilly most of the day, Rebecca showed up again in early afternoon and cleaned up all the beds around the house. Today, she was bundled up in a farm jacket, muffler, and knit cap. Watching her wiry movements, I imagined she must be feeling the chill more than I, especially after spending the past three months in Belize. Every year, she spends the winter there, taking in the sun and the warmth, getting room and board by working for a wildlife research project of one kind or another. Last year, it was a study of baboons. This year, manatees. When I asked what took her there in the first place, she said, "It was the warmth to begin with, but now it's the natives I know and the water and the wildlife." Listening to her talk about Belize, I couldn't help thinking about the wild life she's cut out for herself, gardening up here during the mild and warm seasons, living sparely in a refurbished Elk lodge by the river, then working during the winter for research projects in Belize.

When I was Rebecca's age, twenty years ago, it never occurred to me that I might cut loose from the moorings of my secure academic job. Though I chafed under its obligations, the closest I ever came to throwing it over was in moments of idle speculation when I talked about becoming a forest ranger, or a nurseryman, or a South Seas expatriate with Kate, borrowing the limit on our credit cards and skipping the country for good. So, it seems, I've been a straight arrow most of my life, "a 1950s person," as Kate calls me in moments of exasperation, though I'm actually a product of the 1930s and '40s when I grew up, and of my orphanhood which I sought to overcome by avoiding the risks of a freer, more venturesome life like Rebecca's. So I'm still planting my garden in straight rows, one end balancing the other, as if it were a neoclassical construction. Last year, though, I started growing cosmos in the middle of the vegetables and sunflowers along the back of them. And this year, I'm thinking of scattering some flower seeds throughout the garden. Still, the old ways die hard, and I'm not yet ready to give up my string line, my row covers, or my neoclassical design. What would I use in their place?

SUNDAY *April 9*

Thunder and lightning late last night — loud enough to panic Pip — but no sign of rain that Kate or I could see out the window or hear on the roof. Come morning, though, the topsoil in all the gardens was replenished with a quarter inch of rain. Perfect timing, now that all the onions and peas are in, along with early crops of lettuce, radishes, and spinach — the coolest of the cool-weather vegetables in the spring garden. Actually, anything less hardy would hardly appreciate the weather we're having right now. Overcast skies, temperature in the thirties, and a northwest wind gusting up to thirty-five miles an hour. So I don't expect to be doing any outside gardening for the next several days, until the temperature warms up and the ground dries up enough to be workable.

People in the supermarket this morning were grousing about the cold, and I couldn't blame them. The wind's been a chilly and noisy presence all day long. But the continued coolness has also helped to keep the perennials, shrubs, and trees in check — and the squills in bloom — far longer than I can ever remember. Now, it seems, we're having a northern spring like the kind I remember from years past, a long-drawn-out affair, gradually rising to the heat of early summer, but with occasional periods of cooling off. Not the one-night stands and the quick burnouts we've often witnessed in the recent years of premature warming, blooming, and shedding of blossoms.

In a spring like we're having right now, I sometimes feel almost blissfully at ease with the fullness of time that seems available for the vegetables outside to develop to maturity. But I also feel edgy with an awareness of all the seedlings inside, pushing to be moved into larger containers, or into the outside cellarway, or outside on the terrace to be hardened off before being transplanted into the garden. The patio tomatoes that I started in early February are now beginning to open their blossoms in the outside cellarway, so they'd much prefer to be in larger pots, taking the sun outside on the terrace. The broccoli and cauliflower plants, also in the outside cellarway, would benefit from being transplanted into the garden if the weather were a bit warmer. Even the hardier tomato seedlings I moved down there a week or so ago had to be moved back to the dining room, because the undersides of their leaves were turning purple — a telltale sign that the chill air was depriving them of phosphorus. Everything's yearning for a bit more warmth, a bit more sun, a bit more space to grow in.

MONDAY *April 10*

Now, as I sit here after dinner composing this report, the weather seems calm for the first time today. Nothing outside but the sound of silence and nothing inside but the buzz of tinnitus in my head. But oh! what a day it's been until now. "A Götterdämmerung," according to Kate. And words to that effect from everyone I ran into on my errands around town. For me it's been chiaroscuro all day long — light then dark then light then dark then light then dark. For Pip and Phoebe, it's been traumatic from beginning to end, with each dark episode preceded by thunder and followed by a different kind of downpour. First hail, then sleet, then snow, then rain. And each light episode beset by winds, gusting up to fifty miles an hour. A day of violent contrasts in the center of a weather system throughout the plains and the Midwest created by extraordinary horizontal and vertical contrasts. Warm air above, cold air near the ground, warm weather blowing in from the south, Arctic weather blowing down from the north, winds from the south colliding with winds from the north. The perfect ingredients for a tornado. Also perfect ingredients for what the weather reporters are now referring to as "thunder sleet" and what I thought was "thunder hail" when I felt the tiny round beads of it striking me on the terrace this morning.

Looking down at the vegetable beds from my perch in the attic, I imagined myself enclosing them both in a gigantic spun-bond polyester garden cover, with metal hoops large enough to keep it suspended in midair, like a greenhouse or a retractable astrodome. Had my wish come true, I'd not have had to revisit the gardens after each weather sweep, to lighten the load on the row covers, or pull them tighter across the hoops, or add more hoops to give them more structural support, or lay down more bricks to keep them from blowing off in the wind. By midafternoon, I felt more like a gimcrack architect than a genuine gardener. And now that darkness has come, all I can hope is that nothing more tempestuous besets the place this evening.

In the midst of this stormy day, I devoted myself to finishing the federal income tax — a task that would have been stressful enough had I done no more than add things up and fill in all the slots on the four or five forms that I usually file. But no, I had to see what would happen if I ran my figures through one of those newfangled computer tax programs, which rivaled the day by concluding with a storm of its own that dumped thirty-five pages of forms in my lap before the printer signed off. Kate meanwhile devoted herself to concocting a hearty cassoulet out of lamb shanks, salt pork, and large dried lima beans, in a tomato-lamb broth flavored with a dried red pepper, garlic, parsley, and our own fresh rosemary and bay. A perfect counterpoint to the weather.

TUESDAY *April 11*

Pip got his spring haircut this morning, so his body's looking sleek enough, his beard and eyebrows jaunty enough, to prance around a ring. But lacking a show ring, we did the next best thing and pranced around the block this evening, taking in the moist night air, the mild breezes, the calm after the storm. Today seemed benign compared to yesterday, even though we had some heavy downpours this afternoon. Kate said it felt like the first spring rain, and I felt the same way, especially because the temperature this afternoon got up to the low fifties, a far cry from yesterday's blustery winter storm.

Everyone I ran into today seemed excited by yesterday's weather — the thunder and lightning, the swirling clouds, the sudden darkness, the unpredictable downpours of everything from rain and snow to sleet and hail. People seemed energized just by the experience of having weathered the storm and witnessed its convulsions. Especially an early phase of it that Kate and I slept through or that didn't strike our neighborhood — a heavy outbreak of thunder and lightning around three-thirty Monday morning, followed by a downpour of hail almost as large as golf balls. David, a graduate student in my essay course who lives eight miles east of here, was transfixed by "the boldly forked lightning" that preceded that downpour. "It's so different from the finely delineated lightning we have in California." His fingers moved rapidly to show the difference. Others were excited by the color of the sky, the fury of the wind, and the omnipresent possibility of a tornado.

But not the newspapers. The *Daily Iowan,* the university's student-run newspaper, headlined its account with a self-pitying lead: "I.C. suffers through odd weather blitz." The *Iowa City Press Citizen* was even more explicit about personifying the storm as a sadist and the city as an innocent victim: "Icy rain lashes Iowa City." And the *Des Moines Register* displayed a full banner head, personifying the storm as a trasher — WINTER'S LEFTOVERS DUMPED ON IOWA — and a bad sport into the bargain: "Though an April Storm Isn't Rare, This One Seemed Unfair, Following Warmth and Spring's First Buds."

Romantic poets and painters of the nineteenth century certainly wouldn't have looked upon yesterday's storm as an occasion for the weepies. They'd probably have considered it a sublimely convulsive event, worthy of artistic depiction or extended literary description. And my hunch is that despite what the newspapers have to say, many people still have it in them to admire such a dramatic storm, to be swept away by its sublime power and natural beauty. I certainly was — when I wasn't fussing over my row covers.

WEDNESDAY *April 12*

Now that the sublimity of it all is past, I'm waiting for the cold and waterlogged soil to dry out, but that's not likely to happen for at least a few days after the sun reappears. It's scheduled to show again tomorrow, and it can't come too soon as far as I'm concerned. Not that I'm particularly eager to work in the garden, but all the seedlings in the house and the outside cellarway are hungering for sunlight. All the bushes, trees, and perennials that have been holding back the past few weeks could safely open now without being ahead of schedule. Even the stuff under the row covers seems to be standing still for lack of direct sunlight and warmth. And I wouldn't mind a few rays myself to break up this week-long run of overcast skies.

Still, these gray days have produced a landscape whose colors and textures are more vivid than they would be under a sunny sky, as Pip and I discovered on a midafternoon tour of the back yard. Yellow-green moss starting up again on the terrace, under the maple tree, along the brick edging of the herb bed, at the north end of the gazebo. Yellow daffodils along the north lot line and forsythia in the distance stand out against the newly greened-up lawn. Tufts of green in Kate's sixty-foot flower border stand out against the rich dark color of the wet soil. Light green, dark green, blue-green, silver-green, yellow-green scattered from one end of the bed to the other. Swollen or partially opened buds on the bushes and trees stand out like a yellow-green filigree on all the branches. The delicate traceries of early spring, echoed by the flutter and clatter of migrating birds, momentarily covering the upper branches of trees on their way to the wilderness park a few blocks away.

I on the other hand am on my way to the post office with my federal and state tax forms in color-keyed envelopes, one yellow, the other white. The rite of early spring fulfilled, a ritual that will bring me greenbacks sufficient to pay my local real estate taxes. So I'll recycle the harvest from one set of taxes to pay off another, which I'll use in turn as a deduction on next year's income taxes, which will help me once again to get a refund for the real estate taxes due next year at this time. And so on. It never occurred to me before, but it seems as if I'm composting my taxes. The only problem, of course, is that money ain't garbage, and the recycled taxes never really wind up in my own garden. They're just passing through my hands, like so many other things that come and go in the mail. But they're gone, and that's cause enough for celebration.

THURSDAY *April 13*

The clouds are also gone, and that's another cause for celebration. But when I went to get the paper this morning and put Phoebe out for her constitutional, she didn't look as if she was ready to celebrate anything. In fact, she dashed back in, her owly eyes aghast, even before I could shut the front door. Frail as she is, the old girl still has a few quick moves in her, especially when the air's too chill for her liking. A throwback, no doubt, to the cold, wet days she spent as a castoff before Kate and my daughter Amelia found her on a pile of mulch bags outside one of the local nurseries. So I figured that Phoebe's dash back inside was just Phoebe, overreacting to the lingering chill of the past few days. But a few minutes later when I went out to check on the vegetables, I noticed a touch of frost on the ground and my breath condensing in the air. And not much warmer an hour or so later when I walked into school, my face and fingers chilled to the bone, thanks to a wind gusting in from the north.

But the ache in my fingers did put me in the right frame of mind for this morning's class discussion of E. B. White's "Spring," a piece he wrote in April 1941, reflecting among other things on the difference between a day that promises warmth but delivers "a bitter little wind," and one that actually fulfills its promise, "when no wind blows either in the hills or in the mind." Reading that line and others like it, I also couldn't help feeling that something more than the chilly air must be bothering me. But I couldn't put my finger on the problem right off, because the essay went so well in class, everyone picking up on the various ways that White's apparently casual "notes on springtime" — on the nursing of lambs and the brooding of chicks — actually turn out to pit his barnyard vision of renewal against the Nazi idea of rebirth. Not until I got back to the office and started reading articles in today's *New York Times* about President Roosevelt on the fiftieth anniversary of his death did I realize where that cold wind had been coming from in my mind. Kate set it in motion when she told me at breakfast about the ceremonies honoring Roosevelt. Though I didn't realize it just then, some part of my memory must have been retrieving my youthful feelings about the world, which seemed to me back then to be so clearly divided between right and wrong, good and evil, that I had no doubts about our government or our president. It's been a long time since I've felt that way about things — so long that I can't even imagine myself thinking of the warmth in my row covers as something I could pit against the forces of evil, whereas White evidently felt he was pitting the warmth in his brooder stove against the Nazi idea of spring. The thought of that loss has chilled me all day long.

FRIDAY *April 14*

L ettuce so rarely makes the front page of a big city newspaper that it caught my attention the minute I saw the headline in the *Des Moines Register* — LETTUCE PRICES ARE HEADING THROUGH THE ROOF. A three-column piece running over to four columns on the back page, chock-full of grim facts about "historic" price levels — $1.99 to $2.49 a head in Iowa, $5.00 a head at some stores in New York City. Then on late night TV, I heard the bad news again, this time featuring a bunch of human interest stories, like the one about lettuce salads being dropped from school menus for the rest of the year, and the one about the produce man who'd won the affection of his customers by dropping lettuce altogether from his offerings. "They're thanking me in the aisle," he said. Lettuce, it seems, has suddenly become caviar in the produce section, thanks to the mid-March floods in California that destroyed most of their early spring crop. So El Niño has come home in the form of outlandish lettuce prices.

And my early-early lettuce crop, the one I started in February and transplanted outside in mid-March, has suddenly escalated in monetary value. Forty heads of lettuce at a minimal price of $2.00 per head means I'm sitting on a cash crop of almost $80. Now I'm motivated not only to keep a close eye on the ones under the row covers, but also to transplant all the others I started in March and that've been crowding each other in the outside cellarway. So I spent a few hours at the kitchen sink this cool, overcast

morning, carefully moving each of those precious seedlings into its
own slot. And the result is that I have another batch of eighty-six
lettuce seedlings ready to move into the garden in the next two or
three weeks. A cash crop of $172. Maybe I should retire right now
and become a greengrocer or a truck gardener.

Actually, such notions have fleetingly crossed my mind the past
few years in midfall, when I've had such a postfreeze surplus of
basil and red peppers, thanks to the row covers, that I've been able
to market my stuff to the local co-op and gourmet restaurants. I
especially remember how good it felt a couple of years ago one
crisp fall day, selling my basil at the co-op to my neighbor Steve,
who manages their produce department, and then using the cash
to buy some fresh swordfish and white wine right on the spot —
almost like bartering. The only problem is that I don't enjoy the
hassle of calling around to hawk my produce, not to mention the
bother of picking, bundling, and trucking it to market. My graduate student Dan also thinks I should be uneasy about selling the
extra produce because "it puts you in a different relationship to
your garden." It must be that he thinks of me as having some kind
of platonic relationship with my garden. But, let's face it, I've been
consuming my produce for so many years that a little cash crop
now and then seems like a delicious prospect, like the first fresh
head of lettuce in a lettuceless spring.

SATURDAY *April 15*

Today started out so much like yesterday — completely overcast and a slight nip in the air — that I spent the morning
transplanting the pepper seedlings into wider and deeper
six-packs, large enough to hold them until they're ready to go into
the garden. By noon, though, the overcast was breaking up, and
after lunch when the sun came out the day turned so warm it felt a
bit uncomfortable. Actually, it was only in the low seventies, and
the lingering clouds were lovely to behold. But when I stopped to
chat with Jim who was working in his garden, he complained
about the heat. "I'm sweltering. Aren't you?" Jim and I have been
living back to back for twenty-five years now, visiting with each

other in our adjoining yards spring, summer, and early fall. But when the fall turns cold, Jim's gone hunting, I'm gone teaching, and we don't get together again until the warm weather brings us back to our yards and gardens.

Jim was so inspired by the warmth that he put in a bunch of broccoli plants, onion plants, and even several pepper plants, as well as seeding in a couple of rows of beans. His wife Carol was shaking her head a bit about his putting in beans and peppers so long before the last frost date, and so was I. But Jim has his own way of doing things in the garden, and somehow he usually gets away with them. "I done it the same time last year. The same day as this. Remember?" And I did. I also remembered bringing him up some bottomless plastic water jugs to protect his pepper and tomato plants during a long cold spell. But then as if in explanation, he waved his hand majestically at the south side of his garage, the magical sun trap. And I couldn't disagree with him, especially in view of all the radishes I'd planted alongside it, now beginning to swell up. More to the point, the soil in his beds felt ten or twenty degrees warmer than my clammy stuff.

I guess the difference wouldn't have gotten to me so keenly had I not spent the morning transplanting my tender seedlings into larger six-packs, while he was putting his store-bought plants right into the ground. When I mentioned it to Kate, she spoke like an echo of Jim. "He did it the same time last year. Don't you remember?" Of course I remember and that's part of the problem. I also know there's a perfectly rational explanation for his ability to defy the frost dates and get away with it. Different locales, different soils, different soil temperatures. I also know that I'm trying to do a different kind of gardening — starting all my peppers from seed, and growing a wide range of varieties that aren't locally available. Ace bell, Biscayne cubanelle, Ecuadorian relleno, Italian bullhorn, and Salsa. But even granting all those differences, there's still that old competitive side of me, I guess, just below the surface, waiting to be aroused, even on so genial a day as this one seemed to be.

SUNDAY *April, 16*

aster Sunday, but hardly a day for an Easter parade, what with overcast skies again and a light rain around noon. By late afternoon, though, the clouds broke up a bit, the sun shone through a bit, the air warmed up a bit, as if to grace the day and our Easter dinner with a last-minute reprieve. Even before that brief clearing, the day was marked by the emergence of the Green Arrow shell peas that I planted a couple of weeks ago and the blossoming at last of the maple tree just outside my attic window, yellowish-green fringe dangling now from all its branches. Easter gifts brought on by yesterday afternoon's warm-up.

But the major gift was Kate's festive dinner this afternoon — beginning with a salmon mousse, fresh cucumbers, and Calamata olives, served with slivers of pumpernickel and Italian white bread; then roast leg of lamb, basted with olive oil, lemon, garlic, and our own fresh rosemary, accompanied by boiled new potatoes dressed with our own fresh chives, lamb gravy, asparagus dressed with marinated roast red peppers, and fresh radishes (not yet our own); concluding with a crisp, low-cholesterol brownie torte served in wedges with fresh Guernsey cream that I picked up from a local dairy, and fresh strawberries flavored with a little crème de cassis. Sauvignon blanc with the mousse, pinot noir with the lamb, Kona coffee with the dessert. And a beguiling but haunting afternoon with our guests, namely Kate's mother Lib, and Lib's acquaintance Margaret from the retirement community where they live.

Lib and Margaret evidently met through an occasional bridge group, and don't yet know much about each other. But when Kate asked Lib to bring a guest who might be lonely on Easter, Margaret was the one most obviously in need, what with her daughter who teaches here on a research leave in England, and her other children living out west. So, on the way over in the car, Lib and Margaret were asking each other a few leading questions. "Do you like to cook for yourself?" "Not at all. Never have. If it hadn't been for this wonderful invitation, I'd have stayed in my room and pitied myself all afternoon." And over dinner, they continued to get acquainted with stories about their growing up, their college educations, their marriages, their children, their losses, their physical afflictions, environmental convictions, and political beliefs. So much condensed into a few hours it was thicker and richer than the chocolate-filled Easter baskets Kate made up for each of them. Though Kate and I took part in the conversation, it seemed to me as if both of them were reaching out for something that neither of us could possibly provide, something that one or the other of us might also be looking for some Easter afternoon.

MONDAY *April 17*

Easter leftovers. So many of them in the icebox when I went to get some milk for my cereal that I was sorely tempted to have dinner for breakfast, or at least a bit of the salmon mousse. But I'm glad I restrained myself, since Kate evidently had the mousse in mind for our lunch today, and the lamb for our dinner. The meal is ended but the memory lingers on.

So does the overcast sky and the slightly chill air. A perfect day for moving broccoli and cauliflower seedlings into the garden, especially since the National Weather Service predicts another week of overcast skies and temperatures in the fifties. Now that they're in, protected with row covers, maybe I won't even have to watch them go into their panicky heat wilts when the sun finally does come out. But I'll have to peek under the covers now and then, because I want to compare Packman broccoli, which I'm trying for the first time this year, with Green Comet, an All-American hybrid I've been growing for the past several years. Already, Packman has proven itself to be a faster germinating and quicker growing variety, with much better root development. The question now is whether it produces better broccoli and more side shoots. At the end of the growing season, their overall performance will be evaluated by the Vegetable Review Committee.

One thing for sure is that our neighbor Linda is not just the gruff person I once thought her to be. Actually, I think she may be an overworked social worker who can't resist an opportunity to do a good turn. A few days ago, when I was out walking Pip, I saw her forking a load of shredded tree clippings off her truck and asked where she'd gotten it. "It's free for the taking at the city's mulch pile." I thanked her for the information and thought no more of the matter. But Linda being Linda evidently took it as a hint, and on Saturday afternoon there she was pulling up in our drive with a truck full of mulch, her face red from having loaded it herself, telling me what to do with it. "Don't unload it now. It's too hot. Just keep the truck until tomorrow and put the key in my mail box." So the first thing yesterday morning, I unloaded her truck, cleaned it out, and returned it with a jar of Kate's strawberry jam. And this morning when I put Pip out on his leash, there was that pile of mulch at the end of the driveway, reminding me again not to put any stock in my first impressions of people — or of anything else for that matter. Packman looks like a winner right now, but it may come a cropper before the season's over.

TUESDAY *April 18*

Now all we need is a little sun. That's what I was thinking this morning after I checked the rain gauge in the vegetable garden and discovered that last night's storm brought us three quarters of an inch. But Kate beat me to the announcement, and well she might have, for the sun has shone so little the past few weeks we might be setting a record for overcast days in April. Shortly after her announcement, as if in defiance, the sky turned dark, and the rain started coming down so hard I took the car rather than walking. Just after I got to the office, though, it started to clear, and the sun came out for several hours. So our wish was granted after all, except during a couple of brief downpours in mid- to late afternoon. The only problem is that we forgot to say anything about the wind, which gusted up to fifty miles an hour all day long. But it blew some spectacular cumulus clouds our way, so it wasn't an entirely ill wind.

Besides, it's hard to feel out of sorts with the wind, when all the early spring crops are in the ground, under the row covers, unfazed by the breeze. Now I can relax a bit and get in the rest of the spring garden over the next week or two — beets, potatoes, Swiss chard, and the second crop of lettuce and radishes. Actually, the cool, showery weather that's forecast this week will probably compel me to relax a bit about the garden whether I want to or not. And the graduate theses that are now coming to fruition will leave me no leisure for fussing over the vegetables. This time of the year has always been a strange one for me — such different things coming together in my life. Seed time in the garden and harvest at school. Vegetables just starting, while students are finishing, some of whom I've worked with for several years, now on the verge of graduating. A bittersweet time of comings and goings.

And next year at this time, I too will be finishing up, leaving school for the first time since I entered kindergarten some fifty-eight years ago. Graduating at last — in celebration of which I've been thinking about putting on the carnelian robe, doctoral hood, and cap that Kate and Lib gave me for my fiftieth birthday and marching one last time in the academic parade. But I've also been thinking about teaching a course every year or two after I retire, to keep in touch with the students and keep myself stimulated by the challenge of the classroom. Keeping a hand in, as it's called. So perhaps I shouldn't march in the parade, since I don't really plan to leave school after all. Or perhaps I should make a clean break with it once and for all. Or perhaps I should just stop worrying about it for now, since there's no telling how I'll feel next year at this time, or the year after. It all depends on the weather. And today it's been blowing hot and cold all day long.

WEDNESDAY *April 19*

The only thing that blew in today was Rebecca, who stopped by just to pick up a few bags of leaves and other yard rakings in exchange for a dozen or so of my spare tomato plants and a few eggplant seedlings. But inside the house, a light breeze must've been wafting up from the kitchen to the attic. How else to account for the delicious aroma I've been smelling up here of a Mediterranean fish stock that Kate concocted from the heads, frames, and tails of three fresh red snappers, our own canned tomatoes and tomato juice, garlic, thyme, fennel, orange peel, and saffron? The promise of bouillabaisse and cioppino in months to come.

But my mind has continued to be ruffled all day by thoughts of retirement, partly because I found myself having dinner last night with a retired colleague from the zoology department, partly because I was reading this morning's newspaper account of Joe Montana's retirement from professional football. Two such entirely different persons I'd have thought they had nothing in common. Yet they both seemed bent on putting their careers behind them once and for all. My colleague decided to move out of his office the minute he retired and not "try to keep a hand in." Montana decided it was "time to move on, call it a day for the NFL," without even considering another season. I could easily see why Montana decided to leave, especially after Kate reminded me at breakfast of what a mess his body must be in after all those years of playing pro football. And I could see why the zoologist felt left behind by the important work now being done in molecular biology and DNA. Yet it didn't seem possible that he could mentally walk away from a field that had absorbed him his entire professional life. And as I gradually discovered during our conversation, he has continued to keep up with the research, even if he isn't actually doing it himself.

So what fascinates me, I now realize, is not whether Montana or my colleague have tried to continue doing something they're no longer able to carry on, but how they talk about or think about the work they've left behind. I hear in their remarks a note of defensiveness that I've sensed in some of my own comments — as if one could actually close the door, move on, and not look back. Maybe some of that defensiveness is necessary — a way of dealing with the day to day reality of making a new life for oneself outside of a football stadium, a research lab, or an academic classroom. But the more I think about the matter, the less it seems possible for me to ignore the work I've done in the personal essay, or to stop doing it, or even to talk about it as if it's something I no longer have a hand in. It seems as vivid to me as the aroma of that fish broth — as compelling as the thought of the Creole baked snapper I'm going to cook right now.

THURSDAY *April 20*

T he next time I'm worried about keeping a hand in, I think I'll just pay a visit to our ancient pear tree, as Pip and I did today on our morning rounds. Fruitless last year and threatened by the chain saw, it's now covered with blossoms just beginning to open. It also has a couple of new branches that Kate and I think we can train to replace the ones it lost a couple of years ago when a heavy load of fruit caused one of its main arms to rip off in a high wind. Until that loss, it was so symmetrical that its branches seemed to form the shape of an elongated A-line skirt. A graceful showpiece in the center of the back yard. More recently a one-armed relic of its former self, but still capable of bearing fruit and putting on a good spring display. The only good show of the day.

By the time Pip and I finished our tour of the yard, the clouds had started moving in front of the sun, the temperature dropped, and the wind was blowing in from the east. And by the time I started walking to school, the sky was completely overcast, the air so cold that I wore my winter jacket, muffler, and gloves. A gloomy day made all the more dark and distressing by newspaper and TV reports of the bombing in Oklahoma City. "Evil" is the word on everyone's lips from the president to the Congress to my colleagues, my students, and myself. And "the death penalty" too. A rare consensus in these divided and divisive times. But at what an extraordinary cost to the victims and to the fabric of society itself, now turned panicky at the thought of other such bomb-ings at other federal buildings and public places throughout the country.

Suddenly, the peaceable spring landscape of the Great Plains has been disrupted by the terrorism that's been all too common throughout the rest of the world — from New York City to Dub-lin to Munich to Beirut to Sarajevo to Chechnya to Tokyo. The center of tornadoes has been struck by the even more destructive violence of a horrifically malign human intent. The only wonder is that it's taken so long to reach the heartland. Perhaps I might be more surprised, more appalled, had I not read a student essay last night about the Holocaust and taught an essay today reflecting on the thought that "history has been filled with examples of equal bestiality differing only cosmetically." Still, the newspaper articles and the pictures of dying children left me in tears.

And now I find myself craving anything that might sweeten my view of experience, or at least distract me momentarily from the sickness of the human heart. So I'm pleased at the prospect of digging a hole deep enough and wide enough to hold the dwarf sweet cherry tree that arrived a couple of days ago, then digging a trench for the seed potatoes that came in the mail this afternoon, then burying the roots and planting the tubers as firmly and carefully as possible. Then hoping for the best.

FRIDAY *April 21*

Not even hope can contend with a wind-chill in the mid-teens. No wonder Kate came in from getting the mail this afternoon with the announcement "It's awful out there." No wonder my fingertips turned white every time I went outside today. No wonder the *Des Moines Register* had a piece complaining about the "cool-off." But it's not just the cold that's getting to people. It's also the overcast skies. The absence of sun. And for me it's the cold, waterlogged soil, so heavy with the recent rains that I can't possibly plant those seedling potatoes that came yesterday or the dwarf sweet cherry that's been cooling its heels since Monday afternoon.

But the cool weather does have its bright side — in the continuing bloom of the yellow daffodils and white narcissus along the north lot line and the coral quince blossoms on the south side. And despite the chill air and the overcast skies, everything in the back yard continues to make headway. The early green onions nearly ready, the early radishes at Jim's place now swelling, the snow peas two inches tall and beginning to put out tendrils, the Walla Walla onion plants putting out new top growth, the shell peas almost an inch above ground, and the Dutch onion sets starting to break ground. Record growth this early in the season, thanks to the row covers. But the most surprising news is that the dwarf North Star pie cherry I planted last year already has several blossom clusters on it, so it might actually bear some fruit this summer, a year or two early — if the weather's not too cold for the bees to be out when its blossoms open. And that's a big "if" now that the pear's in the process of blossoming during so cold a period that no bee in its right mind would be out gathering nectar.

Today's cold weather also brought us a would-be foundling, courtesy of Linda the Gruff, who showed up at the back door shortly after breakfast with a little black kitten on her shoulder. No more than three or four weeks old. "I just found it down in the park, screaming its head off. It must've gotten separated from its mother." I told her we couldn't possibly take it in, given the two pets we already have and Phoebe coming to the end of her life. "That's why I thought you'd be interested. You'll be needing another cat." I called upstairs to Kate just to have her look at it. "It's out of the question," she said. But a few minutes later she was downstairs worrying over it on the back porch. And later this afternoon she was wondering whether Linda had found a home for it. And wondering about other things as well. "We couldn't possibly take it in, could we? Pip wouldn't stand for it." And neither would Phoebe. And neither, I guess, would I. But it sure was a good-looking kitten, except for the pus in its eyes. I just wish Linda hadn't come knocking on our door, not on so cold a morning as this.

SATURDAY *April 22*

"It's a good thing you didn't take it in, not with pus in the eyes like that. It was probably diseased and wouldn't survive." Jim had seen the kitten himself, and was trying to make me feel better about my refusal. But somehow that only made me feel worse about the matter, even though the day itself had everything I'd been hoping for — blue sky, bright sun, mild breezes. Clearly, the only thing to do was to distract myself by planting the dwarf sweet cherry.

Seven feet south of Kate's flower border, I marked the spot for it, to balance the dwarf sour cherry tree at the other end of the border that I planted last year. And then I began the planting ritual that Kate and I have used for all our fruit trees and bushes. A ritual so absorbing that the moment I pushed my shovel into the ground, I felt entirely cut off from everything around me but the tree, my shovel, the wheelbarrow, and the soil. First removing the top soil, to be mixed later with compost and put at the bottom of the hole for the good of the roots. Then removing the clay subsoil, to be used for filling in sinkholes around the yard. Checking the size of the hole now and then by putting the tree in it for a second and then back in its plastic bucket of water. Digging down, then shaving the sides, digging and shaving again and again, to produce a hole wide enough and deep enough to hold the roots with room to spare. Room to spare. Kneeling by the edge of the hole, like a supplicant, to dig and remove the last foot of subsoil — so cold and clammy to the touch I suddenly found myself thinking about the hole I'd soon be digging for Phoebe. For Phoebe. Just then, Kate arrived with Pip to call me in for lunch, and what a lunch it was — an improvisational soup made from her own chicken broth, the meat of the red snapper heads, bits of salt pork, diced potatoes, peppers, celery, onions, garlic, thyme, and our home-canned tomatoes. Were it not for that timely lunch break, I'd probably have given way to the gloomy reflections that were then arising in my mind about the cycle of growth and decay, beginning and ending in the soil.

The postlunch planting was a breeze by comparison. But a carefully plotted ritual just the same. First mix the topsoil with our well-rotted compost and some twenty-year-old cow manure from a local farmer, then center the roots on a pyramidal heap of that sacred mixture, then adjust the limbless trunk of the tree to stand vertical all around, then cover its roots with more of the mix and firm the soil with hands and feet, then water, adjusting the trunk once again, then fill and firm and water again, adjusting the trunk once again, then fill and firm and mulch and shape the surface like a saucer to catch the rain. The rain. So much fuss over a thing that looks like a mere stake in the ground, especially from the distance of the back porch. But up close, its firm green buds are filled with promise. And the fussing now will bear sweet fruit for us and the birds for years to come.

SUNDAY *April 23*

Ever since we stopped feeding the birds a week or two ago, it seems to me that more of the display birds have been coming to feed outside our kitchen window than at any other time this winter or early spring. Maybe everyone else has stopped feeding them too, and the chilly weather has kept them coming to our place because they can grub among the heap of scattered seed and shells on the lawn around the feeder. Whatever the cause, it's gradually dawned on me that most of the birds are coming in pairs — two blue jays, two cardinals, two chickadees, two mourning doves, two redpolls, two red-bellied woodpeckers. And this morning two mallard ducks, sitting out in the back yard by the newly planted cherry tree. If I didn't know any better, I'd have said they were a good omen, but they're a mile and a half from the river where they belong with the hundreds of other mallards that congregate there throughout the year. Not only are the birds getting together, but the bees were out this afternoon, working incessantly over the pear tree, most of whose blossoms are now fully open. Spring is definitely in the air, no matter how chilly the air's been these days.

But the buzz of this afternoon's springtime activities was nothing compared to the fizzy ceremonies we attended yesterday afternoon at "the first annual presentation of the Truman Capote Award for Literary Criticism." A gala event put on by the Truman Capote Literary Trust and the University of Iowa Writers' Workshop in the Senate Chamber of the Old Capitol Building at the center of the university pentacrest. There in the stately, pillared neoclassic halls of Iowa's territorial capitol, the spirit of Truman Capote held sway for a couple of hours. And not just in the extravagant $50,000 award, nor the free-flowing champagne, nor the fey manner of the Cambridge don who received the award and then immediately turned the podium over to his sleek-voiced companion, who delivered the don's short paper on literary criticism, while the don looked on as if he were hearing his thoughts for the first time. No, the spirit of Capote was there in the madcap quality of the crowd itself. A festive gathering of display birds —

from Hunter, the fine-beaked university president, to Frank, the beetle-browed workshop director, to the well-preened New York City friend of Capote and his black-suited lady companion to the rabbinically bearded member of the selection committee to the crew-necked congressman to the covey of local academics and their mates, all decked out in their spring finery, to the motley flock of workshop students, and their fledglings too, all atwitter in the glitter of the staid Old Capitol, pecking away at the lavish hors d'oeuvre in the light of the descending sun. *Sic transit gloria Capoti.*

MONDAY *April 24*

Come to think of it, the glory of champagne and fresh strawberries lodges in the memory long after the bubbles are spent. I'm thinking especially of the late night, black tie party that Kate and I put on in my bachelor's apartment right across from the Old Capitol some thirty years ago — a fizzy event, floated with my winnings from a high-stakes poker game, and served up in her mother's antique Fostoria goblets and plates. The university president and the workshop director were also at our little affair, but there weren't any speeches or big awards. Just a festive gathering of display birds, all decked out in their evening feathers. Now my old bachelor pad's been turned into the second floor of a Land's End low-cost outlet. *Sic transit gloria Klausi.*

There weren't any birds around at all this morning when I went to work on the raspberries, not with all the dark rain clouds overhead. But a light breeze and mild temperatures made it perfect weather for putting the bed in order. And order is what it needed. So many suckers coming up everywhere, except in the two hedgerows themselves, that it looked like a randomly scattered array of plants, rather than the carefully planned bed I established three springs ago with the plants Kate gave me for my birthday. So I went at it this morning, digging and relocating about eighteen of the thirty-six plants, to produce two parallel rows. A tricky job, because red raspberry plants multiply by means of underground runners. So they don't readily yield to being dug up and moved, except by deep spading with a sharp-edged shovel and a quick thrust of the spade. After a couple of botched diggings, I got the hang of it, watering them in with a high-phosphorus fertilizer to prevent root shock. Then I weeded in between the plants, mulched them down with a couple of inches of well-rotted cow manure, cleaned up the brick edging, and the bed looked like a display of raspberry plants on parade. So I went into lunch feeling like a master sergeant, fully in command of his troops.

Such good feelings about the garden that I never imagined the afternoon would make me uneasy about what I'd been doing this morning. But the dissertation defense I attended was concerned with women nature writers. And the discussion gradually came to focus on the ways that men seek to dominate nature, especially since the woman doctoral student who had once been a member of the National Park Service was reflecting on the ways that the male-dominated Park Service has traditionally sought to subjugate the land under its control. In the midst of that discussion, I began to feel like one of those creepy males that she and the others were talking about, and I wondered what they would think if they'd seen me dominating my raspberry bed this morning. But I also wondered what they'd do with a crowded, weed-ridden berry patch, so overgrown the plants couldn't be conveniently trained or harvested. I didn't have the nerve to bring up my berry plants on so august an occasion, so I kept my peace until I got home and raised the problem with Kate. She quickly assured me they must be thinking of men who go into the forest with chain saws and pesticides and paving machines. Still, I sometimes worry about how I cultivate my garden, even the unruly raspberries. The act of cultivation involves so many tools of control and subjugation that even a plowshare sometimes seems like a sword.

TUESDAY *April 25*

Yesterday's thoughts about gardening and subjugation had me so flustered that I forgot to mention the green onions I harvested for lunch, just after finishing up with the raspberries and roses. Most years, I don't even get the sets planted for green onions until mid-April, so it was a rare pleasure to pull some yesterday, the dark, moist earth still clinging to their roots. More pleasing to note that despite my gloomy thoughts about Phoebe being gone by green-onion time, here she is still walking from the front porch to the back porch for her morning constitutional, still coming in and whining for her breakfast bowl, still heading upstairs for a nap on her favorite chair in the TV room or her favorite pillow in the guest bedroom or her favorite nook in the attic, still eluding Pip's affectionate overtures. She doesn't have any of her former vigor, and I keep fretting about that, but then again Kate keeps reminding me she's almost twenty years old. So what do I expect? I guess the problem is that I've never lived with anyone of advanced age, or witnessed anyone of advanced age (or any age) enduring the afflictions of a mortal disease day in and day out. Nothing schools us for such experience but the experience itself, and in this area I feel almost as uneducated as a child. But Phoebe teaches me about it every day.

The changes from one day to the next are so slight as to be almost imperceptible, as indistinct as the changes that have been taking place outside these past few weeks, when the daytime temperature's been somewhere in the fifties and the nighttime temperature somewhere in the thirties, with a moderate breeze and some clouds overhead. So it's often seemed as if everything was in a state of suspended animation — as if the trees were on hold, the lawn standing still, the daffodils hanging on to their blooms indefinitely. When in fact the sap's been rising in the trees, the grass putting up new growth, the daffodils fading just a bit every day. So today the pear is in full bloom, the grass needs mowing, and the daffodils only look good from a distance.

Nothing is on hold, as I could tell from the five dozen perennial divisions that Kate and Rebecca dug up and potted for donation to a local gardening club sale — Jacob's ladder, purple coneflowers, rudbeckia, and Siberian iris. But even before I came home and beheld the gazebo floor covered with the fruit of their labors, I discovered at the office that nothing is on hold, when I slipped as I was stepping up onto my desk to water the donkey's tail that hangs by my fifth-floor window and started to fall headlong into it, breaking the fall only by falling directly on my chest, on the edge of a large clay pot of dracaena. A fall so abrupt, so blunt, that it was momentarily stunning, as if I'd broken or ruptured something. Probably I've just bruised a few ribs and injured a few muscles, judging from the pain that comes from lifting my arm. But the pain, I can see, will be with me for several days, reminding me again that nothing at all is on hold.

WEDNESDAY *April 26*

This is the time of year when I'm often trying to get something planted or transplanted before an oncoming rain. Beat the rain, and it waters things in. Miss the rain, and it muddies things up. So when I got home yesterday from school, I was hoping to seed in the Swiss chard and a second crop of radishes before the rain that was predicted to start in late afternoon or early evening. The only problem is that I made the mistake of telling Kate how I slipped and fell in the process of watering the donkey's tail. "Nothing doing. You're not going to start planting seed when you may have a broken rib. Just think of the damage you might do when you bend over to plant the seed. Besides, it's just starting to rain, and I need your help roasting the turkey breast." In the face of such logic, I could hardly mutter even a single "but." So today I've been watching the rain fall, wishing at first that I'd gotten the chard and radishes in, then grateful that I didn't, because the rain's been falling so steadily and heavily at times — two inches total so far — that it might have washed out the seed. Gardening, it seems, has led me to refine the art of rationalizing almost any turn of events.

Today's rain, for example, arrived at just the right time to water in the cherry tree I planted Saturday and the raspberries I transplanted Monday. But happily it didn't arrive yesterday until Kate and Rebecca had finished all their digging and refilling. Yet the rain this morning was light enough that it didn't get in the way of a gardening visit from my colleague David, who came over to dig up a dozen spare raspberry plants for a new berry bed of his own. And it was still falling lightly enough when David left for him to get them transplanted this morning and watered in by the rain.

I'm also glad that it rained all day, because I couldn't do any gardening today, what with my arm still feeling a bit sore from the fall and my chest hurting a bit from a contusion that the doctor told me is probably filled with at least a half pint of blood. Painful though it was just to lift my arm or walk uphill or breathe in deeply yesterday afternoon, I was pleasantly surprised to notice how quickly the pain from such exertions diminished today. So as strange as it seems, I'm even somewhat grateful that I injured myself yesterday, because it gave me a chance to see how durable and resilient I still am. Also to find out from the doctor that my heart sounded good, my lungs clear, and my blood pressure normal. His report was so upbeat I momentarily found myself wondering what further injuries I might be willing to endure just to find out the limits of my tolerance for trauma and pain. But my imagination failed me just then, and I was left wishing, after all, that neither I nor the rain had fallen, so the radishes and the chard would be in the ground, working their way toward germination.

THURSDAY *April 27*

My playful wish that the rain hadn't fallen has turned out to be a wish in earnest, for the rains we've had over the past few weeks have raised the level of our local rivers and reservoirs so high they're on the verge of flooding the next few days. So the TV and newspaper reports are suddenly fraught with reminders of the 1993 deluge. Hard to believe, when just a month or so ago we were running only forty percent of our normal rainfall. But the recent statewide storms have brought our local rainfall up to normal and pushed river levels well above normal, especially given the influx of water from areas north of here. No wonder the ground was so oozy at the base of the hole I dug for the cherry tree.

Talk about things welling up from below! A new theory has recently been proposed for the origin of El Niño, attributing it to fiery lava eruptions coming from between tectonic plates on the floor of the Pacific Ocean. According to this theory, the volcanic heat released by eruptions from the earth's interior starts a chain of events that culminates in El Niño. Such intensely hot eruptions presumably raise water temperatures enough on the surface of the eastern Pacific to lower the air pressure, weaken the trade winds, and release a pool of warm water in the western Pacific and the stormy air above that it comes rushing across the ocean. El Niño, then, is somewhat like a creation of the earth's subconscious, a powerful force so irrational and uncontrollable that it's capable of producing bizarre weather throughout the globe.

The geophysicist who proposed this deep-lava theory of El Niño would probably not be very comfortable with my psychological analogy, especially because his theory is already under attack from meteorologists and oceanographers who describe it as complete nonsense. But it sure does make sense to me that the seething cauldron within the earth might be responsible for some of the most irrational weather on earth. This morning's air, for example, was so cold and blustery — temperature in the thirties with a northwest wind of twenty miles an hour — that it felt like the beginning of March rather than the end of April. A strange sensation, given the height of the sun, the green of the grass, the white of the pear, the purple of the redbud, the yellow of the maples looming in the background. The standard explanation is that the northern jet stream has been dipping farther south than usual at this time of year. But why it dips and when the dip will end seem like mysteries of the deep — unfathomable.

FRIDAY *April 28*

The lawn is mown for the first time this spring. I noticed it yesterday the minute I started walking up the street toward our house. I checked it out the minute I got home. I stared at its dew-covered surface this morning the minute I got up. I'm surprised by how important it is for me to behold the lawn, freshly cut, sweeping up toward the back of the lot. In part, of course, it's pleasing just to see the contours of the land in the slopes and ripples of the newly cut grass, to see the beds and borders sharply delineated by it, to see the shrubs and trees stand out against it, like the aged pear, still blooming white in the center of the yard. The newly mown lawn is like a foil, a ground, that pulls everything together and sets everything off, so I can see the layout of our yard as distinctly as if I were looking at a tinted schematic of it.

But our lawn is not so green or weedfree as the sleekly mown carpets in the gardening ads. And that's part of the pleasure too — to see the dandelions blooming now along the edge of the north lot line, the blue flowers of the creeping Charlie and wood violets scattered throughout the grass, and the white clover to come a month or so from now. All of them noxious weeds to a lawn purist, but I've never put any weedkiller on the lawn, because I don't want to poison the ground or the worms or the birds or our pets or ourselves. Besides, most of the weeds can be controlled by cutting the lawn high enough to suffocate them. And that's part of the pleasure too — maintaining a lawn in a natural way. A lawn that's also self-feeding because the clippings are pulverized and scattered like green fertilizer. But that's only part of the story.

Fifty-five years ago when I was growing up near the Cuyahoga River in Cleveland, in a brownstone walkup with my Uncle Manny, Aunt Celia, and her husband Uncle Ike, I yearned to live in a house in the suburbs with a lawn — a lawn as green as the ones that surrounded the homes of my cousins and my Hebrew school friends who lived in Cleveland Heights. A lawn, I now realize, embodied for me then not just the American dream of comfortable well-being, but also the green, green world of a home and parents like all the other kids whose lives I envied endlessly. So, after my uncle Manny died and I went to live with my uncle Dan and aunt Ruth in a house with a lawn in Cleveland Heights, I was dismayed to discover that a lawn didn't go hand in hand with happiness — especially if it had to be mowed every week with a hand-pushed reel mower. Now as I sit here looking back at that lawn and looking down on this one from our attic study, all the lawns of my life roll out before me, and I see that here, far from where I imagined I might find it, I've stumbled upon the right one for me. It's not so lush as the one of my childhood dreams, but it's green enough for me. And thanks to my heart attack, I no longer mow it myself.

SATURDAY *April 29*

All day yesterday when it was sunny, and the temperature hit the sixties for the first time this week, I had to be in the office. And I chafed all day, longing to be home for just a couple of hours, to plant the radishes and chard before the thunderstorm that was predicted for last night. I chafed so long that by the time I got home I was in a miserable mood, especially because there wasn't enough time to help with the dinner and also get in the seeds. So irritable I didn't even take any pleasure in a surprise royalty check from a textbook I thought had run its course. How compulsive must I be, I wondered, to let a minor frustration become so consuming a preoccupation, especially when the garden should be a source of pleasure and relaxation. But then it occurred to me that even if I couldn't plant any radish seeds, I might find a few radishes ready to harvest up at Jim's. And I did find a half dozen each of French Breakfast and German red, all so crisp and mild they tasted like spring rain. A taste that got me back in a good mood, especially when I realized we were beginning to eat our first crop of radishes just about the time that I usually seed in the first crop. Again thanks to the row covers and the lucky run of warm weather in mid-March.

And the good luck continued this morning, when I got up and discovered that it hadn't rained overnight, so I could seed in the chard and radishes after all. Though the sky was overcast and the air a bit chill, it looked and felt just right for putting in such cool-weather crops. And it was, except for the pain I felt in my injured chest. I figured it would hurt a bit to work up the soil, but I certainly didn't expect it to twinge every time I reached out to put down a seed. Twenty feet of radish seeds at the rate of about twelve seeds a foot adds up to a lot of twinges. No wonder Kate didn't want me to plant those seeds back on Tuesday.

The twenty feet of chard was painless by comparison — only one or two seeds a foot. A breeze except for having to keep track of the planted seeds lest they blend into the soil before I could get them covered with compost. Keeping my eyes so fixed on the soil, I soon found myself fascinated by the bits and pieces of decaying stuff in it — scraps of leaves, shreds of straw, shards of acorns, stems and roots of rotting plants, twigs, and bark, all going back to the source from which they came. An endless cycle taking place before my very eyes. But no matter how closely I looked, it was impossible for me to see the process itself taking place. All I could see were the bits and pieces themselves — the evidence. And a few of the creatures assisting in the process — a black ant that crawled out of the soil just then, a worm I'd come across when I was leveling the soil with my hands, and my hands themselves, planting the seed and covering it with compost. From chard it came, to chard it shall return.

SUNDAY *April 30*

L ast night after dinner, the rain started to fall — so gently that Kate and I and Pip went for a walk in it. And it continued falling gently until sometime past midnight. A half inch of it that watered in the chard and radishes without even the slightest sign of any pounding or washing. The sky was still overcast when I got up this morning, but an hour or two later it cleared up completely, and the temperatures rose into the high fifties.

Perfect weather for touring the yard. So I checked out the pear tree, still in full bloom, and the Dolgo crabapple that came into full bloom this morning, the dwarf sour cherry just starting to open its blossoms, and Jim's aged redbud just behind our lot covered with its diminutive purple blossoms. And when I wasn't gazing at the blossoming fruit trees, or the bloodroot along the north side of the house, or the white narcissus along the north lot line, or the yellow tulips and white daffodils in Kate's flower border, I was checking under the row covers, and noticed we're probably only a week away from being able to pick some fresh lettuce. The broccoli and cauliflower plants seem to have doubled in size just in the two weeks they've been in, and the snow peas as well as shell peas are growing so vigorously they'll soon need some brush to twine around.

This April, after all, has been an idyllic month for gardens and gardeners. Never a day above the sixties, only a few days below the fifties, and only a couple of damaging days during the Arctic cold snap early in the month. A cooler April on average than in recent years, when the temperatures have often risen to the seventies, eighties, and sometimes even the nineties, coupled with dry weather and harsh southwest winds. This year, by contrast, those drying winds have never come, and the seven inches of rainfall have more than made up for the shortage at the beginning of the month. So everything in the garden has come on slowly but vigorously, and the flowering bulbs, bushes, and trees have held their blossoms far longer than usual.

Looking back over this month, I was reminded of some other Aprils here in the early 1970s, cool and moist like this one. But before I knew it, I was also remembering so many other things from that time — our first dog Crispin, our first cat Calliope, the old gray shed where the gazebo now stands, the old gray barn where Jim's garage now stands, our neighbors to the north, our neighbors to the east, our neighbors to the south, our neighbors to the west, all dead or departed — that the passing years were more than thought could bear. Still, it was a fine April, well worth remembering, at least for the moment.

M A Y

May day but the May Day tree no longer stands outside the kitchen window. Victim last year of a seventy-mile-an-hour wind that wrenched one of its main limbs from the other, split its trunk down the center, leaving one half sprawled in the driveway, the other half standing, both bleeding dark sap for the next week or so before we could get anyone to come and put the tree out of its misery. Just when it was on the verge of opening its long panicles of aromatic blossoms. Kate and I planted the tree some fifteen years ago, and though it often bloomed a week or so in advance, its cream-white blossoms usually lingered long enough to sweeten the air as if in tribute to the day itself. It wasn't the first tree we lost, and it surely won't be the last. But none of the others wrenched me quite like the May Day tree. At first I thought it was the blossoms, or the pleasing spread and arch of its branches, reaching all the way up to the north bedroom window, or the perch it provided for birds, or the support it provided for bird feeders, or the suddenness of its demise, or its dark sap pooling on the ground. But now I think it was the presence of the tree so close to the kitchen window it was a part of our lives *every day of the year*. And a shady spot for Pip, sitting or standing on the low stone wall under its branches. Now in its place stands the dwarf Prairie Spy apple that Rebecca and I planted last year on a cool, overcast day like today, a tree so slow to unveil itself that only a few of its leaf buds have opened so far. A late bloomer, bred to protect its buds against the harsh springs of a prairie climate. So small a tree right now its main branch couldn't even support the weight of a house sparrow that tried to perch on it this morning. Oh, what a falling off was there! And the loss was borne in upon me again this morning not just by the day itself, but also by my walk down to school, when I passed a May Day tree, fully in bloom, just a block away from our house.

It never occurred to me before that having lived so long in one place I'd find myself reflexively looking backward so often, like one of those mallard ducks snoozing along the river bank with its head turned in toward its tail, like the old folks who've sometimes tried my patience with their interminable recollections. But memory, after all, is irrepressible, and the longer one lives in a single place the more, it seems, that place becomes a landscape of memories. Spots in time. Sites of remembrance. Every tree or bush burdened with the fruit of recollection. So the yard for me has become a daybook or a yearbook or a lifebook that I read every time I walk within it now.

But the image I want to hold in mind today is nowhere in the yard. I saw it for just a minute or so when I awoke after an apocalyptic dream of the sky gone permanently dark, looked out our bedroom window, and found it entirely suffused with pink. May Day — at least for a minute or so.

TUESDAY *May 2*

May seems to be picking up right where April left off — cool, moist, and overcast skies. A boon for the garden, especially for the spring vegetables under the row covers, where the temperature is closer to normal. But row covers are no help for the farmers whose fields have been wet for so long that they're now a few weeks behind on their field work. And they're not any help for people living along the flood plain, whose property is beginning to flood once again. And they're not even any help to me in dealing with the plants hunkered down in the Plexiglas-covered cellarway — the eggplants, the peppers, the tomatoes, and the second crop of lettuce — all waiting to be moved to the terrace to harden off, and then into the garden. In a few days or so, they'll have outgrown the space, and the space itself will be so heavily shaded by the maple tree, now beginning to leaf out, that the cellarway will be intolerable for the plants. Everything seems to be crowding everything else for space and time in the sun.

And not just in the garden. It's a universal condition, of course, most virulent these days in the continuing territorial conflicts within the Mideast or among the states in the former country of Yugoslavia. But I feel it most in the increasing tensions of youth and age. Perhaps I'm a bit more aware of it right now, because I was teaching an essay this morning about generational conflict, and the tensions were evident in the remarks of the students not only about the essay but also about their parents, their children, and people of their generation. I can also remember a couple of years ago when a young neighbor directly addressed me as "old man" and let me know he'd be living in the neighborhood long after I was gone. And I in turn can't say I was sorry to see him move away last summer. Even in the supposedly more humane and tolerant community of our department, I heard it reported last year that one of my younger colleagues openly declared everyone over forty-five to be out of date. Though I could easily dismiss such a report as rumor, exaggeration, or fatuous posturing, it's hard to ignore the fact that retired faculty in our department no longer can retain their offices, as they once did, by offering to share them with a young teaching assistant. Now we must move out immediately and confine ourselves to a three-room ghetto for all retired faculty. So our department is no longer like an extended family, and I, it seems, am facing retirement in more ways than one.

WEDNESDAY *May 3*

I just got into school after a brisk walk down — a mile and three quarters in twenty-two minutes on a cool, overcast day — and I'm wondering why some of my colleagues and students think of me as being old. I don't feel old, don't think I look all that old, don't even think my body's all that old. The twinges from my fall last week have completely disappeared, the yellowish-purple bruises on my chest are gradually fading away, and I'm sitting here at my computer batting out this report, having just finished scanning a few weather maps and projections that I pulled up on the Internet. Up-to-date mind in an up-to-date body. Sound enough to know that what I'm writing right now sounds mighty defensive. But my hackles are up, raised by the cultural stereotyping that I feel all around me, that wafts by me in the halls, that I hear in remarks about the older generation, and in some of my younger colleagues' public statements about "racism" in the department. As if I knew nothing of bigotry. Given my age, I can claim the special privilege of having been told some forty-two years ago by my undergraduate honors advisor at Michigan that if I aspired to a university position in the field of English, I'd best try to get into an eastern graduate school, given "the problem" of my Jewish background. And I can remember being one of the two or three token Jewish faculty in my first job at Bowdoin College. And I can remember how I was subsequently investigated by the dean and his minions there when I raised questions about the branding ceremony being used at one of the college fraternities. They didn't particularly like my comparisons to cattle cars and concentration camps. In the history of bigotry, there is no beginning and there is no end. My younger colleagues here, especially the minorities and the women, worry intensely now about racial and gender stereotyping, and with good cause. But I wonder if they worry at all about how they stereotype me and others of my age, as I, alas, now seem to stereotype them and others of their age.

If I thought there were any solution to such deeply ingrained ways of thinking and feeling, I'd not want to withdraw forever to the garden. Right now, for example, I'm thinking again about the aged pear tree in the center of the yard, still covered with white blossoms, now unfurling its shiny green leaves. And I'm remembering again how we thought about cutting it down at the end of last summer, because it hadn't borne any fruit, but our faithful tree surgeon Leon assured us that it still had some good years left in it. Now, finally, I think I'm beginning to understand Christ's parable of the fruitless fig tree. I only wish it were applied as often to people as it is to trees.

THURSDAY *May 4*

As if the misty weather weren't enough, yesterday's mail brought a notice from The Temple in Cleveland that today is the anniversary of my mother's death and that her name — Caroline Klaus — will be read at kaddish services tomorrow night. Her name will be read, though neither I nor my brother Marshall, nor any of her widely scattered nephews and nieces, grandchildren or great-grandchildren, will be there to hear the reading of it. Her name will be read every year at this time, so long as The Temple stands and the kaddish is recited. If a tree falls in a forest and no one is there to hear it, is there a noise?

I've often wondered what her voice sounded like, but I was so young when she died — five going on six — and she'd been afflicted with breast cancer and the searing effects of excessive radiation for so long that I can recall only a few early memories. Her giving me a dish of Jell-O, cubed, with whipped cream. Her playing popular songs on the Steinway grand that her parents gave her when she got married. Her riding in the back of the ambulance with me and my brother Marshall, after he'd been hit by a car. No voice. Just images. And not very many at that. No wonder I used to dream of walking up to her casket to look in, only to see it start spinning, end on end, before my very eyes.

And the handful of pictures I'm looking at right now don't tell me much more, although now that I notice it she seems a bit camera shy or uncertain of herself, whether she's at home in Cleveland, at the beach in Atlantic City, or at a house in the country, whether she's standing alone or side by side with her father, a girl friend, a boy friend, or her younger brothers, my uncles Norman and Raymond. Her lips are always parted, her teeth usually showing, but the smile never seems full, relaxed, exuberant. Always a bit contained. And the same is true of the way she stands or holds her arms and hands — always a bit posed, stiff, never quite fully at ease. So, it seems, I share at least one trait with her. I'm camera shy too.

But her letters to her older sister, Leah, are something else. Every one of them filled with gossip, zip, and zesty exclamations — "Ha! Ha!", "Oh boy!", "oh-oh-oh!", "Wow!" Everything so "wonderful" or "grand" or "marvelous" that it's hard to believe she was dead at thirty-five. A few years after she died, I can remember lying under the trees at summer camp, looking up into the scattered clouds, trying to see if I could discern her there or some sign of her there. And later on I can remember wondering what life might have been like had she lived. But I always wound up being so different from myself that the thought was inconceivable. Now I sometimes wish she could see the back yard on a day like this — the pear tree still in bloom, the dwarf cherry opening its blossoms, the narcissus still holding on (she "adored" the narcissus my father gave her) — just to hear one of those marvelous exclamations.

FRIDAY *May 5*

Every spring, usually in mid- to late April, usually after a run of chilly, overcast days, comes a singular day when the sky's so clear, the air so mild, the wind so calm that everything seems momentarily stilled, breathless, briefly at rest before the run up to summer. Today was the day. A week or two late and therefore all the more special when it settled in around nine this morning. Then, at last, I knew it would be safe to move all the plants from the outside cellarway to the terrace. And none too soon, since they were all on the verge of bumping up against the Plexiglas door. Then I knew it was also time for another of my spring rituals — setting up the old circular wooden picnic table on the terrace to provide a squirrel-free place for my vegetable plants and Kate's flower seedlings. And none too soon, since the squirrels have been digging for walnuts in Kate's seedling trays. They've also been biting off tulip blossoms, so her ire's up and with good cause. "They've already destroyed all the tulips at the edge of the terrace and now they're going after my marigold plants. There's no point in my starting these things if the squirrels are just going to destroy all of them. You've got to set up the table."

Actually, the squirrels this spring have been much less damaging than they were during the drought years of the late 1980s. Back then, especially in 1989, they multiplied far beyond normal, as if they were reproducing against the prospect of a massive die-off. Then they started digging incessantly at everything in the vegetable gardens and the flower beds, plucking off tulip heads all around the lot. I went after the horde with a Havahart trap, rotating it around the yard near their favorite haunts, first at the edge of my garden, then under the pin oak tree by the compost bins, then under the maple tree by the terrace. The first day of the trap, April 29, I nabbed four squirrels and relocated them all in the country. The next day five more. The next three months, another fifteen, for a grand total of twenty-four. My tally also included one blue jay, two cardinals, two raccoons, and Phoebe. By the end of July, my vigilance produced a completely squirrel-free yard and an eerily quiet landscape that lasted for about a month. Then the squirrels from nearby yards gradually started to relocate themselves at our place. Nature abhors a vacuum.

So I've decided to set up the trap first thing tomorrow morning, and clear out the critters before they do any more damage. I don't expect to nab as many as I did during the great roundup of 1989. But anything's better than being victimized by tree rats. Then all I have to do is keep spraying things with Hinder, the organic deer and rabbit repellent. And pray that nothing else moves in from the wilderness park over the hill. No wonder I fret about the garden.

SATURDAY *May 6*

After I set up the table yesterday and put all our seedlings on top of it, I spent most of the day in the attic commenting on a set of student essays that came in a couple of weeks ago. Occasionally I looked longingly out the window at Kate, planting and transplanting things along the front of her flower border. And occasionally I walked around the newly mown yard, smelling the grass, checking on the fruit trees and berry bushes, wishing I could stay outside and work in the vegetable garden on such an idyllic day. But yesterday was the last day of the semester, and I'd promised to return those essays by late afternoon, a few days at least before the final essays are due next Wednesday. Some things about teaching I won't miss, and one of them is the paper load, even the evocative essays I usually receive from our graduate students in the nonfiction program. Forty years of responding to student writing has sometimes left me feeling as if I've run out of things to say. As if I've overdrawn my bank account. And at moments like that, I want to stop teaching altogether and not even think about keeping a hand in after I retire.

But today I was free to garden with a clear conscience, and I went at it all day, working to beat the thunderstorms predicted for the next three days. This morning I put in a row of potatoes, the first time I've grown them in fifteen years. There's nothing quite so delicate as small potatoes, freshly dug, but the garden space back then was so tight I didn't feel I could keep growing them. Now that I've got two vegetable beds, and the seed companies have come up with fingerling potatoes, I'm eager to see how they taste, say, with some fresh peas from the garden and a roast leg of lamb. There's also nothing quite like hoeing out a trench deep enough and wide enough for potatoes, so by lunch time I was ready for a break. But not before I baited the Havahart trap with a couple of cracked walnuts covered with peanut butter — the lure of choice for an errant squirrel. After lunch, I planted the second crop of greens — another double row of arugula, buttercrunch, Carmona butterhead, purple oak leaf, radicchio, romaine, and Simpson green leaf. These like the Swiss chard are just a few feet away from the gazebo, where the shade of the roof will protect them from the heat of the mid- to late afternoon sun. By late afternoon, even in the shade of the gazebo, I was wilting a bit from the heat, which reached the mid-seventies for the first time this spring. So, after covering the lettuces to protect them from deer and rabbits, I checked the trap, as yet untouched, scattered a few additional walnut crumbs toward its entryway, and called it a day. Come morning, a squirrel will probably be waiting for a ride to the Iowa countryside. And I'll be free to provide it, now that all the spring vegetables are in.

SUNDAY *May 7*

Neither a squirrel nor a storm was in evidence when I got up this morning. The sky, in fact, was as clear as the trap. So clear that the sun cast a sharp image of my shadow on the grass as I stood at the back of the yard, looking down toward the gardens and the gazebo. So much for the weather forecasts and my own squirrelly projections. Late in the morning, though, Kate saw a squirrel in the trap, and together with Pip we took it out to the countryside, to a belt of trees with a creek meandering through it. And by midafternoon, the sky had clouded over, presaging the rain that started falling shortly after dinner.

But the main event of the day was the annual spring cleaning of the gazebo and the return of the terrace and gazebo furniture from the basement. Easy tasks with pleasant results. Domesticity in the garden. But whenever I start sweeping out the brick floor of the gazebo, cleaning up everything that's gathered over the winter from squirrels and birds and my own comings and goings, I invariably remember myself sweeping out the cracked concrete floor of the old rectangular shed that used to stand on the same spot. Kate stripped that tarpaper-covered thing to its cobbled studs before we moved into the house and turned it into a makeshift summer place for plants, garden tools, tomato poles, fishing rods, dozing cats, cocktails, snacks, and occasional student conferences. For nineteen years, I stored so many things in the rafters of that place and spent so many hours in it contemplating the garden that it truly felt like a second home, though its weathered timbers, criss-crossed with supports to steady it against the wind, actually made it look like the set for a backwoods drama by Tennessee Williams.

Now in its place, on the rise of land behind the terrace, stands a structure as elegant and strong as the other was rickety, shabby, and finally unsafe — a neoclassically proportioned structure that Kate designed six years ago when she was recovering from breast cancer surgery and chemotherapy. Its four-sided sloping roof is supported by six solid wooden columns in an Etruscan style — columns that Kate retrieved from a house that was being torn down several blocks away. Columns just like the ones supporting the roof on the front porch of our house. "Buy me those columns," she said, "and I'll make something of them." And make something she did, though for ten years they sat in the basement, looking like a kit for the Parthenon. Spaced between the columns, on each side and at each end, stand trelliswork panels that filter the light and cut the wind. Though we call it a gazebo, others have referred to it as a pergola, a pleasance, a folly, or a summerhouse.

And now once again it's ready for summer, for the affirmation of life that inspired it.

MONDAY *May 8*

L ast night's rainfall was also inspiring, at least on our sloping lot. It started falling lightly just when Pip and I went out for an afterdinner walk, and it lasted until sometime around four or five this morning. Long enough to yield almost two inches in eight hours, to refill the lily pond, resaturate the soil, and match our normal rainfall for May, though there's still more than three weeks to go before the end of the month. So the peril of flooding is again on the rise. And the mood of farmers is again on edge — most of their fields still unplanted. But it could've been much worse, given the fact we were just on the edge of a massive weather system that killed twenty-five people, spawned six tornadoes, and produced violent thunderstorms everywhere along its north-eastern path from Texas through Oklahoma and Missouri. And before this three-day blow has run its course, there's no predicting what damage it might do around here.

So far, it's been a boon to everything in the yard, judging from my checkups this morning and late afternoon. Overnight, it seems as if all of the spring vegetables have grown visibly larger. And the same is true of the red raspberries and all the perennials in Kate's flower border. Last week, she was fretting about the absent balloon flowers. Now they're three inches above ground. Everything rising, I think, in response to the first warm rain of the spring. Even the leaves of the pin oak tree, which were just beginning to open late last week, are now the size of mouse ears — a sure sign the soil is warm enough to begin planting corn. And the grass which was mown just three days ago is tall enough to need mowing once again.

But the most visible gift of the storm is the color it's strewn everywhere in town. Kate first noticed it last night when she saw the wind blowing white blossoms from the Dolgo crabapple all across the front lawn. I first noticed it this morning when I saw the terrace littered with chartreuse blossoms from our maple tree.

Then on my way down to work, when I passed a lawn strewn with the hot pink petals of a flowering crab. Then as my colleague Miriam was driving me home this afternoon, I gradually began to notice streaks of color not only on the lawns but also on the street sides and curbs and gutters — the streaks becoming longer, the colors more intense, the shadings more varied with every passing block. Hot pink, white, and yellow-green. Hot pink, white, and yellow-green. As if a madcap modern painter had been jogging through the city, jazzing up the streetscape. No special messages. Nothing like graffiti. More like confetti. A coincidence of rain and wind and blossoms on the loose.

TUESDAY *May 9*

"The sky is falling! The sky is falling!" Or so it seemed all afternoon. The sky so dark, the clouds so low, the thunder so loud, an angel of the Lord seemed to be passing over me. And then the rains came, drenching the river directly below my office window. And then they passed as suddenly as they came, the sky clearing a bit before it darkened again and thundered again and rained again. And again. In the interim between the downpours, I nabbed an umbrella from the lost and found, jogged to the bus stop, mailed the monthly bills, and took a bus home, just in time to beat the next series of downpours. All quite brief, but heavy enough to add another half inch to the tally.

Pip in a panic, Phoebe on the couch, plants on the porch, and Kate in a swivet at the kitchen counter, deboning lamb shanks for a white bean casserole for our friend Trudy, who's coming tomorrow on her annual spring trek from New Jersey to her summer cabin in Wyoming. "All Things Considered" on the radio, passing on news about the overnight deluge in New Orleans — eighteen inches in six hours. Local newscasters breaking in to report on regional conditions — tornadoes in Muscatine County, tornado warning in Linn County, and tornado watch here in Johnson County until eight this evening. And Kate breaking in to report on local conditions — "pea-sized hail on the terrace earlier this afternoon."

But now as I sit here in the attic, drafting this report, there's a clear blue strip of sky on the western horizon, big enough for the sun to be shining through it, spotlighting the gazebo and illuminating the entire back yard. The lawn so lush, the leaves so fresh, the greens so varied, the yard seems like variations on a theme, except for the lavender of the redbuds at the corner of the back lot. And now from behind his garage, Jim suddenly appears, wearing a black jacket, beige pants, and a farmer's cap as red as a cardinal. Up and down the red cap bobs, as he bends over his broccoli plants and his pepper plants and his onion plants and his ancient dachshund Peaches.

The calm between the storms. The pin oak, the pear, the larch, and the spruces motionless. A slight flutter in the maple. Not a ripple in the row covers. All quiet on the eastern front. But the storm will come again, as surely as this morning's clear skies gradually gave way to the clouds and clamor of this afternoon. In the meantime, it's time for me to go downstairs and broil some hoki fillets, steam some jasmine rice, slice some tomatoes, and harvest some arugula, green leaf lettuce, purple oak leaf, romaine, and scallions for a salad with tarragon vinaigrette. The first garden lettuce of the spring. Fresh as newly fallen rain.

WEDNESDAY *May 10*

It's hard to believe that just two months ago I was worrying about abnormally high temperatures, abnormally low rainfall, and abnormally dry soil — conditions so troublesome I imagined myself having to water the garden from May on, as if it were a replay of the 1989 drought. But now the temperature's below normal, the rainfall's above normal, and the soil's so waterlogged I wonder when it'll dry out enough for me to tend things in the vegetable gardens. It's hard to believe that the weather could change so much that I'm now worrying about a deluge rather than a drought.

It's also hard to believe that the conditions of our lives could change so much that where I once believed I was teaching in a friendly and relaxed department, I now sometimes feel as if I'm working in the midst of an edgy and uncomfortable place. A place where people are so alert, and legitimately so, for signs of the prejudice that has poisoned our country that some of my colleagues have recently detected evidence of what they believe to be racism even in John, the retired eighty-seven-year-old chair of the department who transformed it in the sixties and early seventies by his appointment of twelve women and five African-Americans to a department that previously had none. And what is the evidence of his racism? At a recent departmental award ceremony, I gather, he told a self-deprecating story about how he had misjudged a black student when he was a young instructor back in 1936. But in telling the story, he evidently used some words or phrases that led some people to perceive him as guilty of racial stereotyping. How is it possible, I wonder, that someone could be seen as reinforcing racial stereotypes when he tells a story about the dangers of racial stereotyping? How is it possible, I wonder, that someone could be so harshly judged even in the process of openly judging himself?

Heavy rain and too much ozone? Or changing weather patterns? Or just a freakish event, like thunder in January or snow in June? I wish I could figure out why Ed felt compelled to send John a letter telling him that his story was offensive to many members of the department, why he couldn't just have given John a call to chat with him about it. Especially since opinion seems to have been divided among people who heard John's remarks — some intensely disturbed, others not. But at this point, it's clear to me that I don't know enough about the weather to explain it. Still, I can certainly see and hear a bad thunderstorm when it's coming my way, and I know enough from years of living in the midst of clashing weather systems to watch out for tornadoes, especially at this time of year. I wish it were just a case of people being a bit too sensitive about some of the hot words and phrases that usually betoken a racist attitude. But as several of my colleagues said to me today, they fear it's a sign of deeply generational conflicts. How else to construe Ed's memo asserting that John's story "undermined the kind of community this department has become and is becoming." Sounds like changing weather patterns, and I wish they'd blow over. But I fear they're with us for some time to come, like global warming and acid rain.

THURSDAY *May 11*

"No, that's wild phlox over there. You can tell by the width of its leaf and the color of its flower. See how delicate the leaf is on this one?" Actually, I could see the difference, once I knelt down to look at it, but only after Kate had pointed it out to me. I could also see that the hot pink color of the Bouncing Bette I was looking at clearly differed from the whites and lavenders of the phlox several feet away. But initially I thought it looked like phlox, much as I'd been mistaking one wildflower for another all the time we were out looking at them this afternoon with Trudy. The three of us were making our annual visit to Rochester Cemetery, a well-known burial place some twenty miles east of here, staked out by the earliest settlers in this part of Iowa. Their weather-beaten tombstones lean all over the rough and rolling hillsides, majestic white oaks shading the cemetery's upper terrain, and prairie wildflowers rampant on virtually every square inch of its surface. Shooting stars, wild anemone, wild columbine, wild geranium, birdfoot violet, white violet, buttercup, blue-eyed grass, May apples — I can barely remember all the names, though I kept asking Kate and Trudy to identify them at every turn along the way. Mostly what I remember is the feeling of ignorance I get whenever I go wildflowering with the two of them — Trudy comparing her eastern and Rocky Mountain varieties with Kate's midwestern ones. "Your shooting stars are so much larger than the ones we have in Wyoming." Plant size, leaf shape, color range, Latin names bouncing back and forth, like a field guide to the wildflowers in the form of a duet.

It's not that either of them set out to make me feel ignorant. In fact, at one point, Kate asked me to identify some plants which were clearly not wildflowers but cucumber seedlings that probably got started from the residue of fall picnickers or wild birds. And at another point, I noticed several wild raspberries that both of them had overlooked. But in the act of noticing those cucumbers and raspberries, I couldn't help realizing how completely I've trained myself to see food plants, and by doing so have almost blinded myself to the subtler differences among wildflowers. Walking out of the cemetery, though, I called their attention to a fascinating pair of arched stones, standing side by side. No names on them. Just MOTHER on one, with a rounded pair of wings below, and FATHER on the other, with the sharply pointed masonic symbol below. But Kate and Trudy were uncertain about the symbol on the mother's tomb. Trudy thought it might be a pair of leaves, rather than wings, but Kate didn't agree. Now I don't know what to think. Maybe it was just a pair of long hair combs.

FRIDAY *May 12*

Another wave of rainstorms is predicted to move in tonight and hang in for the next ten days. So it's beginning to look like the deluge again, and no quick relief in sight. At moments like this, I wonder why I've let myself become as wrapped up in the weather as if I were a farmer, hanging on every forecast to determine the fate of my well-being. Just as the farmers right now are aching to get their cornfields planted before it's too late to bring in a decent crop, I'm aching to get my tomato plants in the ground before they get leggy and root bound from sitting too long in a three- or four-inch square of potting soil. If worse comes to worst, I might even transplant a few to larger pots, so they can keep on growing without being thwarted during the coming rains. But what a fusspot thing to fret about while my colleagues and friends are heading off to the mountains or the seaside or the continent, or anywhere else but here. Trudy to her cabin in the Rockies, David and Rebecca to Spain, Stavros to Greece, Miriam to Stratford-on-Avon — so many people going somewhere for a month or two or three, while Kate and I stay home, as usual, tethered to our gardens.

I guess it was putting in the pea brush this morning with Trudy that got me thinking about how Kate and I have subordinated our lives to the needs of the yard and the gardens. Every spring, I go through this ritual of building a cathedral-like structure along each double row of peas, to provide a support for the vines to twine around as they grow upward on their way to producing peas. And the structure has to be built before the vines get so tall that they're twining all over each other, pulling themselves to the ground. Looking at the vines over the past few days, I could see the snow peas were approaching a critical height, so I felt compelled to put in the pea brush for them today, given the rains predicted for the next ten days. That meant an entire morning devoted to cutting the forked twigs of brush three or four feet tall, then sticking them in the ground every three or four inches between the rows as well as along the outside of each row. Not exactly what I wanted to be doing this lovely morning, even though it was a pleasure to do it with Trudy, even though the finished A-frame structure was pleasing to contemplate, even though the contemplation of it reminded me of my long-dead neighbor Herman, from whom I learned it some twenty-five years ago. But when I told Trudy about feeling trapped by the garden, she was quick to remind me that her cabin in Wyoming is also a trap — a trap without a vegetable garden, given the lack of soil and the chilling temperatures all summer long. So when I looked at the snow peas later this afternoon, I didn't feel quite so resentful, especially when Trudy showed me how alive they were, already twining, already traveling toward the top of the brush.

SATURDAY *May 13*

"The days of the three ice kings!" Kate doesn't ordinarily make such dramatic entrances, but those were the first words out of her mouth as she swept down the stairs this morning in her purple paisley robe. Trudy and I, chatting in the living room, were both taken by surprise, Trudy because she'd never heard of the three ice kings, and I because I'd completely forgotten about them. According to local legend, probably a heritage of the Bohemians who settled our neighborhood, May 13, 14, and 15 are the days of the three ice kings — days when the weather often turns cold enough to produce a light frost or even a heavy freeze. Not exactly the conditions we had this morning, with temperatures heading toward the sixties or low seventies. But then again, there was a point to Kate's announcement, given the thirty-mile-an-hour wind and rain that were blowing our way this morning. Enough to register another three quarters of an inch in the rain gauge, and force a postponement of the neighborhood park cleanup that had been planned for this morning.

Actually, the rain started falling late yesterday afternoon, when we were visiting our friend Mary, who lives out in the country in a remodeled one-room schoolhouse and writes about life among her Amish neighbors. Kate, Trudy, and I had gone to visit Mary and to meet the latest members of her barnyard family — a huge overly friendly dog named Bear, who recently adopted her, and a little flock of ducklings, goslings, and baby turkeys, all so young they were still more down than feathers. Together with her three pygmy goats and four lambs, Mary's whole batch of critters seems a bit like Old MacDonald's farm, except for want of a milk cow, a horse, and a pig. But the image that sticks in my mind is of Mary, standing at the edge of her white-painted henhouse, shooing the little flock inside with a mock cackle in her voice, fretting about the storm.

And the storm was also on Trudy's mind this morning when she was loading up her Jeep before heading off to Wyoming. "The spring snowstorms have been so heavy this year that the man who looks after my place tells me there are four-foot drifts on my road. So I'll probably have to park the Jeep a mile away and hike in." No wonder she was a little uncertain about accepting one of the patio cherry tomato plants that I potted up yesterday. Still, it was a pleasure to watch her pack that plant right next to the gearshift just before she drove off. None of my vegetable plants has ever gotten farther than a few miles from here, certainly not to a snowbound cabin in the Rockies.

And today none of my vegetable plants and none of Kate's flower seedlings even made it off the back porch. This year, the days of the three ice kings have turned into the days of the three rain kings.

SUNDAY *May 14*

By late afternoon yesterday, the air had turned so hot and heavy that Kate and I were both fretting about the possibility of a violent thunderstorm. But the air outside was nothing compared to the atmosphere we encountered a bit later in a crowded Victorian parlor at my colleague Garrett's home, where a surprise party was being staged for Ed, celebrating his retirement as chair of the English department. The atmosphere at Garrett's was still heavy from the storm that had erupted over John's remarks at the honors ceremony, everyone on edge from all the letters and public statements of the past two weeks, including one I wrote and circulated among the senior faculty from John's era, conveying to him our belief that his remarks were undoubtedly well intentioned. Maybe that's why none of the junior faculty came near where I was standing, as if the air around me were dangerously charged. And the tension gradually increased with the entrance of John, the entrance of Ed, and the movement of the two to greet each other, two distinctly different generations confronting one another, all smiles, as if lightning had never passed between them. But surely the most charged event at the party took place a few moments later, when Dee, the incoming chair, stood up to read a two-page statement celebrating Ed's splendid service as chair — the two facing each other, with John seated between them, and Kate standing ramrod straight next to John, like a loyal liege. No wonder Dee's hands were shaking as she read those remarks. No wonder Ed, who's ordinarily so articulate, was briefly at a loss for words in responding to her. No wonder Kate and I were eager to leave after that for dinner with John and my colleague Carol — eager to get outside, where the sky had cleared, the air turned dry, and the evening was aswarm with high school and college graduates performing their own rites of passage in tuxedos and tennis shoes, cocktail dresses and evening gowns.

By comparison with yesterday, Mother's Day today has been a diversion from the generational struggles in the department. Most families, of course, have their own generational warfare, and mothers are often at the center of it. But driving to the Amana Colonies today for a German-American country dinner with Kate and her mother Lib was a genuine blessing. The northwest air, the clear skies, the mild temperatures, the lush Iowa countryside — everything in tune with the spirit of the day, even the roadside motel sign, THANK   FOR THE   EMORIES.

MONDAY *May 15*

A perfect day for gardening, with temperatures in the seventies and mild southern breezes. But I had other things on my mind. Like paying the overdue real estate taxes, taking Phoebe to the vet for an inspection of her cancerous growth, and going to the cancer clinic with Kate while she had a pea-size growth removed from her chest. The taxes turned out to be the easiest part of the day.

The vet was openly surprised that Phoebe's still alive. "I never thought she'd last this long, so I wouldn't want to predict what might happen. She could go on for a while, or everything could change tomorrow, if the growth begins to interfere with things, like her ability to urinate. It's much bigger now. But she hasn't lost much weight, and she still looks good for a cat her age. Most cats don't live beyond thirteen or fourteen, and she's almost twenty." An interesting statistic, but not much solace in the long run, especially when I thought she might live to be twenty-five. So each day now seems more precious than the one before. This afternoon, she spent a few minutes lounging on the warmth of the terrace, as she used to do for days on end in the long hot summers of her youth. Tomorrow she might really take to the stones, since it's predicted to reach into the eighties for the first time this spring. But then again, who knows what she might do tomorrow?

Kate's cancer surgeon reported to her that the growth he removed was "not obviously cancerous" to him or the people in the biopsy lab, but the results won't be clear until Wednesday when they've made a permanent slide of the tissue and examined it under a microscope. If it does turn out to be cancerous, there are various options, from doing nothing to attacking it with everything. But they won't even discuss the options until a week from now if that turns out to be the case. So many uncertainties and so many delays that all the way home in the car, I kept wishing he'd said it was "obviously not cancerous." Or words to that effect. Oh, what a difference a few words can make, or just the arrangement of a couple of words.

So, except for the real estate taxes, uncertainty seems to be the rule of the day on this home front. Late this afternoon, though, when I was planting a row of shallots at the east end of the vegetable garden, I found a volunteer seedling that definitely appeared to be a sunflower, growing in exactly the same spot where a volunteer sunflower emerged last summer. I showed it to Kate, and she agreed that it was definitely a sunflower. So there's one sure thing — at least for the moment.

TUESDAY *May 16*

Last night at midnight when I went for a walk with Pip, the full moon was visible in the southern sky, backlighting the edges of all the cumulus clouds nearby. A sight so striking I stood in the yard and gazed at it through the walnut trees, just beginning to unfurl their leaves. But the moonlit clouds were hardly so surprising as the small flicker of light I noticed at the edge of a neighbor's lawn just a few minutes later. Could that possibly be a firefly so early in the season? I walked back a few steps to check, and as if to satisfy my curiosity, it flickered again. The first firefly of the year. Another sure thing to go with the sunflower I discovered yesterday in the garden. But I also wonder if it's a harbinger of bugs to come, given the unusually warm winter this winter.

This morning when I awoke, the sun was lighting the edges of the clouds with an aura of coral pink, as if to announce another good day for gardening. But I had to turn in final grades this morning. Besides, the soil in the back vegetable bed was still too wet and chilly for planting the tomatoes, and the tomatoes themselves still need a few more days of hardening off before they'll be ready for the garden. So I've moved them from the terrace, now mostly shaded by the maple, to the edge of the gazebo, where they're sitting in trays with the peppers and eggplants, getting more accustomed to the sun and the breezes that constantly play across our back yard. And Kate's moved her seedlings to the top of the stone retaining wall at the edge of the terrace.

Every spring we go through this process of acclimating our seedlings to the strenuous summer climate on our west sloping lot — moving them from the house to the back porch to the terrace to the gazebo and the retaining wall and finally into the garden. A process that sometimes tries my patience to the limit, but I've learned from a few premature planting escapades that there's no point in trying to force the summer vegetables. Jim got away with it last year, but this year he lost his pepper plants to a light frost a few days after he put them in. So, a couple of days ago when I went up to harvest the last of the early radish crop to make room for his tomatoes, he was sounding more cautious than ever before. "I'm gonna wait a few more days before putting them in. Maybe even a week. I'm not even gonna buy any yet, so I'm not tempted by having 'em around."

I wasn't tempted today, for the sudden warm-up had me hustling around to remove the row covers from the broccoli, the cauliflower, and the shell peas, lest they cook under the extra heat. And once the peas were uncovered, I had to put in all the brush for them to climb on, before the rain that moved in again late this afternoon. But the garden at last is beginning to look like a real garden of green vegetables, rather than a ghostly series of white row covers.

WEDNESDAY *May 17*

The minute I got up this morning, I was already on edge, wondering when Kate's doctor would call with the results of the biopsy. But I put it in the back of my mind, figuring he would call soon enough. And I threw myself into the morning chores, hustling Pip and Phoebe out for some fresh air, moving Kate's plants from the porch to the terrace walls, pulling mine from inside the gazebo to the sunny edge of its brick floor, feeding the animals, checking the rain gauge, keeping busy. The skies were still overcast from last night's rain, but the rain had been light, producing only a tenth of an inch. So I figured the sun might come out this afternoon and the soil be dry enough by then to do some planting.

The rest of the morning I devoted to weeding and resetting the forty-five-foot border of bricks along the north edge of the main vegetable garden. Not a good choice for keeping myself distracted, since it was Kate who laid the entire brick border around the garden some twenty-five years ago. But I didn't immediately remember her creating that brick frame, for I was thinking of the spring day just a few years ago when several of my writing students came out to fix up the border from the years of rain and soil erosion that had gradually undermined it, especially along the north edge. How quickly it eroded again! Still, it was a pleasant task, and I finished it quickly, though not so swiftly as Rebecca cleaned out the big shade border where the Virginia bluebells and the pink-cup daffodils and the pheasant-eye narcissus and the wild single buttercups are now in bloom and the gigantic spreading leaves of the hosta *Sieboldiana elegans* are fully opened along with the arching leaves of the comfrey. For a moment there I was pleasantly distracted by it all.

But shortly after lunch, just as I was heading outside, the doctor called and reported that the growth did have some cancer cells in it. So next Tuesday, Kate will have the full battery of bone scans and blood scans to determine whether it has traveled anywhere else in her body. And then based on the results of the tests, the doctor will outline her various options. Kate, it seems, was expecting the bad news, for she has ever been more realistic than I am. I, as usual, was planning a celebration of the good news that never came. And even when I heard the news, I looked for the best possible outcome — that the cancer might be confined just to the growth, while Kate was facing the uncertainty itself — "I'm in limbo, man."

After the news, I tried to distract myself by spading up the annual side of the herb bed and raking it out. But working the soil hardly compared with a walk in the wilderness park, where Kate, Pip, and I suddenly came upon a hillside of wild geranium in bloom — lavender blossoms dappling the wooded landscape like sunlight as far as the eye could see, while the sunlight itself was illuminating the flowers through the flickering leaves of the trees overhead. An impressionist scene so striking it sent me back home distracted enough to plant some curly and flat-leaf parsley, two rows of nasturtium seeds, and a couple of tomato plants, a Big Beef and the fabled Brandywine. Those are the only certainties for now.

THURSDAY *May 18*

"You're not going to fall apart on me now, are you?" Kate had a slight smile on her face when she asked me that question. I wondered what could possibly make her think I might do such a thing when I was just standing at the kitchen counter concocting Phoebe's breakfast. "Something about the look on your face, or maybe the way you were holding your shoulders, like you were about to crumble, or something." Actually, I think it was just the cold air this morning that was making me hunch up my shoulders to keep myself warm. The temperature outside was then in the mid-forties after an overnight rain that dropped another three tenths of an inch, and I'd just come in from a chilly walk around the yard to check on the parsley and tomatoes I planted yesterday afternoon. But that little tour of the yard did get me thinking about some of the things we said to each other yesterday, the gallows humor that passed between us then, and perhaps the memory of those words had played across my face. I was thinking especially of how Kate had responded to my remark that the news would bring new life to this daybook — "You mean new death to it?" At the moment, I'd thought she was speaking mostly in jest, turning my words back on me with a twist of black humor. But later yesterday evening, I didn't think she was joking when she read my piece for the day and said, "It's beautifully written, but it sounds like an obituary, and I'm not dead yet, not by a long shot. But let's not keep focusing on it like this. There'll be enough to focus on next week after all the tests are in."

So this afternoon, after the rain passed over, and the sky cleared up, and the sun came out, and the wind died down, I focused again on the garden. A squirrel must have been digging in the potted artichoke plant, so I reset the Havahart trap under the maple tree, where a pair of the critters have been frisking with each other the past several days. Then I moved all the seedlings to their sunbathing spots and gave them a drink of water. Then seeded up a six-pack of yellow pattypan and green zucchini. Also six-packs of three different pickling cucumbers — Cross Country, Homemade, and Liberty — so we'll be sure to have a decent crop this summer, rather than the puny pickings of the past few seasons.

Enough, I hope, for Kate's bread-and-butter pickles, my kosher dills, and fresh cucumber salads. Late in the afternoon, the soil was dry enough in the back bed for me to move another pair of tomato plants into the garden — another Big Beef and Kate's dark Russian heirloom, the Black Prince. Then after picking some spinach for a salad to go with Kate's rabbit cacciatore, I thought the day was over. But the clatter of the squirrel trap meant an afterdinner ride into the countryside. Now I hope I can catch its mate, so I can reunite them in that lovely stretch of woods with the creek running through it.

FRIDAY *May 19*

Late this morning, Kate and I were walking by a house that used to have a continuous display of annual and perennial flowers — daffodils, narcissus, tulips, peonies, and roses in profusion — and she noticed it had completely reverted to a bare green lawn. "Remember how different that place used to be? Everything is so evanescent." I'd been thinking the same thing from the time that Rebecca came over this morning and we started to work on what used to be the perennial side of the herb bed, but had reverted to nothing but a patch of weeds, a host of scraggly mint plants, and a few other scrawny herbs, like oregano and sorrel that simply couldn't do very well under the afternoon shade of the maple tree. Twenty-five years ago, when we first moved in, the maple was so young it cast almost no shadow at all. Now the terrace is almost continuously under its shade, and the herb bed is gradually being shaded out by it. So, for the time being, I turned it into another lettuce patch. An emblem of evanescence.

And not just in the garden, but in our lives, even in ourselves, as I discovered anew at lunch with Kate and several of my graduate students — Becky, Dan, John, Maura, and Rebecca. A surprise affair at which my students gave me an extraordinary gift — a computer-printed and hand-bound collection of letters and essays that they and former graduates of the nonfiction program had written in honor of my retirement last year as director of the program. Even in my daydreams, I never imagined that anyone might write anything in my honor, because I've never had the kind of scholarly career that calls forth such celebratory collections. But I can remember thinking that the only kind of collection I'd ever want, even if I deserved such a thing, would be the kind that no one would probably ever think of putting together — a collection of personal essays. So I was doubly surprised and moved by the gift. When I got back home and started reading the pieces, I felt a bit like the white cat in Mr. McGregor's garden, or like Narcissus, looking at my image in a pool of water. The only difference is that my students are such honest writers, so unflinchingly accurate in their memories of me, that I could hardly be captivated by some images of myself that I saw in the pool of their writing — browbeating one student, coddling another, ranting around the building about groundhogs in my garden. So many different memories of me, so many different versions of me, that I suddenly realized I was as changeable as the garden, as ephemeral as everything else. The only things that did not change from piece to piece were the vividness of their memories, the liveliness of their prose, the resonance of their voices. Gifts that made me think I should want to keep my hand in, after all, given the presence of such gifted writers.

SATURDAY *May 20*

Another idyllic day. Just right for getting together with neighbors to relocate a hundred-fifty-foot privet hedge at the neighborhood park. A hedge we planted two years ago to mark the boundary of the park, but after the city parks department acquired an additional twenty feet of land, we decided to move the hedge to mark the new boundary. The park is just a couple of houses north of us, so we can easily see it by looking straight out our kitchen windows. During the twenty-five years we've lived in the neighborhood, it's been Kate's most enduring civic project. Twenty-four years ago, she and our neighbor Sarah came up with the idea of creating a park on what was then a vacant piece of land that the city was planning to trade to a developer, who intended to put six duplexes on it. In order to prevent that trade from going through, Kate and Sarah organized more than two hundred neighbors who collectively petitioned and harangued the city to let them turn it into a neighborhood park. A people's park, the first of its kind in the state — created, planted, supported, and maintained largely by neighbors rather than city planners. During the years since Sarah moved away in the late seventies, Kate has often herded the neighbors and hounded the city staff, like an anxious border collie, to contribute labor, material, money, and services sufficient to acquire trees, create flower beds and borders, build a gazebo and a children's play area, and procure more land, as well as a drinking fountain, a grill area, an antique light pole, and a lightbulb in the gazebo. So it's a neighborhood park in more senses than one.

Now, in fact, it's so important a place in the life of the neighborhood that at least fifteen or twenty people are always ready to lend a hand or anything else that's needed to spruce things up in the spring. Today, folks started showing up around nine-thirty, some with wheelbarrows, everyone with shovels, ready to take on the task of transplanting a hundred or so privet bushes they'd planted just a couple of years ago. Initially the work proceeded mostly in silence, except for a few brief hellos. Some people were digging new holes along the line where Kate had marked out the spots with wooden stakes, others were digging up the bushes she'd been pruning back to reduce the stress of transplanting. Once the work was underway, the chitchat started — jokes about moving all those recently planted bushes, brainstorms about creating a neighborhood landscaping group, talk about summer plans, vegetable gardens, and the nursery school next door. By noon, when all the plants had been moved and watered in, everyone was talking about the neighborhood potluck to come and a job well done. After everyone had left, Kate made her last announcement of the morning — "It's time for lunch."

SUNDAY *May 21*

Sometime in May, usually toward the end of the month, a miraculous moment occurs when everything in the yard comes together — when the lawn's freshly mown, the trees all in leaf, the beds all weeded, the brambles and fruit trees and herbs and perennials and vegetables well underway — and the place suddenly looks as if it were not our scruffy yard, but one of those glossy spots that flourish in the pages of a gardening magazine or grow in the daydreams of a gardener who yearns to create a fabled landscape, a garden beyond compare. It's an illusion, of course. But for a moment or two it seems to be there, the thing itself. Like Friday afternoon, when Kate and I returned from that surprising lunch with my students and not only found the lawn freshly mown, in diagonal sweeps, but also beheld the orange parrot tulips abloom along the terrace wall, and the fern bed by the cellarway, the periwinkle bed by the lily pond, the herb beds by the gazebo and the edge of the hillock all freshly weeded, planted, and rearranged by the nimble Rebecca, who must have been putting things in order all the while we were away. But Saturday morning as I gazed at the terrace, its *parterre de Versailles* pattern obscured by weeds and twigs and dried-up maple blossoms and the leavings of winter, I suddenly realized that the moment hadn't yet come, and wouldn't come until I weeded and swept its entire surface. So I weeded every crevice and swept every inch of its nine-hundred-square-foot surface. But still something was missing, though I didn't know what. Then, at long last, when I surveyed the yard early today, all dewy and glistening in the morning sun, in the stilled air, I knew the moment had finally arrived. Or so it seemed, until I walked up the steps to the gazebo and found that a squirrel had been rooting around in a container of compost and scattered it all over the corner of the brick floor. So I swept up the compost and put away the container, but the moment was past. Or so it seemed, until a while later, when I was standing at the back door, watching Kate go from the terrace to the gazebo, placing her trays of seedlings on its sunny edge, just so, and then returning, her hair and her robe waving slightly in the breeze of her movement, her empty fingers pointing outward, just so. Then it was that the entire landscape crystallized around her and radiated out from her, as if what had been lacking all along was the gardener in her garden, like the dancer in her dance. No wonder she thought it a "blessed morning," though only I could see it. Blessedness, of course, is in the eye of the beholder, and it's probably just as evanescent as that moment I beheld this morning. But one thing I've discovered, I think, is that the beauty of a garden can never be wholly seen by its gardener. Perhaps that's why I'm always missing something when I'm alone in the garden, even when it seems most pleasurable.

MONDAY *May 22*

Last night at dinner time, after three days of carefully pilfering walnuts from the Havahart trap, another bright-eyed squirrel finally stepped on the metal food plate, tripping the lever that closed the doors at each end of the trap. Cling-clang. And out to the country I took it, to join the other one I caught last week. So now, at last, the place seems squirrel-free, at least for the moment. More good news this morning, when I noticed that all the cucumbers, pattypans, and zucchini I started in the house last Thursday have already begun to emerge. Also that all the potato plants are beginning to put up leaves.

But the most important news of the day is that I finished transplanting the tomatoes this afternoon. An important milestone for me in the life of the garden, not only because they're the vegetable that lured me into gardening, but also because they've always been the most important single crop both for me and Kate. We can them, juice them, sauce them, dry them, as well as eat them fresh and cook with them throughout the summer and fall. In salads, in sandwiches, in salsas, in soups, in spaghettis, in stews, tomatoes are the sine qua non. The thing without which nothing else is possible. So all of my compulsions are let loose in the growing of tomatoes, especially when it comes time to transplant them. I don't just dig a little hole, put them in the ground, and water them. Nothing so simple as that for me. No way. My plants go in only after I've dug a hole at least twice as deep and twice as wide as they need, only after I've planted an eight-foot-long, two-by-two-inch pole for them to grow up during the summer, only after I've mixed up a batch of topsoil with well-rotted cow manure and a handful or two of slow-release fertilizer, a shovel of which I've put in the hole and watered with liquid fertilizer. Only then do I set the plant in its hole, most of its stem below ground where it will set additional roots. Then I gradually backfill the hole with the special mixture, firming and watering it in when the hole is three quarters full, then covering it with a layer of dry soil as a moisture-conserving mulch. It's an exhausting ritual that I've been performing every May for the past twenty-five years — exhausting because I always try to get all ten, or eleven, or twelve plants set out in a single afternoon. But this year, something inside me kept asking, "What's the hurry? What's the hurry?" So for the past five days, I've been transplanting only two plants each afternoon, and today I transplanted the eleventh and last one in the row. And then it started to rain, as if the weather had been holding back long enough for me to move them in gradually and easily, rather than trying to get them in all at once, in a fanatic and impulsive frenzy. And just to complete this sacred ritual, I set the potted cherry tomatoes at each end of the bed, and noticed they've already set their first tomatoes. Summer is acomin' in!

TUESDAY *May 23*

At eight this morning, at the university hospital's oncology clinic, while I was waiting for Kate to get her blood drawn, the farmer sitting next to me was worrying about how the rain had delayed his field work. "Well, I finally got some of my beans in yesterday, but now I probably won't be able to get the rest in until next week sometime." Heavy rains last night — an inch at our place, two inches at others. And I don't have any of my beans in yet. And it's supposed to continue today and tomorrow, as I heard around eight-thirty, when I was sitting in the nuclear medicine clinic, watching the local TV news, while Kate got injected with irradiated material for her bone scan. Fifteen minutes later, when I was sitting in the diagnostic radiology clinic, while Kate was getting a chest X-ray, I heard the weather report again on a different channel: "Heavy rain." It's the big story here today, as I heard yet again on the same channel in the same clinic, just before we returned to oncology, where Kate had her blood pressure checked, and I heard another family talking about the rain. And the rain itself was falling on the rooftop pavilion, just outside the lounge and refreshment area where we went next, so Kate could get enough fluid in her to disperse the irradiated material through-out her system for purposes of the upcoming bone scan. After she gamely finished off two twelve-ounce cans of lime-lemon spar-kling water — "Here's to radioactivity" — we then went down to the first-floor cafeteria where she had two cups of tea and I noticed that the rain had stopped, at least for the moment.

And for a while some of the uncertainty also abated when we went to the nuclear radiation clinic for the bone scan itself. A high-tech procedure, complete with an animated technician, a finely calibrated body scanner, and a graphic computer display that revealed no evidence of cancer anywhere in the full-length skeletal images that flashed on the screen at the end of the scan-ning. The best news of the day, of the week, even though I was momentarily disarmed by the computer display of Kate, so close to the bone, while she was also sitting on the scanner table, so fully in the skin of her own immediate existence. The technician herself was also so full of life, and her life intersected ours in so many ways — she grew up in our neighborhood, her daughter went to nurs-ery school two doors north of us, her cousin Mike grew up in Kate's home town and was a schoolmate of Kate's brother John — that the disclosures of radiation suddenly gave way to a surprising array of happy coincidences.

But reality took hold again, when Kate finally saw her harried cancer surgeon, who removed her stitches from last week, but put off a discussion of her options until next week, because he hadn't yet seen a report of her blood scan, her chest X-ray, or even her bone scan. Uncertainty had returned, and so had the rain.

WEDNESDAY *May 24*

It's my sixty-third birthday. But at six after three this afternoon, the temperature still hadn't reached sixty-three. Not a good sign for someone like me, who believes in the magical power of numbers and numerical correspondences. Not a good sign for the summer crops either, especially given the overcast sky and the continuing prediction of highs in the sixties, rather than normal temperatures in the seventies and low eighties. But at least we haven't had any more rain since the additional half inch that fell yesterday afternoon. And all the spring vegetables are thriving in this cool weather. Broccoli plants beginning to form heads, cauliflowers just on the verge. Snow peas and shell peas near the top of the brush. Onions beginning to expand, as well as the second crop of radishes. Full heads of buttercrunch and romaine already formed in the earliest of the three lettuce patches, and good-size leaves available on all the other lettuces in that planting — arugula, Carmona butterhead, endive, escarole, purple oak leaf, and Simpson elite. The makings of a colorful salad for my birthday dinner, every part of which included something from the garden — from the pork tenderloin roasted with alternating sage leaves and thyme sprigs on its surface, to the French potato salad layered with chopped French chives and borage, to Kate's fresh rhubarb pie — the first of the season. A birthday feast beyond compare.

Such a tasty climax to the day that I can hardly complain about the lack of correspondence between the temperature and my age, especially given the three-hour clearing of the sky that began when I was planting up flats of basil and dill, and continued while Kate and I were preparing and eating dinner. As if the heavens themselves had conspired to look favorably upon the festivities for a period of time exactly corresponding to the base number in the calculation and representation of my age. Besides, my age is so fraught with mystical multiplicands — three times three times seven, seven times nine, three times twenty-one — that I feel as if I've got karma to spare, enough to share it equally with Kate. Speaking of numbers, I got a card and/or a phone call and/or a present from each of my children, all of them concerned with the weather and my garden. And I got three birthday presents from Kate. The first a set of Punto, the Italian card game based on matching numbers. The second, a pair of seersucker shirts. And the third, an airtight plastic carrying case and storage container for all my seeds, complete with a set of green filing cards and green plastic name slots, so I can make a separate section of the file for each type of vegetable and flower that I grow. A compulsive's delight and a gardener's convenience, especially given the fact that I save my surplus seeds from year to year for as long as they remain viable. What more could an obsessive, retentive, numerologically fanatic gardener want for his birthday?

THURSDAY *May 25*

Workable soil — that's one of the things I secretly longed for on my birthday. It looked so wet and felt so wet yesterday, I didn't expect it would dry out enough today that I might be able to plant the corn tomorrow. But today's dry air and a northwest breeze and the slope of the garden itself all seem to be working in my favor. Late this afternoon I grabbed a handful of topsoil, and it almost felt right — warm and crumbly and just a bit moist. Now if I could just keep my mind on the garden, I might feel even more buoyed than I have been by this bountiful spring.

But I can't stop thinking about all the phone calls I had yesterday — calls painfully torn between one thing and another. First Rebecca the Shy. "Just calling to wish you a happy birthday. Hope I'm not bothering you, but your birthday comes on the same day as my father's, so I can never forget it. And how is Kate? How did the tests come out?" Then Trudy from Wyoming. "I hope I'm not interrupting dinner, but I just wanted to find out how the tests went yesterday." So I give her a quick rundown of Kate's circuitous day at the university hospital, but the roast pork and salad I've just eaten are still so fresh on the tip of my tongue that I can't resist telling her about dinner and my birthday too. "Oh, how could I forget it, especially after last year when I arrived in town on your birthday?" Then a call to Kate's longtime friend Glenda, to thank her for the delicate California olive oil she sent me from her new Mediterranean shop in Carmel. So I tell her how good the oil tasted on the fresh-picked lettuce salad, and how well it went with the bottle of Pouilly Fuissé she gave us a few years ago. "Oh, yes, I'd forgotten all about it. A perfect match. By the way, have you gotten any more reports about Kate?" And then my daughter Hannah from California. "Just calling to wish you a happy birthday, dad. Was it a good one?" So I tell her about our dinner and about Kate's rhubarb pie that was puckering my cheeks and mesmerizing my mouth just when she called, and the garden and the weather and my daybook, and she tells me about the writing that Ben, my first grandchild, has been doing in school, and about her friend Carol, who's been visiting her the past ten days. Hannah doesn't yet know anything about Kate's most recent cancer, so I feel compelled to tell her about it, much as I just felt obliged to report it to my brother Marshall, who called a few minutes ago from California to wish me a belated happy birthday. So like a bearer of ill tidings, I burden them with news they'd rather not hear. What else is new? Maybe I should get an answering service. Maybe I should just pay attention to the garden — to the tulips still blooming along the terrace wall and the spruces drooping with lush new needles, so young they haven't hardened up yet, so light against the dark old growth.

FRIDAY *May 26*

The corn is in, protected with a row cover to keep out the crows and the squirrels. A fourteen-by-four-foot patch of Argent, a knockoff of the great Silver Queen white corn. And none too soon, given the rain predicted for tonight, tomorrow, and possibly even Sunday. I've never planted corn so late. Usually, I get it in the first or second week of May, when the pin oak leaves are just unfurling. But this year the soil's been so cold and wet, even on my windswept hillside, that corn seed planted any earlier than today might have rotted before it germinated. Now that it's in, I can probably look forward to a crop sometime in mid-August, just when the best of the truck garden corn is beginning to tail off. So, come to think of it, I might be better off planting my corn this late from here on out. Possibly even a week or so later.

Field corn, on the other hand, should have been in by now, if a farmer hopes to have a long enough season to mature the corn and dry it on the stalk. But many farmers around here and elsewhere in southeast Iowa haven't even begun to plant any corn, given the water sitting in their fields. That's the story that's been making the news almost every day this week, and I heard it again this morning from Dan, a farmer's son turned carpenter and landscaper, who brings us a truckload of well-rotted manure every year around this time. He's a tall, blond, bright-eyed young man, who talks rapidly as he shovels out the manure. "It's so late now they'll probably have to put in a short-season corn or switch to beans, if the soil ever dries out enough for them to get anything in. I haven't even been able to get any vegetables in at my place. The garden's so flat it doesn't have any drainage, and the soil's just sitting in it all wet 'n cold." But Dan's big story today was the age of the manure he's brought me. "This stuff is probably about a hundred years old. It goes back to the man who built the farm. According to my grandfather, it was there when he bought the farm in the thirties. And now I'm getting to the bottom of the pile, I'll probably run out of it in a couple of years."

I've never before gardened with century-old manure, so I felt a bit in awe of the pile as Dan drove away and I stood gazing at it. Antique manure that's been around since Teddy Roosevelt and his Rough Riders and the Spanish-American war. So I felt a bit hesitant about spreading it on the corn patch before I worked up the soil this afternoon. But then it occurred to me that the manure is about the same age as our house, so in a manner of speaking they were meant for each other. With that in mind, I decided to shovel it on, rake it in, and revel in the thought that I was about to start growing a crop of heritage corn. That I was making history as I pushed the seeds into the ground, row by row, foot by foot, at each of the fifty-five spots. And I'll be eating history sometime this August.

SATURDAY *May 27*

N ow that the corn is in, I'm thinking about the beans. Thinking is all I can do about the garden today, given the downpour we had this morning. I'm thinking it might be dry enough by next Tuesday or Wednesday to work up the soil, but I'm also thinking that I don't want to push things with the beans, because they can easily rot if they sit in waterlogged soil. Or break their necks trying to get through the hard-caked soil that follows a heavy rain and a few days of sun. Things are now so bad off in the countryside around here that farmers quoted in this morning's newspaper didn't think the fields would be dry enough to get started before June 5. And that was before today's thunderstorms. According to newspaper reports, the rains have been so heavy in the southernmost counties of the state that at this point less than five percent of the available acreage has been planted in corn or beans. No wonder the governor thinks the farmers in those areas should be given some kind of federal disaster assistance.

Walking around the back yard this morning, looking at the lush growth in all of our gardens, it was hard to believe that anyone in these parts could be in need of disaster assistance. The lemon lilies are now blooming their heads off along the front of Kate's sixty-foot flower border, the blue Siberian iris are just beginning to open along the back of her bed, the poppies at each end are about to pop, and all the peonies are just on the verge of opening. Several feet away, all the tomato plants I put in last week are darkening up, thickening their stems, forming their first clusters of blossoms. But a quick ride in the countryside is all I needed to help me remember that farm fields and garden plots are miles apart. Most of the rolling land around here, land that's usually dotted right now with young corn plants as far as the eye can see, is still unplowed, untilled, and covered with weeds. No wonder the farmers look forward to going into town every morning for coffee. As one of them put it, "For me, it's kind of mental therapy." The way things are looking right now, I'm afraid the farmers are soon going to need something more substantial than coffee. And I wonder if it'll be there, given the governor's observation that "the movement in Washington is away from special appropriations." At a distance from hardship — even so short as the few miles from my garden to the fields outside of town — it's easy to forget about what it actually looks like, whether it's a weed-ridden field or a run-down school. Easy to think that a balanced budget is more important than a basic human need.

SUNDAY *May 28*

I'm still thinking about the beans, and now I'm thinking it'll probably be Thursday or Friday before the ground dries out enough to be workable, given the drizzles we've been having today and the cloudiness predicted for tomorrow. I'm also beginning to think the cool, moist weather has been pushing all the plants into lusher growth than they'll be able to support very comfortably when the weather turns sunny and warm, as it's bound to do sometime in June. And when it does, the broccoli, cauliflower, and lettuce leaves will surely go limp in the midday sun. Even now, a few of the onion plants have turned pale and droopy as if they were damping off from the excessive moisture and lack of sun.

Most of the people I talked to today also seem to be damping off from the cloudy and rainy weather we've been having. It started with Amelia, my younger daughter, who called me from her home in Wisconsin to find out about Kate and my birthday. But she couldn't avoid the weather. "I can tell just by looking at how the light comes through the blinds whether it's going to be a gray-sky day or a blue-sky day. And it affects me, dad, it really affects me. Like today, when Joe and I got up, I could see right away that the sky was blue and the sun was out, and I was really up for it, especially after all the gray days we've been having up here. But then by the time we got back from breakfast, it was a gray-sky day again, as gray and cold as yesterday. A real downer. Worse than if the sun had never come out at all." Actually, I was feeling much the same way, because I too had been buoyed up by the early morning sunlight glistening on the dewy lawn. And I bustled around the terrace, moving our seedlings from the porch to the gazebo, only to be let down a couple of hours later when the clouds moved in again. Kate didn't get up in time to see the sun, but even without the letdown, I could tell how she was feeling about the weather when I reported Amelia's remark that it really affected her. "You bet it does" was all she had to say, but those four words were quite enough. And when we picked up Lib for brunch this morning, she too had a few sharp words about "it."

But my survey wouldn't be complete without a report of what I heard from Nichelle, a bright-eyed former student who lives a few blocks away. "I love it when it's raining off and on like this. It's just perfect for gardening. You can do anything you want and the plants will thrive. So I've just loved it this spring. There's so much to see, so much to write about. Yesterday afternoon when I was working among my flowers, I was also writing things in my head. I had so much to say I stayed up past midnight writing in my gardening journal, bringing it up to date." I've never stayed up so late working on this journal, but I don't have a husband, a job, and a rambunctious young son to take care of.

MONDAY *May 29*

Memorial Day — so gloomy and overcast when I awoke that I went back to bed again and slept another two hours. Then the clouds were breaking up and the sun was shining through, just as it should be on Memorial Day. And when I drove down to the grocery store to get some milk for breakfast, I noticed the bridal wreath blooming, some flags flying, some joggers smiling, and the streets mostly empty, just as they should be on Memorial Day. But I didn't see any peonies in bloom, as they should be on Memorial Day. Another sign of the cool weather we've been having. Right after breakfast, though, I went out to weed around the baby chard plants, and when I knelt down, the sprightly rhythms of a Sousa march started to waft in the air from the city cemetery three blocks away, just as they should on Memorial Day. Kate said it was a recording, but it sure sounded like the real thing to me. Then I heard the solemn tones of a minister (or was it a public official or a military veteran?), then three rifle shots, then hysterical barking from all the dogs in the neighborhood, then more solemn words, then three more rifle shots, then more hysterical barking, then more solemn words. And then the ever poignant sound of Taps, just as it should be on Memorial Day. A few minutes later, as I was driving back to the grocery store to pick up a roll of film, I saw a young lad coming out of the cemetery with a black trumpet case in one hand and a big white record envelope in the other with MEMORIAL printed on it in bold black caps. But it sure sounded like the real thing to me.

Kate celebrated Memorial Day in her own way. First, by cleaning up the big redheaded woodpecker with black and white whirligig arms that her sister Martha gave me for Christmas two years ago. Then by planting it in the middle of the main vegetable bed, right in front of the corn patch. Its wings spun wildly in the morning breeze, and so did its body. And I spun wildly in the morning breeze when Kate asked me to get some scallions and lettuce from the garden, enough romaine, arugula, and Carmona butterhead for a salade Niçoise. By noon the bird and I were motionless, until Kate called me back into action. "How about getting the table out of the basement, so we can have lunch in the gazebo? It's Memorial Day, and I think we should do something to celebrate the day properly." So we celebrated the day in the gazebo, with a decoratively arrayed salad of lettuces, scallions, marinated asparagus and mushrooms, fresh tomatoes, Calamata olives, and hard-boiled eggs. A side dish of chilled barbecued swordfish with wedges of lime. Sourdough bread. Fumé blanc. Perrier. And the redheaded woodpecker in the middle distance.

Thus restored, I celebrated Memorial Day by planting a ring of ivy starts around the trunk of the maple tree.

TUESDAY *May 30*

A perfect late spring day. Low eighties — the first time this year — light breeze, sunny, and a few scattered clouds in an otherwise clear blue sky. Parsley taking hold. Basil germinating. Nasturtiums breaking ground. Snow peas blossoming. And the first head of broccoli ready for harvest. Soil still a bit cold and moist for beans, but a few more days like this and it'll be just right for planting. The only problem with this idyllic state of affairs is that nothing's ready for temperatures in the eighties — neither plants nor people. The young lettuces were already going limp by eleven this morning, when Kate and I started walking over to the hospital for appointments with her surgical oncologist and medical oncologist. And by the time we finished our two-mile walk, we too were limp. But our leaves turned crisp and our tempers chilled after a few hours of cooling our heels in the air-conditioned hospital, waiting until twelve-thirty for a noon appointment with the surgeon, and then until two-thirty for a one o'clock appointment with the medical oncologist.

The appointments themselves were as perplexing as the weather we've been having. The surgeon was upbeat about the results of the tests. No other cancer detectable anywhere in the system. The medical oncologist was unconvinced by the tests. "A local recurrence in your situation indicates that it's systemic, and what to do with a woman in your situation, no one knows. There just hasn't been enough research." Suddenly I found myself thinking about the mysteries of El Niño and its paradoxical behavior. So I asked him how the tests could be negative but the cancer systemic, and he suggested that I think about a dandelion gone to seed. "Just imagine trying to find those seeds in the grass. You couldn't see them, but you'd know they were there." Never had the dandelion been so menacing a figure of speech. A sign that the medical oncologist probably likes to keep a weed-free lawn. Yet he agreed with the surgeon in opposing a bone marrow transplant, favoring instead the moderate approach of "patching along for several years." Estrogen-blocking therapy combined with a little surgery and light radiation to clean up the site of the recent tumor. The only problem is that the surgeon and the medical oncologist can't be sure the radiologists will agree to give Kate just a light dose of radiation. And Kate doesn't relish the thought of being burned out by radiation like Madame Curie and my mother.

So we're patching along, hoping as the oncologist put it that Kate's "one of the lucky ones who has a good run." Nothing, after all, is certain. But after all that uncertainty, the definite sin of a charcoal broiled steak sure did help, as did a head of butter-crunch lettuce from the garden, sliced down the center, its leaves of growth gradually but distinctly fading from dark green to light green to yellow to the white at its core.

WEDNESDAY *May 31*

Another sunny day in store, I thought at breakfast, but Kate didn't agree. "It's muddled, hazy, just look at the sky." Yes, there were strands of haze obscuring some of the blue, but I thought they'd burn off in an hour or so. And they did, at least while I was visiting a senior English class at the local high school. The sky then seemed as bright as the students themselves, who were peppering me with questions about the textbook they were using — a literature anthology I've had a hand in for the past twenty-five years. Telling them about how the book had come to be and how it had changed over the years had me feeling as if I were suddenly in a flashback and then a fast forward, reliving all the twists and turns in the life of the book and some of my own as well. Actually, I was thrown back a ways as I walked up to the school, its red brick exterior and stone trim so much like the one I attended in the forties that it could have passed for a replica, or nearly so. And the same inside — the long, wide hallways, the rows of lockers, the shiny dark wood trim in the main office. But the resemblance quickly faded when Aisha, my neighbor's daughter who had asked me to visit, led me toward her classroom in the modernized section of the school. And the modernized interior was nothing compared to the contemporary awareness of the students themselves. With students like that, I could even imagine trying my hand with a high school class or two.

An hour later, though, when I was home again, pushing my one-wheel plow through the areas I'd set aside for beans, that fleeting high school visit seemed like an illusion, as transitory as the morning sun, which by then had completely given way to clouds. The beans seemed so pressing, given the rain predicted for later this evening, that when Rebecca turned up around noon I pressed her into service to help with the planting. So now they're all in and sooner than I imagined — a double row of the Hutterites for Kate's bean soups, and a double row of Greencrop, Jade, and Rocdor bush beans, a mixture ranging from flat green to round green to yellow wax. And late this afternoon, while Kate and Rebecca were working on the back flower border, I managed to get in half of the pepper plants — fourteen Ace bells — also earlier than expected.

Early enough to buoy me up after the vicissitudes of yesterday — until I discovered that an early hatching of cucumber beetles had been swarming and feeding on the cucumber and zucchini seedlings, surely infecting them with the deadly bacterial wilt. So it's two steps forward and one step back. Back to starting the cucumbers and zucchini all over again and remembering to keep them dusted against the invasion of beetles that seems to be with us this year. Bittersweet reminders of how up and down this month has been from start to finish. But just to give May its fair due, I want to remember that right before the rain this evening,

Kate picked a big bouquet of the white Festiva Maxima peonies that started opening in her perennial bed. And now they're not only gracing the dining room table, but their fragrance — their sweet fragrance — is permeating the entire first floor of the house with an aroma that cannot be matched even by the most skilled perfumer.

J U N E

El Niño is on the wane, according to the weather folks, but you couldn't prove it by me. More rain last night, today heavily overcast, and so fierce a downpour this evening that Pip is shuddering in the TV room. All week long, in fact, the news has been dominated by Niñoesque stories of the weather. Tornadoes in southwestern Iowa, flooding along the Illinois, Missouri, and Mississippi rivers, a record-breaking mix of cool temperatures, heavy rainfall, and cloudy days from the beginning of March to the end of May — ideal breeding conditions for a record-breaking hatch-out of mosquitoes in June and July. Even the TV financial reporters have been featuring the flooded fields and delayed planting. "Given the current situation," said the bright-eyed market analyst, "I foresee the possibility of a significant run-up in agricultural equities over the next six months." Every cloud has a silver lining. Especially for people who are far from the cloud.

But the overcast weather was nothing compared to the obituary reporting the death of my retired colleague Sherman, who was born and raised in Cleveland some twelve years before me. A nationally distinguished scholar of American literature and culture, he wrote or edited more than twenty books, most of them concerned with writers who engaged nature in the most challenging and compelling terms — "the green American tradition," as he put it. The obituary lists some of Sherman's best-known work, but it does not indicate that Sherman himself engaged nature directly almost every day of his life, whether he was walking home from school on a winter afternoon or tending the land at his summer place, and later his retirement home, in the boundary-water area of Minnesota. I walked with him often, and his pace was as quick as the shifts of his attention, at one moment telling me, "You should be wearing rubbers in weather like this," as if he were an older brother or surrogate father, at the next moment telling me that "Bibliography is power," as if he were my intellectual mentor, which he was in some ways I've only begun to realize. But the image of him I most remember is from a late afternoon in early September, some twenty years ago, when he pulled up in my driveway in his dark blue Jeep, and pulled out of the back a cardboard box containing four Norway spruces no more than a foot or two tall, each as ramrod stiff and straight as Sherman himself. A few trees from the thousands he was raising at his place in Minnesota. We planted them along the back-lot line that afternoon, while Kate and his wife and Jim were chatting on the terrace. Now twenty years later, those spruces are thirty feet tall, and their lower branches collectively cover a distance of almost ninety feet. Talk about leaving your mark in the world.

FRIDAY *June 2*

Sherman's spruces. They're spaced so evenly across the back of the lot, and they provide such a striking backdrop for Kate's perennial bed, which is centered in front of them, that it's easy to imagine they've been standing there ever since we planted them. And Kate's perennials themselves — the white peonies, the pink Sarah Bernhardt peonies, the dark blue, pale blue, and white Siberian iris, the yellow lemon lilies, the orange poppies, the coral bells — all stand out so vividly right now against the trees, especially on an overcast day like this when their colors are not washed out by the sun, that it's also easy to imagine her border has always been located exactly where it is ever since she created it some twenty-five years ago. But strange as it might seem, neither the trees nor her border have always stood in their present locations. Both have been on the move.

Initially, Kate's perennial border was half its present length, and it was centered in front of Jim's weathered gray barn, a two-story structure, sixty feet long, that ran along the northern half of our back lot. And initially we planted the four spruces just ten feet apart, running along the southern half of our back lot. So, for several years, the spruces and the flower border were completely separate from each other. The flowers were nostalgically high-lighted against the old gray barn, until Jim was forced to tear it down by the city building and zoning inspector in 1979. And the spruces grew slowly at first, thwarted initially by the old alley bed that ran a few inches beneath their roots. But once they broke through that layer of cinder and dirt and gravel, the spruces grew so well and so wide that by the mid-eighties they were crowding each other for space. So our tree surgeon Leon undertook the massive project of digging and relocating two of the four trees along the northern half of our back lot. Then, in response to the extended row of spruces, Kate expanded her flower border to center it in front of the trees. Everything was finally just right — until all the spruces grew so rapidly in response to their increased spacing that their lower branches began to intrude upon the back edge of Kate's flower border. So, in 1989 on an early spring day a couple of months before our yard was to be on display in a city-wide gardening tour, Kate relocated her entire perennial border fifteen feet in front of the trees. That's where it now stands with an alley of grass running like a strip of no man's land between the flower border and the trees. The only problem is that the trees are continuing to encroach on that green alleyway and sometime in the not so distant future will dictate yet another move of the flower border.

Sherman's spruces. Their growth is ceaseless. As unremitting, it seems, as the rain that's been falling again this week.

SATURDAY *June 3*

"Isn't it just awful? I wonder when it's gonna end?" Those were the first words of the mechanic who came to fix our dish-washer yesterday morning. And a half-hour later as he was walking out the door, he uttered the wish on everyone's lips these days — "I sure hope it ends soon." "It," of course, is the rain, and it's been falling for so many weeks that the pronoun has become a shorthand part of everyone's conversation, standing for rain, or water, or moisture, or dew, or any other undesirable condition produced by the excessive amount of it that we've had the past three months. Like Kate's remark that "It's gotten so bad it feels like we're living in the middle of a dense, tropical forest." There's so much of it in the air now that it didn't burn off until nine or ten this morning. And even then the lawn was so heavy with it that I asked the mower to come back a few hours later after it had dried up. The soil's so saturated with it that even though our house is on sloping land, it's started to create problems in the basement, showing up around the edges of the concrete floors, trickling down some of the old stone walls, the dehumidifier now running non-stop around the clock. And early yesterday morning after the heavy downpour, it was halfway up the trench in the potato row and didn't go back into the soil until a few hours later. Hardly surprising, given that we've now had almost fifty percent more of it than normal.

But all the spring vegetables are thriving on it, especially the lettuce and onions, the broccoli and cauliflower. We've got so many heads of lettuce in the ground and so many coming on that even if we had salads three times a day for the next three weeks we'd still have a little left over before the greens go bitter in the heat of July. It's also helped to germinate the corn, settle in the first batch of pepper transplants, and put some more growth on the tomato plants. Though Kate's been fretting about the "stress" it's been causing in her flower border, the peonies, Siberian iris, and lemon lilies have rarely looked quite so colorful, healthy, and vivid as they did this afternoon. Even the fringe tree, the last of the decorative trees to blossom, has seemed to thrive on it this week, suffusing the yard with a fragrant aroma as beguiling as the tropical frangipani tree.

But the real news of the day is the blue-winged, yellow-breasted macaw that moved into the second floor of the duplex just south of us. When Kate saw it sitting on the balcony railing, she said, "It's the most interesting thing that's happened there in some time. It's a real squawker." And she wasn't talking about the rain.

SUNDAY *June 4*

A rainless day — a lucky break for the neighborhood's annual spring potluck, but Kate had other things on her mind when she got up. "They're gonna cut me up again. In the same place. And I wonder if my skin'll grow back right." I assured her it would, and if her surgeon didn't think so, he'd make the incision elsewhere. As usual I was more hopeful than she. Ever hopeful — there's one in every family.

But it was time to get cracking, as Kate put it, to get ready for the potluck at the neighborhood park. Sweep out the shelter, set up the tables, bring down the tablecloths and the ice and the sliced bread and the sliced ham and the paper plates and plate holders and cups and plastic utensils. And have a good time. And we did, watching folks trickle in from noon on, from every part of the neighborhood, singles and partners and marrieds and children, some eighty people in all. Bringing coleslaw, macaroni salad, Indian rice salad, cold spaghetti salad, potato salad, lettuce salad, snow pea salad, sliced ham, lasagna, barbecued spareribs, chicken casserole, baked chicken, spaghetti in meat sauce, brownies, chocolate cake, rhubarb crisp, carrot cake, melon mix — so many dishes I can't remember them all. And a lemonade stand, run by Nichelle and her neighbor's young daughter, to raise money for redbud trees, the Oklahoma state tree, to be planted at the park in memory of those who died in the Oklahoma City bombing. And an impromptu women's softball game, kids against grownups. And neighbors shuffling from table to table, to share the news and the food and the good feeling of a Sunday afternoon. And wherever I went, people asking me what was eating their bean plants or tomatoes or zucchini or roses, and what to do about them. So many questions about maladies in their gardens that by midafternoon, when the picnic was over, I'd begun to feel somewhat like a family gardening doctor. I just wish I could solve some of my own gardening problems as well as I took care of theirs. Why some of my peppers are beginning to yellow, and what to do about the groundhog — terror to all vegetable gardeners! — that turned up in the back yard this afternoon after the potluck.

But no matter how menacing the groundhog, it couldn't offset the good feelings of the picnic and the splendid news that came later in a phone call from my brother Marshall, a doctor, telling me that he and his friend Jack, a medical oncologist, both believe that Kate's cancer is almost surely a local recurrence and not a systemic condition. "If it occurred exactly at the site of her previous cancer, why assume that it traveled through the entire system to get there? If you hear the sound of hoof beats, would you assume that you're hearing horses or zebras?" Horses, of course, which I much prefer to dandelion seeds.

MONDAY *June 5*

"Was the apple worth it?" So it was that Kate inquired of the possum I caught in the Havahart trap, when she saw it this morning just before I took it out to the country. Given her question, I assumed she was preaching the possum a lesson from Genesis, a new version of the fall, especially for beasts. I just wanted to be done with the critter, so I could get back to getting rid of the groundhog, the main reason for baiting the trap with pieces of apple. Oh yes, I was fascinated by its five-fingered paws, clutching the wire mesh, like diminutive hands, except for the long dark nails at the end of each digit. But the ride into the countryside was so beguiling — the sky clear, the air warm and rich with the feel of summer — that I almost completely forgot about the possum. I wanted to keep driving, just to see the roadside fields and the local reservoir a few miles away. But when I got to my regular drop spot and started unloading the possum, the experience was so disconcerting I completely forgot about the reservoir. The trouble started the minute I opened the trap, assuming the possum would go hustling out through the tall grass, just like the squirrels. It didn't make a move to leave from either end of the cage. So I tilted the trap high enough that it came sliding out on its back in the tall grass, its four feet stiff in midair, its tail stretched out, its head motionless. Obviously dead from the shock of the ride in the darkened car trunk. Guilt swept over me, as I stood gazing dumbly at the carcass of the beast, so fully alive but a few minutes ago. So much for the Havahart trap, I thought, and my fumbling attempts to have an animal-free garden, when a slight nudge of my toe brought a slight movement to the beast, who gradually rolled over and went trundling off through the grass, leaving me with a sudden understanding of what it means to play possum.

When I got back home, I went up to visit Jim, to tell him my story and find out if he'd seen the groundhog around his place. "I saw it once but then it scooted right under one of your spruce trees." And then as we stood by Kate's flower border, looking down toward the trap that I'd baited again, Jim started reminiscing about the groundhogs of his youth. "Used to hunt 'em for bounty. The only way I had to earn any money then, during the Depression. Fifty cents apiece, ten cents a crow, five cents a gopher, a pocket gopher. All of 'em trouble to the farmers, so the counties paid to get rid of 'em. We'd shoot 'em, cut their scalps off with a single-edge razor and carry 'em in a bag to the county courthouse for the payoff. Actually, I like 'em in a way. But they sure do cause trouble in a garden." They sure do, and right now I'd pay far more than fifty cents to be rid of the one that's hanging out under my neighbor's shed, just a few feet from the garden.

TUESDAY *June 6*

Nothing in the trap this morning, but then again nothing in its right mind would have been prowling around last night during the lightning and thunder and rain. Pip hyperventilating on top of our bed, Phoebe hiding under it, and we trying to get a few hours sleep before Kate's early morning surgery at the hospital. More cutting, more tissue removed, more pain this time than a few weeks ago. "This time he must've been cutting close to the bone. There's not much else left to remove. And every time the pain increased, I could hear my heart beating faster on the monitor behind me. Beep, beep, beepbeepbeepbeep. Fight or flight time. But the whole thing didn't take very long. He works fast. And when it was all over, I told him I didn't want to see the medical oncologist again, that I didn't need to hear about being doomed to an early death, when it doesn't make any sense in terms of my present condition and the test results. I told him what your brother said, and he agreed it's difficult to understand how it could be considered systemic." So it's probably a local recurrence. The best possible news, short of having no recurrence at all.

I wish the groundhog were just a local, isolated recurrence, but Jim says "It's a she, and she's probably nursing a litter there under the shed." So, even if I catch her in the trap, there'll be more to follow. There's a snake in every garden, all right, and my snake is a groundhog. The last one that turned up here some five or ten years ago drove me batty until Chris, a neighbor across the street, now dead and gone, took care of it with a shotgun. That's when I first began to understand why Thoreau had no mercy on the ground-hogs in his garden, especially after they did in his beans. My beans just started to emerge yesterday, so I'm feeling especially fretful about the beast whose lair is but a stone's throw from my bean rows. All yesterday afternoon, in fact, when I was planting a row of yellow marigolds along the front of the main vegetable bed, I kept lifting my head to keep an eye on the Havahart trap and the shed right behind it. Also when I was transplanting the reddish-orange cosmos that had volunteered from last year, and when I was seed-ing in the okra in front of the cosmos. My eyes darted back and forth so often between the garden and the shed that my neck was stiff by the end of the afternoon.

Ever vigilant, I've imagined myself boarding up the base of the shed, putting wire mesh over the boards, building a rock wall around the whole thing. But Jim says it would just dig its way out of there. Besides, its compatriots are perennially breeding and thriving in the wilderness park just a few houses away from Jim. So, it seems, the groundhog is systemic. It's here to stay, as heavy a presence as the warm, humid air that's been hanging in all day long.

WEDNESDAY *June 7*

Suddenly it's summer, and I mean high summer — mid-eight-ies yesterday, ninety this afternoon, and humidities to match. As if it were the middle of July rather than the beginning of June. Yet just a week ago, we reached the eighties for the first time this year. No wonder Kate and I and the unwatered eggplant seedlings were wilting this morning. No wonder the snow peas were ready for a stir fry last night, and the tomato plants are all in blossom, and the beans, which just broke through the soil a day or two ago, are already a couple of inches above ground. Everything growing like Jack's beanstalk. But tomorrow, the temperature's predicted to drop into the low seventies. A drop of that magnitude probably won't come without a cold front moving in and a clash of weather systems likely to produce a big thunderstorm tonight, given the clouds piled up in every part of the sky. And several more days of rain, according to the National Weather Service. Worse and worse for southern Iowa, which has now been declared an agricultural disaster area by the governor. Some areas here and in adjoining states are already worse than they were during the deluge of 1993. Meanwhile, Trudy reports that a massive cold front moved into the mountain states yesterday, and the temperature at her place in Wyoming didn't get out of the thirties. So much for the weather service's claim that El Niño is breaking up.

But Kate's on the mend, well enough to take one of her two-mile exercise walks this morning. No lying around for her. And the groundhog hasn't shown his face around these parts since Monday morning, right after I returned from transporting the possum. Good news, according to Jim. "Sounds to me like it might be a traveler. A male. They move from den to den, servicin' the females, getting 'em pregnant and movin' on. I seen 'em movin' like that. And I also seen 'em come back and kill off the young males. Catch 'em at the back of the neck and snap it, just like that. They don't like competition." I don't like competition either, not for the stuff in my garden. So I was glad to learn that the groundhog might, after all, be just a local and transient recurrence. A traveler. On the move.

The more I've thought about it, though, everything seems to be on the move — from the sex of the groundhog to the diagnosis of Kate to the status of El Niño. As if everything in the world were playing possum. Dead one minute, alive the next. So I'm beginning to feel uncertain about the nature of everything I see and hear about. I mean, if I can't trust my own eyes, or Jim's animal know-how, or a doctor's opinion, or the weather service's prediction, what can I rely on? My colleagues worry about problematic literary texts. But right now the whole world looks problematic to me.

THURSDAY *June 8*

L ast night after dinner, during the last hour of daylight, the air was still so hot and heavy and humid and breezeless that I was dripping from the minute I knelt down in the garden to put in the eggplants and the second row of peppers. And the work wasn't really hard. Just digging up a large trowelful of soil, tossing in some slow-release fertilizer, working it into the soil, popping in the plant, pulling the soil around it, watering it in with a transplant solution, and covering the surface with a light layer of dry earth. A few hours later, though, a cool, dry breeze started wafting in from the west, as promised, and by morning the house was so chilly that I hustled around pulling down all the windows we'd left open overnight. But the predicted overnight thunderstorm never arrived, and today has passed with only a few intermittent sprinkles. Not even enough to register a tenth of an inch in the rain gauge. And the temperature just barely made it up to sixty this afternoon, a thirty-degree drop from yesterday afternoon. It felt as if we'd gone from July to April in just twenty-four hours. So I went from wearing shorts and a T-shirt yesterday to long pants, a long-sleeved shirt, and my farm jacket today. At this rate, I wonder if the weather's ever going to settle down this year.

I also wonder if Kate's condition is ever going to settle down. Last night, just before going to sleep, Kate told me that her cancer surgeon would be calling this morning to give her a lab report on the tissue he removed on Tuesday. I hadn't realized that yet another biopsy would be involved, so I suddenly went on red alert, wondering what it would mean if some more cancer cells turned up this time. Would it mean that the medical oncologist was right about it being systemic, that the doctor from hell, as my brother had called him, was not so misguided as everyone had thought? And that question was still on my mind when I awoke briefly around four this morning. Just after breakfast, though, a call came through from Judy, the surgeon's nurse and research assistant, reporting that no tumors were found in the sample. But I'm still sleeping with one eye open.

The other good news is that we're supping more and more on fresh herbs and vegetables from the garden. Last night along with some chilled poached turkey and homemade lemon mayonnaise, we had a fresh head of steamed broccoli and a macaroni salad with minced burnet, dill, sorrel, green onion, chive blossoms, and a tarragon-tomato vinaigrette. And tonight, it was fresh thyme and parsley with the sautéed veal chops, fresh chives with the boiled new potatoes, and a fresh head of buttercrunch lettuce. No reversals in the garden, at least for the moment. And still no return of the groundhog. But I'm still sleeping with one eye open.

FRIDAY *June 9*

Ever vigilant, I've also been eyeballing the big garden for weeds to be pulled and volunteers to be transplanted or thinned. And today was a perfect day for putting things in order — overcast with temperatures in the sixties. So I cleaned up the double row of chard and moved some of the plants around to fill in the empty spaces where the seeds got washed out by the rains. Then I pulled all the weeds in the center of the garden, to make it ready for the cucumber seedlings that should be big enough for transplanting sometime next week. But I left all the Johnny-jump-ups that volunteered over the winter — so many the entire center of the garden will eventually look like a sea of cucumber leaves with Johnny-jump-ups bobbing on the surface. Well, that's what I hope it will look like.

A strange turn of events for me, letting flowers run rampant in the middle of my vegetable bed — letting any kind of flower in, for that matter. Before last year, the only flowers that got into my vegetable garden were the usual row of marigolds along the front of the bed. But last year, something within me said, "Why not? Why not?" Maybe it was all those tempting pictures in the winter gardening catalogues that finally got to me, especially because we usually grow just a few annuals in the yard, like the nasturtiums in the herb bed and the Johnnys on the hillock. Maybe it was the memory of other gardens I've seen around town where vegetables and flowers consort with each other without embarrassment. Maybe it was a hankering for all those new, exotically colored sunflowers that tempted me to plant a row of them along the back border of the vegetable bed. Maybe it was also a hankering for some cosmos waving in the breeze that lured me into scattering an envelope of whites and an envelope of reddish-oranges right in front of the corn patch. But I also think there was something deeper within me, rebelling against the strictly ordered balances and demarcations and segregations of my previous vegetable gardens. A desire to mess around a bit, a delight in disorder among the order. So, all those Johnnys that seeded themselves in are like a welcome colony of immigrants, blown east from the hillock in front of the gazebo. I've also got a couple of volunteer sunflowers at the east end of the bed, seeded in from the bird feeder that hangs off the pear tree during the winter. So many flowers finding their way into my vegetable bed, so many flaws in the carefully worked-out patterns, that it should be a lucky place for years to come.

If the okra's any sign, the luck is already working. It usually takes an average of two weeks to germinate, but it's already coming up just three days after I planted the seeds. Then again, maybe it's just a result of my soaking the seeds and the intense heat that followed. Or something else altogether. The way things have been going recently, I'm feeling reluctant to offer any hard-and-fast explanations of anything.

SATURDAY *June 10*

"It must be really difficult to be faced with two such different interpretations." My son Marshall called this morning, and I'd just finished telling him about the disagreement between Kate's cancer surgeon and the doctor from hell. Initially, it *was* difficult to understand how one doctor could treat her recent cancer as just a local recurrence while the other believed it to be systemic. Far worse was the hopeless future that seemed in store for Kate, according to the doctor from hell, who repeatedly asserted that her cancer was systemic and therefore certain to recur. "Maybe it won't come back for four or five years. Or it could suddenly show up everywhere in the system six months from now." But once my brother explained how unlikely it would be for a cell to travel throughout Kate's entire system and return exactly to the site of her last breast tumor, I've not had any trouble weighing the merits of the doctors' radically different interpretations. Now, instead, I'm troubled by how quickly I was willing to accept the extreme diagnosis of the doctor from hell. Oh yes, I was initially puzzled, so I asked him how all the tests could be negative, yet the cancer be systemic. But once he began talking about the crudity of the tests and then offered me the dandelion metaphor, my skepticism was readily dispelled.

As I look back on that afternoon, I wonder why I was so quick to accept the opinion of someone I'd never met before, even though it contradicted the view of the distinguished cancer surgeon who's been taking excellent care of Kate for the past six and a half years. Partly, I think it was the unusual frankness with which the doctor from hell announced his dire view of things. Partly his highly articulate manner, so different from the uncomfortable behavior of the surgeon, who usually says little and explains much less. But ultimately, I think the dandelion metaphor took me in, for it spoke to me in terms I know from firsthand observation. Kate, as usual, took a more hard-nosed view of things. "Didn't you notice how I was trying to lead him on, to see how far he'd go? I've always known that it can recur, but the way he was talking just didn't make sense to me, not in terms of the evidence from the tests. And besides, he didn't have any research studies to back up what he was saying. Even he admitted that."

So I can't help wondering why I too didn't notice the weakness of his case. I've been chiding students for years whenever they don't provide evidence for their assertions. And why didn't I tell him that his dandelion analogy was badly chosen, for the body is not like a lawn any more than a cancer cell is like a dandelion seed. Maybe it's because the dandelion analogy did embody a germ of common sense — that some things are so small they cannot be detected even by the most sophisticated technology. But a germ of sense doesn't necessarily lead to an epidemic of truth.

SUNDAY *June II*

"Get that trap set and keep it set! I don't want it eating in my garden." Nothing like a groundhog to liven up a lazy Sunday afternoon. And this afternoon, it sure did produce a flurry of activity around here. Kate and I had just gotten back from a leisurely walk downtown, and I'd gone outside to finish edging and weeding the tomato-pepper-eggplant bed, when my neighbor Chris called me over to his yard, which backs up against Jim's. "I just saw a woodchuck or a beaver or something like that. It ran under that spruce tree right behind Kate's flower bed." Chris is a young, high-powered physical chemist, who doesn't pay much attention to wildlife, so it's not surprising that he wouldn't know the difference between a groundhog and a beaver. But I could feel the adrenaline rise as I scurried around, looking for the groundhog, looking for Jim. And it only got worse when I saw the critter emerge from the tree and start heading toward Kate's flower border. A groundhog all right, but distinctly smaller than the one I'd seen earlier this week. So I ran around the bed to head it off in another direction, and it ran back under the tree. Again, I tried to find Jim, but no luck. So I went to tell Kate, and she immediately issued the command about getting the trap set. Then back to Jim's place, but again no luck. Then to my wheelbarrow, which I loaded with bricks to block up the entryway under my neighbor's shed, figuring that at least I could discourage it from hiding out near my vegetable gardens. Just then, Chris's wife Lynne came running toward me. "Do you know what that animal is? We've been chasing it around our garage. It's big and fat, but it sure moves fast. And now it's under the deck by the Russians' place." The Russians moved in next to Chris and Lynne a few months ago. A happy coincidence, because Lynne is a specialist in Russian language and literature. So she ran over to find out if they'd seen the beast. And I went looking again for Jim, to give him a quick description of the criminal and its likely whereabouts. The Russians, as it turns out, were gone for the afternoon. But I did eventually find Jim, and he as usual was interested in speculating about the critter. "Sounds to me like it might be a young one. Born earlier this year. But it might be almost full grown by now. They mature pretty quick. That other one's probably long gone, someplace else. I seen a couple going between Turner's pasture and my place, and I bet this is one of 'em." Jim got a spotlight, and we both checked under their deck but couldn't find a sign of the beast anywhere around. Later, Jim discovered that it lives under the porch of a house across the street from the Russians. So I went home and gave a full report to Kate, who was of the opinion that "It's time for Our Gang to wash up and get ready for bed." And I agreed.

MONDAY *June 12*

"What is so rare as a day in June? Then, if ever, come perfect days." And cool nights. Three in a row, without even a hint of rain, and this one the best of all. Dry air, light breezes, mild temperatures, clear skies. Just right for a midmorning walk with Kate. And spring vegetables to match. Last night, a wilted spinach salad, tossed with olive oil, tamari, lemon, and garlic. This noon, a head of buttercrunch, halved down the center, and topped with fresh onions, radishes, tomatoes, olives, anchovies, and grated parmesan. This evening, stir-fried snow peas. Tomorrow, perhaps, more broccoli from the heads accumulating in the ice-box. So much bounty that Kate took some snow peas, lettuce, scallions, and radishes to her mother this afternoon. And a Car-mona butterhead, ruffled red and green, to one of her mother's friends the other afternoon, who returned the favor with a dozen brown country eggs. Cast your vegetables on the water.

Now if only the animals were in sync, the days would seem complete. But this morning began with a gentle wake-up re-minder from Kate, sometime around six-thirty. "Now's the time to set that trap, when it's likely to be out, looking for things to eat." Not an auspicious way to begin the day, but I brought it upon myself, leaving the trap unset after all the flurry of yesterday after-noon. So I baited it with a chunk of corn and a slice of apple, "delicacies" according to Jim, and took it up to the spruce tree where the critter was hiding out yesterday, right near the juncture of Jim's back yard, Chris's back yard, and ours.

Then I went to put Phoebe out the front door for her morning walk, and the threat of a groundhog seemed trivial by comparison. Every morning now, I dread the business of going to get Phoebe in the half bath where she sleeps, uncertain of what I might find. The tumor is growing larger, her hind quarters smaller, but she continues to soldier on, as she did this morning. A few reproving squawks, then the purring when I picked her up and stroked her neck and petted her head, then the quick hops down the front porch steps, a visit to the shade border, and a stroll to the outside cellarway, her "safety zone," according to Kate, where she's always waited, like a sentinel, to be let in the back door. Then a quick hop up to her counter in the half bath, peering out at the kitchen while I open a can of cat food and mix in an antibiotic pill. But her days are clearly coming to an end. Now she spends most of her time sleeping on one of the window beds in the attic, or on the window sill next to my computer, where she took this morning's sun. And we have begun to talk about the day, not so far off, when we should put her to sleep forever. "What is so rare as a day in June? Then, if ever, come perfect days."

TUESDAY *June 13*

Still nothing in the groundhog trap, but no depredations in any of the gardens. Now if only the doctors could get their act together, the days would seem complete. It all started harmlessly enough, when Kate headed off this morning to have the stitches removed from last week's surgery. In her brown denim overall-jumper, green and white striped T-shirt, and matching green socks, she looked like a member of Our Gang. But three hours later when she came in the back door, her jaw set, her cheeks flushed, her eyes glaring, she looked like one of the Furies. I could see right away that she wasn't wrought up just by her three-mile walk home in the noonday sun. "You won't believe what happened. First of all, he was late again, shooting the breeze in the hallway with an old colleague who stopped by. Then after removing the stitches, he sat down in the chair and told me he'd just conferred with the radiologists, and they refuse to give me the light dose of localized radiation that everyone else recommends. They want to do something more extensive. He also said there's nothing he can do, except to arrange an appointment for me if I want to talk with the radiologists about it. I'm mad as hell with the radiologists and the system, and I told him so flat out, several times over." But the worst was yet to come. "And when I asked him why a light course of radiation isn't available to me, he told me 'It's probably economic, but don't quote me on it.'" Radiologists more hellish than the medical oncologist. "I feel like I'm caught in a crapshoot. But I refused to go along with it. I told him a heavy dosage of radiation didn't seem to do much for Madame Curie in the long run, and I'm not going to roll over like all the passive women they usually deal with. So I asked him if he'd call Marshall's friend Jack, and confer with him about what's needed. And he agreed to, but doesn't have Jack's number." I called the surgeon, gave him the number, and then we sat down to have lunch. But the most surprising news came just a bit later when the surgeon quickly called back after conferring with Jack and reported to Kate their agreement that no radiation is needed.

Heavy dose, light dose, no dose. And no explanations for any of the options. Talk about a crapshoot. An ending so absurd I decided to cook a celebratory dinner — charcoal-broiled tuna with fresh rosemary, spaghetti with pesto from last fall's garden, fresh stir-fried broccoli with ginger, garlic, tamari, and lime juice. And after dinner, a walk up the back yard with Pip, where we found a hand-printed note in the Havahart trap: "HOG, THEY'RE TRYING TO CATCH YOU. FRIEND." When I showed it later to Kate, she suggested the following reply: "FRIEND, I DON'T SCARE EASY. HOG."

WEDNESDAY *June 14*

Now the big question is whether it was Hog's friend or the groundhog itself that tripped the lever on the trap last night. I noticed the problem the minute I checked it this morning — one end of the trap closed, the other open, and the piece of corn moved off the central metal plate. My hunch is that the groundhog paid a visit, but got away because the doors didn't close at the same time. So I adjusted the lever a bit, reset the trap, tried it a few times to make sure the doors were synchronized, and continued around the yard for my early morning checkup.

No dew on the grass, no clouds in the sky, the air a bit heavier. All the signs of a high pressure system, likely to hang in for a while, bringing on summer a few days ahead of the solstice next week. All the plants in the back bed visibly reflecting the transition from spring to summer. Plum tomatoes showing on the Enchantments, cherry tomatoes swelling on the potted Prestos, blossoms opening on the slicer tomatoes. Eggplants and pepper plants putting out new growth. And all the spring vegetables still thriving in the moderate temperatures and moisture-laden soil of the last several weeks. Cauliflower beginning to head up. Walla Walla sweet onions and Dutch red onions beginning to form bulbs. Shell peas beginning to swell. Green Comet broccoli heads ready to eat, now that the Packmans are done and putting out side shoots. And more snow peas ready to harvest. Spring coming to a climax just as summer's on the verge of arriving.

A pivotal moment in the large vegetable garden that I decided to honor by weeding and cultivating it again this morning, then removing the row cover from the corn patch along the north side of the bed. The last one to go, as Kate immediately noticed on her own inspection tour. "It's about time. Now when are you planning to get the cucumbers planted?" And she might have added the pattypans, zucchini, and melons to that question. I don't like to transplant young seedlings in the face of a rising thermometer, so I'm waiting for a few days, hoping for a slight break in the weather, to ease their way. And once they're in, all the summer vegetables will be in the ground. Everything in sync and in season. But even now, as Kate says, "You can really tell it's summer from how silent it gets in the afternoon heat and how dark it is in the house." Also from the yellow swallowtail that wafted over the terrace this morning.

THURSDAY *June 15*

"Can you believe it? I been waterin' the past two days. And just a week or two ago we was worryin' about having too much rain. But when I dug down with my fist this morning, there just wasn't anything there. I just don't understand it, how it changes so fast. And I don't like it, don't like it at all. It's supposed to hit ninety today, mid-nineties over the weekend. And no rain in sight. It looks like that drought you was talkin' about back in February." Jim's land drains into mine, and his soil is less clayey than mine, so it always dries out more quickly than mine. And he starts fretting more quickly than I. But even I started watering last night after dinner. The lettuce and Swiss chard, the herbs around the gazebo, the parsley and nasturtiums in the herb bed next to the gazebo. And this morning, I went around checking the soil in both of my vegetable beds and Kate's flower border. Dry on the top inch or so in most places, still wet enough below to ball up firmly. But a day or two from now, the ground will surely be drier, especially given the above-normal temperatures and the breezes wafting in the from west. So I'm now figuring on a stretch of watering far sooner than I ever expected. And I don't like it either. Lugging the hose two hundred feet to the back of the lot, then setting up the sprinkler strip along the full length of Kate's sixty-foot border, first in the front, then in the back. Then gradually working my way back down the lot, water wand in hand, deep watering all the red and black raspberries, the two young cherry trees, the currant bushes, all the plants in the eggplant-pepper-tomato bed, everything in the big vegetable bed, and in the herb beds. A two-day routine. And then a day or two later, working my way around the lot, cultivating the soil, to keep it from baking in the heat. Another two-day routine. Suddenly, I'm remembering the summers of '88 and '89, years of the drought, when I was tethered to the hose for weeks on end. Time to start mulching, far sooner than I expected. Summertime.

The season is visibly coming on in Kate's flower border, the yarrow turning yellow, the delphinium bluing up, and only the coral bells and rich blue salvia still in full bloom from the late spring phase of her garden. But the surest measure of the season and the heat is Phoebe, always addicted to it ever since Kate found her shivering in a cold rain some twenty years ago. So, come summer, Phoebe always prefers the warmth outside to the cooler air inside. Even — especially — on the hottest of days. True to form, she went to the back door in midmorning, asking to be let out, and ever since then she's been flaked out on the stone terrace, soaking up the warmth of the day. Kate and I are also about to take the warmth of the day by taking part in something called the Great Railroad Caper aboard the Silver Solarium — a sunset ride to the Mississippi and back. I just hope it's no warmer in the solarium than it is outside.

FRIDAY *June 16*

My colleague Jix, host with his wife Jean of the Great Railroad Caper, greeted us at the tracks with the good news. "It's air conditioned." "It," as it turns out, was a remodeled dome car, built in 1948, its antique stainless steel exterior glittering as if it had just come off the production line, its aquamarine windows as polished as its silver surface. Its name — SILVER SOLARIUM — painted in black letters on a stainless steel panel directly below the windows, its legendary train name painted in large black letters on a panel directly above the windows — CALIFORNIA ZEPHYR. The name immediately brought a rise from Kate. "That's the train I took to school on the West Coast." It was also the train we took to the coast during the early seventies when Kate gave me my first guided tour of northern California. But the old Zephyr was never quite like this spiffed-up dome car, with its newly upholstered chairs, its modernized galley, its specially designed shades to block the intense heat of the sun at any angle in the sky. A dream car, for an early summer dream ride across the Iowa countryside. A caper, a fantasy, a world apart, made possible by the Iowa Interstate Railroad, the fruit of Jean's long-term efforts to preserve an east–west train line throughout the state. Thirty-three of us were scattered around the dome car and the lower lounge, together with a caterer and her small crew, slowly being pulled by two diesel engines past farm fields, small towns, and railroad intersections, cars stopping to wave at us as we waved back along our stately progress. Our whistle blowing — two longs, a short and a long, two longs, a short and a long. Sixty miles to the Mississippi in two and a half hours. Pop songs and forties jazz playing in the background. Thirty minutes on a railroad bridge directly over the great father of the waters, while the diesels uncoupled themselves from us, trundled over to the Illinois side of the river, switched tracks, trundled back, and hooked up in front of us for a three-hour return trip in the setting sun. Leisurely enough to make our way through a four-course dinner, and drinks, and singing. Leisurely enough to behold the farmscape rolling out on both sides of the tracks, the fields so far behind the season they looked like early May rather than mid-June. Corn plants no more than a week or two old, green lines of them running into the distance against the dark brown soil, row after row, like a study in perspective, a geometer's delight, a reminder of what Grant Wood might have beheld some sixty years ago as he gazed out over this undulant landscape. A reminder of what I beheld some fifty-five years ago as I gazed out the train window, alone, on my way from Cleveland to my aunt Leah's in Evansville, Indiana, for an early summer vacation. But I don't remember a sunset anywhere near so rosy as the one last night. Nor do I remember deboarding a silver car gleaming against a darkened station and a glittering sky.

SATURDAY *June 17*

Up at sunrise, gardening at the edges of the day — today, yesterday, and the day before. Sure signs that summer is here. Yesterday morning I put the sprinkler strip along the front and back of Kate's bed and let it run for an hour or so in both places. But the salvia in front and the yarrow in back got so bent over from the weight of their waterlogged blossoms that I had to turn off the hose before the soil was deeply soaked. So I'll have to make yet another tour of the bed, water wand in hand, to make sure everything gets enough to last through the next four days in the nineties. Even watering has its rules. Water too shallow and the

roots run shallow. Water too often and the plants become depend-
ent. So, in weather like this, I try to limit myself to watering just
once a week, deeply enough that it'll hold until the next rain or
watering. Yesterday morning, I took care of the eggplant-pepper-
tomato bed — a deep drink that stopped the eggplants and peppers from going through the midday wilts, as well as greening and
heightening them up a bit. Given the moisture that Jim and I
found in the soil just two days ago, it's surprising that the water
should have made so much difference. But the visible difference
reminds me that moisture residing in the soil doesn't give plants
the boost they get from the easily available water of a substantial weekly rain or soaking. So this morning I continued the watering — three hours with the wand in the big vegetable bed, long
enough to saturate everything and to take stock of all the plants.
Onions bulbing up. Shell peas swelling. Snow peas still putting
out new pods. Broccoli forming side shoots. Cauliflower making heads, three already large enough to harvest for a cauliflower-
broccoli stir fry tonight. Potatoes beginning to blossom, loveliest
flowers in the edible nightshade family — lavender with yellow
centers.

But the real news of this weekend is the visit of my daughter
Amelia, the only one of my children to really be bitten by vegetable gardening. Maybe she picked it up from me, or from detassel-
ing corn during the summers of her youth, or from tending the
gardens at Scattergood, a Quaker high school ten miles east of here
that she attended for two years, or from studying agricultural
journalism at the University of Wisconsin. Or maybe just from an
exuberant love of the vegetables themselves. For whenever Kate
and I go to visit her and her husband Joe at their big old frame
house in Wisconsin, I always notice that her vegetables are growing rampantly, bearing fruit abundantly, with a joyous sense of
abandon that I envy almost as much as her love of this insufferably
hot weather. "Winter," she says, "I'm often depressed, but summer
I really flower. The heat makes me sweat, and the sweat's cathartic,
so this is my favorite season."

SUNDAY *June 18*

Father's Day, which I celebrated this morning by picking several heads of lettuce for Amelia to take home with her this afternoon. Lettuce from the earliest crop that I started inside in mid-February and transplanted outside in mid-March — still crisp, tender, and tasty despite the recent heat wave, despite being three months in the ground. Reminders of the extraordinarily cool, moist spring just past. Amelia, as if to match my gift, gave me a bottle of Italian balsamic vinegar and a plain glass cruet to hold it, thanks to a hint from Kate. We've recently taken up the old-fashioned expedient of oil and vinegar in cruets. And the salads now seem more tasty to both of us than before, probably because we're using much less oil and vinegar than ever before. Just a sprinkle or two rather than a tablespoon or three. Maybe less really is more, especially in the dressing of salads.

But more definitely is more in the watering of gardens, as I noticed again early this morning when I went out to check the vegetables, all of them distinctly more erect and showy than before. The visible difference made me curious about how long it's been since the last measurable rain, and I was surprised to discover that during the past two weeks we've had just a quarter of an inch. No wonder some of the plants have begun to seem parched. Subsoil moisture is one thing, and we still have plenty of it, but surface moisture is another, and we're now badly hurting for it, especially in this continuing heat wave. So I spent a few hours with the water wand, drenching all the plants in Kate's flower border.

Early morning in the flower bed, still in the shade of the spruce trees directly behind it, still suffused with the mild overnight air. The buzz of insects around my head. The soft rush of water at my feet, pooling up as I move the wand around each plant and then move on. Birdsong coming on, but no sounds yet of traffic in the distance or mowers in the neighborhood or neighbors in their yards. I'm alone with the flowers. Nothing to eat here. A feast only for the eyes. Especially right now the pale gray mulleins, four feet tall, like sentinels down the center of the bed from one end to the other, their base leaves like flannel, their tall columnar stalks like velvet, covered with yellow-petaled flowers from top to bottom. A bee flies into the center of a mullein flower. A flower falls from a mullein stalk — a sight I've never seen before. Is the fall of a blossom like the fall of a sparrow? Is there a divinity in it? I don't know, but it sure did feel heavenly just then.

MONDAY *June 19*

"Mostly sunny and continued very warm" all the way through Friday, according to the National Weather Service, and "no rain expected." So I continued my watering and cultivating routine this morning. A sprinkler strip along the red and black currant bushes, while I pulled my three-pronged claw through most of the rows in the main vegetable bed that I watered on Saturday. Tomorrow morning, I'll claw up the flower bed and then start the cycle all over again, mulching the summer vegetables with straw right after I water them. Usually, I don't mulch them until late June or early July, for fear of insulating the soil when it's still too cold for the good of the plants. But the soil two or three inches down is already warm to the touch. Red alert, I feel like I'm on red alert, especially because I've also been keeping all the cucumber and zucchini seedlings on hold, waiting for a break in the weather that was supposed to be coming in a couple of days. But now it looks like I'll just have to start putting them in the garden, protecting them with the cedar shingles I use to shield things from the worst of the sun and wind. And hope for the best.

Talk about hoping for the best, I took Phoebe into the vet this morning at the suggestion of Amelia, who's studying to be a nurse practitioner and thinks the old girl might live comfortably into the fall if we can keep her on cortisone to reduce the irritation. "It's a big tumor, dad, and it's just going to get bigger, but the cortisone will stop her from aggravating it so much." And the vet agreed. He also gave her a shot of fluid to plump her up a bit, and now she's back out on the terrace taking the heat of the day — soulmate of Amelia in her love of the heat. So, it seems, this abnormally warm weather is good for something.

Actually, the best news of the day came from my brother Marshall, who called Kate this morning to report that he'd spoken to another oncologist friend of his. And this doctor also believes that Kate's recent tumor was just a local recurrence that usually occurs in about ten percent of such cases — definitely not grounds for assuming her cancer is systemic. Good news for sure, but now I'm even more curious as to why the doctor from hell would make such an extreme and outlandish diagnosis. The most plausible and disturbing explanation I've heard so far came from Amelia. "If you ask me, dad, he was just trying to cover his ass, giving the worst-case scenario, so you couldn't ever take him to court for not giving you all the possible options. Was there anyone in the room when he told you that stuff?" Well, yes, I told her, one of his residents was there, taking notes. "See what I mean, dad?" So the doctor from hell might have been diagnosing with far more concern for his own well-being than for Kate's. Given such a devilish approach to diagnosis, I sure am glad he's not predicting the weather. It's already bad enough as it is.

TUESDAY *June 20*

Our state climatologist is finally in sync with the weather, having announced just yesterday that "The threat of major flooding in Iowa this year is over." Now we have something else to worry about. "Hot weather and even the possibility of a drought." The National Weather Service, not to be outdone in declaring the obvious, has just announced that during the last week "Iowa moved directly from early to midspring into summer." The effects of that move are visible everywhere in the vegetable garden, everything suddenly speeded up in its growth. All three crops of lettuce now headed up. Shell peas now almost plump enough for harvest when a week or so ago they were just beginning to swell. Snow peas all finished with their first crop and beginning to put out new growth toward a second. Broccoli heads all harvested as of last week and first crop of side shoots all harvested yesterday. Cauliflowers almost all fully matured, their pale white heads beaded with dew under the gray-green leaves I've folded over to keep them blanched.

But nowhere is the sudden spurt of growth more noticeable than in the tomato plants, all of them about three feet up the seven-foot poles. So I've already started the process of training them to the stakes — another one of my rituals, as painstaking as the pea brush routine, and as functionally pleasing from beginning to end. The problem in this case is to discipline a tropical vine that wants to grow rampantly. In fact, the indeterminate varieties I favor will not only grow indefinitely high, until killed by frost, but they also put out an indefinite number of stems, known as side shoots or "suckers," and every sucker will produce an indefinite number of tomatoes. Seemingly a gardener's wildest dream fulfilled. But a wildly growing tomato plant is an invitation to disease, rot, small fruit, and delayed ripening, as I discovered from my first few vegetable gardens some forty years ago. More, in this case, turns out to be less. So, rather than letting my tomato plants grow an indefinite number of side shoots, I limit each plant to just two or three stems, pinching out all the other suckers as they emerge. Then I tie each stem to a separate side of the stake or to the front with a soft piece of cloth or plastic tape. The leaves on each stem produce enough shade to prevent the tomatoes from sun-cracking, yet they let in more sunlight and air than a plant covered with the foliage of many stems. When the vines are five or six feet tall, with tomatoes swelling and ripening up and down both sides of the stake, they're a spectacle to behold. A festoon of fruit, a tower of tomatoes. Now they still seem a bit dwarfed by the poles, as if they were aspiring beyond their limits. But soon enough the poles will be too short for them, especially given these tropical days on which they thrive.

WEDNESDAY *June 21*

"The sweat's in my eyes, and my eyes is burning." That's the way Jim saw it this afternoon when he was weeding around one of his flower beds. That's exactly the way I felt this morning when I was mulching the eggplants, peppers, and tomatoes after I gave them another soaking. Kate and I were both sweating even before we got out of bed this morning, because the overnight cool-off never arrived. A few more nights like that, and we'll probably be running the air conditioner around the clock, despite our distaste for sleeping in the artificial breeze and the jetlike roar of our air-conditioning system.

The hottest day of the year. The hottest day we've had in four years. Mid-eighties by midmorning, high nineties by late afternoon. And it's supposedly just the beginning of summer. A paradoxical occasion, when the earth is farthest from the sun, yet the longest daylight period of the year, because the Northern Hemisphere is tilted most directly toward its light. This afternoon, it felt like we were not only tilted toward the sun, but its rays were focused exactly on our back yard, heating it up to the point of combustion. The grass is already beginning to turn brown, as if we were in the midst of a July or August heat wave, though there's still more than a week to go in June. As the weatherman said last night, "That's the way it's been all year. All mixed up."

In a heat wave like this, even the tropical vegetables are unhappy. Though tomatoes presumably originated in western South America, they usually stop setting fruit when evening temperatures exceed seventy, as they did last night. And the same is true of most peppers, though the bell variety I grow, namely Ace, will continue to set fruit even in weather this hot. Its name is well earned. But the Black Prince tomato from Siberia is displaying the signs of its origin, its leaves beginning to go limp by midmorning. Well, it's a long way from home, and it looks like it's going to be a long, hot summer. So, I wonder if the Prince will survive long enough to produce one of its black beauties. The fabled Brandywine, on the other hand, sitting right next to the Black Prince, seems to be completely unfazed by the heat, despite its discovery by a New England seedsman.

"Remember last summer? How perfect it was?" Actually, I'd momentarily forgotten, but when a clerk at Pleasant Valley Nursery reminded me this morning, as he was loading bales of straw into my trunk, I remembered all the statistics exactly as he was giving them to me. "Just a few days in the nineties, in mid-June. And the rain came like clockwork, once every week or so, sometime overnight, so we never had to water." And I never had to mulch. Remember? How could I ever have forgotten?

THURSDAY *June 22*

"It looks like we should probably be having some all-vegetable meals." Kate had just opened the refrigerator door this morning and seen the shelves bulging with some of the stuff I'd just harvested — shell peas, cauliflower, a head of red oak leaf lettuce, and two heads of green Simpson lettuce, not to mention broccoli, snow peas, radishes, and other salad greens in the two big vegetable crispers right below the shelves. The climax of the spring vegetables usually produces a brief congestion in the refrigerator, but never so abundantly as this year, what with the three separate lettuce patches and a crop of rabbits so cretinous they haven't yet touched a leaf of it.

We almost had one of those all-vegetable meals last night, when I broiled a chicken breast and served it with the first fresh shell peas of the spring, a salad of mixed greens, and a head of steamed cauliflower dressed with olive oil, garlic, lemon, paprika, and grated parmesan. For lunch today, Kate made a salad of mixed greens, feta, olives, and tomatoes. And for dinner this evening, I cooked some more fresh peas and steamed another head of cauliflower, which I topped with sautéed red peppers to go along with a few bratwurst. But even if we had all-vegetable meals for every meal, we'd still not be able to deal with all the spring vegetables that are out in the garden right now, especially given the way they're being forced into maturity by the hot weather. So we're casting more vegetables on the waters.

This evening after dinner, Kate took some up to our neighbor Judy, to thank her for hosting a little get-together at her house yesterday afternoon, where another neighbor, Margaret, who's in her mid-eighties, showed Judy and Kate how to make cheskys (pronounced shiss-keys) — an old Czech fruit pastry that looks and tastes very much like a fancy raspberry turnover. Margaret, as it turns out, had offered to put on the show as a way of repaying Kate and Linda the Gruff for planting some flowers at her house several weeks ago. But Margaret didn't feel her own kitchen was large enough, so she dragooned Judy, whom she knows from church. After the chesky episode, Kate then drove out to Lone

Tree, a small town about ten miles south of here, to pick up a half-dozen free-range chickens from Carol, a farm woman she'd heard about after giving some lettuce to her mother's friend Janet.

So, it seems, my spring vegetables are making their way around town and coming home to roost in the form of cheskys, chickens, and fresh brown country eggs. "Just passing it around," as Kate says.

FRIDAY *June 23*

Nine days in the nineties and still counting. A blessing for Phoebe, whose heat-hunger has led her to camp out on the terrace, especially now that we've been running the air conditioner day and night. But a curse for everyone else. Last night, it got so bad that Kate and I went to the movies, not for the air conditioning but the escape to a world so remote from ours — the medieval Scottish highlands during the time of the rebel patriot Wallace — that I thought it might be a cooling distraction from the continuing heat wave. But tempers ran so high through most of the story it made me hot just to watch all the blood being spilled. And it wasn't any better this morning in the un-airconditioned church during the memorial service for Connie, the wife of my retired colleague Bob. Neither a cardboard hand fan, nor the open stained-glass windows, nor the light touch of the pianist, nor even the thought of Connie's unflappable self-composure and inner strength could stop the sweat from dripping down my forehead and temples from the first hymn to the final benediction. The forecasters have been promising a break this weekend, but they've been promising one ever since the heat wave began.

Whenever the weather used to act up like this in the seventies and early eighties, I'd talk it over with Herman, a retired farmer who immigrated to this country shortly before World War I, and who spent his later years tending a garden crammed with flowers and fruit trees and brambles and grape vines and vegetables just a block away from our house. A garden that he planted and tended entirely himself, all the way into his late eighties, despite having to walk on crutches and lean over a wooden sawhorse because of severely damaged hipjoints. After a day of gardening, Herman would get cleaned up, put on a white shirt, a clean pair of overalls, his black leather shoes, and sit out on a red metal garden chair, which he placed on top of an elevated wooden flat in front of his five-in-one apple tree. And every summer evening on my walk around the block with Crispin, our first terrier, I'd stop and listen to Herman reminisce about the past. Turns out he'd kept a log of the weather and his crops during all his years as a farmer. So, whenever I was fretting about a long run of hot, dry days like we're having right now, wondering when it would end, he'd always have something worse to report, like "the summer of '36" or "the dust bowl days." And then he'd let me know he was "just takin' it one day at a time." When I first heard that expression, I thought it was just a way of talking about how to get through a long run of bad weather. "One day at a time." But the more I've thought about the matter, that apparently shortsighted view of things may be one of the best long-range bits of advice I know. Especially if you're keeping a daybook.

SATURDAY *June 24*

"It's not like him, not like him at all. I never seen him behave like that." Jim was cradling Pip's head in his arm, checking his gums, feeling his stomach, trying to figure out what had caused him to vomit a few minutes earlier and then suddenly go into something like shock. Kate and I were both kneeling on the ground, looking at his glazed eyes and his limp body, so alert just a few minutes earlier. Kate had tethered him to a tree while she was working on her flower bed after dinner yesterday, and when I came out to tie up a few tomato plants the wave of her arm and the expression on her face immediately alerted me that something was wrong with Pip. So I went to get Jim, who knows more about animals than anyone around, and after a few minutes without much improvement, we all agreed that a trip to the vet was in order. And it was. Evidently, Pip had eaten something that caused him so much pain and panic he'd almost gone into a severe shock. So today, tomorrow, and Monday, he's on stomach relaxants, fluids, and light food. And he's been acting the part whenever he sees me. Head hangdog, tail between his legs, moping over the absence of his usual rations and treats, especially the rawhide chips that probably caused some of the trouble.

But the real trouble that's got me feeling a bit hangdog myself is that Pip's clearly aging, as Kate's been trying to tell me whenever we have an episode like this. "I keep telling you I've been running a geriatric ward around here the past year." But I guess I've been ignoring her, because Pip has generally had such a good constitution, so few illnesses, such a handsome, well-marked coat — full black saddle, reddish-brown legs and head — that he often seems to be just a few years old. And often he still behaves that way, wanting to get ahead of us on a walk, even when he doesn't have any idea of where we're going, sometimes taking the leash in his mouth and jumping around with it, like a young puppy. But he's ten years old — old for his breed, according to the vet. His eyes are beginning to cloud up a bit, his stomach is evidently beginning to act up a bit, he doesn't wake up early anymore, and he doesn't try to run away much, as he did just a year or two ago. It used to be that instead of calling Jim to diagnose an ailment, I'd be imploring him to help me track Pip down, usually at ten or eleven in the evening. Probably that's why Jim was so surprised by his behavior last night.

But I don't mean to be writing an obituary here. I'm just taking stock of things, noting the seasonal changes. Besides, Jim's help last night gave me a good excuse to give him and Carol one of the five heads of cauliflower I harvested this morning. One good head deserves another. And it was especially good at lunch today, when Kate served one steamed and cooled, dressed with a Creole vinaigrette.

SUNDAY *June 25*

"I'm going home to water from a drying-up well. That'll bring it on." Rebecca came over this morning with a jarful of mint transplants in trade for the spare pepper plants and eggplants I've been holding for her. She likes to barter, and I like to find a

good home for my backup seedlings once I'm sure all my transplants have taken. But she wasn't here a minute before we were
talking about the lack of rain, now that we've gone without it the
past three weeks — commiserating with each other in our envy of
the nearby towns that got some yesterday. I told her that Mount
Vernon, just twenty miles north of here, got two inches yesterday
afternoon, when all we got were the rumbles of distant thunder
and overcast skies. "Well, can you believe they also got it south of
here in Kalona? And right next door to us in Coralville?" Then
Kate came out with Pip on the leash and supplied one of the
refrains that've been on our lips the past few days. "It's clouding up
and passing over us again, falling everywhere else but here." So I
started watering Kate's flower border again, then the parsley and
nasturtiums in the herb bed, before the three of us went in to have
a late morning breakfast and talk about other things in our lives.
But the rain was still on everyone's mind when Rebecca went
home, voicing the superstition I've often believed — that watering
is the best way to break a drought. Probably because so many
people water during a drought that some folks are sure to be doing
it right before a rain.

An hour or so later, the first few drops were so faint, I wouldn't
have noticed them without Kate's skeptical question, "Is that
rain?" But soon it was coming down so well that Kate remarked on
the delicious aroma. "It sure does smell good." Then on the scope
of it. "You can't do that with a hose." And I was thinking about the
multimillion dollar rains of yesteryear. Only Pip was distressed, his
tongue distended its full length, hyperventilating nonstop. But
when the wind picked up, and the thunder and lightning started
exploding all around us, and the rain blew in with the force of a
violent monsoon, both of us were on the verge of hyperventilating
too. Then Kate was singing a different tune. "Rain, rain, go away,
come again some other day." And I was panicking about all the
damage in the garden. And not without cause. For an hour later,
when the storm had passed, I not only discovered that three and a
half inches had fallen, I also found tomato stems broken, the corn
laid flat, bean plants askew, chard and lettuce bruised. The entire
large vegetable bed disfigured by rain, wind, and runoff. A mess
that put me in mind of Kate's other remark during the storm,
about "asking for things that we may not want when we get them."

MONDAY *June 26*

Jim was sitting astride the peak of his garage, right behind our spruce trees, touching up his weather vane, when I first saw him this afternoon. But even from a distance I could see a twinkle in his eye, when he called out what was also on my mind just then. "I guess we won't have to be waterin' for a few days." Last night on top of the big one yesterday, we got another three quarters of an inch, for a total of four and a quarter inches in twenty-four hours. And even now as I write this report, the rain is falling again, though far more gently than yesterday afternoon. Elsewhere yesterday there were flooded streets, blown-out power lines, uprooted trees, and hail-shredded plants. No wonder Rebecca was happy it completely missed her yesterday afternoon, especially since she picked up a couple of inches of the gentle stuff last night and today. This morning, I too was half wishing it had missed us yesterday, especially when I went out to examine the corn patch and found all the stalks still flat on the ground, pointing in all directions, like a bad throw in pickup sticks. Telltale sign of a dangerous twister. Jim wanted to know what I did about the corn, especially after he'd talked to a local farmer this morning. "He told me he just lets the sun pick 'em up. Is that what you do?" I tried that method a couple of times, as I told Jim, but each time the plants never really made it all the way back up, bending themselves instead into an L-shape, reaching for the sun. So this morning I used my own method. I knelt down on an old strip of plywood at the edge of the corn patch, propped up each corn stalk one by one, and pulled a couple of handfuls of muddy soil around the base of each plant to hold it steady when the next downpour comes through. Fifty-five corn stalks and an hour later, I could easily see why the farmers just leave it to the sun. Then I worked on the double row of bush bean plants, their leaves weighted down with soil clinging to their undersides. I didn't want to touch the leaves for fear of spreading fungus when they're wet or breaking their brittle stems, so I just walked down each side of the row, gently tapping the undersides of the leaves with the long wooden handle of my hoe, tiptoeing through the straw-mulched muck. Then I took on the last of this morning's salvage operations — the lettuce patch by the gazebo. All the red oak leaf and green Simpson plants so bruised by the violent force of the wind-driven rain that their leaves were pockmarked with dark green translucent spots, cell walls shattered, as if they'd been through a hard frost. Rain-bruised lettuce — a spectacle I've never seen before, but I consoled myself, as I fed it to the compost, with the thought that it had already begun to go bitter from the heat.

TUESDAY *June 27*

Now, two days after the storm, the perennials in Kate's flower border and the vegetables in both of my beds have recuperated from the violent wind and rain, most having pulled themselves up straight all on their own. Most garden plants, after all, are more durable and resilient than I sometimes imagine. They probably don't need all the fussy reconstruction work I lavished yesterday on the corn patch. They certainly confront the weather more directly than I do, and they certainly put up with its rapid changes more capably than I do. Now they're visibly thriving not only on the readily available moisture, but also on the drastically reduced temperatures — in the mid-seventies rather than the mid-nineties the past two days — and on the overcast skies rather than the searing rays of the sun. As I write this report, more thunder is exploding around them, and more rain is falling on them, but without any wind to speak of. So the heat wave and drought have been broken. And there's probably enough moisture in the soil to last us through the end of July. "Through the middle of July," according to Rebecca. And now we seem to have returned to the cool and rainy weather that prevailed much of the spring. But then I remember with the help of Kate that we often have a week or two like this every summer, when a cool front settles in, saturating the soil, filling the yard with a swamplike atmosphere. On days like this, there's not much one can do in the garden, except for weeding, which Rebecca did this afternoon, scrambling around the border of the gazebo in her dark green gardening clogs. I took on the terrace this morning in my summer pajamas, pulling all the weeds and sweeping up all the stuff that had collected on it since my last cleanup a month or so ago. Now there's nothing left to do but enjoy a break from the garden.

For as long as I can remember, such days as these have always offered a break from something. At summer camp during my childhood, they were the only thing that could liberate us from the incessant kicking exercises in the swimming pool. "Craft day," our counselors announced and herded us into the wooden lodge, where we whiled away the hours wood-burning and leather-working. And when I wasn't at camp, I can remember my cousin Howard and me retreating to his screened-in porch, where we set up a card table and played board games and card games for days on end. Monopoly forever. Maybe this is the time to break out the Punto set that Kate gave me for my birthday. Or maybe I'll try my hand at the beadworking kit I gave her for Christmas three or four years ago that's still sitting unstrung on the tall dresser in our bedroom. Or maybe I'll set up the filing cards in the seed storage case she gave me for my birthday. So many choices, I don't know what to do. Craft days are here again.

WEDNESDAY *June 28*

"Look at that deer print!" I can distinctly remember myself looking at it yesterday, when Rebecca showed me its heart-shaped signature right under the thyme at the corner of the gazebo. And I can remember thinking nothing more about it, except that I hadn't seen one in that spot before. Oh yes, we've had quite a few deer around here for a number of years, ever since a pair started propagating in the nearby wilderness park. Jim's been keeping track of the herd, which now numbers in the forties or fifties, and he occasionally tries to keep them from feeding on our gardens by supplying them with apples. From time to time, though, we've seen them in the back yard, or seen their droppings in Kate's flower border or under our apple tree, or seen the results of their nibbling at the young beans. I've been able to keep them under control by spraying things with Hinder, the only organic compound that's capable of doing the trick because the deer can't stand the intense smell of its ammonia-based mixture. Just a couple of days ago, I told Jim he should try some of the stuff after he told me about their doing in one of his bean patches. The only problem is that Hinder has to be reapplied every three or four weeks or after a heavy rain such as we had on Sunday. But until the clearing that took place this afternoon, it's not been dry enough to reapply the stuff. All of which explains the sad spectacle I found this morning when I was making my early rounds of the yard and discovered that the dwarf sweet cherry tree I planted this spring had been severely pruned by a visiting deer. Every one of its four main green branches was cropped at least in half and several of its leaves were stripped off. Kate was surprised when I showed it to her and Rebecca today. "I've never heard of them feeding on cherry trees." Neither had Rebecca, and neither had I until last summer when I found a couple of badly nibbled branches on the dwarf sour cherry I planted last year. Just as I was telling them about last year's episode, Rebecca looked down at the base of the tree, encircled by a narrow wire hoop to protect it from nibbling rabbits, and again exclaimed, "Look at that deer print!" Now I'm wondering whether I should hold the deer at fault or the rain that washed the Hinder off the tree. Or the fallen apples that Kate noticed under our apple tree just five or ten feet beyond the cherry tree — fruit that probably lured the deer to walk by it in the first place. I think this must be one of those cases that logicians or lawyers might love to debate. As for me, I took the episode as a warning to reapply the Hinder to the young cherry trees, the antique roses, the young hostas, the red raspberries, and the beans, as well as to dust the okra, cucumbers, pattypans, and zucchini with rotenone. This is war. No time for craft days.

THURSDAY *June 29*

The heat wave, the rainstorm, Pip, and the deer — they've all made me so fretful I haven't noted any of the buoyant summery events that've taken place in the vegetable gardens the past week. So, without further ado, I intend to catch up on the good gardening news. No bad news allowed, not even the septoria leaf spot that showed up yesterday on the bottom of the tomato plants and sent me scurrying to one of the nurseries today to get some copper fungicide. That and the cool, dry air that blew in late this afternoon, the first such breeze in more than two weeks, will keep that blight in check. And it's supposed to stay around all the way through this Fourth of July weekend. Mild days, clear skies, cool nights, and gentle breezes. So only good news from here on out, such as the cucumber, pattypan, and zucchini seedlings that I finally transplanted into the large vegetable garden last Saturday, the day before the storm. The rains helped settle them in so well they're already putting out new leaves, crawling around among the Johnny-jump-ups. And they're all safely dusted with rotenone against the return of cucumber beetles and squash vine borers. So all the summer vegetables are now in and heading toward that special day when everything is ready at once for the first fresh ratatouille of the summer. Which reminds me that the back vegetable bed is finally in its exclusive summer mode of eggplants, peppers, and tomatoes, now that all the spring lettuce is gone. The eggplants have doubled in size just since the rain and are ready to blossom. The peppers are all comfortably settled in, blooming and setting fruit. No more wilting for them. And the pole tomatoes are continuing to set fruit all along their four- to five-foot height.

How could I ignore their continuing fruit set, when yesterday just as I was fingering a cluster of tomato blossoms, a bumblebee came buzzing into one of its flowers, right next to my thumb and forefinger? So intent upon his business he seemed to ignore me completely, as if I didn't even exist in his world. But he sure did in mine. Up my hand the whirring went, and then my arm, and then my chest, abuzz with its vibrations, one part bee and one part me, holding on, holding tight until he let go. Then for a moment, it seemed as if I knew what it might feel like to be pollinated, even though I will never know how it feels to have fruit clinging to one's vine. As for fruit, the first ripe cherry tomatoes were ready last Thursday, earlier than ever before, thanks to starting them in February. Jim and Rebecca also got fruit the same day from the spare Prestos I gave them a couple of months ago. A hybrid that performs by the clock! And now both of the plants are covered with so much fruit they'll keep us in tomatoes until the pole-bearing plants start ripening in late July or early August. What a buzzy life they must have led the past few weeks.

FRIDAY *June 30*

J am-time, jam-time. And jelly too. Red currant bushes so burdened with fruit their branches are splayed out almost to the
point of lying on the ground. No wonder Kate took one
glance at them this afternoon and said, "Those bushes look badly
stressed." The currants themselves are almost as bright as holly
berries, but far more abundant on the bush, hanging on numerous
panicles suspended from every branch. A nuisance to pick, especially the smaller Red Lake variety, but one of the most piquantly
tart fruits for jellies and fools. And rarely ever available at the
market. The fruiting of the currants is doubly special, for it also
marks the beginning of Kate's annual jam- and jelly-making season, when she hovers over her strainers and her stir pots, her pectin
and her sugar, her jars and her lids, her canners and her racks,
making things out of the various fruits we grow in our yard. Before
the summer is over, she'll put up a hundred to a hundred fifty
cups of jelly and jam. From our apples and black currants and
red currants and cherries and crabapples and black raspberries
and grapes and rhubarb and whatever else attracts her fancy at the
market or in the surrounding countryside. Usually strawberries.
Sometimes elderberries. Sometimes wild grapes. Sometimes cor-
nelian cherries.

Each fruit gets its own special treatment. Jam from strawberries,
jelly from currants, butter from peaches. But every summer at this
time, she concocts a unique combination, known as June jam or
July jam, from the currants, black raspberries, green apples, and
mulberries that are simultaneously available on our lot. Given the
turn of the month that's now upon us, I guess it'll be July jam this
year. Sometimes other combinations too, according to her fancy.
Tomato-basil jelly, orange-mint jam, pear chutney. And this afternoon, when I was hoeing and weeding the big vegetable garden,
she whetted my appetite for a special kind of preserve named
bar-le-duc after the French village near Verdun where the confection was first devised. "It's a preserve made of whole fruit carefully
prepared to retain its shape when put in a clear jelly. How would
you like black raspberries suspended in red currant jelly? I've been

reading about it for several years and thought I'd try making some this time."

No, we don't use all the jams and jellies ourselves. Kate, in fact, rarely eats any of it herself, and I go through only one jar a month on my breakfast muffins. So all the rest goes to relatives and friends in special Christmas mailings of eight or nine jars a family and occasional care packages during the year. But woe to the ones who don't return their jars in a year or don't return them at all, as I discovered when an elderly aunt of mine returned her empty jars two years later with a note of apology. How, I wondered, did she know to return the jars and apologize for the delay? "Any good housewife would know."

JULY

In the cool of the morning, just when I was beginning my usual tour of the grounds in my pajamas and bare feet, the stones in the terrace and the dew on the grass were so chill I almost hustled back in the house. But the yard was so peaceful and the borders so immaculate from Rebecca's weeding the past few days that I kept to my course, gazing at everything along the way, from the recently opened pink and rose hollyhocks in front of our neighbor's peeling white shed, to the yellow Hyperion day lilies just beginning to open behind the currant bushes, to all the summery colors and shapes on display in Kate's perennial border, now at the climax of its third bloom phase. The tall fuchsia spikes of the lythrum, the sky blue of the stirrup-flowered delphiniums, the navy blue of the salvia spikes, the violet blue of the veronica spikes, the orange and pink and white of the tiger lilies, the yellow of the yarrow, the white of the small-petaled feverfew. So many colors and shapes so carefully arrayed from back to front, from one end to the other, I was momentarily transfixed by the spectacle.

Gazing at that colorful sight, I couldn't help thinking about some of the earlier and smaller versions of Kate's border, until I soon found myself spinning back some twenty-five years, when we had just bought the place and nothing existed in that spot but an untended yard. Or in any of the other back yard spots where our gardens and borders and shrubbery now exist. No raspberry beds, or herb beds, or shade borders, or yew hedges. Nothing, in fact, but a handful of trees and an old tool shed. Lord of all I surveyed from that highest point on our land, I was suddenly filled with pride for all we had brought into being during the past twenty-five years. A place of light and shade, of flowers and fruit, all radiating out from the lily pond, the terrace, and the columned summer-house. A world so complete unto itself, so perfectly articulated on this rare summer day, that it seemed at that moment to be immutable. But the illusion lasted only for a moment, and then I was filled with dismay at the prospect of how things might look some twenty-five years from now, especially to someone else who would probably be standing in that selfsame spot instead of me.

Such a depressing thought, it drove me back in the house again. Still I couldn't stop looking out the back door at the yard and the flower border, until Kate came downstairs and I told her it all looked so beautiful this morning I was depressed by the very sight of it. "How foolish can you be? Why not enjoy it while it's there to be enjoyed? Or would you rather I take you to the nursing home right now?" Given the choice, I decided to enjoy it. How foolish could I be?

SUNDAY *July 2*

What is so rare as a day in July that feels like one in May? Thanks to El Niño, the cool wave continues here in the Midwest, while the Pacific Northwest is baking in ninety-degree temperatures, according to my friend Chris, who tells me his homegrown Oregon pepper plants are sulking in the heat. And the upper elevations of Wyoming, according to Trudy, are still piled high with so much snow that areas she hiked in last summer are completely inaccessible. So chilly here this morning I needed a full-length pair of pants and a farm jacket on top of my shirt when I went to do my errands at the supermarket and the recycling bins. Even in midmorning, when I was harvesting currants again in full sun, the air was still so mild I wasn't at all hot in my spring outfit. Seasonal confusion again.

But there's nothing confusing about the cycle of life in a vegetable garden. All the spring cauliflowers are now harvested, and only a few are still left in the refrigerator. And last night, we had the last of the shell peas with tandoori rabbit and a curry of cauliflower, potatoes, and onions. So this afternoon I deconstructed the row of pea vines and pea brush, removed all the cauliflower plants right next to them, fed the refuse to the compost pile, and cultivated the empty rows for the fall plantings to come. Now the big vegetable garden is looking more summery than ever, the corn waist-high, the cosmos beginning to open right in front of it, and only the snow peas still standing as a reminder of spring, on the chance of another crop. Now, with the three-foot-tall shell peas gone, more sunlight and air will be available all day long for the summer beans and cucumbers growing in the center of the big garden. In the rhythm of a full-scale vegetable garden, the seasonal rotation is inexorable. So while it felt like spring this morning, I was thinking about fall this afternoon, especially after I'd cleared out the refuse from the pea and cauliflower rows, and contemplated the beans that would have to go in there very soon if I hope to have a good crop of them come September. And the thought of those beans made me realize that I should seed up a little flat of Brussels sprouts right now if I expect to have a crop of them this fall. And the same for broccoli and cauliflower. The seasonal compulsions never end.

Meanwhile, just to make sure I didn't lose touch with summer, I worked on the herb bed, transplanting the dill and basil seedlings I started in late May. Actually, Kate's been nudging me to get them in for the past few weeks, but once the heat wave hit, I didn't want to put anything into such stressful conditions. Now that the basil and dill are in, the herb bed's almost complete, except for some additional borage and dill that Kate wants me to seed in. And the fall basil I'm planning to grow under row covers for a possible cash crop after the first frost. The seasonal compulsions never end.

MONDAY *July 3*

"Let me tell you, Klaus, America is out there shopping. The streets around here are quiet, but just get out on the highway leading to any of the big shopping centers, and the cars are lined up bumper to bumper. The stores are jammed. And not just with families in their campers, stocking up for the holidays. Also with little old ladies in high heels, hose, and earrings, their shopping bags full." Kate had just returned from hunting around town this morning for some wide-mouth jelly jars to hold the precious bar-le-duc she put up this afternoon. But her mind was as much on the holiday shopping craze as on the jars she'd been looking for the past two days. And on the strangeness of this day itself — supposedly a regular workday, but for many people a self-created holiday by virtue of coming between the holiday weekend and July Fourth itself, which doesn't take place until tomorrow. All day long, I've been pondering the strange nature of today, or even tomorrow for that matter, given the way that Lyndon Johnson and the Congress rearranged the calendar to create a yearlong series of holiday weekends, many of which don't coincide with the holidays themselves. Sometimes they just come nearby, especially when the holiday occurs in midweek, as with this year's Fourth of July. So when are you supposed to celebrate it? I asked Kate. "Well, from what I hear, many people are taking off almost a whole week, from last Friday through this Tuesday, and just calling in sick or taking off tomorrow." As I discovered this morning, when I called the doctor's office and the receptionist told me my physician would be back in the office again on Wednesday. Actually, I was less interested in how much time people can finagle from their jobs than the question of when the festivities are supposed to take place — the fireworks, the picnics, the band concerts, the ice cream socials, the flags flying. All that stuff. Early yesterday morning, for example, I couldn't help noticing that flags had suddenly appeared block after block at the edge of lawns all along the one-mile stretch of road leading to the supermarket. They sprouted overnight like morning mushrooms. And last night at the city park, the annual fireworks went off on Sunday as usual. Now as I sit here writing this report, I can hear some firecrackers going off around the neighborhood. This evening the Russians are having an outdoor party. And tomorrow afternoon, Kate and I will be going to a July Fourth picnic at my colleague Alan's house in the country. But it also felt like a holiday when I was picking the black raspberries this morning, and it felt like one when I was picking the currants yesterday morning. And it'll probably feel like one tomorrow, even if it rains as predicted. Maybe it's not so confusing as I first thought. Independence Day every day of the year.

TUESDAY *July 4*

How often, I wonder, does it rain on the Fourth of July? And not just a light drizzle but a long, gentle soaker that went on until midmorning. Perfectly timed after last week's storm to give all the flowers and vegetables another good drink and keep them spruced up for another week or so. Also perfectly timed to give me a break from the garden — a crafts day, a holiday. Actually, the sky was so dark it put me in a perfect mood to hunker down over the dining room table and do the monthly bills. Some craft. But by late morning, the clouds blew out, the sky cleared, and Kate confronted me in the dining room. "Some way to celebrate Independence Day. How about going for a walk? How about doing something in the spirit of the day?" I made a few owly remarks about being in the spirit of the day all the time it was raining, while she was upstairs whiling away the morning. But the weather, after all, had gotten in sync with the holiday, so off we went for a walk to the river with Pip. The air soft, the streets quiet, except for Pip barking at the scent or sight of every dog. Pip on parade, ears flapping, tail wagging, all swagger, declaring his independence for everyone to hear, pulling on the leash as if he were the master and I the dog. He certainly had more hoopla in him than anything else around, for the streets bore no hint of the holiday. Not a flag in sight, where just two days ago they'd been hanging from the porches and sticking out of the lawns. Actually, Pip wasn't the only one sounding off, for on the walk home the weather also had a few things to say, rumbling in the west before it started raining again for another hour or two. But not enough to discourage us or others from gathering under the red and white striped marquees at Kris and Alan's place in the country. There, at last, we found the Fourth — on the long outdoor tables spread with potluck dishes surrounding the barbecued beef and turkey and ham prepared by Kris and Alan. And the keg of draft beer. And the blankets and chairs spread on the rolling lawn. And there again, as if to grace the festivities, the rain again blew over, the clouds blew out, and the sky again turned blue. And we talked — what else? — of gardening. And my colleague Linda told me of how she was learning to do it for the first time in her life, working eight to ten hours a day under the charismatic influence of an organic truck gardener, and discovering that "it's a total way of life." She talked to me of learning to make a straight row and of mulching her crops with straw and of planting her beans for the fall, and I knew she'd been converted, even if I hadn't seen the fire in her eyes. Fireworks enough to light up any fourth. And now as if to cap this noisy holiday, the weather has produced its fiercest and loudest storm of all. Fierce enough, I fear, to level the corn patch once again. Farewell Fourth. Come on fifth.

WEDNESDAY *July 5*

Not a stalk out of place in the corn patch, and nothing else amiss in any of the other crops, despite winds of seventy miles an hour and a heavy downpour that brought yesterday's total to an inch and a half. The first sight of everything standing so straight had me clicking my fingers and skipping around the yard. On closer inspection, though, I noticed a whole swatch of blighted leaves on one of the potted cherry tomatoes in the back bed — too much moisture in the cramped quarters of all those stems, stakes, tomatoes, and foliage. Then on the way in for breakfast, I noticed what appeared to be a row of dog prints right where the shell peas were standing just a few days ago. Probably the neighbor's aged Labrador retriever, I thought — it often wanders into our yard when it's having an airing. Just to make sure, I walked around to the front of the garden, and from that angle I could see they were deeply indented hoof marks, obviously made after the rain. So deep I could imagine Rebecca exclaiming over them — "Look at those deer tracks!" Suddenly, I felt the urge to put a fresh sprinkling of Hinder on the beans and a fresh dusting of rotenone on the cucumbers, right then and there. But the skies were so heavily overcast, it seemed foolish to put anything on that might soon be rained off. Yet it also seemed hapless just to stand by and let the critters have their way, as I knew they would without any kind of deterrent. But why waste the deterrent in the face of another possible downpour?

Standing there at the edge of my garden, I suddenly felt confused and stymied by the forces of nature. And it didn't get any better an hour or so later, when I picked up Phoebe from her pillow in the attic, to take her to the vet, and she let loose a gusher down the side of my pants. When it rains, it pours. But the news from the vet was better than my water-soaked expectations. "She's doing quite well, especially under the circumstances. Better than I'd expected. So much better in fact that I didn't have to plump her up with any fluid." Given the condition of my pants just then, I could hardly disagree.

By the time we got home, my pants were drying, the sky was clearing, and by late afternoon I decided to redust the cucumbers and zucchini. But no sooner had I put on the rotenone and come up here to start writing this report than the rain started up again, heavy enough to wash it all off. Shortly after dinner, the sky seemed clear enough to try another sprinkling of Hinder. And now, having just returned from a midnight walk with Pip, I'm pleased to report that the stars are out and the moon is up in the western sky. No need to panic about the deer — at least for the moment. And maybe the rain will bring us a few more snow peas as crisp as the ones I picked this morning and stir-fried for dinner this evening. A bit more of spring in summer.

THURSDAY *July 6*

Or a bit of the mountains in the prairies, given the cool, dry air that blew in this morning and blew everyone away. Rebecca: "Can you believe this air?" Jim: "This air sure is something else." Kate: "Good breezes all day long." And I thought so too, except when I found a robin's nest blown down under a pine tree, its soft oval depression still slightly warm, its mud daubing still slightly moist, its shattered blue eggs a few feet away, scattered among the needles.

On a day so rare as this, it's always hard to reckon with fallen nests and shattered eggs, as I discovered when Kate and I were coming home from a walk with Pip, and we saw a young man so crippled, it seemed, by some profound neural disorder that he could barely keep himself upright. He was walking unsteadily on the balls of his feet, arms outstretched, as if every step were a balancing act, and he about to fall. Kate saw him first and said, "Let's cross right here. I don't want him to think we're staring." And neither did I. Something deep inside me also didn't want to see his anguish, so I was happy to cross right there.

And something deep inside me didn't want to hear Jim's story of the deer any more than he wanted to tell me about it this afternoon. But when I went up to let him know about the tracks I'd found in the garden yesterday morning, he told me, "I seen it going down to your place the other evening. It's the same one that's been coming to my bean patch night after night, the whole past week. Right through Tom's old pasture, across my driveway, down to your place for those sour apples, then back up by your raspberry patch, and back into my bean patch." Then he looked at me hard with that faraway stare he sometimes gets in his eyes when he's about to tell one of his hunting stories, but he didn't say anything more.

Rebecca had a more buoyant story to tell when she arrived this morning. "I've just come from a meeting with Mickey, an hour long. And he wants me to get up a proposal for a greenhouse big enough to supply herbs for his bakery and all his restaurants. Can you believe it? Me? And he wants a proposal in ten days, with costs for two thousand square feet, eight thousand square feet, and everything in between. Just like that. Can you believe it? I told him I have to be free to do other things too. But how can I pass it up? Sometime in my life, I have to take something seriously." So we talked about greenhouses big enough and varied enough to grow herbs on a scale large enough to supply five restaurants and a bakery with parsley, bay, rosemary, and thyme — and basil galore. And I agreed to barter some of my think time for some of her gardening time. But the image that sticks in my mind right now is of Kate bounding into the kitchen this afternoon with a fistful of sage, parsley, and thyme, saying, "There's your bounty for you. Just smell it, and see what I mean." And I did.

FRIDAY *July 7*

That fistful of herbs was just a foretaste of the bounty yesterday and today. Last night with dinner, we had a bowl of fresh cherry tomatoes from the garden. Also a Walla Walla sweet onion, a Dutch purple onion, and sprigs of dill in a marinated beet salad that Kate made with her own red wine vinegar. And this morning, I harvested another meal's worth of broccoli shoots, another picking of snow peas, and two quarts of black raspberries. But it's not just the bounty that makes the difference, it's the harvesting too, as I discovered again this morning, back in the corner of the lot, behind the larch tree, picking the raspberries. The cool air, the little fruit clusters, red, purple, and black, the beaded surfaces of the ripe dark fruit lit by the rising sun, the thorns brushing my shirt sleeves, the slight rustle of leaves, the seclusion. A rush of sensations that momentarily answered all my questions about our gardening and our summer-long attachment to this plot of land. But no sooner did I feel so content than I was thinking of a conversation I had outside the co-op yesterday morning with Linda the Gruff. She was miffed about her big blue pickup truck, the one she brought me the mulch in, but behind her anger was a fascinating side of Linda I'd never imagined. "I've been waiting weeks for it to be repaired and now it's back in the garage, still not working right." Frustrating, I thought, but no reason to be so upset, especially given the little red truck she has to haul things around in. "Well, that one's all right for driving around town, but it's not heavy-duty enough to get me up to this land I own in northern Minnesota and lug around the stuff I need to work with when I'm up there." I was curious about the land and how she'd acquired it. "It's fifteen acres, twenty miles or so outside of Duluth, that I bought in five-acre parcels, years ago when I was just out of college. I found out about it in a newspaper ad, and got it all for about sixty-five hundred dollars. I didn't have that kind of money then, but the man who owned it let me pay it off at fifty dollars a month. And then I got an old caboose car for hardly nothing — all wood, tongue and groove, built in 1938 — and I got a guy to haul it all the way to my land for just nineteen hundred. And I've been restoring it ever since. That's why I need that blue truck of mine." Boy, did I want to see that place. "You'll never see it. That's where I go when I want to get away from it all. Most people don't even know I own it. But I'll show you some pictures of it." If pictures were enough, I wouldn't still be cursing myself for passing up a nineteenth-century lobsterman's house on the coast of Maine, on a two-acre lot covered with roses, that I could've got for five thousand back in 1962. A place where I too could've gotten away from it all. All summer long. But then I remembered how I felt this morning when I was behind the larch tree, at the corner of the lot. Just me and the brambles, away from it all.

SATURDAY *July 8*

Today, almost three months after planting them, I decided it was finally time to pull up the snow peas. Another handful of pods this morning together with yesterday's harvest gave us enough for our last dish of stir-fried snow peas this season. And in celebration of the event, Kate and I planned an Oriental meal around them that we served ourselves in the gazebo. Charcoal-grilled mahi-mahi marinated in canola oil, lime juice, garlic, and our own lemon grass; steamed basmati and jasmine rice with chopped garlic chives from the herb bed; a special side dish of fermented black beans mixed with chopped ginger, hot pepper flakes, and oil that we prepared this morning; a bowl of fresh cherry tomatoes from the garden, standing by to cool our palates, just in case; and a salad of sliced cucumbers, marinated in a vinaigrette of sesame oil, rice wine vinegar, sugar, tamari, and Tabasco. So much fuss was ne'er lavished over a bunch of pea pods.

Now that the snow peas and shell peas are gone, the other legumes, the beans, are no longer overshadowed by them. Now, in fact, all the beans are in bloom, so in a week or two we can look forward to fresh yellow and green bush beans, tender enough when fresh to need only a few minutes of cooking. But the beans that are on my mind right now won't be ready until sometime in October. Dried white beans — Hutterite beans — named after

the Moravian Czech immigrants who brought them to this country in the middle of the eighteenth century. Though Kate discovered those beans two or three years ago, it wasn't until last summer
that she cajoled me into growing some. I can still remember my
resistance to growing that little packet of Hutterite beans that
she bought from Seeds for Change. The blurb about them producing a "thick, white, creamy soup" left me completely cold,
especially on the warm, sunny morning a year ago last June when
I set up my line, drew my finger through the slightly moist soil,
and pressed the white seeds into the dirt one by one. And the pods
they eventually produced didn't look any more appetizing as they
swelled, dried, and turned brittle over the months that followed.
But that was before I tasted the soup she made of the beans
themselves on a bitterly cold day this February — a bean and ham
soup so creamy in texture, so delicate in taste that I wished right
then I had planted a lot more of those heirloom beans, as I did last
month. Now I understand why the Hutterites carried them all the
way from Europe to this country. What I don't understand is why
they taste so much better than an ordinary white bean from our
local co-op. I'm tempted to think it's because they're homegrown
and home-dried. But my hunch is there's some unique genetic
code in them that will assert itself in any garden, in any soup pot,
in any country, in any century.

SUNDAY *July 9*

"Hey, Klaus, do you realize we're eating a lettuce, tomato,
and sweet onion salad from our garden earlier than ever
before?" Actually, I'd been thinking the same thing a few
minutes before, but I didn't want to mention it, because Kate was
reading me an article from the co-op newsletter and I didn't want
to interrupt her. Besides, Kate doesn't ordinarily have much patience with my calling attention to the first of this or the best of
that. Too competitive for her taste. But then she said it again. "I
don't think we've ever had lettuce and tomatoes together this
early." Usually, in fact, it doesn't happen until much later, when
the fall lettuce crop is ready. This year we were able to pull it off in

midsummer, thanks to the cherry tomatoes coming so early. The only problem is that I don't have any more greens left in the crisper, except for a few heads of radicchio. So this first is probably also one of the last for a while.

Then again, we may not have to wait as long as usual, because just a few days ago, I seeded up a flat of arugula, Simpson green leaf, and purple oak leaf lettuce, hoping to get another crop of greens ready by late August rather than October. And just this morning, they all started to emerge. So in a few days I plan to put them under grow-lights for three or four weeks, and then transplant them outside under a dark mesh shade cloth that's supposed to cut down on the heat and sunlight of summer. I've never tried such a thing before, but if polyester row covers can conserve the heat, why can't shade cloth dispel it, and thereby create a little bit of spring right in the middle of summer?

Juggling the seasons, having them both at the same time, is what it's all about. And for me it's not just a matter of being first or last, though I do admit to such a competitive instinct. It's also a matter of seizing the day, as the Romans used to say. Making the most of time, whatever time remains. Getting the most out of one's garden. So, last Thursday, I also seeded up some flats of broccoli, Brussels sprouts, and cauliflower that I plan to get under grow-lights as soon as they emerge. Then in mid- to late August I'll move them into those open spots in the main vegetable bed that are waiting to receive them. Which reminds me again that I should also get the beets and beans planted soon if I hope to have a fall crop.

My mind, it seems, is doing double time, or triple time — spring, summer, and fall converging in my thoughts, competing for my attention. But how can I do otherwise, when everywhere I turn I'm caught among the seasons? It's not just the spring-summer salad we had for lunch, or the summery black raspberries I picked this morning, or the red raspberries coming on for this fall, or the spring-planted broccoli still bearing shoots. It's the convergence of seasons, the fullness of time, in everything that grows.

MONDAY *July 10*

This morning — low sixties, mild breezes, cool overnight air still lingering around the edges. This afternoon — low nineties, dead air, rising humidity. From late spring to high summer in eight hours. And worse to come during the heat wave now gripping the mountains, plains, and Mississippi valley. So I distracted myself by looking two months ahead, seeding in a crop of fall beans where the shell peas once stood, and a crop of fall beets where the snow peas just moved out. Then I distracted myself by staring into the face of the volunteer sunflower at the southeast corner of the big vegetable garden, a few drops of dew still lingering in the center of it and two bees gathering pollen from the anthers, their legs so covered with yellow they seemed like a part of the flower itself. Talk about bridging the seasons! That sunflower must have been growing there at least since mid- to late April, for when I first noticed it in mid-May, the seedling was already a few inches tall. I also have a hunch that it was probably seeded in by the volunteer sunflower that turned up in the same spot last summer, for its leaves are just as expansively arched, its toughly ridged stem just as sturdy, muscular, and tall as its predecessor, which I suppose was seeded in by the bird feeder that hangs in the nearby pear tree throughout the winter. So, in a manner of speaking, it's been a long time coming, but it's been well worth the wait, especially to watch the day by day unfurling. First its green outer sepals, then its yellow petals, then the growth of the petals, and the thickening ring of stamens and pistils now taking place. And inevitably the formation of the seeds that come from the union of those sexual parts. It began opening a week ago, and now that its bright yellow petals are all unfurled, it measures almost a foot in diameter. And it's almost six feet tall, so I can look it directly in the face without bending over. A striking visage, now perpetually facing east, toward the rising sun, ever since it locked itself into that position a couple of weeks ago. Jim also stopped to look at it when he was down in our yard this morning. "When I was a kid, we used to pick the seeds right out of the center, just like that." Suddenly he was sticking his thumb and forefinger right into the center of it. "They grew along the alleys, and we'd stuff our pockets with 'em. They weren't salted like the ones in the stores nowadays, but they were so tender and tasty we'd chew the whole thing." When I was that age, I didn't even know about sunflowers, much less that I might snack on their seeds, and now that I do, the cardinals and squirrels usually beat me to the snack bar. So as I was listening to Jim, I was also thinking it might be time to rebait the Havahart trap with peanut butter for the squirrels, especially because of the temptations offered by the volunteer sunflower at the other end of the garden. Come fall, I'd like to pick a few of those sunflower seeds myself.

TUESDAY *July 11*

"**O**wning a greenhouse isn't my only dream. It's just one of many." Rebecca came bounding into the kitchen in late morning holding a bunch of carryout packets from the co-op, ready to have a little potluck lunch with Kate and me, so we could continue the conversation we started late yesterday afternoon. And a big smile spread across her suntanned face when she made that announcement. So radiant that Kate said, "I've never seen her lit up like that before." Yesterday, Rebecca and I talked with Ted, a long-ago English major who now owns a local fruit market as well as a big greenhouse operation, specializing in lilies. And Ted helped Rebecca to calculate the high costs and risks of trying to start up a large greenhouse specializing in herbs. But it was clear from something she said yesterday afternoon that Rebecca couldn't let go of the idea — "Even if I maybe don't want to get involved in taking on something big for Mickey or anyone else, I'd still like to have a greenhouse of my own. Just one bay, not five or ten. I've always wanted a greenhouse so I could grow herb plants and fresh herbs in the winter and sell them around town, just like I sell my basil now in the summer. But I don't want to be so tied to it that I couldn't just close it down whenever I wanted to." So, when she showed up this morning, making that declaration of independence, I understood what she meant, especially because she was wearing a tie-dyed blue T-shirt with BELIZE printed across it in big white letters. But as we made our way through her takeout packets of couscous, tabbouleh, and baked, marinated tofu, along with our leftover rice, grilled fish, snow peas, fermented black bean relish, fresh watermelon, cherries, and grapes, it gradually became apparent that the greenhouse dream was still very much on her mind. How else to explain her silence when Kate asked, "What are some of your other dreams?"

Kate rarely asks people such personal questions. I was so surprised by it that I've been wondering how I'd have answered the question. And the very fact I've been wondering all afternoon and part of the evening has given me pause. Have I no dreams? Am I really the 1950s person Kate sometimes accuses me of being? Or have I reached a point in my life beyond the realm of dreams? Oh yes, I think about traveling around the world with Kate when I'm fully retired, but that's not really a dream — just a matter of waiting a year or so for it to happen. And the same is true of my yearning to be done with this daybook and my book on the personal essay. Occasionally, I dream of living on the West Coast, north of San Francisco, or the north shore of Kauai, or in a villa in Tuscany, dreams I can't possibly imagine coming true. And whenever I ponder such dreams, I'm beset by nightmares of regret about leaving this place. So maybe I'm living my dream, but this heat wave sure feels like a nightmare.

WEDNESDAY *July 12*

The deer or the heat? I wonder which is worse. Yesterday, Jim was complaining about the deer the minute I saw him. "You should see what they done to Lynne's tomato plants last night. Cropped them all off at the top, just like that. It's something awful. Then they came over to my place and nipped some branches off a couple of mine. You can see their tracks right here." Another pair of them from the herd in the wilderness park, roaming around the neighborhood vegetable gardens. "I never seen 'em eat tomato plants like that, not this time of year when there's so much other stuff to feed on." I'd never heard of it either, especially given the poisonousness of tomato plants. "There's some-thin' strange going on, been going on now for several years. Deer just don't behave the way they used to, coming so close they don't even care if you see 'em or get close to 'em, eating stuff they'd never eat before. Too many of 'em around for their own good." I told Jim about some studies I've read on overcrowding in animal and human populations, and how it usually leads to pathological behavior of one kind or another. "Well, it sure has with the deer. They're just not acting right. I told Lynne to get some of that Hinder stuff you've been talking about, and I guess I'll have to get some of it too." Which reminded me to douse all the tomato plants with it last night and give the beans another sprinkling of it, just to be on the safe side.

But there's nothing one can sprinkle on to keep the heat down or drive it away. Low nineties Monday, mid-nineties yesterday, one hundred this afternoon. The humidity so high the heat index is running around one hundred ten. The first time since 1991 that Iowa's had temperatures of one hundred and above. No wonder Kate came back in midmorning after doing only a few blocks of her two-mile walk, with Pip panting at the other end of the leash. Earlier this morning, when I was just watering things — no exertion at all — the heat was so unpleasant I couldn't stand more than an hour of it. Rebecca, who showed up for the first time in shorts, worked only an hour, though she'd planned to stay longer. Only Phoebe thrives on the heat, so enamored of it she's now taken up full-time residence on the terrace — morning, noon, and night — as in days of yore. Even now, I can see her sprawled out there under the cocktail table, and she'll only come in under duress when Kate or I bring her in for brief cool-downs and food breaks in the air-conditioned house. We used to think her heat-hunger grew out of the cold, wet days of her orphanhood. But last night Kate discovered that cats have a normal body temperature of one hundred two and therefore thrive on the heat. So the current heat wave feels like Phoebe's last hurrah, a burnout bigger and better than any she's ever had.

THURSDAY *July 13*

Not even Phoebe could take a whole day outside today, as I discovered late this afternoon when I heard her screechy meow on the other side of the attic. I thought she was at her usual post on the terrace, but when I heard that single meow, I knew things must be worse than usual and went down to get an update from Kate. "When I brought her in after lunch, she didn't ask to go out again, but just curled up at my feet on the living room rug. It's a hundred and two out there, like a desert." And the heat index, as I discovered from the Weather Network, was one hundred twenty-five. No wonder she decided to stay in. No wonder a thousand cattle and twenty thousand turkeys died yesterday in southwest Iowa, when the temperatures there reached the record highs we're having here today. Only Jim seems acclimated to this weather. This morning when I was outside watering Kate's flower border and the red raspberries, he stopped down to visit, wearing a green farm cap and a pair of long pants, but nothing on his suntanned chest. Jim in his high-summer mode. And he'd been watering too. "I just finished hosing my tomatoes and peppers. It's hard on the plants, but I love it like this. Always have. I was out here yesterday until three in the afternoon." I wonder how long he was out there today.

Bad as it's been today, it couldn't equal last night when Kate called up to me in the attic around nine in the evening. "The air conditioner's not working." I was just finishing yesterday's report, but she was still in the midst of processing and canning a batch of peach jam she'd been working on since midafternoon. The air in the kitchen was stifling — from the oven where she'd been thickening the jam to the cooktop where she was processing the jars. The problem, I thought, was just a circuit breaker, stressed out from the overload. But a few clicks of the circuit switch in the basement brought only momentary improvements — start up, break down, start up, break down. Then I thought it might be the condenser motor outside, overheated from having to overcome the congestion of hostas and ferns blocking the air flow around it. But digging out the plants again brought only momentary improvement. Then I thought it was just a blown fuse or two. But an emergency replacement of the outside air conditioner fuses — Kate holding the flashlight, I changing the fuses — again brought only momentary improvements. Then, when it was almost ten-thirty, I called the repairman who arrived at eleven and by eleven-thirty had identified the problem as a faulty capacitor and replaced the broken gizmo. I'm still not sure how a capacitor works, but I gather it's a device that's supposed to store energy temporarily. And when your capacitor's broken, your condenser can't do much more than turn itself on and off fitfully. Maybe that's why I felt so bad today whenever I went outside. Maybe I need a new capacitor.

FRIDAY *July 14*

Whenever the weather turned hot, excessively hot, my long-gone neighbor Herman and other old-timers around here would talk almost in tones of reverence about "the summer of '36." Nothing could possibly compare to what it was like back then. But now according to the newspaper reports, we've been making some new records of our own, with the heat index running higher than it ever has before. So, in years to come, when I've turned into a genuine old geezer myself, I can rock back and forth in an old metal lawn chair, speaking in tones of reverence about "the summer of '95," or at least about this week of spectacular highs — "the worst heat I ever felt in my life." For the past few days, in fact, I've been trying to remember if I've ever felt anything like it, and this morning when I was picking the last batch of black raspberries a memory came back to me from forty-five years ago. It was a Saturday morning during the fall of my sophomore year at Michigan, and I was badly hung over — the first time in my life I'd ever gotten so drunk. On rum and Coca-Cola — what could be worse? In desperation, I took the advice of a college chum and went to the steam bath at the Michigan Union. And there, in the white-tiled room, sitting on the wooden benches, I succumbed to heat, wet heat — a steamy embrace — the likes of which I'd never felt before or since, until this week. No wonder people often refer to a heat wave as feeling like a steam bath. "That's why the cliché's a cliché," as Kate reminded me this morning. Especially when it comes with the impressive humidity of this one.

Right now, with the temperature at one hundred and the heat index at one hundred seventeen, there's nothing quite so comforting as our stone-walled basement and the outside cellarway that leads up from the basement to the back terrace. Oh yes, the basement's an incredible mess right now — the fruit room cluttered with canning jars and freezer cartons, the furnace room stacked up with cardboard boxes and packing material, the laundry room overflowing with all the clay pots and plastic six-packs and other gardening stuff we've accumulated over the years. But it's cool and dark, cool and dark. And right at the foot of the outside cellarway sits the flat of fall broccoli, Brussels sprouts, cauliflower, and lettuce that I moved under the cool pink glow of the grow-lights on Tuesday morning, just before the heat wave moved in. The spectacle of those tiny seedlings coming on under the lights is so comforting and reassuring I've decided to spend a few days as close to them as possible, cleaning up the basement. And by then, maybe, the heat wave will have passed, or at least abated a bit, so I can safely emerge from my underground lair and take to the garden again.

SATURDAY *July 15*

Today was a day for taking stock of things, and it began with the newspaper's body count of Iowa livestock killed by the heat — one and a quarter million chickens and turkeys, five thousand head of beef cattle, one thousand hogs. According to the article, all those deaths were caused by "scorching heat and high humidity." But if heat and humidity were the sole villains in this case, there'd have been far more deaths than those. Looking at a picture of some two hundred thousand chicken carcasses on the front of the newspaper — all those carcasses from one massive chicken farm — I couldn't help wondering how many of those deaths were attributable to the stifling conditions that poultry and other livestock must endure in many large feeding operations. No fresh air, no shade trees, no space to move around in, no water to cool off in. Mass production under such confining circumstances seems likely to inflict massive suffering and die-off in a heat wave such as this. Buchenwald in the farm belt. But the representatives of agribusiness talk only about the "economic disaster," and their employees talk only about needing "a cast iron stomach" to clear away the carcasses, as if the agony of the animals had never even occurred to them.

Though this morning's newspaper also claims there's enough subsoil moisture to prevent crops from suffering heat stress, a heat wave of this magnitude must be traumatic for anything that's exposed to it day in and day out, morning, noon, and night, even under the most spacious and protected conditions. So I wasn't surprised to see that the pole-climbing Big Beef tomatoes have stopped setting fruit and that some of their earliest fruit is beginning to turn white rather than red — a sign of cooking rather than ripening on the vine. The eggplants and peppers are also throwing their blossoms. And all the plants there are almost dry on the surface, despite the heavy watering I gave them just a few days ago, and despite the straw mulch surrounding them from one end of the bed to the other. But a few of the Enchantment tomatoes are beginning to ripen early, and as usual they do "look like Fabergé eggs," just as promised in the seed catalogue. In the big vegetable bed, the first crop of beans looks like it'll produce enough for a meal next week, and the fall crop emerged yesterday, just four days after being planted. So the heat wave's not entirely bad, but most of the vegetables look like they're just trying to survive until it breaks — the beans, chard, cucumbers, and zucchini transpiring in the noonday sun, only the okra standing up to the heat, true to its deeply tropical origin.

Late this afternoon, though, the western sky began to cloud over, and a wind picked up around dinner time — breezy enough and cool enough to turn the outside tolerable for the first time since Monday. So at last the air conditioning is off, and the silence, the silence, is a blessing.

SUNDAY *July 16*

What a fair-weather friend am I! Yesterday, I didn't want to be out in the yard at all. So I made a quick tour of the gardens, no more than fifteen or twenty minutes in all. Just long enough to water the seedlings in the gazebo, check the soil in each vegetable bed, eyeball the plants to notice any gross changes in their leaves and fruit, and glance at the red raspberry patch. Today, on the other hand, I spent almost five hours working in the two vegetable beds, watering, weeding, dusting, mulching, checking on the recent development of each plant. And in the process of getting reacquainted with things, I discovered how mistaken I'd been yesterday about the state of the vegetables. Today, nothing was quite so stressed out as it seemed yesterday, and some of the stuff was much further along than I thought. Cucumber vines covered with miniature fruit, eggplants also beginning to set a few fruit, bell pepper plants covered with little peppers, okra about to blossom, ruby Swiss chard so crisp and colorful that our neighbor Wendy couldn't resist taking a close-up snapshot of it, and enough bush beans to give Wendy a bunch for dinner and still have enough for ourselves.

How could I have been so mistaken about things? Especially about things as familiar as the back of my hand or the lines on my face. Haste, I suppose, had something to do with it — not wanting to put up with the heat and humidity, not wanting to look too closely at my stressed out plants for fear of getting more stressed out myself. Kate said I'd have been crazy to spend any time outside. "It was dangerous out there." But I could swear there was also something bizarre about the appearance of things that made them unpleasant to look at during the intense heat. Kate said there was a "brassy light" that glared on everything, as through a haze, harshly, transforming the visual appearance of things as strangely as the black light during the solar eclipse last summer.

Now that the heat wave is past, it's a pleasure just to look at things again and behold the tone of their natural colors, especially right now with the hundreds of tall yellow day lilies marching up the north lot line in their full lemony glory, like a grand procession, leading to Kate's perennial border. And the sixty-foot border itself, now in the midst of its fourth bloom phase, contains a dazzling array of day lilies from the short scarlets along the front and sides to the tall peach yellows along the middle, and the tall dark pinks along the back. Interspersed with the blue balloon flowers and the purple coneflowers and the rudbeckia goldsturm, they certainly didn't seem flattened or washed out any longer by the glare.

Nor for that matter did the doe that I saw this afternoon seem flattened or washed out, as she stood under the shade of the apple tree, munching on fallen fruit. The almond color of her coat, the long arch of her neck, the precise movements of her head were beautiful to behold, at least for a moment or two, until I remembered the fall crop of beans that emerged yesterday and the bright new leaves just opened on the sweet cherry tree that one of her cohorts devoured a few weeks ago. Then I sent her bounding away with a clap, and went running for the Hinder — and for Jim. Life here is definitely back to normal.

MONDAY *July 17*

And the weather's gone back to late May or early June. So cool and dry by contrast with the past few days that Kate had goose bumps on her arms when she came down for breakfast. Cool enough to bring the broccoli, Brussels sprouts, cauliflower, and lettuce seedlings up from the cellarway, where they've been getting a bit leggy under the grow-light. Already they seem more at home in the natural air and sunlight of this springy day, especially since I spent the morning transplanting them into a dense potting soil where they can grow even stronger the next few weeks. Cool enough for the lawn mower to show up sporting his new heat wave haircut, down to the scalp. "Everything was burning up last week — the lawns, the engines, and us. We're catching up today." And off he went, bounding up and down the lot in less than an hour.

Pip felt so invigorated by the air that when Kate put him out on his chain this afternoon, he broke the metal loop on his collar and went bounding up the yard, heading for Jim's. I was in the attic, just on the verge of starting this report, and the moment I heard Kate yell — a single "Hey!" long and loud, followed by the slam of the back screen door — I knew what had happened. Or thought I did, especially when I looked out the attic window and saw Pip so far in front of Kate she'd never be able to catch up, much less keep an eye on his bounding movements. Actually, as I later discovered from Kate, it all started with Phoebe shrieking in the gazebo and the screech of another cat, both of which I mistook for the screeching of our neighbor's macaw. When Kate heard the catfight, she snapped Pip on his chain and ran out to break it up, but suddenly Pip was bounding off in front of her. On the way downstairs, I put in a call to Jim, the help call of yesteryear, and Jim reported he'd just seen Kate in his back yard but no sign of Pip. All I could think of on my way up to Jim's was how beautiful a day for such a calamity to occur, half-blind Pip bounding toward his demise. By the time I got to Jim's place, Kate was heading up the street in front of his house, shaking her head, holding her hands up in resignation and dismay, calling "Pip, Pip," but not as if she believed it would produce any results. Neither he nor any of our other terriers has ever come when we call them in the midst of such an escapade, so why should it have been any different today? But then, just as the three of us gathered in the street in front of Jim's house, Pip came up behind us, panting hard, his tongue hanging out, eager to be caught and held. I wondered what could have produced such a strange turn of events, and Jim's answer left me as fretful as I was thankful at that moment. "He must've run into that big groundhog up in Tom's pasture. It's an old one, a beast, twenty-five pounds at least."

TUESDAY *July 18*

Sometimes I think Jim might be putting me on about the size of those groundhogs in the pasture, but he didn't think I was kidding about the doe under my apple tree. Now he's put stakes around his bean patches, ringed the stakes with ammonia-dipped rags, and hung ammonia-dipped rag strips from the rags. They're not much to look at, but ammonia's the main ingredient in Hinder, so it should do the trick, unless the deer just bend over the rags and go after the unsprayed beans. There's no telling what'll keep them away. So many of them and so many other troublemaking animals — groundhogs, moles, possums, rabbits, raccoons, squirrels, as well as birds and insects — that necessity's been the mother of numerous inventions, as I was reminded last Saturday, when I started sorting through all the gardening stuff we've accumulated in the basement since I last tidied it up two years ago.

No cruel contraptions or synthesized chemical poisons are allowed in our gardens, so the things I found, or remember from years past, run the gamut of ingenuity, from the artful to the mechanical. Among the artful, I'm especially fond of the black metal scare-cat my daughter Hannah gave me several years ago. Dangling from the end of a cane pole rod, its glass eye glitters in the sun. And the plastic inflatable owl from Kate's sister Martha — also on a pole, its body waves back and forth in the wind. But they're both so unrealistic I wonder why I've never tried something more plausible, like a life-size scarecrow. Maybe I shouldn't have thrown away my old overalls and farming jacket or my hole-riddled tennis shoes. I could've created something in my own moth-eaten image.

It's one thing to look scary, it's another to smell bad or taste bad, and that's where some old-fashioned chemical and biological controls come in — like the Hinder, the citronella candles, the hot red pepper potions I used to spray on the cucumber and melon vines, and my favorite one of all — the plastic rings dipped in tiger piss (Kate says it was fox piss), dangled from stakes every ten feet around the garden. A sure-fire deterrent for deer, except they cost so much I couldn't afford to keep replacing them every few weeks. Besides, I couldn't get 'em on the stakes without smelling up my fingers something awful.

Last but not least, a contraption that apparently sounds unbearable to the beast in question — the New Improved Mole Chaser from my son Marshall. Its "wind-driven blades create a constant vibration that moles find absolutely intolerable and that sends them in urgent search of a more tranquil environment." I haven't yet set it up, but I'm wondering how it might sound when I'm wearing my new improved hearing aids. Will I also find it so intolerable that I urgently go in search of a more tranquil environment? Maybe Kate's right, maybe all these contraptions "are more for the people than the animals."

WEDNESDAY *July 19*

A luscious morning in the garden, more like June in the mildness of the air, the softness of the breezes. But more like July, like high summer, in the height and development of the plants. The corn that was just waist high on the Fourth of July is now six feet tall and beginning to tassel. The Enchantment tomato plants that were five feet tall at the beginning of the month are now almost seven feet tall, near the top of the poles — ripe, red plum tomatoes on their bottom clusters, green fruit five feet up, yellow blossoms the rest of the way. Their main stems are so tall and fully developed, I'm allowing a few additional side shoots to grow and set more fruit between now and the beginning of September, when I top the plants so they put all their energy into ripening before the first hard frost. Even one of the Big Beef slicer tomatoes is almost ready to pick, a week or so earlier than usual, thanks to the recent heat wave. The two Ichiban eggplants are waist high, taller than ever before, their purple-veined leaves as big as hand fans, their finger-shaped fruit emerging, their lavender blossoms opening in profusion. The Ace bell pepper plants are covered with small and medium-size fruit. Everything's almost ready for the first all-fresh ratatouille of the season, except the pattypans and zucchini, which are just beginning to put out blossoms.

So many vegetables are coming on right now that Kate and I were able to put together a large salad platter for a potluck tonight at my colleague David's, almost entirely from our own gardens. A heaping bowl of the cherry tomatoes that I started back in mid-February — surrounded on one end of the platter by steamed, chilled cauliflower clusters from our last head of the spring crop, dressed with a Creole vinaigrette; on the other end by a beet and onion salad in a red wine vinaigrette with our own purple onions and dill; and on each side by our own yellow and green beans, dressed with a lime and marjoram vinaigrette. A wheel of color from spring to summer.

And the potluck itself was such a colorful gathering of graduate students and faculty in the nonfiction program that I was having second thoughts about early retirement, especially about giving up the opportunity to work with gifted writers like Mary and Rebecca, whose graduation from the program had occasioned the party. Not only gifted writers, but in their case thoughtful editors as well, whose careful reading and suggestions have often helped me with my own manuscripts. So the festivities left me feeling as churned up as the big storm that blew in from the northwest just an hour or so before the party began. A storm that began with such a violent clap of thunder that it sent Pip running down to Kate. And me too.

THURSDAY *July 20*

Another outburst late this afternoon, this time from Kate, when I came back from a workshop on social security and retirement investing, and told her about what I'd heard. First, a laid-back presentation by a representative of social security. Then, a hyped-up pitch from a mutual fund representative about saving and investing more during retirement. That was the part that provoked her. "Why do we have to save any more or invest any more than we've already got in your retirement funds? Don't we already have enough?" More than enough, I explained, not only to maintain our current standard of living, but possibly even to live better in retirement than we're living right now. Enough to travel and remodel the bathroom and buy a new car after thirteen years with our present one.

"Live better in retirement? I can handle that, no problem. Travel to Bora-Bora and Tahiti and Australia and New Zealand and the rest of the South Pacific and Pacific Rim? I can handle that. And a new bathroom finally? I can handle that too. An end to thirty years of scrimping and saving? What's the problem? Don't you believe in the reward at the end of the trail? What else have we been saving it for? Just to save some more? I may not be here a year or two from now. And the same goes for you. It could all end tonight, and then what would we have to show for it, but a lot of money to pass on to people which would probably do them more harm than good? I'm for spending it now and enjoying it while we can. We've earned it." What an outburst from Kate, as sudden as yesterday's rain and just as refreshing. A big smile on her face from start to finish. It buoyed me up as much as the flowers and vegetables after yesterday's downpour. And it was almost as surprising, given her ordinarily careful way with money.

But upon reflection, it seemed to me she was being just as sensible as she's always been, especially when she reminded me of her father dying at the age of fifty-six, and when I thought of my own father having died at the age of fifty-four. This week, in fact, is the anniversary of my father's death, according to the announcement I received from The Temple a couple of days ago. It took me by surprise, as it often does, coming at the height of summer, at a time of such abundance. Speaking of abundance, I discovered after supper that even the fingerling red potatoes are now ready, when I scrabbled with my fingers a couple of inches down and found one glistening in the soil. And when I brought it into Kate, she scrubbed it, cut it in half, and insisted we try it right away. Why wait? It was as crisp and moist as a spring radish.

FRIDAY *July 21*

My father, Max. A phantom I pursue every July, when the notice comes from The Temple. I don't say kaddish, but I do seek knowledge. He died when I was two. So how can I know him, except from a few remaining snapshots and word of mouth? In one of the shots, he's standing by an operating table, a surgical mask on his head, anesthetic paraphernalia in his hand, looking every inch the doctor and anesthetist. In another, he's standing outside an apartment building, in a suit and vest, his head thrown back, a broad smile on his face, holding my brother Marshall high above him, so it looks as if he was a proud and loving father. In the third, a formal, full-face portrait, I can see he has a high, broad forehead shaped much like mine, so it looks as if he was also my father, though he was old enough to be my grandfather when he conceived me at the age of fifty-two. How like a bastard child I've sometimes felt for want of knowing more about him, or my connection to him, than I do.

My mother, twenty-two years younger than he, doesn't say much about him in letters to her sister, except to gush about a bouquet of flowers or a painted valentine he's sent her or the expensive clothes he's urged her to buy for herself or the house he's bought and decorated "just like the movies." So perhaps there's some truth to the report that he was an extravagant husband, a twenties millionaire — until he lost it all in the crash of '29. But did he really have a ticker tape in his medical office? And were there really thousands of people at his funeral? And did he really work his way through med school by lighting gas lamps? All I know for sure is that years after he died, people would tell me, "What a wonderful man your father was! Always smiling! Always fun to be with." Except, according to my brother, when he sometimes didn't speak to our mother for a week or two. I wonder if he was a Gemini like me.

Most of my life, it seems, I've been seeking my father. First in his older brother, my uncle Manny, also an anesthetist and general practitioner. A quiet man. Devoted to his patients — and to the fresh vegetables that came from the open-air market just two blocks away. But he died five years after I went to live with him. So there were others. So many others, so many disappointments. Until Ernie, the cardiologist who pulled me through ten years ago, shortly after my heart attack, by rousing my competitive gardening instincts one early spring afternoon in his cardiac care unit. Six years later when he was dying of cancer, I kept wishing I could do something to help pull him through. But all I could do was to help put his garden to bed that fall and stop looking for any more fathers. Still, it was intriguing yesterday to hear my brother talk about Max on the phone, especially about the fruit and tomatoes he used to bring home from the open-air market. "Maybe that's where you got your interest in gardening. Who knows?"

SATURDAY *July 22*

A rained-out tree pruning workshop this morning sent Kate scurrying to the farmers' market nearby, where she found some fresh leeks, red potatoes, and small pickling cucumbers. Nice-looking produce, all right, but when I first saw it in the brown paper bag, I felt the slight twinge of jealousy that often rises within me whenever she brings home fresh vegetables during the gardening season, especially in high summer. And I told her so. But I couldn't deny her retort. "Well, you decided not to grow any leeks this summer." I didn't grow any, because I didn't want to go through the hassle of deep trenching and gradual backfilling that's required to grow a properly blanched crop of leeks from start to finish. Laziness, I guess. But the cucumbers are only a few days away from being ready. "I just felt like having a fresh cucumber salad tonight, and yours aren't ready yet." That was the remark that got to me, for I too have been hungering after some fresh cucumbers. It also reminded me that I missed the boat with my first crop of seedlings — the ones that got done in by the cucumber beetles, because I didn't keep them dusted with rotenone. So I had to start all over again, and I lost two or three weeks in the process. But now that I listen to myself mulling over our conversation this morning, I can't help noticing how much my thoughts are driven by those old competitive urges — "I missed the boat," and "I lost two or three weeks." So maybe it's not jealousy, after all. But then again, I can't help remembering how sweet it felt when she tasted a slice of her cucumber. "It's bitter. Do you think that's because they came on in the heat wave?" Probably, but I told her not to worry because the salting process and her vinegar marinade would surely take care of the problem. How good to feel magnanimous about a rival cucumber! Still, there's nothing to equal the satisfaction that comes from growing the vegetable of choice. So I felt even better this morning when Kate went out to the garden and pulled a fresh purple onion to put in her cucumber salad. Or when I went downstairs this afternoon and discovered that she'd harvested our one small artichoke from the potted plant, to include with her steamed, chilled leeks in a Creole vinaigrette. It was almost as pleasurable as watching her from up here in the attic yesterday afternoon, when she was harvesting some cherry tomatoes, a cooking onion, and one of the first green peppers for last night's dinner. More satisfying, even, than when I picked our first full bunch of Swiss chard for last night's dinner. What's going on here, I wonder? Isn't it enough to grow a bunch of fresh vegetables and eat them when they're ready? It should be, God knows, but sometimes it seems I have a way of complicating even the simplest of things.

SUNDAY *July 23*

If it were just a simple matter of having fresh, tasty, organically grown vegetables, I'd have given up gardening several years ago, when the co-op and the farmers' market started selling a wide variety of locally grown produce, just a fifteen-minute walk from home. Last night, for example, the leeks that Kate got at the farmers' market tasted as earthy and fresh as the ones I've grown in recent years. And the flat green beans we had from our own garden didn't upstage the leeks, even though I'd carefully dressed them with a light coating of olive oil, a sprinkling of marjoram, a squeeze of fresh lime juice, a twist of grated pepper, and a dash of salt. That austere dressing balanced the intense Creole vinaigrette on the leeks and artichoke, and together they provided a fitting accompaniment to the charcoal grilled swordfish.

But when we were sitting in the gazebo last night, dining on the fish and the leeks and the beans and the cucumber salad and the beet salad, it was a special pleasure to look out at the vegetable garden just a few feet away and behold the row of plants from which I'd harvested those beans. I could see the source from which they'd come and savor everything pulsing in them, from the afternoon at the end of May when Rebecca and I had pressed the oblong white seeds into the soil and covered them with compost to the moment when I harvested the long, flat green beans yesterday afternoon. The rain that fell overnight after we planted them and then the sun and the rain and the sun that drew them forth just five days later — all of it was there in those beans. And not just the weather, but the straw mulch insulating them and the Hinder protecting them from the deer. And the plants themselves

— my eye was feasting on the plants themselves, their dark green leaves face-up, like palms raised toward the sky.

Well, not to put too fine a point on it, I felt more deeply connected to my beans than to someone else's leeks — almost as deeply as Thoreau to his fabled bean field, perhaps because I ate my beans sitting in a summerhouse the same size as his place by Walden Pond. Fifteen feet long, ten wide. My lily pond, of course, is diminutive compared to his pond, and I only have a couple of goldfish in it. But I didn't have to eat my beans in solitude, which may explain why I savored mine more than he evidently enjoyed his. In an entire chapter about his beans, Thoreau mentions eating them only once, in passing, at the end of a very long sentence. Kate went so far as to say that the beans at the farmers' market didn't look anywhere near so appealing as mine, and perhaps that also made them seem so tasty. Come to think of it, I've rarely had beans that can match the ones from my garden, but maybe that's just a quirk of beans, which need to be picked and eaten immediately to be at their peak, as they were last night.

MONDAY *July 24*

Now, when conditions are just right for the big-time growth and fruition of high summer — ample moisture in the ground, ample heat in the air — I'm suddenly on edge again with signs of trouble. A cucumber vine in deep wilt from one end to the other — probably bacterial wilt spread by the cucumber beetle — so I pulled out the vine and redusted all the others with rotenone. A pattypan plant missing four of its elephant-ear leaves. Probably the work of deer, feeding on one of the most unlikely of greens, so I sprinkled Hinder on everything in both vegetable beds. The waterlily tub tipped over on its side in the lily pond. Another deer, or a possum, or a groundhog, or raccoon, or possibly Phoebe, who's always lapped from it like a tigress at her private watering hole, though I doubt she has enough strength now to tip it over on her own.

Nothing to be done about the waterlily plant, except to set it right side up on the concrete block in the pond and hope that the nighttime visitor doesn't start coming to eat as well as drink. In

years past, I've found lily pads chewed around the edges or completely bitten off and floating on the surface of the pond. And I
can also remember the waterlily getting enough sunlight each day
— six hours at least — that it produced a continuous bloom of
lilies during July and August, sometimes three or four at once. But
now it's so heavily shaded by the maple tree that it gets only a
couple of hours of morning sun. Now I'm content just to behold
the surface covered with lily pads and the two resident goldfish
swimming in and out of their canopy.

Twenty-five years ago, I dreamed of having a place large enough
for a pond of my own, where I could paddle around in a little
rowboat or stand by the shore and fly-fish for bluegill or bass. And
bring a few in for dinner along with the fresh vegetables. But the
dream could never have come true except in the form envisioned
by Kate, who gave it to me for my birthday some twenty years ago
— a circular hog-watering tank, four feet in diameter, two feet
deep, its galvanized surface glistening on the terrace when I came
home that day from work. "There's your fishing pond. Dig a hole
between the porch and the outside cellarway large enough to
contain it, paint the inside with black epoxy paint, fill it with
water and fish, ring it with bricks, and you'll be ready to go." And
I did. And gradually we created an ecologically balanced system
with snails and clams to filter the water, oxygenating plants to
aerate it for the fish, a waterlily to shade the fish, and sometimes
other bog plants to please the eye. One year, a painted box turtle
paid it a short visit on the way to the Iowa River two miles away.
And another time, our nephew Peter, then just two or three, tried
to walk on the lily pads, with splashy results. But now the only
visitors are a cast iron toad, memento of a visit to Carmel, and the
critters who come in the night.

TUESDAY *July 25*

No overnight visitors to the pond, or perhaps more accurately
no telltale signs of overnight visitors. How do I know what
might have come by without leaving its calling card? But a
deer visited the other pattypan plant last night and took a few
bites. And another deer, or perhaps the same one, left its mark in

the back garden, this time four and a half feet up the Whopper tomato plant, where it chewed off a bunch of leaves, stripped the branches as clean as if it were a tomato hornworm. But I couldn't find a worm anywhere nearby. Besides, the clean-cut bites on the stem clearly indicate a deer. So they're dining higher than I thought it was necessary to sprinkle the Hinder. Now I know better.

But why am I fretting about such a minor loss — just a bunch of leaves from a single plant that occupies no more than two square feet of space out of fourteen hundred square feet in both vegetable gardens? A minuscule fraction — one seven-hundredth — of all the area under cultivation has a little damage in it, yet my attention veers inexorably to that trouble spot rather than to the splendid things coming out of the garden right now, especially from the nearby tomato plants. Last night, for example, we had the first full-size slicer of the season, a Big Beef from the plant right next to the Whopper, and it was as piquant, meaty, and juicy as if it had come on two or three weeks later when the full-season tomatoes usually reach the peak of their flavor and texture. The heat wave, no doubt, has brought all the tomato plants along one or two weeks earlier than usual. And the slices of Walla Walla onion we had with the tomato were as sweet, crisp, and juicy as a piece of fresh fruit. And the green and yellow bush beans were as meaty and tender as French filet beans. And Kate's stuffed pork chops, featuring a mix of anchovies, rose peppercorns, and our own shallots, winter savory, sage, thyme, and parsley, were redolent with the life of the herb bed.

Given such varied delights, why do I think about, much less write about, a trifling bit of damage? Why do I go out each morning looking for troubles rather than triumphs, losses rather than gains? And then having found a few, why do I blow them out of proportion, even make them the point of departure for my daily reports, as in this one and yesterday's? Why don't I begin instead by mentioning the first batch of fresh cucumbers I harvested today, one of which turned up in Kate's pasta salad this noon, and the eggplants ready for picking and the corn fully tassled with the silks emerging? Why don't I just shrug my shoulders and concede a little bit to the animals, like a tithe? But no sooner do I start thinking that way than a little voice inside me says, "Give them a leaf and they'll want the whole branch and then the whole plant and before you know it there'll be nothing left. Besides, whose garden is it, anyway? Yours or theirs?" So the old ways die hard, even — perhaps, especially — in the midst of abundance.

WEDNESDAY *July 26*

A busman's holiday, I thought, when I saw the newspaper piece about vegetable plots at the Johnson County 4-H and FFA Fair. So Kate and I had a day at the fair, where I stuck my hand in the middle of the big tomatillo plant and gaped at the Violetto pole beans in the kids' garden, their purple-veined leaves and lavender blossoms vining near the top of the eight foot tepee. A gaudy bean, fit to serve as a centerpiece in next year's garden. But the Muskovich tomato plant was no match for our Black Prince, its earliest fruit now changing from green to orange to reddish brown. Actually, none of the vegetables could compete with the livestock. The rabbit barn — a colorful display of bunnies from so many different origins, it looked like a harey version of the United Nations. The English Spot, the Flemish Giant, the Florida White, the Holland Lop, the New Zealand Black, and don't forget the Fuzzy Lop, with fur to match its name. The sheep barn filled with freshly shorn blackface. The poultry barn a winner too, especially the wild turkeys and the Grand Champion Pen of Three for Egg Production, one of which laid a brown egg right before our very eyes. And the cattle barn — how shall I ever forget the young farm boy, bedded down on straw with his animal, cradling its head in his neck, stroking it, stroking it, against the time when he would have to part from his beloved at the sale barn. The cycle of life and death playing itself out at the fair, grandparents and parents sitting or standing by, playing their part in the cycle. But oh! what a treat it was just a few minutes later biting into a grilled beef brat in a bun with sauerkraut, ketchup, and pickles, thanks to the enterprise of the county cattlemen's association. Almost enough to make me forget the boy in the cattle barn. The hog barn, alas, was "too smelly" to visit in the noonday sun, but Kate was hot to find the commercial exhibition hall where a local monument company was giving away yardsticks. "Get one of those for your garden and stop using the one I got for the house." We also got a free wooden ruler and a yellow plastic fly swatter, thanks to the county sheriff — gifts that seemed to suggest he was advising us to "Go straight or I'll swat you dead." And so many other gifts that Kate was almost completely disarmed. "Just think of how much we got to see, got for free." We also got an ice cream cone with a scoop of butter brickle for fifty cents and shared it all around the midway, from the games of skill to the breezy rides. Some things never change, like the Ferris wheel, the tilt-a-whirl, the merry-go-round and the carny hawker, imploring everyone to "Throw a Ping-Pong ball into a fishbowl and get a free goldfish." For a moment, I was tempted, just because we have room for another in the lily pond. Now I wish I'd tried, especially after I hefted a wooden mallet but passed up a chance to "Ring the bell" and then saw a sign reminding me that "You can't win if you don't play."

THURSDAY *July 27*

"It reminds me of my grandmothers, it really does — my Edwardian grandmothers, with their ample bosoms and their corseted bodies and their layered undergarments even in the heat of summer." Kate was euphoric about the Brandywine tomato that I harvested this morning and we sampled at lunch together with Rebecca. An oblong wonder, six inches long, four inches wide, pink on the outside, coral red within. So tasty and spicy it needed no salt, so meaty and tender that Kate thought its texture was "sensuous," so moist its juices oozed from each of the four thick slices I cut and layered on a bed of romaine, but not before I photographed the whole thing in its full rotundity. Always one for a little competition, or at least a comparison, I also prepared another plate with four thick slices of a Russian Black Prince, a smaller, more globular fruit, also ready this morning and photographed before slicing. When Rebecca first saw it in the kitchen, its dark green shoulders merging into its dark orange-brown skin, she was almost as carried away as Kate had been by the Brandywine. "Look at that color! It's so odd, so strange!" And just as strange on the inside, its reddish-brown flesh surrounding greenish juice and pale seeds, with a milder, more delicate taste than the Brandywine, but a peppery finish, like watercress, that Kate and Rebecca thought would make it perfect for a salsa.

Now, as I sit here looking back at our lunch, which also featured a bowl of leftover paella I made a couple of days ago and a fresh melon and blueberry fruit salad that Kate concocted this morning, I'm wondering if it was all an illusion, a fizzy sensation, springing from the chilled bottle of champagne that Rebecca gave me when she arrived this morning. A gift — some gift — for my help during the greenhouse caper a few weeks ago. I opened it right before the meal, and we began by toasting the heirloom tomatoes and the good food and the weather of July that had brought us such bounty. And the weather of August to come. And our good health. And so many other good things that maybe we were ready to be swept away by tomatoes beyond compare. Who knows? One thing I know for sure is that right now I'm planning to grow both of those tomatoes next summer, champagne or not.

Actually, even before lunch, I was already a bit high from a bumper picking of cucumbers, and a first little harvest of okra, and a couple of lengthy eggplants. So, when the pattypans and zucchini begin to swell up, all the summer vegetables will be doing their thing. Even without those vegetables, I think I'd have been carried away by memories of the county fair that Rebecca and Kate stirred up when they were talking about it on the back porch this morning — the youngsters with their livestock, grooming them with their parents, readying them for the show and then for the sale barn, and then the letting go.

FRIDAY *July 28*

"Thirty-two of 'em. Can you believe it? Thirty-two." Rebecca was talking about the tornadoes that hit northeast Iowa yesterday, and I could easily believe it, especially given the increasing heat and humidity of the past few days, the violent thunderclouds that passed over our place late yesterday afternoon, and the slightly cooler breezes that moved in overnight. A collision of hot and cold weather fronts, basic ingredients of a tornado, the big story last night on local TV news. Uprooted trees, downed power lines, twisted homes and barns. The landscape rearranged wherever a funnel touched down. Kate told me later about an area weather watcher who, when asked by an earnest TV reporter to explain what could possibly have moved a century-old barn three feet off its foundation, said, "Well, if it wasn't a tornado, it sure was a strong wind."

The wry turn of that remark got me thinking about the way people describe the weather in their daily chitchat. So I was careful about the spin I put on it this morning when my haircutter Chris asked me how my garden was affected by the evening storm that moved through here on the Fourth of July. Thanks to all this record keeping, I remembered the seventy-mile-an-hour wind, the driving rain, my fear of the corn being leveled again, but most of all my surprise the next morning when I discovered the storm hadn't disturbed anything, even a single corn plant. When she heard my little report, Chris let go like a sudden downpour, complete with lightning and thunder. So turbulent it momentarily brought my haircut to a halt. "It completely destroyed my husband's garden. Completely. We not only had the wind and the rain, we also had hail. Golfball-sized. You can't imagine what it did to our place. Shredded my chard, shredded the beet greens, shredded the broccoli and left the hostas riddled with holes." A sad story, all right, so I tried to encourage her with the thought that the hostas would endure and that some of her crops might do better than she feared. But as soon as I tried to comfort her, she told me, "The only crop failure so far has been the cucumbers. The beetles got 'em." Otherwise, she's harvested beans, beets, celery, chard, and tomatoes.

Not bad for a completely destroyed garden. It made me wonder what we gardeners would do without the weather to excite us. This afternoon, for example, Rebecca told me that when the storm hit her place last night, she could hear the big tractor-pullers at the fair, a mile away, come to a grinding halt. "Grrrrrrrrrrrrr." We didn't get any of the rain on our side of the city, but when Kate and

I saw the towering storm clouds to the south, we both thought they looked like trouble, big trouble. And there's more trouble on the way with the heat wave that started today. Kate warned me it was coming, but I didn't believe her. And now it's here. Really big trouble. Really.

SATURDAY *July 29*

If I'd heeded Kate's warning earlier this week, I'd have been watering a couple of days ago, rather than at six this morning. How quickly the weather changes! And how quickly I respond to it! Only a fretful vegetable gardener could be so slavishly tied to every twist and turn in the weather. But without my compulsions, what would become of all the immature cucumbers, pattypan, and zucchini, waiting to swell on the vines? The cucumbers would turn bitter, the squash would probably shrivel up. Even yesterday afternoon, just a few days after the rain, those vines were wilting severely in the heat.

No wonder I couldn't help thinking about the tyranny of vegetable gardening, when I was in the nearby city cemetery just an hour later, on a guided tour sponsored by Kate's Heritage Trees project. Fifty of us, most of us in our fifties or older, were looking at a remnant of native forest, an extensive grove of trees, most of them between ninety and a hundred seventy years old — basswood, bur oak, black oak, swamp white oak, black maple, sugar maple, eastern red cedar, and shagbark hickory. So old their bark was deeply indented or furrowed, their branches reaching way beyond us, a canopy shading us from the heat of the sun. And we were walking in the oldest area of the cemetery, where many of the tombstones bore the dates of people who'd been born in the late eighteenth century, more than two hundred years ago. Looking at those tombstones, walking amid those trees, chatting with others in the group, I couldn't help thinking how impervious this landscape is to the daily twists and turns that've been ringing my alarm all spring and summer.

But listening to Mark, the young forester from Iowa State, it gradually occurred to me that those durable trees were shaped as much by momentary things as my transitory vegetables. An ill-timed cut or a careless bit of pruning early on, and the health or structure of a tree will be damaged for life. So Mark turned out to be as fussy about pruning and all the other things that shape the life of a tree as I am about watering and all the other things that bring a vegetable to fruition. Talk about fussiness! How could I forget the passionate account of growing cecropia moths that I got right before the tree walk from Jeff, a botanist who raises them from start to finish? "It all depends on what happens in a few days right before the beginning of summer, when the females lay their eggs, and males need to be present to fertilize them. Then once the caterpillars start feeding, they need to have the same kind of leaf." And then I discovered the whole process from egg to caterpillar to pupa to moth takes an entire year — for a creature that lives only four days. So much fuss for such a short time! But then Jeff reminded me about all the years that go into the one-day life of a cicada. In every living thing, it seems, the long and short of things inheres.

SUNDAY *July 30*

How could I talk about the long and short of things without mentioning the kosher dill pickles I'm putting up? Yesterday, four quarts. Today, two more quarts. Tomorrow, as many as the cucumber patch will yield. And more each day, until I've got at least two or three dozen quarts of them curing in the basement fruit room. Kate wants me to get up a big enough cache for us to have some left over for next year, "just in case." Just in case I have a crop failure like the last few years. Not likely to happen again, now that I'm planting the cucumber seedlings shallowly enough that they don't suffocate in my clayey soil, and then keeping the vines amply watered and regularly dusted with rotenone. Just the same, a good year is a good year, in cucumbers as in grapes, in pickles as in wines, so I'm putting up enough to have some left over, just in case.

Kosher dills. The name itself sends me reeling back to Cleveland Heights, where I tasted the first one I can ever remember, in a little delicatessen right around the corner from where I lived with my uncle Dan and aunt Ruth. Though my crusty uncle Dan perpetually made me feel as unwanted as a Dickensian child of the streets, my aunt Ruth's secret hungers perpetually sent me to that delicatessen, or another one nearby, for her afternoon snacks. So I became a connoisseur — or more fittingly, a *kenner* — of kosher dills. Of corned beef, pastrami, salami, and knishes too. But above all else, for reasons still unbeknownst to me, a kenner of kosher dills. New dills, full dills, but above all else, authentic dills, made with a pure salt brine — no vinegar allowed — and just the right amount of pickling spices, dill, garlic, and alum for crispness.

The recipe I use was given to me some forty years ago by my brother Marshall. The most cherished gift I've ever received from him, for I'm sure it must have been derived from the first great pickle of them all — the Ur Dill, conceived and refined, no doubt, in the sacred precincts of an Eastern European shtetl. Or perhaps it's based on the pickle barrel that must have graced my grandfather Joseph's grocery store in the flats of Cleveland at the end of the nineteenth century. Whatever the source, the zingy brine it yields is as precious to me as a fine champagne — and like a fine champagne it's aged fully in the bottle. In this particular case, a sterilized wide-mouth quart jar, at the bottom of which I put two level tablespoons of kosher salt, one tablespoon of mixed pickling spices, one large clove of garlic (or two medium ones), and a pinch of alum. Then a little distilled water to dissolve the alum and salt. Then the pickling cucumbers and some fresh dill (both heads and leaves), tightly packed. Then distilled water, leaving an inch of headroom in the jar. Capped lightly for twenty-four hours to release any buildup, then capped tightly for six weeks and stored in a cool, dark place, it yields a cloudy brew beyond compare.

MONDAY *July 31*

The last day of July, and the back yard looks it. Brown spots in the lawn, faded colors in Kate's flower border, weeds in the terrace, and everything just a bit haggard around the edges. And why not, given the lingering heat wave, the second one this month. So hot again, the lawn mower skipped last week and turned up today for the first time in two weeks. The alternating stripes of his mower's track certainly do give the lawn a manicured appearance, but they don't do much for the browning. Only an inch or two of rain and cooling temperatures can really spruce things up. All the weather reporters are predicting a big storm this evening, but right now the heaped-up clouds, towering over the back yard, look more like Hollywood sets than the real thing.

The dog days are upon us, and Pip is in a matching mood, cooped up here in the air-conditioned house for so long he's almost given up hope of getting one of the big-time walks that keep his tail wagging and his bark in shape. But in this kind of heat, he's hardly good for more than a few blocks before he wants to lie down in the grass and cool off in the shade. Even Phoebe, the devotee of heat, got so dehydrated from camping out in the gazebo and refusing to eat that I took her into the vet this morning to get her plumped up with fluids and stimulate her appetite. Still, she had enough in her to douse me again on the way to the car, just as I was wondering aloud if she might give me another sprinkle. But the more ominous message came from the vet, who agreed with me that her tumor's much larger and told me that if the fluids don't work, "we might have to help her out." Looking at her comfortably curled up right now on the rug behind the computer, it's hard to believe she's so far beyond help. But Phoebe's never been one to refuse a bowl of food, so her loss of appetite is a sure sign the day has almost come to help her out of this world.

I've also been looking outside at the back vegetable bed, its tomato vines and pepper plants and eggplants much taller than usual, trying to set them clearly in my mind's eye, for this Sirius day, oddly enough, is also the one I've been longing for ever since the start of this gardening season — the day when all the warm-weather plants are pumping out their fruit at the same time, the day of our first all-fresh ratatouille. "Vegetable stew," as Kate reminded me again this morning, when I told her that the zucchini were finally ready. And as if to commemorate the occasion, Jim showed up this afternoon with a fresh catfish he caught just a few hours before. "All of 'em were real nice, real nice. They didn't want to come off the bottom, just wanted to stay down there. So we had to work at hauling 'em in. A good sign. They cleaned up good, too, and should make a nice meal." A memorable one too.

A U G U S T

L ast night's catfish was so firm, moist, and delicate — not a hint
of midsummer rankness in it — that Kate told me, "You must
call Jim and tell him how good it was. It's the best catfish I've
ever had." It upstaged even the premiere ratatouille of the season,
a star-studded confection not only of eggplant, zucchini, pattypans, tomatoes, onions, and peppers, but also okra and corn.
Eight vegetables married so happily with basil, thyme, garlic, and
a smidgen of hot red pepper that their rich, dark sauce was the
quintessence of summer. Yet the fish, the delicate catfish fillets,
lightly breaded and sautéed, were still on our lips this morning. So
I called Jim right after my inspection tour of the gardens. But the
startling spectacle I beheld in the cucumber patch almost made
me forget to tell him about the fish. Leaf stems sticking out all
along the front of the patch without any leaves attached, each one
cleanly bitten off at the tip, and no residue of the leaves anywhere in sight. What kind of beast could possibly want to eat an
old cucumber leaf coated with rotenone? Even without rotenone,
they're so tough and hairy that nothing in its right mind would
possibly eat more than one or two leaves without spitting them
out. As if to compound the mystery, I also noticed several bare leaf
stems sticking out of the volunteer tomato plants right in front of
the cucumbers. No mystery, according to Jim. "I think it's a pair of
fawns. I seen 'em up at my place the past few nights. I don't think
they know any better. Can you imagine something eating leaves

off my pepper plants? It's crazy, almost as crazy as going after cucumber leaves. I think they must be trying things out. But I'm sick of 'em trying things out of my garden." And so am I. The only problem is that I can't really claim they've done any serious damage yet. Several leaves here, several leaves there, but not enough missing to endanger even a single plant, much less an entire crop. So why am I letting the deer get to me again, especially after I wrote about them just a week ago. It certainly doesn't cost much to keep things protected with Hinder — I've only spent fifteen dollars on it so far this summer. And the Hinder keeps them at bay, as long as I renew it every three weeks or after a heavy rain. Not much money or trouble, really, to have an almost deer-free garden, and less hassle than fencing both vegetable gardens with electric wire. As Kate always says, "Just get out the sprinkling can, and stop fretting." But there's the rub, now that I think of it. Why should I have to get out the sprinkling can at all? Or anything else, for that matter? Why can't I have a garden like Kate's, a garden that's rarely ever bothered by deer and groundhogs and possums and whatever it was that took a bite out of one of the Brandywine tomatoes yesterday, and then had the nerve to spit it out right on top of the straw? Kate says I should rig a camera up to a light sensor, so I can get an automatic snapshot of the beasts whenever they come to eat. But would I feel any better if I knew what was causing the trouble? And would I really feel better if I could get rid of them once and for all? Maybe not, given how empty it felt around here during that month back in '89 when we had a squirrel-free lot. Maybe I need something to fret about, to keep me on edge. Maybe, after all, the critters are as necessary to my gardening as the vegetables themselves.

WEDNESDAY *August 2*

" I think it's a copout when you ask all those questions about the animals but don't really answer them, except with a tidy little concluding statement about yourself." How strange, I thought, that Kate should consider my confession to be a copout, especially when all my questions about the animals were concerned with the fretfulness of my reactions to them rather than with the animals themselves. But just to make sure I wasn't dodging the big questions about animals in the garden, I did a little reading this morning about the ecology of a back yard. In *Noah's Garden,* a visionary work by Sara Stein, I discovered that my problems might be solved by creating a "patchwork landscape," a reconstructed ecosystem, which provides such a varied and complexly dispersed array of habitats that "herb and herbivore, prey and predator play a continual game of hide and seek that keeps the seesaw gently teetering." A lovely vision, I thought, the peaceable kingdom in a children's playground, all the plants and animals keeping each other gently in balance, though of course what she's talking about is nature red in tooth and claw. The only problem is that a patchwork landscape, as Stein acknowledges, requires an environment much larger than a single back yard — a collaboratively developed network linking all the yards and neighborhoods in a natural community. Not likely in my case, when my next door neighbor doesn't even bother to care for the aisle of fruit trees that Kate and I helped to plant on her lot some ten years before she bought the place. Or when my neighbor on the other side spitefully hacks off limbs from the walnut trees on our joint lot line, because Jim and Carol and Kate and I and the city council stopped him from trying to appropriate a landscaped piece of our adjoining public alleyway for his own use. Think globally, act locally — but how is one to do so when the vision falters right at the lot line? Besides, not even a patchwork landscape will reduce the massive and increasing overpopulation of the deer, for which Stein herself admits the need of such alternative methods as "professional culling" or the "high tech solution" of "a birth control vaccine." So I turned to Roger Swain's *Groundwork: A Gardener's Ecology,* another richly informed book, where I found that the only responsible and sure-fire way to keep the animals at bay is a tall, electrified fence. The only problem is that a fence has to be put up and taken down every year, because "galvanized wire . . . rusts too fast if left outdoors year round." And an electric fence, even with warning signs, would probably turn out to be a shocking experience, especially for an absentminded gardener like me. Besides, Kate considers them so ugly, she wouldn't ever allow one in the yard. So, it seems, my only recourse is to Hinder things in the summer, row-cover them in the spring and fall, and fret my heart out all season long.

THURSDAY *August 3*

In the midst of a bumper harvest, it seems a bit strange, even to me, to be fretting about the weather. Especially after a dinner featuring the vivid tastes of fresh slicer tomatoes, fresh green beans, and an Oriental salad of fresh cucumbers and fresh sweet onions marinated in sesame oil, rice wine vinegar, and tamari. But it's beginning to look like the drought of the late eighties. Three consecutive days of overcast skies, three days of darkly threatening clouds, three days of heavily humid air, and only two tenths of an inch so far in the rain gauge. So much promise and so little payoff. So much humidity, but so little else. Like a rain forest without the rain. And not just this week, but also the week before.

Still, the main activity around here continues to be deerstalking. And now it's not only Jim and me doing the stalking. Now even Kate's been drawn into the hunt. Usually, she stands off from the fray, preferring, I think, to calm things down whenever I'm off on one of my frenzies. But last night, around midnight, just when I was putting Pip out for his constitutional, Kate suddenly turned up in the kitchen with the big black halogen flashlight in hand, the one that throws a beam so far it looks like a full-fledged spotlight. "Let's see if any of the deer are out in the yard." And out she went to the back porch, waving her beam back and forth across the yard, up and down the misty, midnight air. No deer in sight, but a vivid tableau just the same — Kate, flashlight in hand, her back slightly arched in a Holmesian stance, and half-blind Pip tugging at his leash, pawing at the terrace, eager to track the invisible prey across the murky upland of our small estate.

Her interest, I think, was sparked yesterday afternoon, when I was showing Jim where a bite had been taken five feet up on one of the Big Beef tomatoes. Just then Kate showed up and got a firsthand view of the deer-bitten tomato, bright green on one side, scabrous on the other, like the phantom of the opera. Her eyes widened, she quickly stepped back, and then pronounced a one-word judgment of it. "Ridiculous." I think she was also drawn in by Jim's remark that "The only remaining predator of the deer is man, and we can't do anything inside the city limits." She reminded him about coyotes, especially the pack that's been going after wildlife and livestock just south of here in Kalona. Jim responded by proclaiming that "A lone coyote's a coward," and as if to prove his point, he told us one of his hunting stories about a buck he'd shot and a coyote that came to feed on it while he was getting some friends to help him lug home the carcass. Jim was apparently so taken aback by the memory of the scavenger feeding on his kill that he paused a few seconds as if to regain his composure. Then with a glint in his eye, he said, "I shot the coyote too." That final twist came as such a surprise it momentarily had all three of us laughing. But now I don't know. Now I'm just thankful I don't have to deal with coyotes as well as deer.

FRIDAY *August 4*

Now, when all the plants and vines are pumping out vegetables like a mass-production line, I'm suddenly tempted to put the gardens on automatic pilot and take a few days break from the constant vigil of tending them. And I mean break — a complete break. No weeding, no dusting, no watering, no Hindering, no cultivating, no pruning, no tying. No checking on this, no fretting about that. Not even any harvesting. No gardening activity of any kind. The yearning to be free of it all takes hold of me every year around this time, brought on no doubt by the long and continuous labor of bringing the gardens to this point of abundance.

But now, in the height of summer, the dog days of August, when the heat hangs on and the humidity hangs in like a wet rag, now is one of those times when the plants and the vines compel my vigilant attention. And not just to keep the vermin at bay, but also to keep the vegetables under control. If the beans aren't regularly harvested, they grow tough and stringy — in just a few days. If the cucumbers, eggplants, pattypans, and zucchini aren't regularly picked, they grow monstrously large — in just a few days. If the tomatoes aren't picked when ready, they go soft and sweet — in just a few days. If the onions aren't pulled and cured in the sun, they begin to rot from the inside and outside alike — in just a few days. Ripeness is all, and the moment of readiness often seems to come and go within a single day. Now's the time when I feel most imprisoned by the garden.

And it's not just the harvest. It's also what has to be done with the stuff once it's been picked. This week it's been cucumbers every day, fifty or sixty so far, all of them to be put up as kosher dills, or used in salads, or given away before they start rotting in the vegetable bins. Next week, it'll be tomatoes to be canned or sauced or juiced or dried. And more cucumbers to be dealt with. And the onions to be dried. And four dozen ears of corn coming on. No wonder I'm often bargaining with Kate to keep things moving out of the vegetable baskets and bins. Flat beans and a Brandywine tomato this evening. Who knows what I can get her to serve up for lunch and dinner tomorrow?

But this year, for the first time in several years, we won't be alone with all those vegetables, thanks to a family reunion of sorts that's now underway. Yesterday, Kate's sister Martha blew in from Florida, and Martha's college-age son Peter drove down from Wisconsin. Come Sunday, my son Marshall will be driving in from New York with his daughter Kathleen and his son Owen, and on Monday my daughter Amelia and her husband Joseph will be arriving from Wisconsin. Enough mouths, thank God, to cope with the cornucopia.

SATURDAY *August 5*

"Would you mind going to the farmers' market for me?" Only Kate would have the nerve — or, should I say, the gall or the chutzpah — to ask such a favor of me. Especially when she knows we're being inundated by our own vegetables, especially when she knows I just finished a piece about coping with the abundance, especially at quarter to seven in the morning when I'm just beginning to wake up and the sand isn't out of my eyes. Some wake-up call. A request to buy somebody else's vegetables. "I just need some kohlrabi for this evening's dinner, for Lib's birthday. You know how much she loves it." So how can I refuse to get some kohlrabi for my aging mother-in-law's birthday dinner? Especially when Kate gives me a little hug along with the request? I'm a sucker for a well-timed hug. "Also you can check out the competition." Nothing like an appeal to my lingering type-A personality. "Besides, you might get something to write about." The most cynical move of all, especially when she knows how much I'm hungering for a break from the garden. So how could I refuse the chance to write about something other than my garden?

On the way out, I snatched a pencil and paper, just in case. Never can tell when the details might be so priceless that every word, every image begs to be captured just as is. And priceless they were, especially the prices compared to the quality of the produce. A dollar a pound for lumpy, overgrown beans. Seventy-five cents apiece for dull-skinned eggplants. Twenty-five cents apiece for Italian plum-style tomatoes, smaller by half than my Enchantments. Twenty cents apiece for cucumbers no bigger than my largest. And full-size slicing tomatoes available only at a couple of stands, in both cases underripe, for a dollar a pound. Only the peppers at three for a dollar, or zucchini at five for a dollar, were notably good buys. And even those I could offer at a lower price. But the thought of underselling the others made me realize I'd let myself get so involved in checking out the competition that I'd almost forgotten to look for kohlrabi. Just then, my colleague Dixie came by and asked me, "What are you doing here? Checking out the competition?"

Well, I did find one place selling kohlrabi. But what I found most of all was a renewed interest in my own garden — so much so that I drove right home and spent the next three hours working in the big vegetable bed for the first time this week. Rather than fretting about the deer, I weeded and watered the entire bed, dusted the cucumbers and beans with rotenone, pulled all the onions, and worked up a good sweat. An hour later, two of the cucumber vines went into a deep wilt, clearly bacterial wilt, and never recovered. So I pulled them both. Suddenly I could see why cukes were going for twenty cents apiece. Suddenly, too, I could see why I'd best stick to writing about vegetables and leave the peddling to others.

SUNDAY *August 6*

I t was a classic summer dinner, just like the ones that Lib used to spread around the big oak table on the air-conditioned eating porch at the old family house in Lisbon, twenty miles north of here — the big, tan brick place with the wide stone front steps and the decorative concrete planters on the walls abutting the steps that made it look like a small-town public library, a Carnegie-era library. How many times did I climb those steps the summers I was courting Kate some thirty years ago? How many times did I drive the twenty miles from Iowa City to Lisbon, by the rolling cornfields lickety-split, sometimes so fast I got picked up in Solon, halfway there, and taken to the local cafe, where I paid the speeding ticket right at the bar? How many times? It hardly matters now. So many gone now who used to sit around the table on the air-conditioned porch. All of them came back to me last night when Kate and I and Martha and Peter and Lib were sitting around the table in our air-conditioned place, eating the classic Midwest summer dinner. A platter of meat, in this case a rolled rump roast. A platter of sweet corn, so juicy and tender I wish I'd grown it myself, but ours is still a few days from being done. And a big platter of fresh vegetables — sliced tomatoes, sliced green peppers, sliced cucumbers, and sliced sweet onions from the garden. And the sliced kohlrabi from the farmers' market. And a special bowl of homemade mayonnaise, made in the same tall-glass, plunger-whipper Wesson Oil Mayonnaise Maker that Lib herself once used — the one with the mayonnaise recipe in raised glass letters right on the glass jar itself. And the basket of bread. And the big fruity dessert — in this case an open-face peach tart of Kate's devising, the edge ringed with fresh blueberries and the center with Bing cherries, glazed with Kate's apricot jam, and served up with sparkler candles. And the jar of Guernsey cream, fresh from the local dairy, to dribble over the big fruity dessert. Some things, thank God, never really do change all that much.

And now my son Marshall's coming back, and the memories are coming back with him as well. Actually, they've been coming on for several weeks, ever since Kate decided to revive the screened-in sleeping porch, the tree-shaded spot where Marshall used to camp out in the long hot summers before we air-conditioned the house. I've spent the past two days vacuuming out the dust and scrubbing off the mold of fifteen or twenty vacant summers. Martha just put up some new venetian blinds on the east side. Kate decked it out with a reading lamp, a reading stand, and a couple of dark green futon/reading chairs. And just a few minutes ago, Marshall called to give me a travel update. "I'm in central Indiana, dad, running a bit late, so we probably won't be in until dinner time. I've been telling Kathleen how the dinners mostly come from the garden. And she's looking forward to it." Some things, after all, never do change.

MONDAY *August 7*

My grandchildren. Those words have been part of my vocabulary for some ten years, ever since my daughter Hannah gave birth to her first child, Ben. Yet the words have always sounded a bit strange whenever I turn them over in my mind — as strange as the statement "I'm a grandfather" or "I have five grandchildren." For I see my grandchildren so infrequently, once every year or two or three, that I can hardly claim them to be mine in any vital sense, though mine they clearly are. A kinship unmistakable whenever I see any of them. I see it immediately in Kathleen's long face, dark hair, and dark brown eyes — her markings much like mine when I was also ten. I also see it in Owen's wide head and broad forehead — so large it looks like my father Max lives on in his three-year-old great-grandson. But a blond-haired, blue-eyed Max? And a trim-nosed me? Now I'm beginning to understand what the breeders mean when they talk about hybrids and the crossing of strains. Now I see myself and now I don't. My love of food lives on in both of them, and so does my way of talking with my hands, thanks to my son Marshall. But was I then so rambunctious as Owen or so curious and knowledgeable of wildlife as Kathleen? Was I so robust as Owen or so poised as the gymnast Kathleen? Was I so intense as Owen or so conscious of my identity as Kathleen? The more I look, the less I see myself in them, and gladly too.

I certainly wouldn't have responded to Jim as Kathleen did this morning, when he called her Kathy. "My name's Kathleen," she said, and that was that. More spunk than I ever had at that age. From that moment on, Jim called her Kathleen, and from that moment on she didn't hesitate to ask him about his duck blind and his decoy ducks, and to listen closely to everything he said, especially when he was telling Marshall why he'd given up coon hunting some four years ago. "I haven't hunted coons since Queenie died. She was my last coon hound. The best one I ever had. After her I never had the heart to get another. I've owned a lot of coon hounds in my life, but you only get one complete hound in your life, and I've already had her." After that story, I think that she and I and Marshall could have stayed at Jim's the rest of the morning, listening to him ramble on about the different kinds of decoy for each kind of duck, and the deer going after his pepper plants, and the gigantic old larch tree in his side yard where he told Owen to "Just go pee behind that one, if you have to." But we were on an errand for Kate, charged with gathering some hickory bark from the nearby wilderness park to include in Amelia's birthday present, and half-blind Pip was tugging at his leash, eager to lead us there and back in time for lunch. Kathleen and Owen did most of the gathering, then Marshall showed them the creek where he used to hang out with his teenage friends, and I stood by feeling for the moment very much like "grandpa Carl."

TUESDAY *August 8*

N ow I'm feeling like a father again, thanks to Amelia bounding in last night with a bag of fresh vegetables, straight from her garden in Wisconsin — a chip off the old block, carrying coals to Newcastle. The only problem is this: when I looked in the bag, I noticed that her peppers are bigger than mine, and some of them are four-lobed, whereas mine have all been three-lobed thus far. What a strange reaction — to behave as if I were checking out the competition again, whereas she was just bringing me a loving daughterly tribute, and maybe even a little payback for all the peppers I've sent home with her in years gone by. Or was she? Maybe she's a chip off the old block in more ways than one, giving me a little giftlike jab to remind me of the problems I had with my peppers last summer. Maybe that's why she also brought me some cucumbers, to remind me of my cuke failures the past two summers. Maybe she's trying to let me know she's taken the measure of my gardening and can best me with one hand tied behind her back, since she's also going to nursing school this summer and working part-time at a nearby hospital. Why else would she tell me last night that "I just put 'em in the ground, give 'em a good start, and then they have to survive on their own. I don't have time to fuss over 'em like you." But then again, she also told me last night about the crop failure she had this summer with her beans — all the leaves chewed off by rabbits. Surely she wouldn't tell me about the beans if she were out to put me down with the peppers and cukes. The minute she told me about her beans, I no longer felt like a competitor as much as a fellow gardener, commiserating over our common verminous problems. And when I started explaining to her how she could keep the rabbits off by spraying her beans with Hinder, I felt like a father again, passing on what I've learned from my firsthand experience in the family garden.

But my gardening experience could hardly compare to what we saw this morning in an extensive series of dioramas, illustrating the geological, natural, and human evolution of Iowa. Dazzling scenes depicting the age of fish and the giant sloth and the earliest native settlements, all in vividly three-dimensional detail. But for me, the most interesting period was the late prehistoric age, when gardening first evolved, and gardening surplus made possible the emergence of stable human communities. Cache pits, drying racks, and the preservation of seeds — those were the sort of things that weighed heavy on the minds of prehistoric gardeners. Weightier matters, surely, than the size of Amelia's peppers compared to my own. But the preservation of seeds inevitably led to the creation of better strains and the development of better gardening methods. So, it seems, Amelia and I are connected to those prehistoric gardeners, like parents and children.

WEDNESDAY *August 9*

A better strain? Last night we had our first batch of home-grown corn — a new white hybrid named Argent, whose silvery name betokens its aspiration to displace Silver Queen as "the quality standard for white corn." A tall order, given that some breeders and testers consider Silver Queen to be the best corn of all. Every spring Kate asks me, "Are you going to grow me some Silver Queen?" And every year until recently I've grown her some, only to have much of it damaged by smut or squirrels or drought or storms before the ninety-five days it takes to mature. The longest span of any sweet corn. So, the last few years, I've been looking for an earlier version of Silver Queen, a corn as tasty, possibly even better. The holy grail of sweet corn. And lo! in one of this year's catalogues, I found the blurb of my desires — "Argent, an earlier Silver Queen . . . matures about a week ahead of Silver Queen, and is rated equal or better in taste by most testers: tender with great corn flavor." An irresistible claim, the clarion call that I and millions of gardeners have been longing to hear.

Now that I've harvested a batch and fed it to a discriminating group of testers — namely Kate, Amelia, Joseph, Marshall, Kathleen, Owen, and myself — I can report the following results. To begin with, it came to maturity in seventy-five days, almost three weeks earlier than Silver Queen, thanks no doubt to the four heat waves we've had this summer. Attractively filled-out cobs from one end to the other. "Very fine looking," according to Kate when she first saw it, "but the ears aren't quite as large, and the kernels aren't quite as white." Also "very tasty" said Kate after her first few bites of it, "very delicate" too, but "not quite as substantial." "One of the best I've ever had," according to Marshall. "This is wonderful, really wonderful" according to Amelia, as she devoured four ears, despite an upset stomach just a couple of hours before. "Very good," according to Joseph, who uses his adjectives sparingly. No comment from the children, who together ate three ears. As for me, I too consider it one of the best I've ever tasted — juicy, tender, delicate, sweet, but not quite as rich, not quite as full-bodied, not quite as chewy as Silver Queen.

So the Queen still reigns supreme. Or, as Kate said today with a knowing smile, "Nothing's as good as Silver Queen." But given her resistance to competitive ratings, she quickly added, "They're just different kinds of corn." Marshall, the great conciliator, also reminded me that "It's all a matter of taste, dad." And I agree. But given the choice between a long wait for a little Silver Queen, or a shorter time for a lot of Argent, I'd prefer Argent. And who knows, it might get even better with a few more days on the stalk. So I'm holding out for a few more days of testing. A better strain is surely worth the wait.

THURSDAY *August 10*

Though Argent is one of those long-lasting — "everlasting" — hybrids that hold several days on the stalk, the other summer vegetables are not holding back, not by a long shot. They're putting out growth and ripening fruit at extraordinary rates, even for this time of year. It's not just the heat we've been having — nineties again this week — but also the rain — another inch on Tuesday — and now all the humidity as well. And it's all showing up in the vegetables. Three dozen Walla Walla sweet onions, most of them a pound apiece, curing in the gazebo. A dozen pickling cucumbers a day for the past several days, waiting to be kosher-dilled. A dozen eggplants hanging on the two Ichibans, and another half dozen in the kitchen, waiting for Kate to turn them into baba ghanouj and poor man's caviar. Two dozen slicer tomatoes and three dozen plum-style tomatoes so fully ripe that Kate spent the afternoon canning, "sweating it out again" in the kitchen. And the Enchantment tomato plants that I topped a couple of weeks ago at seven and a half feet, overreaching themselves by another two feet of growth. So I trimmed them back again this morning and tied up a few more of their side shoots below, to keep the fruit coming through the fall. And so many yellow pattypans heaped up in the vegetable bins that Kate stuffed a bunch of them for dinner last night with a chili- and cumin-flavored mixture of rice, onions, green and red peppers, and sweet corn, baked in her homemade tomato sauce. My chicken thighs and legs, sautéed in a matching set of spices and herbs, and braised in wine and homemade tomato juice, were no match for her pattypans. No wonder Kathleen and

Marshall and Kate and I kept coming back for more of her stuff. But hardly anything's a match for what Kate can do with a batch of homegrown vegetables and herbs.

And nothing's a match for what's going on right now in her sixty-foot flower bed. Snow-on-the-mountain blooming from one end of the bed to the other, their sage- and white-edged leaves so vivid I can easily see each tall and branching clump of them, even though I'm sitting here some two hundred feet away in the attic. And the same is true of the black-eyed Susans alternating with the snow-on-the-mountain. The "cool colors of late summer," as Kate calls them, upstaging the "hot colors of midsummer" — the purple coneflowers and the fuchsia-toned lythrum now fading out, but still visible enough to create an interesting "conflict," especially from this vantage point. Now I only wish a cool front would make itself as prominent as those cool colors, but all the weather predictions call for a continuation of the heat wave at least through next Monday. Still, even the heat has its consolations, and not just in the vegetables, but also in the red seedless grapes that Kathleen discovered ripening just before she and Owen and Marshall left for Michigan. A sweet farewell.

FRIDAY *August 11*

The heat. It's not only ripening the grapes unevenly, but also bringing on the fall crop of red raspberries earlier than I expected. Yesterday, I picked the first two plump ones and gave them to Kate, even though she refused to close her eyes and open her mouth when I asked her to. Next week there should be enough for breakfast and desserts, and later for raspberry jam. A month early. Another sweet gift of the heat. But for everything given, it seems, something's been taken away. Though the Enchantment tomato plants are thriving in the heat, setting new fruit above and beyond the top of their poles, most of the slicer tomato plants — Big Beef, Black Prince, Brandywine, and Whopper — have been throwing their blossoms for almost a month. No wonder all the state newspapers have been commiserating with tomato gardeners. No wonder there were so few tomatoes at the farmers' market last week and the prices were so high. If the heat wave continues, there'll be relatively few slicers available the entire fall. The heat has also burned out the patio cherry tomatoes a few weeks earlier than usual, but the volunteer cherry tomatoes in the big garden have been coming on so strong, we'll probably have all we could want until frost. And a similar give-and-take is going on in the pepper patch. The Ace bells are so burdened with fruit that their branches are beginning to bend and break under the weight of it all. Proof of their reknowned ability to keep setting fruit in the heat, and the assurance of plenty for stuffing and eating fresh. But the Biscayne cubanelles and Ecuadorian rellenos have set only two dozen peppers all summer — and the Italian bullhorns none at all. So we'll not have the abundant supply for sautéing that we've had in the past. Probably the most extreme examples of give-and-take are the fall beans and beets I planted on the tenth of July, just a month ago. The beans are now blossoming and likely to bear fruit a week or two early, but the beets germinated badly and now are completely burned out. And the broccoli and Brussels sprouts and cauliflower and lettuce that I started in early July and transplanted in mid-July? Well, I've been shuffling them back and forth between the heat at the edge of the gazebo and the cool shade under the maple tree, trying to get them enough light without letting them get burned out by the heat. And the same is true for Pip and Phoebe and Kate and me. A little fresh air, a little sunlight, at the edges of the day, but mostly we're all surviving by staying inside in this air-conditioned house. And the house is sounding more and more like a nonstop jet flight, the hum of the blower incessantly recirculating the air as we make our way from morning to evening, July to August, summer to fall, world without end. The heat giveth, the heat taketh away. The snow-on-the-mountain bloometh, the speedwell fadeth away.

SATURDAY *August 12*

And the pickling continueth unabated. Yesterday afternoon, Kate filled a couple of half-gallon wine jugs with her home-made tarragon-shallot-white wine vinegar. A yearly ritual that usually also produces a couple of jugs of her basil-garlic-red wine vinegar. And now that I've put up twenty-one quarts of kosher dills — enough to keep this deli going for another year or two — she's dealing with the continuing crop of cucumbers. So many left even after I finished my tour of duty that they nearly filled up one of the big vegetable bins in the refrigerator. A slew of them are still forming and swelling on the vines, and blossoms galore still lure the bees. So this afternoon, she started work on a batch of her bread-and-butter pickles, slicing up the cucumbers and our small Dutch onions for an overnight brining process. Tomorrow, she'll rinse them and then give them the vinegar, sugar, and spice treatment (turmeric, mustard seed, celery seed, and ground cloves) that produces pickles so crisp and tasty they make the store-bought ones seem flabby and bland. She's also contemplating another cucumber pickle from an old Pennsylvania Dutch cookbook — a recipe that calls for a brew of olive oil, vinegar, black pepper, and mustard, but no other spices and no sugar at all. No sweet indulgences for those German immigrants. And she's been muttering about a seedless pickle relish, to go with the Indian curries I make during the winter. Necessity is the mother of invention, and the necessity of dealing with all those cucumbers has given birth to a flurry of pickling, the likes of which I haven't seen around these parts during the crop failures of the last two years. This afternoon, she also started work on a batch of pickled onions, to cope with the little onions that came from the Dutch yellow onion sets. And I can tell from a question she asked me at lunch — "How's the okra doing?" — that she's also thinking about doing something to them. Gumbo be damned — once she's in the pickling mode, everything's grist for her brine. So the kitchen's beginning to smell and look like a little pickle factory — crocks and jars on every counter. And the air conditioning's circulating the aroma up here to the attic, inspiring me with every sniff, and reminding me of her pickles past — the pickles of yesteryear. First, the month-long picklefests that left her dizzy with the smell of steaming brine. Then, the weekly pickle sales at the farmers' market that helped raise money for the neighborhood park. The dilly beans, yellow and green. The dilled carrot sticks, with and without the beans. The pickled beets, pickled peppers, pickled green tomatoes, pickled cherries, spiced crabapples. All the pickles of her childhood memories — even pickled peaches, the very thought of which seemed a desecration of that noble fruit, until I had them last Christmas with a roast leg of pork. A marriage so delicious, it made me imagine there must be a way of pickling every fruit and vegetable, until I thought of lettuce.

SUNDAY *August 13*

"When are you going to dig the potatoes?" Kate's question took me by surprise, because I didn't know she'd been watching the potatoes closely enough to notice their tops had died back and they were ready for digging. But then I remembered her asking me to grow them again this spring, especially the new fingerling-size potatoes. So, yesterday morning, I dug the buried treasure, eager to see if they actually looked like Giant Peanut Fingerlings, three to four inches long. I shoved my garden fork in the ground, at a distance from the dried tops, not wanting to spear any of the fingerlings with a tine. The soil turned over easily, still a bit moist from the recent rain, and there they all were — peanut-shaped all right. But so small they looked like midget peanuts, no more than an inch or an inch and a half long. Not to worry, I thought. Just a result of being a bit shaded by the pin oak tree. So I moved to the next spot and eagerly turned over the soil, only to find another handful of midgets. And another, and another. And so few potatoes, the whole batch of eight plants yielded no more than two or three meals' worth. The six red potato plants produced a somewhat better yield. Still, I felt as if the Irish potato famine had been replayed right in my own back yard. But when Kate saw the midget fingerlings, she reminded me of how bad the weather's been, and then told me they'd make a fine potato salad for dinner, lightly steamed and dressed with a vinaigrette and fresh chopped herbs. And they did make a fine salad, intense with the earthy taste condensed within their little skins. A perfect companion to the charcoal broiled marlin, as well as the fresh sliced peppers and tomatoes. The cooked and the raw.

A memorable meal, especially given the silent presence of Phoebe curled up just a few feet away in the bottom of the antique wooden dry sink, where she's been holing up the past few days,

calmly taking her leave of us. Barely eating anything, not even a
scrap of marlin she'd have squawked for just a few months ago. But
purring every evening when she curls up on the tambour between
us in the TV room and we pet her gently. And sleeping every night
on the terrace. A night owl still. And greeting me each morning
with the single squawk for which she got her name. Her eyes
bright, but her body gaunt, and the suffering sure to come. So the
indecisions and revisions about when and how to help her out —
Monday? Or Tuesday? At the vet's? Or some other way? Until
suddenly, it seemed, we were talking about where to bury her on
the lot, and Kate resolved it all at once. "I think we should take her
in first thing Monday morning, and before we go you should dig a
hole behind the old apple tree, in that depression of land where
the rabbit warren used to be. Remember the rabbits she used to
catch out there? She'll be right at home. And it won't damage the
tree, because it's dying too." So tomorrow first thing, I'm digging a
hole for Phoebe, right where the rabbits used to be.

MONDAY *August 14*

Six-thirty in the morning, the sun not yet above the trees, but
the air still heavy and warm from the lingering heat wave. A
long way from the snowy day in January when we learned
that Phoebe had an incurable tumor, and I thought we'd lose her,
just like the others, before the ground had thawed enough to bury
her on the back lot. On my way out to dig the hole, I hear her
squawk, see her coming toward the porch, let her in the back door,
and pick her up to pet her, but she's intent on curling up again in
the bottom of the dry sink. Taking her leave, in her own fashion.
So I go to the gazebo, gather up a spade, a shovel, and the pillow
from her sleeping basket, put them in the big black wheelbarrow,
and wheel my way up to the chosen spot behind the apple tree.
With the pillow on the grass to guide me, I spade out a rectangle of
sod, two feet long, one foot wide, and set it under a nearby yew.
To the right of the bush, I suddenly notice all the magic lilies,
risen from the ground, lavender pink flowers atop their tall green
leafless stalks — naked ladies as they're sometimes called around

these parts — standing among the white blooming hosta lilies. A quiet place, off the beaten track. Then back to dig the hole, shoveling the soil into the wheelbarrow. Jim told me yesterday that "Two foot's deep enough to stop anything from digging her up. I've got some of my own buried up here like that, and they've never been bothered." Two feet deep, easy as pie, like doing the dwarf sweet cherry tree this spring, except I didn't figure on running into broken bricks and stone a foot down. And I didn't figure on breaking into a heavy sweat a little farther down. Deep enough, I think, lest I turn into a job for some other gravedigger. Then back in for breakfast and some time with Phoebe, an hour or so until the vet will be done with her morning surgery. Then the quick drive over with Kate — Phoebe in the basket with the towel we'll wrap her in, both of us petting her all the way, assuring ourselves we're doing the right thing. A few minutes alone in the examining room, then the vet with her assistant, then all of us petting Phoebe. Then the shot going slowly in her leg, Kate holding her head and shoulders, saying, "There she goes." The eyes clouding over, the legs going limp, the body collapsing in the arms of the vet and her assistant — so calmly, so swiftly, a wave of relief sweeps over me and "Thank you" heaves out of my mouth. Then the vet wraps her carefully in the towel and the tears come welling up. Then the quick drive home and Kate carrying the basket to the spot and I lifting her out and into the bottom of the hole and Kate hefting two shovelfuls of soil over her and I filling in the rest. Gently tamping it, then watering it like the cherry tree, then replacing the sod, and gently tamping it down. There's a hump there now, and some gaps around the edges, as there always is when the soil's disturbed, but Kate says that in time the hump will sink and the grass grow back until we hardly know it's there at all.

TUESDAY *August 15*

No sooner had we buried her than both of us hustled around, getting rid of all the visible reminders — her water bowl, her food bowl, her dry food, her canned food, her pills, her sleeping pillow. As if we could put her out of mind by putting her things out of sight. But no sooner had we gone out to lunch to repair our spirits than we were talking about her again. And again at bedtime, Kate cutting to the quick. "Do you realize that no one will ever look at you that way again? And no one ever chirp at you that way again?" Kate was talking about "the mystery of her spirit," of anyone's spirit, and the irrevocability of its passing. "Here one second, gone the next." I as usual react in somewhat more sentimental terms. The squawk is ended but the melody lingers on. I could hear it this morning, the minute I went out to check on things in the gazebo. But it was just the macaw next door, screeching to be fed. And I could hear it again when I went to pick cucumbers, and our neighbor's cat went scuttering through the leaves. So I went out to the hump and walked around its edges, just to firm it up a bit before the rain we were supposed to get today. Nothing like rain to water things in. And nothing like a change of subject to get one's mind off things.

A temporary cool front moved in yesterday afternoon and will be here for a day or so before the next heat wave predicted for Thursday or Friday. So, right before dinner, I trimmed up the basil seedlings I've been tending for the past couple of months and finally planted eighteen of them along the front of the large vegetable bed. Enough for ourselves and some postfrost sales to the co-op. And I gave them a good soaking, given my gloomy view of our chances for rain. I also checked on the month-old lettuce seedlings I started last month, only to discover that a little green worm, like a cabbage worm, had chewed up most of their tender central leaves in just a couple of days under the grow-lights. A new kind of loss for me. So I'm about to start another batch of lettuce, this time for fall rather than late summer, and the minute they're up I'll dust them with Dipel, the organic bacterial deterrent of cabbage worms.

No sooner had I come inside after that loss than Kate asked me how the Brussels sprouts were doing, and I had to report that they too had been devoured during the past few days, so I'm down to just the broccoli and cauliflower seedlings. "Aren't we going to have a fall garden — no leeks, no turnips, no beets?" Not if the heat wave comes back for another two-week scourge. Still, there's nothing like a challenge — and the veiled threat of alien produce from the co-op or the farmers' market — to spur me on. So during the next few days I'm springing into action for fall. Transplanting the broccoli and cauliflower seedlings, starting bok choy and lettuce seedlings, planting beets, radishes, spinach, and turnips. And hoping for better things to come.

WEDNESDAY *August 16*

I hadn't seen my colleague Linda since the Fourth of July, when she was still learning her way around a vegetable garden. But yesterday, when I saw her in the English department office, she momentarily seemed larger than life, as if she'd been growing all summer long, right along with the crops she's been raising. Maybe it was the large bag of vegetables she had in hand — yellow patty-pans, green zucchini, and cubanelle-shaped Gypsy peppers as colorful as their name. Or maybe it was her generosity in offering them to the secretaries and anyone else who came by, including me. I was tempted by those Gypsy peppers, especially given my own puny crop of cubanelles and bullhorns. Looking at Linda's ample crop of Gypsies, I remembered growing them several years ago myself, when they first came out — an "All-American winner" and deservedly so. Crisp, tasty, and abundant. But after a few seasons, I was lured away by the Biscayne cubanelle, a longer and, I imagined, more abundant variety, even though the catalogue made no promises on that score. I also remembered being seduced by the Italian bullhorn-shaped peppers, especially Corno di Toro, father of all the bullhorns. Had I been paying closer attention to the maturation times — sixty-five days from setting out plants for Gypsy, eighty days for Corno di Toro — maybe I'd have had second thoughts about the matter. Especially since an eighty-day pepper usually does most of its blossoming right at the peak of our summer heat waves, when sweet peppers refuse to set fruit. No wonder I've had such trouble with those bullhorns, compared to my fifty-day Aces. But it wasn't until I looked into Linda's bag that I began to make sense of the problem. So much depends on a chance encounter and the run of one's memory.

Like the spectacle of Pip parked right outside the dry sink where

Phoebe spent her last five days. Or the paw prints I saw this morning on the dusty Plexiglas door of the outside cellarway where Phoebe was standing just a few mornings ago. Ghostly reminders of how right Jim was when I told him Phoebe's age. "Twenty years! That's like family. Like family. It'll be hard." Rebecca also took it hard this morning when she saw the hump behind the apple tree. She came to work just when I was beginning to transplant the broccoli, in the overcast and drizzles of the past two days — a good time for transplanting. But she quickly reminded me that the temperature's predicted to go back up to the mid-nineties tomorrow and stay there through Saturday. Not a good time for transplanting or starting any cool-weather crops. So I put aside the broccoli and turned my attention to weeding the garden, deadheading the marigolds, trimming the onion tops, cleaning up the gazebo. So much depends on a chance encounter.

THURSDAY *August 17*

This morning on my way from watering the peppers and tomatoes to soaking the red raspberries on the other side of the yard, I couldn't help noticing the colorful display in Kate's flower border. Especially the vividness and height of things in its late summer phase. Snow-on-the-mountain much snowier than it was just a week ago — so intensely white I hardly noticed its sagey lower leaves. Lythrum surprisingly colorful up close — more intensely fuchsia-colored than it seems from my distant view in the attic. Hardly fading out so much as I imagined, else it wouldn't be aswarm with cabbage moths, butterflies, and bees. And the purple spider flowers a striking two-tone combination of purple and white. Up to my neck in height, like the lythrum and snow-on-the-mountain. Tall enough to make me feel as if I were on the verge of walking into a stand of prairie wildflowers, and well I might have been, given so many hybridized versions of them in Kate's bed. The goldenrod, the three varieties of black-eyed Susan, the purple coneflowers, their big copper-green cones glistening in the sun. Standing there at the edge of Kate's border, I felt again the admiration — and the envy — of a compulsive vegetable gardener. Admiration for the striking colors, textures, and shapes, for the repetitions and variations from back to front, one end of the bed to the other — four different kinds of rudbeckia on display against a backdrop of lythrum, snow-on-the-mountain, and spider flowers. Even in my most contrived structuring of the big vegetable bed, I've never been able to achieve something quite so formally intricate as Kate's display. And whatever I'm able to devise, I have to start anew each year. My materials are perishable, hers perennial, and therein lies the source of my envy.

Or maybe it would be more accurate to say my vegetables are fragile, vulnerable — and not just because they're annuals, but also because they're more at risk of attack from animals and insects. Just this noon, on the way to getting a tomato and onion for lunch, I discovered once again how vulnerable things are in my garden, when I noticed one of the two yellow pattypan plants suddenly in a deep wilt, despite being as erect, floriferous, and fruit-covered as its mate just a few hours earlier. I'd watered it and dusted it with rotenone just this morning, just like the other one, but now it was gone. So I cut it off, bisected its main stem, like a plant pathologist, and there I found what I expected — the hatched-out borer that had secretly been chewing its way up and down the main channel, invisibly sapping life from the plant until it had nothing left but to collapse in the ninety-five-degree heat of the noonday sun. I gave it a proper burial in the compost pile and went in for lunch, hungering for the years that bring the philosophic mind.

FRIDAY *August 18*

"Years that bring the philosophic mind" — a line from Wordsworth that I hadn't thought about for some twenty-five years, and suddenly there it was yesterday afternoon when I was writing about the demise of my yellow pattypan plant. I never expected that Wordsworth's poetry would come to mind at that moment, and I imagine that Wordsworth himself would probably have been a bit dismayed to hear me invoking his great ode about immortality and mortality on the occasion of my expiring pattypan. But the mind has a strange way of taking its own course, especially my own. To make matters even stranger, I then began to wonder how long it would take me to achieve the philosophic mind. Not the kind of speculation my college English professors would have indulged in me some forty years ago, for literature, as they taught it, was concerned with great ideas and great cultural traditions — not with the immediate circumstances of one's own life. But I've been on my own for so long, I couldn't resist the temptation of wondering what it takes to attain a philosophic mind. And suddenly, as if out of nowhere, popped my aunt Ada. Actually, she's not my aunt — she's my mother's first cousin — but she might just as well have been my aunt, given the weekends she lavished on me after my mother died. She's also my oldest living relative — ninety-four years old this month — old enough to have attained a philosophic mind. She already seemed philosophic when Kate and I attended a celebration of her ninetieth birthday, four years ago this weekend, a weekend just as witheringly hot as this one. But it wasn't just the heat and her age and her wry wit that got me thinking about aunt Ada yesterday and today. It was also the three-vegetable dinners she always served me on those weekends long ago. Beans, potatoes, and tomatoes, or carrots, potatoes, and peas, or some other combination, so lovingly and deliciously prepared I could hardly resist them. Oh yes, there was always a tasty meat dish and a scrumptious dessert, but those vegetables come to mind right now, because Kate and I have been eating so many meals with three or more vegetables — and not just at dinner. A couple of days ago for lunch, I made thin-sliced vegetable sandwiches of tomatoes, cucumbers, and sweet onions with sliced cheese and our own homemade mayonnaise on whole wheat bread from our neighbor Marybeth, served with sliced pickles from the first jar of kosher dills. And yesterday for lunch, Kate and I had smoked trout on melba toast with fresh tomatoes, sliced green peppers, and chopped purple onions from the garden. Three vegetable meals so tasty I wish Aunt Ada could travel here to enjoy them. But at least I can call and tell her about them and also send her my written recollections of them — those three-vegetable meals that bring the philosophic mind.

SATURDAY *August 19*

In the midst of a summer-long heat wave, neither the consolations of philosophy nor the satisfactions of a three-vegetable meal are quite so comforting as a breezy cool front that lowers the temperature from the mid-nineties to the mid-seventies. The breeze arrived this morning, as if on command, just when I was hanging my aloha shirts out to dry in the four corners of the gazebo. But the heat wave's scheduled to return in a day or two. So I hustled around, picking cucumbers and okra, weeding the river rock at the top of the driveway, dousing the broccoli and cucumber seedlings, cultivating Kate's flower border to conserve the water I soaked it with yesterday morning, tying up the tomato plants and firming up their stakes to support the heavy load of fruit they're now carrying.

Looking at the Enchantments just then, I was momentarily transfixed. I stood and stared at them, laden with egg-shaped fruit from the bottom to the top of their poles — and a foot beyond in midair. But gazing, after all, is never enough. Then I wanted to know exactly how many tomatoes they've produced — a type-A kind of yearning I forswore after my heart attack. Yet the spectacle of all those plump tomatoes — most of them three inches long, two inches wide, dangling from the vine in clusters of four, five, or six fruits a bunch — weakened my resolve, though not so completely that I became obsessive about the counting. I counted the fruit on only one of the five Enchantment vines and multiplied by five to reach an approximate total of the yield. Well, the fruit on that plant was so honeycombed around the vine and in the tangle of stems above the pole that it was impossible to get a full count without prying into the clusters and possibly damaging or breaking off the fruit. So all I could say for sure is that one of the plants has produced at least one hundred twenty-five tomatoes. By extrapolation, I figure that the five plants have produced at least six hundred twenty-five tomatoes, not counting the three dozen that Kate canned last week, and the three dozen or so we've eaten over the past month, for a grand total of at least seven hundred tomatoes in all. An impressive yield in any year, but especially this

summer when homegrown tomatoes are in short supply. So impressive I was just on the verge of agreeing with a garden columnist
who recently proclaimed that a tomato plant's "beauty is in its
bounty." But then I gazed again at the vines, surrounding the poles
like garlands of dark green leaves, sprinkled with starlike yellow
blossoms, and entwined with clusters of Fabergé eggs — red, or-
ange-red, orange, pale green — and they seemed quite beautiful
just as they were. A vivid spectacle, and a reminder that beauty,
after all, is not the same as bounty, except in a mercenary view of
things. Then again, I'd hardly disagree with Kate's enthusiasm for
the plumpness, meatiness, juiciness, piquancy, peelability, uni-
formity, and abundance of the Enchantments she's canning right
now. Sometimes, after all, beauty and bounty do go hand in hand.

SUNDAY *August 20*

The more I think about it, the more bothered I am by that
columnist's maxim about the tomato plant — "Its beauty is
in its bounty, and its scraggly foliage is a badge of honor." It's
meant, I realize, to put gardeners at ease about the curled and
blighty foliage that tomato plants often develop this time of year.
But it puts so much emphasis on the productivity of vegetable
plants that it seems to ignore their natural beauty. And not just in
that remark, but in this one too — "Your tomato plant is a work
horse, not a show horse. Some general ugliness in the midsummer
vegetable garden is inevitable." Though I don't think of my vegetable plants as show horses, I do believe that a healthy, well-tended
vegetable plant has a shape, color, texture, and habit that's as
showy and captivating as any of the plants in Kate's flower border. Just this morning when I was watering the peppers again, I
stopped to look at the Ichiban eggplant bushes, their dark purple
stems branching upward and outward, their purple-veined leaves
reaching upward and outward, their light purple blossoms and
dark purple fruits hanging downward — every part of them so
colorfully coordinated and balanced they seemed like studies in
purple. Except for the striking contrast of their olive-colored
leaves. The eggplant, of course, is one of the most ornamental

bushes in the world of vegetables. But even the lowly cucumber vines have a visible appeal. Even now when they're stressed out from the heat and from a month of pumping out a dozen fruit a day, their dark green leaves still float above their bright yellow blossoms and dark green fruit below, somewhat like waterlilies. But improperly planted and tended, as mine were last year, they're a sorry sight, and fruitless too. If the plants themselves are potentially beautiful, why should I believe that "some general ugliness . . . is inevitable" in my garden? George Washington evidently didn't put up with ugliness in his neoclassical vegetable garden at Mount Vernon. My colleague Keith from the art department didn't put up with ugliness in the circular vegetable garden he created so long ago — a mandala of pie-shaped wedges with companionable herbs and vegetables at every point in the circle. And I've never felt free to put up with ugliness, ever since Kate carefully framed the big rectangular vegetable bed with a border of antique bricks some twenty-five years ago. I've noticed, in fact, that whenever my vegetable plants seem to approach their greatest potential beauty, they also produce an extraordinary bounty, like the Enchantment tomatoes this year.

But maybe I'm just huffing and puffing about form and function in the vegetable garden, because I'm getting myself in the mood to start teaching again this week, and my leaves are feeling a bit scraggly from forty years of fretting about form and function in my students' writing. Even so, I'm not willing to believe that ugliness is inevitable — either in my gardening or in my teaching.

MONDAY *August 21*

"Pretty soon I'll be wearing socks, and you know what that means." Rebecca was pointing at her rope-sandaled feet just to make sure I didn't miss the drift of her remark. Actually, the air was still so cool when we were talking this morning — still in the upper fifties — it was all I needed to remind me of the changing weather, the turning season, the chillier days to come. Still, both of us were a bit puzzled by the up-and-down temperatures we've been having the past several days, trying to figure out when to seed in our fall vegetables. Both of us were worried about the spinach being bitter if it germinated in hot weather, yet both of us worried about missing the best season if we didn't get it in soon. All I needed to convince me was Rebecca's count of the days from seeding to picking the first batch of fall spinach. "Forty-two days it takes at least, and that's early October." Not even the thought of my row covers could justify a delay. The covers don't work without a crop to cover. And just a bit later, Kate weighed in with a report from her sleepless, hayfeverish night — "All night long I heard the crickets. They're mating, getting ready to die."

What a haunting time of year this is — so full with the abundance of high summer heat that Kate picked almost a bushel of Big Beef slicers to can from just four tomato plants, yet so full with harbingers of the cold to come that I know there won't be enough time to ripen any new fruit they set just a week from now. A pivotal time not only in the garden but also in my life, as I was reminded again last night at our first departmental meeting of the fall semester, when our new chair, Dee, announced, "We'll be saying farewell this year to a couple of our distinguished senior colleagues." After the meeting, I talked with my colleague Jix, who's also retiring this year, and we both were struck by the feeling of estrangement in a department that once felt like home. So few of us, so many of them, I suddenly felt like a late summer tomato in an early spring garden. But maybe the distance arose from differences of interest. Both of us are known for our work in nonfiction writing, while most of our colleagues specialize in some kind of literary or cultural theory. Maybe that's why the only others who came up to chat with me were also in nonfiction writing. David, just a few years younger than I, congratulated me on beginning my last year of teaching. Patricia, some twenty years younger, was curious about my plans for the future. I talked about the possibility of keeping a hand in, of teaching a course every fall. But listening to myself just then, it didn't seem as if I was all that hot about the prospect. Only fifty-some days to the first killing frost, and I'm not sure I want to spend it in a classroom — not with all the fruit I've got set, waiting to ripen on the vine.

TUESDAY *August 22*

I was standing by the photocopying machine, making handouts for my course, when she came into the office, plomped down on a chair, pulled off her sunglasses, and looked at me as if she were on the verge of tears. My gardening colleague Linda — so buoyant just a week ago, like the yellow pattypans she'd been giving away in the office, but now suddenly depressed. Dressed in a pair of black slacks and a black overshirt, as if in mourning. And she was. "It's my squash plants, the pattypans and zucchini. Nineteen out of twenty suddenly dead, just like that, just a day after I saw you." I've never grown so many squash plants, so I've never had such a massive die-off. But I know what it looks like when their elephant-ear leaves collapse. I saw it again on Sunday, when I checked the garden at noon, and discovered the wilt in a large section of my one remaining pattypan. And I know the panicky feeling that wells up in me whenever I see that wilt, or a limp cucumber vine, or a deer-bitten tomato, or a woodchucked cantaloupe, or a squirreled-up ear of corn. It's the fear of losing control, the terror that anything and everything might suddenly go wrong, and there's nothing I can do about it. When I told that to Linda, it was just what she needed to hear. "That's exactly how I felt, how I feel, like my whole garden's at risk, out of control." I asked her if she had cut open one of the plants, just to get a clear view of the enemy, the squash vine borer, chomping its way through the inner core of the stalk. "It's so bad I can't even stand to go out and look at the place." I asked her if she'd been keeping the plants dusted. "I did, until there weren't any more bugs in sight." Finally, I had the answer to her problem, and suddenly I felt like a gardening consultant and therapist, explaining to her that the squash vine borer's not a one-time threat, but a summer-long menace, so the main stalk has to be kept dusted all the time, and sometimes even that's not enough as I know from my own pattypan plant, but I learn what I can from the losses and try not to let them get me down as bad as they used to. That little bit of advice brought such a smile to her face, and such words of acceptance, that I momentarily thought I had found my calling, my postretirement career. I could be a therapist, specializing in the treatment of depressed vegetable gardeners! I could help others to cope with anxiety, insecurity, loss, and the other stresses that arise from trying to contend with the uncontrollable forces of nature. A new mission that inspired me all the way home, until I walked in the back door and found Kate standing in the kitchen, her cheeks flushed, her hair limp from a morning in the neighborhood park. She'd been watering the drought-stricken annual bed that I'm supposed to take care of, but when she tried to turn off the faucet, the spigot came off in her hand, and a gusher came right in her face. "Like a broken fire hydrant." As I listened to her story and looked into her eyes, it occurred to me that she didn't need any therapy just then, except for me to make lunch quick and keep my mouth shut.

WEDNESDAY *August 23*

Another segment of my remaining pattypan bit the dust this morning, but this time it wasn't the borer's dastardly work. It was the gardener's sloppy hand, or, to be exact, the watering wand extending from his hand that inadvertently got hooked onto the stem and ripped away its tenuous connection to the main stalk. So I now have another opportunity to practice my gardening therapy, this time on myself. Physician, heal thyself. Well, it's not the first time I've done in a plant when I've been trying to do it some good, and it probably won't be the last. I guess it's just one of those paradoxical aspects of gardening — and living. Sometimes we tend things to death. Besides, the main stalk is still alive, and might turn out to be more vigorous and productive without being sapped by the segment I did in this morning. And even if the plant doesn't become more fruitful, it'll probably bear more pattypans than we can use, especially given the three zucchini plants and the volunteer squash plant still healthy and pumping stuff out. It wouldn't have happened, of course, if I'd been more attentive. But it was one of those long mornings in the garden — from seven-thirty until noon, except for a brief drive to one of the gardening stores. And my mind was drifting, carried away by all the emblems of the turning season. The suntanned coed by the bus stop, dressed for campus success, in a dark brown skirt and an olive drab overshirt, with a cigarette dangling from her lips. The garden store stocked for success, with bulbs for fall planting and birdseed for winter feeding. The flower border stripped for success, airier than it's been since early June, in the wake of Rebecca's recent dead-heading and trimming of all the midsummer plants. Spider flowers fading, their seed pods swelling. Snow-on-the-mountain glimmering with fireflies, one atop the other, mating on the snowy leaves, as if to remind themselves of the coming winter. Jim out by his garage, repainting and recamouflaging his duck blind, his mind on the fall hunting season. Kate gone to Lone Tree, southeast of here, picking up a dozen farm-raised chickens to carry us through the winter, the farm wife killing and dressing them all the while I'd been out in the yard. And I? Watering the flower border to encourage the fall bloom, watering the red raspberries to swell the fall crop, watering the tomatoes to set some more fruit. And checking on the flats of fall lettuce I seeded up yesterday, pulling up the summer beans and planting the fall spinach in their place, buying beet and bok choy and purple-top turnip seed to be planted tomorrow. And thinking about everything coming full circle — the spinach seeded in where the spinach carried over last winter, the raspberries fruiting up that I pruned and transplanted last spring, and the sun arcing lower in the sky so that now in late afternoon the entire south side of the yard is in shade, as it was in late April, when the early spring garden was just taking hold. So much happening, so much on my mind, it's no wonder I did in the pattypan.

THURSDAY *August 24*

"And you haven't missed a single day? Or just skipped one?" My colleague Jim had asked me what I was working on when I encountered him at the co-op yesterday, expecting, I think, that he'd hear about my book on the personal essay, or some other academic project. So when I told him about keeping this daybook, this gardening memoir, his eyes lit up with surprise. But his eyebrows went up and those questions popped out when I told him that I write a 500-to-600-word piece every day and revise it before bedtime, so I'm ready for the next day the minute I get out of bed. And this morning after class, I got almost the same look and the same incredulous question, in unison, from Ellen and Marilyn, two graduate students from last semester, studying with me once again, both of them wondering about the daybook. "And you still haven't missed a day!" If they were the only ones to question my behavior, I could probably dismiss it as just a temperamental difference. But right from the start my relatives and friends and acquaintances have raised their eyebrows or given me some well-meaning advice about the dailyness of it all. I distinctly remember my brother Marshall, asking me one night on the telephone, "Every day?" And my colleague David, suggesting early on that "You needn't feel obliged to write one every single day. Occasionally, you might just skip a few days, just to break the rhythm a bit. You know what I mean — it's the kind of liberty that most contemporary writers feel free to take." But something in me didn't feel free to take it just then. Nor did I feel free to take it a few months later when I was talking on the phone with Trudy, who gently told me, "Don't be upset with yourself if you miss a day now and then." Nor did I feel free a month ago, when my retired colleague Don invited me to a poker game, and I had to beg off because of this daily commitment. Don put the question in its most challenging form — "Why can't you just skip a day?" Given that compelling question, I've been wondering myself why I can't just skip a day. Is it just a compulsion, or an addiction, that I can't let go of it for a single day? Perhaps it is. But then again whenever I ponder the question of why I can't skip a day, the answer always seems inescapable. The sun doesn't skip a day, the vegetables don't skip a day, Kate doesn't skip a day, and Pip doesn't skip a day. Only Phoebe has been skipping days, and not, God knows, by her own choice. So how could I possibly fail to seize this day — or any other? The fall crop of wax beans was ready to pick, and two pattypans were ready to cut, and the fall crop of arugula had just begun to sprout, and the heat was plain oppressive when I walked down to teach, and Kate was just beginning to compose a seven-vegetable salad when I got back home for lunch.

FRIDAY *August 25*

Sometimes the daily grind of the garden is harder to take than this daybook. Especially right now, when I'm trying to get the fall vegetables started at the same time that I'm trying to get my fall course underway. Seedlings on the one hand, students on the other. And the weather's too hot for all of them. Too hot and stuffy in the classroom, too hot and humid in the garden. But the salad greens are continuing to sprout, as they must, if they're going to produce a good crop by October — endive and green leaf lettuce today to go with the arugula that showed up yesterday. I've been hovering over the seedlings, trying to get them enough sun lest they quickly turn leggy, but without burning them out in the ninety degree blaze we've been having the past three days and are scheduled to keep having the next several days as well. And it's not just the heat that I'm up against in the garden. It's the drought as well. Just an inch or so of rain the past month, during a period when we ordinarily have four or five inches. Heat and drought so persistent that lawns all over town are turning brown during a period when they ordinarily begin to green up. And the soil is turning hard during a period when it usually begins to soften up. This morning, for the first time since the droughts of the late 1980s, I spent some time watering strips of bare ground in the big garden, so I can loosen the soil enough in the next few days to make it ready for planting the beets, bok choy, and turnips. And next week, I suppose, I'll have to water some more bare ground to make it ready for the fall radishes.

Even under the best of circumstances, it's a challenge to launch the fall garden. Hard to summon the energy again after a spring and summer of planting and tending the crops. Harder still to envision the coolness and moistness to come in the midst of a late summer heat wave and drought so persistent as this one. So intimidating and frustrating it puts me in mind of the Garden Game, a British board game I played with my son Marshall and my granddaughter Kathleen, the night before they left. "The object of the game is for each player to plant seed packets in his or her garden until the garden is full, with plants that do best together."

But after an hour of playing it, neither Marshall nor Kathleen nor I had a single packet in our gardens, because we kept landing on the wrong squares — Weeds, Bad Weather, Soil Too Hard to Dig, You Tread on Wrong End of Rake, August Drought, all of which force one to Lose a Seed Packet. And when we weren't losing a seed packet, we were losing our entire gardens to an Act of God card. So we gave up the game in frustration. I've not yet given up on the fall garden — it's still too early in the game to do that. But I sure am doing some heavy imaging exercises right now, trying to remember how crisp and tasty the lettuce and radishes were last fall.

SATURDAY *August 26*

U p early this morning to play the fall gardening game. I've decided to think of it as a game, because that way my competitive instincts might be roused enough to continue this absurd venture of trying to sustain vegetables that thrive on temperatures between fifty-five and seventy-five in a climate that's presently running highs between ninety and ninety-five. So the object of the game is to defy nature, to garden against the odds — to get as many cool-weather vegetables planted and germinated as possible in the midst of a heat wave, and to keep them growing and thriving until the heat wave breaks and the weather cools, assuming, of course, that it will. Though the game has just begun, I'm already scoring points. This morning, my flats of escarole and oak leaf lettuce were covered with new sprouts. Together with the others that have already come up, I now have five flats of different greens underway, and I'm waiting only for the buttercrunch and Carmona butterheads to pop before I start transplanting the seedlings to their individual slots in the plastic four-packs and six-packs. I also scored points this morning when I discovered that the spinach I seeded in the garden on Wednesday had already begun to emerge. Just a few shiny green sprouts so far, but I'm keeping them watered and lightly covered with straw, to keep them as cool as possible. Kate wants me to spray them with Hinder, but they're still so small I can't believe the deer will ever find them under the straw.

The game is so new I'm still uncertain about whether or not to award myself bonus points for special efforts to ensure the crop, like Hindering the spinach or soaking the beet seeds overnight in a bowl of tepid water, to soften them up before I planted them this morning. But it sure was a mess to handle all those wet seeds — harder, I think, than trying to keep my eyes on the little turnip seeds that I planted in the other half of the row. By comparison, it seemed easy to seed up a row of two dozen bok choy plants. Still, it was already so hot and sticky the whole time I was putting things in that I couldn't help thinking wistfully of spring, when it wouldn't have been necessary to soak the beet seeds, or cover the rows with straw, or make believe I was playing a game.

Actually, it didn't feel like a real game without competitors. So I looked for Jim, but couldn't find him. Then I called Rebecca several times without any luck, and I figured she too must be out starting her fall garden. But when I finally got in touch with her after dinner this evening, she was so depressed about the weather she could barely stand to talk about it. "My ground's like concrete. The contractors say it's dry as dust three and a half feet down. We need rain, professor, and we need it bad." Listening to Rebecca, it didn't feel like a game at all. It suddenly felt all too real, like a reminder of the droughts we went through in '88 and '89, like a sample of what the East Coast has been going through all summer long, like a taste of what's been going on along the Rio Grande and in southern Spain for longer than I can bear to remember.

SUNDAY *August 27*

"Just look at them all out there. Look through the binoculars. I feel like I've done my good deed for the day." Kate had just come in from filling the birdbath beneath the walnut tree, and the edge of it was already ringed with sparrows, waiting to splash in the center. A lunchtime spree. Actually, the bird bathing started in midmorning when I went out for another round of watering. Emergency measures to stop the cucumbers from going bitter, the thyme from burning out, the red raspberries from shriveling up. After ringing the raspberry patch with a soaker hose, I came in to cool off for a while, and immediately noticed a clutch of lady cardinals on the terrace, bathing in a shallow pool of water that had collected below a leaky hose joint. A strange sight, given the fiercely territorial behavior of cardinals. Once the cardinals got wind of it, the word must have gone out to all the feathery precincts. An hour or so later, Kate and I noticed a colony of sparrows gathered in the same spot — so many, so obviously desperate for water, that she immediately went out to fill the birdbath. Before this morning, neither of us had been aware that the birds were in trouble, for they hadn't shown up to drink from the lily pond or bathe in the water from the hose.

The birds and the crops have evidently reached a point of critical need, all at the same time. How else to account for some of the cucumbers being bitter despite my keeping them watered once or twice a week? And the thyme turning brown despite being watered just a few weeks ago, despite its ability to thrive on the dry, stony hillsides of Italy and Greece? And the raspberries shriveling despite my weekly waterings and a four-inch mulch of composted cow manure? Telltale signs of drought, when the topsoil and the subsoil are so dry they behave like a wick, soaking up whatever moisture comes their way or comes nearby. Watering in the midst of such conditions, as I discovered during the late eighties, is at best a mere holding action, at worst a futile activity. Like trying to fill a rat hole with sand. Only a full-scale rain — preferably a long, gentle soaker — can fill all the pores of ground so dry as ours has now become.

And only a rain together with a cool front is likely to fill the yards again with the sounds of human life. I've been vaguely aware of the silence, of the absence, the past few mornings, but a question from Kate made me think about it more directly than before. "Did you see anybody outside this morning?" No one this morning, or come to think of it any other time this week, except for Wednesday when I saw Jim working on his duck blind. What a strange thing it is to look out at our back yard right now and all the yards around — filled with flowers and vegetables and fruit trees and shade trees, all the signs of human habitation and intention. And not a single soul in sight. Like a science fiction nightmare — or dream — of what the earth might suddenly look like bereft of human beings.

MONDAY *August 28*

"Everyone's gone to the air-conditioned malls," according to Kate. Or they're holed up in their air-conditioned homes like us, pickling and eating our way through the record breaking temperatures and humidities of this lingering heat wave. Two days ago, Kate filled a half-gallon wine jug with her homemade basil-garlic–red wine vinegar — two large cloves of garlic and a whole stalk of basil leaves resplendent in the crimson brew. Then we divvied up a vegetable bin full of pickling cucumbers, and she started work on a batch of her family's garlic–grape leaf dills. A crisp, no-nonsense pickle, chilled overnight in cold water, then packed in pint jars and processed in a brine of cider vinegar, distilled water, kosher salt, and alum — each jar decked out with one large clove of garlic, a sprig or two of dill, a small dried hot red pepper, and one large grape leaf from our vines. And yesterday, given my ceaseless commitment to perfecting the salt-brined kosher dill, I put up another four quarts of them, this time reducing the salt measure slightly from two tablespoons per quart to one and five sixths tablespoons, in order to compensate for a slightly excessive saltiness in the first two quarts we've eaten during the past two weeks. But just now, in the interests of scientific curiosity, I ran downstairs to sample a jar from the second batch of dills, and it seemed to me that the slightly excessive saltiness might be a byproduct of the alum — perhaps a bit too big a pinch — especially given the fizziness of the brine when I opened the jar. Ever fretful, ever fretful, in quest of the perfect brine. Yet a brew even now that's almost fit to drink, and four more quarts waiting to be capped tight for testing a month or so from now.

Meanwhile, the fresh vegetables are perfect just as they are, especially the Ace bell peppers now turning red, glistening so vividly on the bushes I can see them all the way from my attic lookout. Close up, their skins are so lustrous, so glossy, they seem to have been varnished by the sun, tinges or streaks of green still faintly visible, like blushing recollections of their former guise. But in the mouth, they're something else again. We sliced one to go with our three-vegetable sandwiches this noon. Crisp, moist, and mildly sweet, like the one I diced up in a cabbage, onion, cucumber, and tuna salad a few days ago. Not yet like the full winy sweetness of the darker ones to come. Nor like the bright, briny sweetness of the minced ones in the pickle relish that Kate concocted two weeks ago. Nor like the succulent squares of the one I included in a ratatouille last week. Nor like the rich smoky taste of the one that Kate charred, skinned and sliced for a bouillabaissean spaghetti sauce of crab meat, squid rings, and charred, skinned, green pepper slices — all combined in a reduced tomato broth flavored with garlic, grated lemon rind, lemon juice, thyme, hot red pepper, and saffron. Mirror, mirror, on the wall, who's the most protean one of all?

TUESDAY *August 29*

Change. For a moment, I thought it might be embodied in the gaudy transformations of a bell pepper. But then I found myself thinking about the birdbath, so altered by the weather and the years we rarely bother to fill it anymore, much less to cast our eyes in its direction. It's off the beaten track to all the garden beds, so who cares? Besides, it's better not to look that way, lest all the ghosts come rushing back. Actually, it didn't begin as a birdbath, but as a disparate array of old things. A stately elm tree that stood on our neighbor's front lawn for about a hundred twenty-five years, until the Dutch elm disease did it in some twenty years ago. A scattering of bricks, strewn around the yard, dating from when our house was built about a hundred years ago. And a very large concrete saucer, about two feet in diameter, with a hump in the center of it, so it looks like a gigantic orange juicer, though it was probably a mortar for grinding things up. Probably also dating from when the house was built, it turned up six years ago, directly under the foundation of the old shed where we were excavating for the foundation of the gazebo. An elm tree, a scattering of bricks, and an old concrete mortar — who but Kate would turn them into a birdbath? Actually she didn't make a birdbath to begin with. She started by making a very large table that sat in the corner of the old shed, a metal armchair on each side of it. The table consisted of a squared-off pile of the old bricks, supporting a thick slab of trunk from the old elm tree. An outdoor cocktail table of mythic dimensions, some fourteen feet in circumference. Large enough for books and papers and drinks and food, but mostly a place for our first cat, Calliope — an elegant calico — to lounge away the summer afternoons in queenly splendor. "Shed duty," as we used to call it, while Phoebe, who came along in Calliope's later years, guarded the terrace, waiting for her time upon the throne. Phoebe eventually held court there, until the shed was about to come down and Kate decided the old table didn't quite fit her neoclassical gazebo, that it might look better under the walnut tree on the other side of the lot. So the table turned into a piece of garden sculpture for a few weeks, until the mortar turned up. Then Kate made the sculpture into a birdbath by placing the saucer-shaped thing atop the slab of old trunk. A millstone also turned up in the excavation, and it took up residence beside the birdbath — a place for walnuts, dried corn, and a carved stone turtle from Thailand. Kate's wildlife shrine. But the years and the rains have gradually worked their way upon the old slab, with waterlogged chunks of it fallen away and only a small piece of the original still intact, just large enough to hold the mortar. So we've asked our treeman Leon to bring us another slab, when he finds one. But the more I think about the thing, the more it looks like a fitting emblem of the way things are — the bricks holding, the trunk rotting away, so there wouldn't be room enough on it for a cat, even if we had one.

WEDNESDAY *August 30*

It was a bit after midnight, and Kate was in the TV room with Pip, watching a late night movie. I'd turned off the bedside lamp some ten or fifteen minutes earlier and rolled over on my side, hungry for sleep but filled with memories of dinner — the grilled swordfish I'd marinated in lemon grass, garlic, oil, tamari, and lime juice, the green beans dressed with olive oil and marjoram, the little red potatoes dressed in minced burnet and chives, the sliced Russian tomatoes straight up, all decoratively arrayed from one end of the dark stone platter to the other, with a couple of lemon wedges to brighten it up. No wonder I couldn't get to sleep.

My mind was somewhere else, somewhere else, squirrel-caging as usual. Spinning around my wheel — last night's dinner, this morning's gardening, today's report, tomorrow's class, the lingering heat wave, wondering what I'd write about — when the ear-splitting sound of my name came bellowing from the other room. "KLAUS!" And again, louder and longer, *"KLAUUUUS!!"* Actually, there's no way to represent that sound in writing, except to note that the *au* part, prounounced *ow*, was long drawn out, as if in pain. And I suddenly knew, even before I heard the rest of the outburst, that the bellow was Kate's panic button, announcing the arrival of our annual summer bat. And no sooner did the word come to mind than I looked up toward the ceiling, and there it was flying around the room, right above my head, jagged wings outspread — circling, circling, up and down, in the half darkness, a bigger wingspread, a much bigger spread, it seemed, than its forebears. Circling to find its way out.

My heart pounding, the adrenaline rushing, the old fight-or-flight response surging through my body, I jumped out of bed, ran out of the room, pulled the bedroom door tight behind me. And there was Kate standing in the hallway right behind me, asking the selfsame question that was then ringing in my mind. *"Where's the badminton racket?"* Not in the guest room, not in the TV room — all the way down in the basement, for God's sake. By the time I returned, racket in hand, Kate had heaped up a bunch of bedsheets to block the crack between the door and the floor. And there she stood, Pip beside her, both of them waiting to usher me back in and close the door behind me, while I would rush toward the lamp, turn on the light, stab my racket in the air, and hope to stun the bat rather than kill it. So familiar a script that all of us perform our parts like well-rehearsed actors. The bat soon flies into the racket and falls to the bedroom floor. I, shaking with stress and remorse, quickly pick it up between a couple of paper towels, run downstairs to the front door, its body quivering slightly between the pieces of paper, and let it loose on the front lawn. Kate calls me her hero. But all I can think of at that moment is the long essay I read several years ago on the gentleness and timidity of bats. Then I'm ready for sleep. And so is Pip.

THURSDAY *August 31*

This bat-infested, deer-bitten, heat-plagued, drought-ridden month is finally coming to an end — with an enchanting break in the weather. Now, for the first time in a week, the temperature's dropped from the mid-nineties to the mid-eighties, a dry breeze has blown out the humidity, and the sky's been clouding over all day, as if it might even be working up to a rain. Now, for the first time in a week, the air conditioner's silent, and the house is cool enough on its own for Kate to be canning another batch of Enchantments. Now too, just when the weather's relented a bit, the deer have returned, for the first time in a month, this time going after the fall beans I dusted yesterday to keep off the grasshoppers that have been nibbling them the past few days. If it isn't one thing, it's another.

Still, it was such a pleasure this morning just to walk around the yard without being oppressed by the intense heat and humidity, or just to stand in the kitchen this afternoon, chatting with Kate, mild breezes wafting in from the north, playing across my cheeks, that I was suddenly on the verge of giving way to some of my most sentimental impulses. Like ignoring the deer-chewed beans and thinking instead how special it is just to be alive and well on one of those so-called average days that the weather folks repeatedly talk about. So this is what it's like on an average late August day. I'll have a few more, thank you. And some rain too, if possible.

I'm not the only one who's fretting about the drought. Kate's cancer surgeon was worrying about it during her checkup today. "Do you hydrate?" he asked. Kate says, "I did a double-take, wondering who or what he meant to hydrate." My internist was also worrying about it during my checkup today in somewhat plainer language. "And what are you doing about the lack of rain?" But I'd sooner have them discussing the lack of rain than the other more worrisome problems that might have arisen during our double dose of doctors today. For the time being, at least, we seem to be in somewhat better shape than the yard — neither so dried as the grass, nor so cracked as the ground.

Maybe it was the good omen that came yesterday in the mail, in a small rectangular box. No return address and no identifying mark on it, except for the familiar printing of my daughter Amelia, and the label indicating it once contained a blood pressure gauge — a "pocket aneroid sphygmomanometer" — a message itself from the nurse in training. Inside the box, carefully wrapped in paper towels, two full heads of homegrown garlic, with bigger cloves than I ever grew in my garden and a brief message: "Fresh from the garden." A heart-healthy tribute and a one-upping gift from Wisconsin. Kate wanted me to plant them for a crop to be harvested next summer. But I'm all for eating them now, beginning with the chicken I'm about to broil. A clove a day keeps the doctor away.

SEPTEMBER

FRIDAY *September 1*

Nothing like the farm forecast to start one's day. "Above-average temperatures with limited precipitation expected during the first ten days of September in the corn belt. The overall effect will be continued degeneration of crop conditions and some crop withering." Some hope withering, too. At this rate, I won't be able to transplant the broccoli, cauliflower, and lettuce seedlings until it's almost mid-September, so they won't have a chance of coming to maturity until November, even with the polyester row covers in place. I also noticed this morning that the spinach seedlings I was bragging about several days ago were actually weed sprouts. In fact, only one seedling is up in the entire fifteen-foot row. Spinach, after all, is a cool-weather crop from start to finish, preferring to germinate at temperatures between forty and fifty degrees. So, if I hope to get it going this fall, I'll have to pregerminate the seeds in wet paper towels in the icebox, or seed up some flats in the house and try to transplant them later on. I'll also have to reseed the beets, because most of the sprouts burned out the last few days of the heat wave, despite my daily waterings. But there's no point in trying to redo the beets or start the radishes until the upcoming heat wave is past.

No wonder our elderly neighbor, Mr. Wells, turned over his vegetable garden today and told our neighbor Marybeth that his droop-headed sunflowers were "in mourning." No wonder Jim was shaking his head yesterday about "this weather. The worst I've ever seen this time of year." No wonder my doctor, a flower gardener by preference, was looking at me sympathetically yesterday when I told him I'm a vegetable gardener. He was thumping my chest just then and stopped for a moment, looked me squarely in the eye, and told me in his most earnest tone that he's always considered vegetable gardening to be a good bit harder than flower gardening, "especially in weather like this." For a moment there, I thought he might be giving me a heart-healthy warning, prescribing a change in my gardens. Consigning me to the perennial border, like an old horse put out to pasture. But it was probably just the fellowship of gardeners. Besides, I wouldn't have taken the hint, even if he'd been giving it. There's still enough willfulness in me to thrive on the challenge of this droughty weather. Otherwise, I wouldn't have been up early this morning, watering the red raspberries, watering the perennials, watering the beans and the cucumbers and the bok choy and the turnips and the basil and the parsley and the rosemary and the thyme. If Amelia can grow garlic in Wisconsin, surely I can grow a fall garden in Iowa.

SATURDAY *September 2*

"I think we need some bouquets in here today." I was dusting and vacuuming the living room when Kate came downstairs with a load of laundry under her arm and made that flowery announcement. And out she went to the back yard, to the row of hybrid sunflowers, now all in bloom for the first time this summer. A few minutes later she was back in the kitchen clutching a handful, every one a different color — pale yellow, bright yellow, yellow-orange, brown and yellow, purple and yellow, rust and yellow, rust — poking them into a frog in the center of a tortoiseshell bowl. Then she placed the bowl in the center of the dining room table, turning it around a few times, rearranging a few stems, until she had sunflowers looking out in every direction. Variations on a theme that put me in mind of another bouquet she made twenty-eight years ago today, also on Saturday, September 2 — a cheerful gathering of zinnias and other late summer flowers, sitting pertly in the center of Lib's dining room table at the old family house in Lisbon. A centerpiece for the buffet meal that followed our wedding in front of the living room fireplace, right below the bas-relief of the four seasons dancing in a ring. August back then had been so hot that the bas-relief was perfectly in keeping with the season — the figure of Summer barely draped in cloth. But no sooner was I thinking of that other bouquet, that other time and place, that gathering of relatives from miles around — so many of them now long gone or moved away — than out she went and picked another bouquet. Black-eyed Susans, sprigs of lythrum, and a piece of mullein from the flower border, several stalks of white-flowering garlic chives from the herb bed, and a few stalks of lavender hosta lilies from the hillock by the gazebo. How sad, I said, compared to all the flowers she might have picked had August not been so hot and dry. "How insulting," she said. "My flowers aren't sad at all. They look as if they've just come from a field of wildflowers. Just you wait and see." When she finished arranging them, they did look like a gathering of wildflowers, more buoyant than both of those other bouquets, the one on the table in the dining room and the one on the table in my memory. A conundrum — that flowers so pathetic in the hand should turn out to be so sprightly in the vase. Maybe it was the green glass vase that made the difference. Or the diminutive flowers themselves. Or her deft arrangement of them in the vase. So many colors, so many shapes, concentrated in a single spot, as in a field of wildflowers. Something she said about them also caught my attention. "These are the flowers we have. We don't have the others. So there's no point in talking about them." A maxim for all seasons, especially the coming fall — and all the falls to come.

SUNDAY *September 3*

F all. You'd think it was already here and summer had taken its leave, given today's newspaper summary: "The hottest summer in Iowa since 1988 — near-record humidity in July." I didn't need a newspaper to give me that update. All I needed was to look at my utility bill, which told me that the average July temperature this year was nine degrees higher than last year, and that my air-conditioning costs for the month were $200 more than last year. But it was heartening to learn that "The heat index soared to 131 degrees July 13 — about as bad as it's ever been here." That's the evening our air conditioner broke down while Kate was canning the peach jam. No wonder she seemed a bit edgy. Henceforth, whenever I spoon that jam on my English muffin, I'll remember the quintessential July evening it was made and the sweat of the brow that went into its making.

But I don't want to lapse into the past tense when I'm talking about summer. Not yet. No matter what the newspaper says, it didn't sound as if summer had passed last night when the TV weatherwoman predicted temperatures in the low nineties this week. And it didn't feel like summer had passed when Kate and I and Pip were walking down to the co-op this afternoon. We hadn't even gotten a block from the house when Pip started panting and Kate said, "I thought it was cooler than this." From then on, she led us along the shadiest route all the way down and back. "Cross here." "Turn right here." But it sure was breezy under the maple tree this morning when I was transplanting the lettuce seedlings into their separate slots. So pleasant that right before lunch a wasp dropped into my glass for a sip of wine and seemed visibly refreshed when I picked him out and sent him on his way. The overnight air so cool that Kate asked me to close one of the bedroom windows early this morning. Cool enough that even the vegetables were looking as if they'd been stiffened up a bit by the evening.

So what's going on here? According to my weather books, American meteorologists don't any longer mark the beginning of the seasons in terms of the solstices and equinoxes — June 21, September 21, and so on. They date summer from the beginning of June through the end of August, fall from the beginning of September through the end of November, and so on. That way the four seasons can be neatly boxed up to make four sets of three-month periods. Today, then, is the third day of fall, as our meteorologists see it. But everything in my body and everything in the garden is telling me that we're caught in a transitional phase, somewhere between summer and fall. And I won't feel we've made the transition until the days are milder — mild enough to transplant the fall vegetables, put on the row covers, and stop fretting about the weather for a while.

MONDAY *September 4*

Labor Day, a day of rest, but for me a day to put the tomato plants in order once and for all — trimming them up for the final four-to-eight-week run from now to the first killing frost. Scissors in hand, I strip out the blighted lower leaves, remove all the fruitless blossom clusters, cut off the tops of all the stems, channeling all the energy of the plants into ripening the fruit they've set. A yearly ritual prefiguring the death of the summer garden. No more green growth, no more blossoms, no more setting of fruit. By the time I'm done cutting, pruning, and trimming, my work horses look like show horses again, ready for a fall display as vivid as the turning leaves. But when I step back to admire the row, I notice all the poles leaning this way and that, like a bunch of old geezers on parade. The Enchantments leaning backward from the weight of the fruit-covered stems hanging down behind them. The Big Beef slicers slanting left and right from the clusters of heavyweight fruit at the top of their poles. What else to do but straighten them up before the coming rain?

What else, but I forgot that the oldest stakes are sometimes so rotten they break at the ground just from the slightest pressure of my foot against them. This morning, it was one of the Big Beef slicers — a whole pole of them — that I suddenly found myself holding in midair, then contemplating how to shove it back in the dry ground right behind its broken base, with no one around to help me. A bright September morning, a pair of dragonflies darting overhead, a woodpecker knocking at the apple tree, and there I stood on the verge of doing in one of my tomato plants, all on my own. Summoning my strength, I started to shove the broken end of the pole into the ground, only to realize I couldn't continue, or I'd tear the main stalk apart at its base. Too bad I tied it so tightly back in June. Kneeling on the ground with the bottom of the eight-foot pole in one hand, cutting the cloth ties with the scissors in the other hand, I also felt a strange sense of regret that the plant had set so many new tomatoes during August. But then I looked in front of me and saw my salvation — the black soaker hose a couple of feet away, watering the peppers. So, with the pole still in one hand, I dropped the scissors and leaned forward to pull the hose toward the pole. As I circled the hose beneath it to soften the ground, the entire pole started waving back and forth in my hand. But only for a second or two. Then I took the pole in both hands, shoved it firmly back into the softened ground, stepped back to admire it, and went inside to put my own sweaty self in order.

TUESDAY *September 5*

"*Zuzz, zuzzz, zuzzzz, zuzzzzz.*" The cicadas were at it again late yesterday afternoon, zuzzing all the while I was standing at the kitchen table, making a battuto for the pork tenderloin. Basil, bay, rosemary, shallot, thyme, and zuzz from the herb bed, garlic from Amelia, a dried-up slice of French bread, salt, pepper, and some olive oil to zuzz everything together. When the cicadas are zuzzing, they sometimes zound like they're right inside my head, or at least inside my ear. That's how one of them sounded when I was outside with Kate just a few minutes earlier, picking chard for the special dish she created to go with the roast pork. Well, even if it wasn't actually in my ear, I could've sworn it was right next to me on the ground, but she assured me, "It's up there in the pin oak tree." And later on when she gave me a taste of the chard, I could've sworn it was right outside the kitchen window. But maybe I was so carried away by what she'd done to the chard that I'd lost my sense of direction. A rich, earthy concoction of chopped green leaves and minced ruby stems quickly cooked and drained, then mixed with sautéed onions and shallots, homemade chicken broth, grated parmesan cheese, salt and pepper. Or maybe my in-the-canal hearing aids just don't know how to cope with the cicadas. Or maybe it was the red wine. An hour or so later, when I served up the pork and the chard, along with some fresh Enchantment tomatoes, and a platter of spaghettini dressed with olive oil, garlic, parsley, and grated asiago, the cicadas had been joined by the crickets — the zuzzing and the sissing so wide-spread it sounded as if summer might never end.

Once upon a time, some fifteen years ago, it never did end. That was the year I kept hearing the crickets all through the fall and the winter too. They must've gotten trapped in our bedroom, in the corner opposite the bedstead, I thought, because I always heard them sissing there just when I turned off the light and settled my head on the pillow, heading for sleep. Only later did I realize that those crickets marked the onset of my tinnitus, a sign I was losing my upper-register hearing, even as I was gaining the endless companionship of a summer sound. Not until I got my first pair of hearing aids some ten years ago did I realize that I hadn't really been hearing the crickets at all, but a mindless imitation of them, a ceaseless hiss, without any of their resonance and variance. I'd evidently been out of touch with them for so long that I'd completely forgotten what they sounded like. And the cicadas, too. And the clatter of leaves in the wind. And the wind itself. Now, in the waning days of summer, I can hear the male crickets again, rubbing their front wings together and the male cicadas vibrating the membranes on the underside of their bodies — rubbing and resonating, rubbing and resonating, for the night is coming, and it's coming soon, when they will not siss or zuzz.

WEDNESDAY *September 6*

"Occasionally, you'll be listening to the cicadas going zuzz, zuzz, zuzz, and suddenly you'll hear a zing, a louder, higher version of the sound. That's the outcry of a cicada being stung by the cicada killer. It's not a killing sting, just a paralyzing one, delivered by a giant wasp, the female of the species. An insect large enough to grab the cicada in her pincers, drag it high enough up a tree to launch herself on a flight to her burrow, where she'll then drag it below ground, and lay an egg squarely in the center of the cicada's body." My colleague Jeff in the biological sciences department, is an entomological raconteur, a teller of fabulous bug stories, gathered over a lifetime of curiosity about the behavior of insects. Actually, Jeff is a botanist, a collaborator of

Kate's in the Heritage Trees project, but plants and bugs are so closely involved with one another that his knowledge of insects is hardly surprising. So I called him this morning, trying to get some confirmation for my theory that bad weather, bad bugs, and bad harvests go hand in hand. And before I knew it we were off on a tangent, zuzzing and zinging about the cicadas. As for my theory about the weather, the bugs, and the crops, I don't know what made me think of it. Maybe the squash vine borers, or my sun-burned bok choy seedlings, or my burned-out spinach, or my bug-eaten crop of fall beans, or the gigantic hornets' nest at the top of the dormer right outside my attic window. Or this morning's newspaper article about the average high temperature this summer being eighty-eight, and August being the fifth-hottest one in 123 years of state record keeping, and the borers being much worse than normal, and the corn and soybean crops in some areas so drought-ridden they're either dead or beyond help from rain. Jeff immediately reminded me of the droughts, plagues, and famines in the Bible, suggesting they could probably be explained by eco-logical disruptions like the ones we've been having the past few years. The same, he said, for the recent downturn here in the butterfly population — probably caused in part by the deluge of '93, then the heat wave and drought of '95. But even Jeff was surprised to hear my story of the aerial attack I witnessed yester-day in Kate's flower bed, in the midst of the lythrum, where a handful of white and sulfur yellow butterflies were clinging to its few remaining flowers. A pretty sight — the pale-winged butter-flies against the fuchsia-colored blossoms — but not apparently to a squadron of honeybees that flew in and started divebombing them, again and again and again. Shooing them away from the flowers. Two months ago, at the height of the summer bloom period, before the heat wave and the drought, the butterflies and the bees fluttered peacefully around the lythrum, day in and day out. But the drought and the heat have so reduced the crop of flowers that the bees have become aggressive. Not enough nectar to go around. Fortunately, the asters and anemones and mini-ature chrysanthemums are all on the verge of blooming, and the weather is now in the process of turning — thundering and drizzling all morning long — so perhaps the monarchs will finally return and the flower border once again become a peaceable kingdom.

THURSDAY *September 7*

All the way down to campus this morning, I could tell it had finally arrived — the birds moving south, the squirrel with the walnut in its mouth, the coeds in their oversize sweatshirts. The long promised cool-down of fall, down to the sixties and low seventies, just as the TV weatherman predicted last night. The northwest breeze, the overcast skies, the falling leaves, the chill in the air — everything convinced me to put on my shoes and socks and a long-sleeved shirt and zippered windbreaker for the first time in a couple of months. The autumn breeze was already moving in yesterday afternoon, when Pip and I were out walking, and we ran into our neighbor Linda the Gruff. I hadn't seen Linda since we talked in early July about her secret place in northern Minnesota, so I wondered if she'd been summering up there. "No, I've been around here most of the time. It's just been too hot to be outside much. But even when I'm not up there I'm up there in my imagination." A swell place to be, I thought, especially during a summer like this one. I still had a foot in this miserable summer, but Linda, it seemed, had been somewhere else all along. The mere thought of her imaginary escape had me moping again about that nineteenth-century lobsterman's house in Maine that I could have bought some thirty-five years ago. "It would've been worth every nickel of it." And then as if to echo Linda's reproof, Kate's cousin David called from Minneapolis this afternoon, just before dinner, to tell us about the cabin he'd just bought on an eight-hundred-acre lake, two hours away in Wisconsin. Suddenly, it seemed as if everyone but us has a place up north, or a place down east, or a place somewhere else — a place they can be whenever the weather turns bad. But then I got to thinking about the meal we had last night, a six-vegetable dinner inspired by the cooler air that was then blowing in. A little stew of chicken breasts and sliced red peppers, somewhat in the manner of my Hungarian ancestors — sautéed in olive oil, garlic, black pepper, basil, and a generous amount of paprika, then braised in white wine and a diced tomato. And a side dish of sliced pattypan, zucchini, and onion, sautéed in olive oil, basil, salt, and pepper. And a few red potatoes, boiled and served with chopped chives. A real meal from a real vegetable garden, not an imaginary meal from a garden somewhere else. As vivid as the day itself, as real as the pot of leek and potato soup that Kate was stirring up on the stove this noon when I came home today for lunch. "Let me tell you," she said, "it's really cold out there." I didn't need any telling, not after my walk home from campus. But a bowl of that soup, laced with yogurt, spiked with bits of hard salami, perked up with chives from the garden, and both of us were ready to face the season head on. A few minutes later, a light rain started to fall, as if to suggest that it was time to get back in the garden again and get on with the rest of the fall planting.

FRIDAY *September 8*

Six-thirty in the morning and I'm fully alert, ready to get on with the fall garden. Actually, I've been half awake for the last hour or so, twisting and turning about yesterday's piece, this morning's planting, Kate's hay fever, the crisper full of cukes, the pain in my back, congestion in my nose. Nothing like a restful morning in bed to prepare for a day in the garden. Kate as usual is sleeping the sleep of the innocent, oblivious to the world, especially after a night of hay-feverish suffering, her eyes so red when she went to bed that one was nearly half closed with irritation. So I tiptoe around, dressing for a day in the garden. For the first time since spring, I'm putting on my blue and white striped overalls with the bronze buttons and snaps and the blue bandanna in the front pocket that Kate gave me for my birthday last year. I want to look the part when I'm out in the garden. Also a warm cotton flannel shirt — I want to feel the part too. I know it's going to be crisp from the chill that moved in last night, but the air that greets me when I open the front door to pick up the morning paper is almost like the shock of a walk-in meat freezer. No prebreakfast garden tour this morning. I'll just put Pip out on the back porch, grab a bite, read the news, and wait for things to warm up a bit. But the paper itself is as chilling as the air, especially the front-page article about depressed people my age being heavily prone to strokes. I hadn't thought I was depressed, but the list of symptoms sounds a bit too close to my restless mind, my sleepless night, my pain in the back. Better get a few seed packets, get outside, and start dealing with things in the garden. The spinach that didn't germinate, the beets that burned out, the turnips gone leggy. But the sun is now up and the air is warm and the sky is clear and the breeze is mild, and it feels like the promise of spring all over again, until I kneel down to seed in the spinach and notice the zucchini plants to the left, most of their leaves chewed off overnight. Then I remember Jim telling me just two days ago that the deer had come back and eaten his whole back patch of beans. Time for a quick therapy session, focusing on the remedy of Hinder, and the recognition that my zucchini plants are still alive, still bearing more than we can eat or give away. Back to the spinach, so buoyed by the sweetness of the morning and my self-help treatment that I finish the row in a trice and hustle my way up to reseed the beets and turnips. As I kneel down to plant the nubby beet seeds with the sun at my back and the warm coffee cup in my hand, the sensations of the moment are so comforting that my mind is filled with a renewed awareness of the truth that one cannot force nature, as I had tried to do during the late August heat wave. There's a time to plant and a time not to plant, and now at last is the time to do it. The only problem is that I've just pulled the muscle or the ligament or the tendon at the back of my knee, and I can't stand up without excruciating pain.

SATURDAY *September 9*

Nothing for pain like a bottle of champagne. So when Rebecca turned up yesterday at the cocktail hour, with two bottles in hand, she seemed like a double dose of exactly what the doctor had ordered. And a good thing too, since my chiropractor doesn't keep office hours on Friday. Actually, by the time Rebecca arrived, the pain had already subsided enough that I was able to seed in the turnips and plant up a row of onion sets that Kate had discovered at the grocery story, labeled as a box of pearl onions for cooking. Green onions to come from the fall garden — as if it were spring. Fit companions for the radishes and lettuce yet to go in. As for my leg, the only problems that remained were the vague terror of what it might portend about my aging body, and the real terror of going up and down the terrace steps and the stairs of our three-story house. Each step somewhat like touching an electrified fence. But after a glass or two of Rebecca's inspiring champagne and several crackerfuls of Kate's inspired baba ghanouj, the vague terror disappeared, and the real terror was relieved by the procedure I used for stairs shortly after my triple bypass. Little steps for little people. Problem Solving 101. After that, I was unfazed by the outraged bumblebee that came in the house on a bunch of sunflowers and then found himself trapped right in front of me on the kitchen screen. A jelly glass placed over the whirring bee, a three-by-five card shoved between the glass and the screen, and lo! I was able to carry the bee to freedom as easily as the stunned bat. Another glass of champagne, and I was able to stuff a batch of our red peppers with a mixture of ground lamb, minced anchovies, bread crumbs, flat leaf parsley, rosemary, and garlic, baked in a purée of Enchantment tomatoes, served with a platter of linguinettine dressed in olive oil, and a salad of romaine with sliced cucumbers. Some champagne. Rebecca had brought it for a belated celebration of our wedding anniversary, but with every passing sip all I could think of was the buzzing moment itself. Rebecca talking about the geese she'd seen moving south — "So early. I wonder what they know that we don't." And the monarch butterflies she'd seen on the violet sprigs of the butterfly bush that she brought us. Kate showing all the fallen nuts she'd gathered from our neighborhood trees. "Just look at all the different acorns, bur oak, black oak, red oak, pin oak, swamp white oak." I hustling back and forth to Hinder the deer-bitten vegetables. The chill air returning at sunset. And the full moon gradually sneaking up on us until there it was right behind the spruce trees at the back of the yard, just when we were sitting down to eat. All swollen and bright in the darkening sky. And right above me, when I was out with Pip for a midnight walk. And right behind the spruces in the front yard, when I went out to get the newspaper. Everything gradually coming full circle, like a ring of time, like the turning year itself.

SUNDAY *September 10*

My leg was so much better this morning that I felt only a twinge or two going downstairs in normal fashion. And no pain at all going up. No more little steps for me. Not in the house, or in the back yard when I was out watering my newly planted beets, onions, spinach, and turnips. But a few hours later, when I was outside planting the German radishes, there it was again — another jolt, and another — just when I was bending over to cover the seeds with some compost I'd just dug out of the bin. A shocking little reminder that it hadn't really gone away, as I'd thought, hadn't yet healed itself. And here I was aggravating it again, without any champagne in store this afternoon. A few careful moves, and I could see it was still just a minor pull of some sort, likely to heal itself in several days if I don't put too much stress on it. I could still transplant the broccoli and cauliflower seedlings this afternoon, as planned, and the lettuce seedlings a day or two from now. But then I started wondering what it would be like if it wasn't just a minor pull or a thing that would gradually heal itself. And there they were again — the panicky thoughts that ran through my mind when it happened on Friday, thoughts that had me so depressed yesterday I could hardly write about it. It's not the leg, of course, but what the leg portends. I saw it this morning in Carol and Jim's seventeen-year-old dachshund, completely blind, barely able to walk or take its constitutional on this beautiful fall Sunday. I saw it yesterday morning at the checkout line in the supermarket — the man who used to mow our lawn some twenty years ago, when he was in his early sixties, now so frail he couldn't write a check on his own, or recognize me when I said hello. And that got me thinking about my retired colleague Bob, a longtime friend and fishing companion, point-device in every way, now in a nursing home, beyond the point of any seeming thought. Oh yes, I know, these are extreme cases. Still, they embody the truth I once took so lightly that twenty years ago

I jestingly set up a World War I wheelchair in the old shed as a throne for Lib, who was then in her early sixties, as I am now. She took the jest in grousing good humor, but yesterday it wouldn't have seemed so laughable to me. The old wheelchair's down in the basement these days — not in keeping with the style of Kate's neoclassical gazebo. But even now I can stand in the gazebo, about where the wheelchair used to sit and look out at the deer-bitten zucchini plant, healing itself, putting out new leaves, setting new fruit, as if the frost would never come. The killing frost will come, of course, no matter how many row covers I use, and even before that the crippling ones will take their toll. Until then, I expect the zucchini to keep putting out new leaves and setting new fruit. What else is there to do?

MONDAY *September 11*

If I could vegetate like a zucchini plant, then aging and retirement would be as simple as photosynthesis. I'd bask in the sun, soak up the rain, mindlessly leafing and flowering and fruiting every day until the frost came. But it's not that simple, as I was reminded the other day when Kate asked me if I was planning to teach a course next fall. The same old question I've been trying to answer the past year or so. Do I want to keep a hand in after I retire? Or do I want to start a new life — get out of school for once in my life? No more classes, no more books, no more students' dirty looks. Actually, the graduate students I teach are so talented and stimulating that the prospect of teaching one course a year seems like a luxury, something I've sometimes imagined myself doing just for a token salary. Even during the departmental turmoil of last semester, when the weather in the building was as turbulent as the spring thunderstorms, I still thought I wanted to keep a hand in, just to keep in touch with such gifted young writers. Also to try out some ideas about writing that I've gotten from keeping this daybook. Now, several months later, I don't know if I'm even up to teaching a single course anymore, fussing over the growth of my students as much as I'm hovering over my fall lettuce seedlings. Maybe, it's because I'm presently facing the first batch of writing from my class, and I'm feeling a bit rusty from the summer break. Maybe it's because forty years of reading and responding to student writing, even the best of it, has left me feeling like the cucumber vines are looking right now — burned out and weatherbeaten, tired of putting out fruit. Maybe it's because I'd rather put all the energy and time I have left into my own writing, the writing I'm doing right now. Yet I also know that in many ways the classroom is a seedbed for my own work, a hothouse of ideas about prose that nurtures my own. I bear fruit in one place because I bear it in another. Still, I wonder how much time is left before the hard frost comes. So, as my colleagues might say, I'm conflicted. And so I couldn't give Kate an answer when she asked me that question last Friday. Fortunately, I don't have to answer the question right now. And for all I know, the question may not be mine to answer, because it all depends on whether the nonfiction program has any need for me to teach and the department has any funds for me to teach. And those questions won't be answered until this spring, when a new gardening season's just getting underway. There's a time and a place for everything, and right now, it seems, I should seed in the Cherry Belle radishes and start reading that first batch of writing from my students. Who knows, the answer to my question may lie somewhere in their prose.

TUESDAY *September 12*

"Just look at those tomatoes, another whole basket of them, all of them just as large and firm as before, in spite of the drought. And that many more still on the vines." Kate was standing at the foot of the attic stairs yesterday afternoon, right below where I was sitting at the computer, so I could easily lean over the oak railing and see her holding up the basket of Enchantments for me to admire, as glowing as the smile on her face. A bumper harvest all right, but I couldn't help thinking about the downside of Kate's remarks — the continuing drought. And it wasn't just because I was in a fretful mood right then, working on yesterday's piece about retirement. The fact is that it's been more than a month since our last inch of rain, and that inch is just about all we've had for the last eight weeks, except for an occasional drizzle like we're having today. So dry that the statewide corn crop estimates have fallen by twenty-five percent. So dry that when I ran into Rebecca downtown this morning and mentioned the rain, she raised her eyebrows, shrugged her shoulders, threw up her hands in despair, and changed the subject, asking me about my leg and telling me how much she enjoyed our get-together last Friday.

As for the tomatoes, they're doing so well because their roots are way down from my deep planting of them, drawing on the subsoil moisture, my occasional waterings, and the surface insulation of the straw mulch. Besides, once tomato plants have set most of their fruit, they tend to ripen better if they're a bit short on water, rather than swimming in it. The deluge of '93 produced the smallest tomato crop we ever had, so it's not surprising that we're having such a good one this year, especially given the ample rains this spring and early summer. And it's generally the same with the peppers and eggplants. Yesterday afternoon, I counted about sixty ripe red peppers on the Ace bell plants, and more on their way. And today, Kate harvested a dozen eggplants from just two bushes and made up four more pints of baba ghanouj for the freezer.

So why am I complaining about the drought? Because of the stress and damage it's inflicting on shallow and deep-rooted things alike. The burned-out grass, the shriveled-up berries, the browned-out leaves falling from many of the trees. A scorched landscape, just at the time that it's usually green. And the fall vegetables struggling to take hold in ground that dries out almost every afternoon despite my watering it almost every morning. So, after I transplanted the broccoli and cauliflower seedlings on Sunday, I immediately threw a row cover over them and the bok choy, not only to keep out the deer, but also to keep in the moisture. Tomorrow, I'm going to cover up the recently seeded beets, spinach, turnips, and radishes to keep in the moisture. And until the drought is broken, I'm leaving the hose strung out in the middle of the back yard between the vegetable gardens and the flower bed, like a big green snake in the grass.

WEDNESDAY *September 13*

eets up, radishes up, spinach up, turnips up, and a few green onion tips just beginning to show — all thanks to the cool weather, the row covers, and yesterday's tenth-inch of drizzle. Just imagine what might happen with a whole inch of rain. But nothing like that is in sight for the next week, so I'm planning to keep all the sprouts watered until they've clearly taken hold. And tomorrow or Friday, the lettuce seedlings will be sturdy enough that I can begin transplanting them, so the fall garden will at last be fully launched. If at first you don't succeed, plant, plant again.

Meanwhile, I'm looking at some gardening snapshots that just appeared in the fall issue of our neighborhood newsletter, the *Goosetown News*. Goosetown was named after the geese that roamed the streets in the nineteenth and early twentieth centuries, when the area was still heavily occupied by Bohemian and other European immigrants. Their back yards and side yards were filled with large European-style vegetable gardens, berry patches, and grape arbors that backed right up to the alleys still running throughout the area. A few of those gardens still remained when Kate and I moved into the neighborhood twenty-five years ago. But with the departure ten years ago of our neighbor Herman, the eighty-year-old retired farmer who taught me so much about gardening, the last of those European gardens came to an end. As a tribute to that tradition, our neighbor Marybeth, Goosetown's archivist and newsletter designer, decided to feature snapshots of some present neighborhood gardens and gardeners, along with the shot of an abandoned Bohemian garden that once contained "rows and rows of cabbage, onions, tomatoes, potatoes, carrots, string beans, lima beans, turnips, lettuce, radishes, garlic, dill, and parsley." Right below that now lonely scene, there's a buoyant shot of our nearby neighbors Margaret and Bob, sitting in front of their heirloom zinnias, with Margaret holding a bowl of freshly harvested tomatoes, glowing in the bright sun of late August. Below that a shot of Jenny and Greg's variegated English flower border. And then a shot of Jim standing next to one of his tall staked tomato plants, looking as proud as if he were holding up a pair of antlers on the first day of the deer-hunting season. Marybeth does know how to produce an evocative layout of shots. On the back there's another spread, including a shot of my tomato, pepper, and eggplant garden, followed by one of Wendy standing beside her giant sunflowers, then one of an unidentified child's flower garden. And last of all is my favorite: a shot of Jim's back bean patch, surrounded by a barricade of things he put up late in August to ward off the marauding pair of fawns — a picnic bench, two large pieces of trelliswork, a long strip of wire fencing, a plywood panel, all arranged in a three-foot-tall rectangle around the bean patch, the bean patch that the fawns leapt into and devoured just a week or so ago. *Sic transit gloria legumi.*

THURSDAY *September 14*

M y old neighbor Herman. The mere thought of him yester-day, and I could see him again in his garden, as if he were still there. His wide German forehead topped by a thinning shock of white hair, his short, broad-chested body supported by a pair of wooden canes — checking on his grapes, harvesting his red raspberries, cultivating his Chinese cabbage, watering his lettuce, or just contemplating his tree roses from the perspective of his red metal chair. His deeply lined face, his icy blue eyes, his large arthritic hands tell all. Though his lot is small — fifty by a hun-dred feet — his ambitions are large. So large that almost every bit of his land is devoted to some kind of gardening, except for a small border of grass around the front and side of his house. Annuals, perennials, flowering shrubs, fruit trees, berries, herbs, vegetables — something of every kind. A cherry tree, a peach tree, a plum tree, a pear tree, a five-in-one apple tree. Everything pruned just so. Everything supported just right, like the green metal stakes for the tree roses, and the notched wooden two-by-fours holding up the branches of the fruit-laden plum tree. Everything used and reused, like his spring tree prunings turned to pea brush turned to kindling for his outdoor grill. Everything turned to more than one account, like the watering can under the downspout, and the picnic table under the grape arbor, and the strip composting under the paths between the vegetable rows. Subsistence gardening — Herman was doing it long before it had a name. But he also had black-eyed Susans and cosmos and daisies and snow-on-the-mountain and spider flowers along the whole length of his house for all the world to see.

Walking by his place this morning on the way down to school, and then again at noon on the way back, I was dismayed to see how barren it had become — only a few flowers by the side door, only a few vegetables in the garden. A white picket fence barricading off the whole back yard, and nothing to behold but a few flowering shrubs and the five-in-one apple. Herman's garden had vanished almost without a trace, visible only in the mind's eye of a nostalgic neighbor, or the records of a neighborhood archivist. If this is what it all comes down to, maybe I should get a new compulsion, start a new life in more ways than one. But then I got to thinking again about Herman's tree roses — those plants so tender, so fragile, they couldn't possibly survive an Iowa winter. Every fall, he'd bury them in trenches, mound them over with dirt, cover the mounds with lumber, and resurrect them every spring. And there they'd be the whole summer long, risen from their graves, blooming their heads off, visible proof of his faith in the mysteries of gardening, in the way things can endure above ground and below if one cares enough to give them what they need.

FRIDAY *September 15*

"Everything in it's from the garden — except for the bread dough, the cheese, and the anchovies." Kate was introducing the pizza she concocted for lunch today, with a sly smile, a slight bow, and a majestic sweep of the plate as she placed it squarely in the center of the kitchen table. "Last year's tomato sauce, this year's tomatoes and onions, and fresh chopped basil." She also had a little side plate of sliced green peppers and sweet onions, along with a handful of Calamata olives. So, it was a three-, four-, or five-vegetable meal, depending on how you count the onions and tomatoes. Not to mention the dried hot red pepper flakes she also remembered after her first or second bite. But all those ingredients — cheesetomatoesanchoviesbasiloninstomato- saucedriedredpeppers — were so well fused it was impossible for me to think of it as a three- or four- or five-vegetable anything, though there's no denying that it was in a sense just that.

If the pizza were the only thing puzzling me today, I'd probably not give it a second thought. But there's also Kate's flower bed that I soaked last night and again this morning to bring on the asters and anemones and perk up the gray leaves of the mullein and yarrow plants. Each time I set up the hose, I stared at the snow-on- the-mountain, grateful it was still glittering from end to end. Especially vivid in the rising sun, and a striking ground for the few other touches of color still remaining — the pink of two or three spider flowers waving in the breeze, the bluish tips of the Russian sage, the yellow of the goldenrod and a few black-eyed Susans on the wane. But when I came in and shared my pleasurable percep- tion with Kate, her response completely surprised me — "The snow-on-the mountain's faded and setting seed. It'll be done in a few days." How strange, yet how could I dispute her. She'd been working in the bed all yesterday afternoon, cutting out the faded lythrum stalks and the dried rudbeckia, to make room for the aster show. So I decided not to say anything for a few days, while the snow continued to glitter. But now as I sit here in the attic, looking out toward the bed, I can see that it's fading like a three- day-old snow.

Nothing, it seems, is what it seems to be, not even this book I'm writing. I was trying to describe it this morning in a report of what I'd accomplished during my research leave last fall. The univer- sity's report form asks one to "specify any new objectives that emerged in the course of the project." So, after reporting on my book about the essay, I tried to explain this one — "I also started work on a memoir, in the form of daily entries about my garden, aging, weather . . ." Just then, Kate announced lunch, and it was only after I finished the pizza that I realized I'm writing a journal about my gardenagingweatherfoodKateteachingwritingmylife. I wonder what the dean and vice president would think of that.

SATURDAY *September 16*

Some things, after all, are exactly what they seem to be. Like the care package that arrived yesterday afternoon from my son Marshall, including a letter about his trip back to New York, some snapshots from that morning in early August when we stopped to visit Jim in the midst of camouflaging his duck boat, and a jug of New York maple syrup. A sweet thank you from my son, the master of nostalgia, for our time together and the waffles I cooked each morning during his visit. But the minute I saw that maple syrup, I remembered the time some twenty years ago when Marshall and I and Kate and Lib were coming back from a vacation on Lake Champlain — a small group cruise on a broad-beamed ketch. And we stopped off in Ithaca, where I'd gone to graduate school and Marshall was born, and there I bought a jug of Cornell University maple syrup from a roadside stand on the edge of town. And then I remembered the maple syrup and pancakes a couple of years ago when Marshall and I took a five-day fishing trip to southeast Iowa. Talk about the master of nostalgia!

And it wasn't any different this morning when I went out to deliver my batch of Goosetown newsletters. I was eager to get them out, not only to boost all the gardening that's going on, but also to make sure everyone knows about the neighborhood "bratluck" that's planned for a week from this Sunday. But no sooner had I gotten to the end of our little street just two blocks away than I found myself looking up toward the 1860s gothic brick house on a two-acre lot that my daughter Hannah and her husband Monty inspected at the end of their Christmas visit last year. And the waffles I'd made for them that winter morning were merging with the ones I'd recently made for Marshall, and the syrup was flowing everywhere. It didn't get any better when I passed the little house just a block or so away where I lived for a year some thirty years ago, shortly after I was divorced, eating my waffles in solitary splendor. And two blocks over, there was Herman's house again, bereft of fruit, except for the high-bush cranberry, its rusty leaves and red berries so irresistible I stopped to pluck a couple of sprigs, just for old times' sake. Down one more block and over, almost home without any more recollections, and I ran into Linda the Gruff . "I need fourteen more newsletters to finish my route." No problem, except when I went over to deliver them, she showed me a picture of her secret place up in Minnesota. And there on a grassy spot in the middle of a woodsy clearing sat the old caboose, its mustard-colored sides, its rusty red lettering, its little square loft so dreamlike in that lush green place that it made me wish I were someplace else — as far, far away as I could get.

SUNDAY *September 17*

Maybe it was the sight of Linda's caboose, or the continuing drought, or the predictions of a harsh winter, or just the simple desire to get as far, far away as I can, especially come the end of December when I'm done with this book — whatever the reasons, yesterday afternoon I suddenly found myself calling the airlines, calling my travel agent, calling Ruth, our friend in Oahu, calling the Paauhau Plantation House in Honokaa, on the north shore of the Big Island, to make reservations for early January. Actually, the impulse didn't arise as suddenly as it might seem. Kate and I have been talking about the possibility of a New Year's trip to Hawaii for several months — back to the place we've been visiting every few years for the past fifteen years. Often to a house on the north shore of Kauai. The garden island. There, just a few years ago, we spent a few days weeding around bushes and young trees on the windswept hillside of the National Tropical Botanical Garden at Limahuli — a busman's break in our holiday — helping them put things back together after hurricane Iniki. Tedious work, digging weeds on that steep terrain, but such a bracing oceanside vista, I'd rather pull weeds there than any other place in the world. Too bad they can't grow decent tomatoes. But now we're looking for a new challenge on the cliffs of another coast. And yesterday for some reason, the impulse was so strong I felt almost desperate to get everything arranged as quickly as possible. Partly it was a sudden fear the flights might be full, or we'd not be able to get a conveniently located cottage along that sparsely settled coast — a cottage large enough for ourselves and our friend Ruth.

But also, I think, there was a panic deep inside me, roused by the thought of my retired colleague Bob, turned eighty today, withering away in a nursing home. Wordless the witty man who once beguiled us all with occasional verse in pentameter couplets. His wife recently dead, his son two thousand miles away, and Bob himself a million miles away, so far beyond the point of no return that when I called his old friend and colleague John to tell him I was planning a birthday visit, he wondered if there was even any point. But John came along on the slim hope that Bob might respond to our visit. And so did my colleague Carol. And Bob did respond in a fashion, after I woke him from his sleep and took his hand in my own, rubbing it and talking to him about our fishing trips of decades past, and after Carol took his hand, rubbing it and telling him how good he'd been to her in decades past. Suddenly there he was, holding my hand tight, then holding her hand tight, holding on to each of us for dear life. But then the sudden anguish on his face, the pain in his eyes, made me wish I'd never woken him in the first place, made me wish I could help him out as easily as I'd helped out Phoebe. But all I could do just then was to hold his hand and rub his forehead and wish I were far, far away.

MONDAY *September 18*

"K laus, you better get home right away." I'd gone down to the office for a few minutes in midafternoon, just to run off some handouts for tomorrow's class, and suddenly Kate was on the telephone, her voice so solemn I thought it must be bad news about one of my children, or her mother, or someone else in the family, or Pip. But no, it wasn't as bad as I thought. "A reporter just called from 'Live at Five' — the TV news program on channel nine. I don't know how they got our name. But they're coming out around four-thirty to do a story about the upcoming frost, and they want to use your garden as a backdrop. Don't worry about being in the picture. They just want to show the garden and some of the things you use, like the row covers." I heard something last night about frost on Thursday, but I didn't think it was so definite they'd be reporting on it today.

So now I'm home, sitting up here in the attic, watching Mike, channel 9's roving reporter, get ready to do his thing. He's standing by the edge of the back garden — in a button-down shirt, a colorful tie, and a casual pair of chinos — fingering the row covers I showed him just a few minutes ago. A clean-cut fellow, his light brown hair brushed straight back, I could tell he was a quick study when he said, "Oh, it's just like layering up when you go outside." But I can also see that he's not quite at ease with the covers, because he's not yet opened one fully enough to show how it can cover the whole front row of pepper plants. He's just holding a folded one up against a tomato plant, gesturing with his other hand, and talking into a make-believe camera, while Steve, the cameraman, is running his wires from the live truck out to the garden. I wonder what Mike would think if he knew I'm watching him from up here, reporting on him, even as he's getting ready to report on my garden. What a delicious reversal of roles — the TV reporter being covered by the gardener! But I can't stay here any longer, because it's time to go downstairs and watch it live on TV.

Exactly five, and there's Mike on screen, standing in my garden, next to the Big Beef slicers, hyping his upcoming report. How strange to be watching him and my garden on TV when I could be upstairs watching firsthand or outside watching up close. But then I wouldn't be able to see how they package the whole story. Oh, to be in all three places at once! Now the anchorman's on screen, talking about the upcoming frost, then turning it back to Mike, who runs through five different scenes — in an apple orchard, in my garden, in a cornfield, a bean field, and then with the county extension agent, talking about the dangers in each setting. All so quick, it's done in a trice. Then the weatherman with an overview of the freeze, two weeks earlier than normal, then another shot of my garden, while the anchorman delivers his wrapup line: "So, if you wanna keep 'em, you better cover 'em." A neat package. But now the brunt of this whole escapade has just dawned on me full force. Highs two weeks ago in the nineties, now a possibility of lows in the twenties. The anchorman called it "a topsy-turvy year." And I just planted my fall lettuce this morning.

TUESDAY *September 19*

This morning before breakfast, I was up in the attic, standing by the tall center window of the gable, gazing out as I often do at the full sweep of the back yard, from the terrace right below me and its stone retaining walls, to the gazebo and the herb bed a few steps up, to the vegetable gardens, Kate's perennial bed, and the spruces along the back. A pleasing vista in every season, its upward sweep, its sloping sides uncluttered, open to the eye, except for the old apple and pear trees. Kate's landscape plan fulfilled. But something about the look of it this morning seemed a bit strange. At first I thought it was the lawn — still brown, like the color of dried wheat, even under the shade of the walnut trees along the south lot line. Then I thought it might be the striking contrast between the pale brown color of the lawn and the rich green foliage of the surrounding trees and shrubs. Or the trees framing a turbulently gray sky for the first time in weeks. But then for some reason my eye was drawn to the pear tree in the middle of the yard, pendulous with ripening fruit. Yet it wasn't the blushing pears that drew me there. It was the wide ring of dark green grass all around the drip line of the tree. How strange, I thought, since I hadn't fertilized it this summer. Then I remembered putting the soaker hose around it a week or two ago for a full twenty-four hours. Kate didn't want to lose the aged tree, not after its almost miraculous recovery from the deluge. Looking at that odd circle of green, like a halo or a wreath fallen to the ground, I began to see strange things everywhere in the back yard — not just the halo on the lawn, but also the peppers in the garden, the juniper on the hillock, the yews in the planter. Everything, everywhere, sticking out, almost as harshly as the stark white row covers now protecting the lettuce and spinach. Oh yes, I realize that things wouldn't stand out so starkly now were it not for the browned-out lawn, normally so green this time of year that it pulls everything together like a carpet. Still, my impression of things sticking out here, sticking out there, made me feel a strangeness I'd never felt before about what we do when we garden. Stick things here, stick things there — a bush, a tree, a bed, a walk, a wall, all in the name of a pleasing space, a fruitful place. And so it is. Until the convulsions of a year like this — the deluge, the heat wave, the drought, and now the early frost — bear witness to the truth that all we do can easily be undone, and that nothing we do can ever be quite so natural, so organic, so in tune with the cycle of things as we suppose. Were I fully in tune with things this year, I'd have turned off my hose, put away the Hinder, thrown out the rotenone, and given up on the summer garden. But then I'd not have had the satisfaction yesterday afternoon of watching Mike chomp his way through a red pepper, then an Enchantment tomato, his eyes alight with the surprise of things that "never tasted so good."

WEDNESDAY *September 20*

"It's too early for this, way too early." Rebecca and I were tromping in and out of the back vegetable bed, draping the gauzy white row covers over the bell pepper plants and eggplants, as if we were disciples of Cristo. Rebecca herself was already wrapped for the cold, in socks, corduroys, a cardigan sweater over her blouse, and a matching fatigue hat. I too was layered, a sweatshirt on top of my flannel shirt, and bib overalls on top of my chino pants. Rebecca figured we could get everything covered in an hour or so. But two hours after she arrived, we'd only done the peppers, eggplants, and three of the Enchantment tomato plants. And I wasn't even being fussy. Before we could start wrapping the plants, we had to harvest their fruit — the ripest red peppers for freezing and all the ripe Enchantments for canning. Once the plants are fully covered, it's a nuisance to get under the covers for daily vegetable picking, much less for large-scale harvesting. So we picked a dozen red peppers and a half bushel of Enchantments. More work for Kate, whose smile seemed a bit strained when she came out and saw them during a break from the leaf illustrations she's been making for the Heritage Trees brochures. Then we started draping the pepper plants, only to discover that a single twenty-foot row cover wasn't enough, because I had lengthened the bed from twenty to twenty-four feet last fall. Why didn't I think about that last fall? And even two overlapping lengths weren't enough, because the pepper plants are so tall this year they also need two overlapping widths. Suddenly, I was contemplating triage in the garden. Not enough row covers to cover everything else in both vegetable plots. Also not enough bricks or poles or overly large pattypans and zucchini to weight down all the covers. By the time we finished the row of peppers and eggplants, I was also feeling it's way too early for this. The garden under wraps, even before the autumnal equinox. All in the name of getting all the bounty and ripening it on the vine. Rebecca saw it a bit differently. "Isn't it strange that we do this, trying to hold it at bay, when we know it's coming, and it can't be stopped." A few minutes later, she too was feeling pressed by the desire to hold things at bay in her own garden, and off she went, having helped me through the worst of the fall covering routine. Well, not exactly the worst. That didn't happen until a few minutes after she was gone, when I was putting a long plastic sleeve over one of the tomato plants and needed a twist tie to pull it tight at the top. So I removed a spare tie from the neighboring pole, and suddenly the entire tomato plant on that pole collapsed from top to bottom, as if it were falling to the ground on its knees. I guess it wasn't a spare tie after all. And after fixing it up, I didn't have much to spare. But I sure was grateful that it rained yesterday. A whole day of it, almost an inch of it. I just wish I could've enjoyed it more today.

THURSDAY *September 21*

Staring at the sheathed tomato plants this morning, taking stock of what still needed protection, I was struck by how different they look from the row-covered peppers. The ghostly white sheets of spun-bond polyester completely hide the pepper plants, so I can't see them unless I hunch over and peer through the covers. Even then I can detect only their blurred shapes and an occasional leaf or fruit close to the surface of the cloth. But the clear plastic sleeves on the tomato plants hide nothing. In fact, they reveal everything — stems, leaves, and pendulous fruit — like a see-through woman's sheath, an in-your-face bit of haute couture from an Italian or Parisian designer. Come to think of it, the row of tomato plants looks somewhat like a parade of avant-garde bridesmaids, each one sheathed in a billow of plastic from head to toe, from the gathering at the top to the one at the bottom. Up close, the effect is even more daring, what with all the holes punched in the plastic to keep the plants from overheating on warm sunny days. But there is no danger of overheating today. Overcast skies, light rain, temperatures in the mid-forties, and a northwest wind, like the end of October or November. Thirty degrees below normal for this final day of the traditional summer season. One of the coldest ends on record.

Cold as it's been the past two days, the hyped-up freeze predicted on Monday, Tuesday, and Wednesday didn't get here yesterday, nor will it descend tonight, and it might not even come tomorrow evening or Saturday morning. And after Saturday, the temperatures are predicted to rise gradually back to normal. So I wonder what Mike and his TV colleagues are thinking today about their feature story of Monday. If I hadn't been through this kind of weather drill before, I'd probably feel badly deceived, especially since I spent the better part of two days moving all the tender potted plants down into the cellarway steps, and protecting all the tender crops with row covers or sheaths — not only the eggplants, peppers, and tomatoes, but also the remaining cucumbers, pattypans, zucchini, and basil. As it is, I just feel mildly put out. But I don't know exactly whom or what to blame — the misleading storm track or the overeager meteorologists. I'm not even sure if I should complain at all, for the covers are now in place, not only protecting things against a frost, but also helping to keep them warm during these cooler days of fall.

The cold weather has also brought a return to Kate's heartwarming soups and stews. This week it was a lentil gumbo, a reddish-brown marriage of the legume itself with her homemade chicken broth, canned Enchantments, chopped celery, onions, peppers, okra, and bits of chopped ham, flavored with garlic, parsley, rosemary, black pepper, and mild jalapeno sauce to produce a brew so rich, so warming, that it comforted me all the while I was outside comforting the vegetables.

FRIDAY *September 22*

U p at seven-thirty for a bird's-eye view of things, looking out the window for signs of a frost or freeze. But I don't see any, except for a faint strip of rime along the roof over the front porch. Just as I thought from yesterday's forecast. The overnight low probably bottomed out at thirty-three or thirty-four. And a close-up check of the see-through tomato sheaths confirms my supposition. All the leaves as green and plump as before. So much for the weeklong hysteria around here. Back in the house for a leisurely breakfast and the morning newspaper. IOWANS WIT-NESS FREEZING END TO SUMMER '95. Bad news for the farmers in western and central Iowa, and worrisome news for us too, especially given the prediction that temperatures here in eastern Iowa might follow suit if the protective cloud cover breaks up. As it already has on this bright sunny morning! Suddenly, I'm not feeling so relaxed anymore. A hard freeze on the way — more than my one layer of covers and sheathing can protect against. And I don't have enough covers to give everything another layer. So I'm off to the local nurseries, looking for more. But I don't have much time to find some and get them in place, because I'm supposed to be down on campus at one-thirty this afternoon to meet with my graduate reading group on the essay. This leisurely day is beginning to feel like a pressure cooker. By the time I find some covers and get back home, Kate's hunched over her leaf illustrations for the sixth day in a row, working against her deadline of this afternoon, when they have to be ready for printing in the Heritage Trees brochures. Seventy-six separate illustrations to identify trees in the oldest neighborhoods of Iowa City. A two-year tree survey she's headed up, now beginning to bear fruit in treewalk brochures for each of the neighborhoods, including Goosetown. Watching her, I feel like a mayfly, trying to hang on to my six-month-old vegetables for another few weeks, while she's trying to preserve the city's historic trees for as many more years as possible. But I don't have time to pursue such reflections, especially after she tells me the local weather station has predicted lows this evening around twenty-seven. A hard freeze! So I'm off to start wrapping the tomato row from one end to the other, and none too soon, given the brisk northwest breeze that's chilling my fingers. And then another layer over the peppers. And then back inside to make lunch. And then Kate's request that I cover her asters and geraniums when I get back from campus. But I don't have any covers left, and I don't have time to get any. So she agrees to drive me down to campus, get some at the nursery store, and leave them for me to deal with when I get back home. By the time I get to my office, I can feel the pulse beating at the back of my head, and it doesn't get any better when I look at my calendar and discover the essay group's not scheduled to meet until next Friday.

SATURDAY *September 23*

I didn't really begin to feel better yesterday until I was standing by the cooktop, stirring up a Creole sauce of pepper, onion, tomatoes, thyme, parsley, and bay, to go over a couple of hoki fillets. By then, I'd covered all the tender things with two layers of cloth. Nothing like double coverage in the world of a fretful gardener. Control. Security. It reminds me of how I felt in the days shortly after my triple bypass — before I discovered that it's not a permanent remedy, but just a temporary holding action, a stay against the cold that's sure to come. But with everything under wraps yesterday, I wasn't fretting about much, except the little pot of rice simmering on the back burner and the sauce right in front of me. Then it occurred to me that I hadn't done anything to protect the chard — a perfect companion to the baked fish and rice — so I ran out to pick a bunch for dinner, leaving only the smallest leaves for the remote possibility of another harvest. Back in the kitchen, Kate was freshening up the old bouquet of sunflowers, so I ran out again to pick her some more. Better to have a bowl of them on the dinner table than a freeze-dried row in the garden. Then at last I felt at ease — so confident I'd picked or protected everything tender that the coming freeze excited me almost more than the coming meal. And later, I could tell the freeze was coming for sure, when Pip and I were out walking at midnight, the sky clear, the stars bright, my breath condensing in front of me as he pulled his way around the block, energized by the cold and his purblind will.

Come morning, I jumped out of bed, expecting to find the lawn completely rimed with frost, a thick white coating of it, but instead found just a trace on scattered portions of the back yard. And a close-up check of the unprotected plants revealed they hadn't been nipped by it, not even the okra, native of Africa. The same at Jim's place, where he hadn't even bothered to pull the sheets completely around his tomato plants. Rebecca showed up around noon and reported the same light frost at her place. This may be one of the earliest cold spells on record throughout the plains and Midwest. It's certainly been one of the most damaging for Iowa's corn and soybean crops. But for me just then it was also one of the most unpredictable and puzzling ones on record. The only things damaged at my place were some leaves at the top of a few eggplants, peppers, and tomato plants. What's going on here? I wondered. Why should any of the protected stuff have even the slightest bit of damage? Rebecca immediately had the answer. "It's the moisture trapped on the leaves by the covers." And then Kate chimed in. "Turned to ice crystals by the cold. But the real damage takes place when the sun comes out and hits those crystals." Like an antiphonal chorus, they chanted the eternal verities, of frost and freeze, of melt and thaw, reminding me again that if the ice don't get you, the sunshine will.

SUNDAY *September 24*

"Do you have anything left?" Hardly the first thing I expected to hear from my neighbor Wendy when I ran into her this morning at a nearby supermarket. And such a distressed look on her face! I was on my way to buy stuff for the neighborhood bratluck this noon — cider, brats, potatoes, charcoal, ice — but she was still thinking about yesterday morning's frost. When I told her I'd lost nothing, she looked as surprised by my answer as I'd been by her question. Who could've lost anything in such a light frost as that? But when she told me she'd lost everything, and much of it this morning, I was even more nonplused. I could hardly believe her. After all, she lives just two blocks south of us, and we didn't have any overnight frost. "Well," she said, "my thermometer was down to twenty-eight this morning. Maybe it's a bit off, but there's no question about my plants. They're all dead. It's as crazy as that eight-inch snow in Denver this week that destroyed all the trees." No wonder she thought we should warm the cider and forget about the ice. No wonder she wanted to look at my row covers and sheaths when we talked again at the bratluck. And she wasn't the only one there with problems. Our neighbor Mary, who lives just two blocks west of us, was asking what she could do with all the green tomatoes she picked from her frostbitten plants. And our elderly neighbor Mrs. Abbott, who gardens near Wendy, was overjoyed with gratitude when I gave her the pattypans and zucchini that Kate and I had brought to weight down the tablecloths at the park. Stranger and stranger, especially when I took Pip for a walk after the bratluck to see things with my own eyes, and discovered a bed of frost-killed tomato plants at my neighbor Roger's place just one block west of us. But Kate, as usual, solved the mystery the minute I told her about it. "Your garden and Jim's are up on a hillside. Theirs are down in that hollow on Center Street where the cold air falls and collects."

Though it did in our neighbor's vegetable gardens, the overnight frost did bring out some of their best cold-weather cooking. Three separate grills covered with brats, hot dogs, and chicken breasts, their skins browning and crackling over the hot coals. And so many dishes to match, all fit for the overcast day, I had difficulty choosing. I certainly couldn't pass up the sliced carrots, spiked with ginger and cilantro. Or the two pots of baked beans, one rich with bacon, the other with brown sugar and spices. Or the three warm potato salads, one slivered with cheddar cheese and onions, another cubed and baked with ham and cheese, and Kate's — thinly sliced, scattered with rings of my sweet purple onions, spiced with dry mustard, salt, pepper, parsley, and four kinds of thyme, dressed with olive oil and her tarragon vinegar, and ringed with wedges of Enchantment tomatoes. Nor could I resist one little brownie, or a sliver of Wendy's warm apple pie, alluringly ringed with a sprig of sweet autumn clematis.

MONDAY *September 25*

Such a lovely fall morning — mild air, clear skies, a warming sun — that I got up first thing, put on my bib overalls and went out to unwrap the peppers and tomatoes. And seed in another batch of radishes. The first batch now coming on so well after last week's rain that Kate and Rebecca were both exclaiming over them last Saturday. "Their leaves are so big, their leaves are so big." Radishes by mid-October. Same for the green onions, so Kate suggested I plant another batch of those too, "right next to the other ones." And why not? With the row covers in place last year, we had lettuce until early December and radishes on Christmas. So why not green onions too? And when those are gone, we can hustle off to Hawaii and keep eating fresh vegetables — and fresh fish — from the Big Island.

Actually, we've already been eating there, ever since I added a few more Hawaiian guidebooks to our growing collection. The colder it got last week, the more we dined off those books, until Saturday morning, the coldest of the week, I binged on Jocelyn Fujii's highlights of the Hawaiian regional cuisine at Chef Alan Wong's Canoehouse. I had even more difficulty at his place than I did at yesterday's bratluck. How could I resist his seared peppered ahi tuna with soy sauce vinaigrette and fern shoots? Or his lobster won-ton ravioli in lemon grass chili ginger sauce? Or his grilled chicken breast with sliced roasted eggplant, Maui onion, tomatoes, and basil or tomato chili pepper water? Talk about mid-Pacific cuisine! And a little while after my east-west binge, Kate got lost in a little snack bar, called Broke the Mouth, right across from the farmers' market in Hilo, where a local farmer and a master chef are bridging the cultures in things like starfruit salsa and spring rolls with basil, mint, and arugula. Maybe Linda the Gruff is right. We can be there even when we're here. By the time we get there, in fact, we might not have to make the trip at all. The voyage is in the planning. The food is in the book. Maybe I can even try out some of those recipes myself, with our own arugula and basil and lemon grass and tamari. Maybe with the boneless pork loin chops that Kate wants me to fix for dinner tonight. Hawaiian regional cuisine right here in Iowa City.

Right here in Iowa City, everything else is running true to course. The fawns are still foraging at Jim's place. This afternoon when I went up to visit, he was shaking his head over the dozen large hosta plants they'd cropped off last week and the double row of wax beans they nibbled at last night. "I'm gonna harvest all the rest this afternoon, so Carol and I get some of 'em ourselves." After last night's assault, Jim finally conceded that he should've been using the Hinder this summer. And it looks like I better get some more on right now, given the two deer-bitten hostas I discovered at our own place just after I finished commiserating with Jim. Some things are always in season.

TUESDAY *September 26*

"There's still so much color there, so many things still in bloom!" Wendy took me by surprise again on Sunday after she stopped off to look at our yard. I thought she'd come to look at my row covers and sheaths. But when I saw her later on my walk with Pip, she burbled on so much about Kate's flower bed that it made me wonder if I'd been missing something. So I've been eyeballing it the past few days, in different lights, at different angles, trying to see what Wendy saw. One thing I keep noticing is that the snow-on-the-mountain, faded though it is, still has enough white in it to billow up and down the whole sixty-foot length of the bed, some of the plants bending over, some still erect. Maybe it was the rise and fall of all that fading white that caught Wendy's eye. Or the little flecks of yellow in their burst seedheads. Or the sage-green color of their leaves. Or the dark red color of their stalks. Or perhaps it was the Clara Curtis chrysanthemums that finally came into their own after last week's rain. They too are billowing up and down the whole bed, along the front of it, their pale pink petals and yellow centers accented by the snow behind them. They look so much like painted daisies that I'm always a bit confused when Kate reminds me that "They're chrysanthemums, not daisies. *Chrysanthemum rubellum 'Clara Curtis.'* And painted daisies are also chrysanthemums. *Chrysanthemum parthenium.*" Whatever they are, there's such a profusion of them now, so much

nectar to go around that the bees are swarming and the butterflies are fluttering all over them as peaceably as if there'd never
been a late August shortage of it. No more divebombing. Maybe,
it was all those sulfury yellow butterflies that Wendy saw, hovering
around every mound. Or the few yellow rudbeckia still scattered
down the center of the bed. Or the handful of purple coneflowers
still in bloom. She certainly must have noticed the lavendar-pink
spider flowers still waving back and forth along the bed. There
aren't many of them left now, but they sure do make a nice complement to the Clara Curtis mums. And now that I notice it, the
four big stands of aster spaced out along the back, make a striking
contrast to everything else — their leaves dark green, their buds a
flat dark purple. I've been so eager for them to bloom that I hadn't
even noticed how strong they look just as they are. I certainly
couldn't see them when they were draped in polyester row covers.
And neither could Kate and Rebecca, who thought they looked
like Casper the Ghost. But I haven't overlooked the Russian sage,
alternating with the asters. Who could? Their tiny blue flowers,
their pale gray stems shimmer in every light. Come to think of it,
the whole bed is shimmering. So much color there, so many things
still in bloom, I wonder how I could possibly have missed it.

WEDNESDAY *September 27*

"You forgot to mention the salvia and the veronica. They're
down along the front edge. Just a few of them in bloom, but
they add some more touches of blue to the bed." Kate was
reading my report last night, checking as she always does for
inaccuracies and oversights. And sure enough when I went out this
morning to see for myself, there were a few spikes of blue at the
edge of the brick border. That oversight made me wonder if I had
missed anything else, and I certainly had, right in the middle of
the bed — a few clumps of goldenrod. And now as I look out
from my attic window, I can also see two rust-brown clumps of
dried lythrum that Kate must have left standing as background
accents. Her flower bed is beginning to remind me of those cogni-
tive puzzles that appeared in the comic books of my childhood —

usually a forest scene with animals optically hidden in the landscape. Even then, I was a little bit hard of seeing. A snake here, a
monkey there, always eluded my attention. But a graphically hidden snake in the grass is hardly the same as a four-foot-tall clump
of lythrum, its rust-brown shape clearly visible for all the world to
see. I wonder what's blocking my vision of things. Maybe it's just
that I don't see flowering plants as well as fruits and vegetables.
Only this morning, for example, when I was out watering and
fertilizing the fall vegetables, did I notice that all the marigolds
along the front of the big vegetable bed must've been nipped by
the weekend frost. Their flowers were still bright yellow, but some
of their leaves were blackened at the tips. Come to think of it,
though, I just noticed this morning that all the okra plants and
tomato plants were nipped by the weekend frost — but only on
the south side where the sun must've hit the frost on their leaves.
Maybe it was more damaging up here than I'd imagined or wanted
to recognize. Then again, the plants are still vigorous, and Kate
harvested another basket of Enchantments to put up this afternoon. So it's not as if I'm seeing things through rose-colored
glasses. Yet I do seem drawn to the brighter things, like the bee that
landed on the inside of my glasses when I was bending over to look
at the marigolds. Also the fruits and flowers themselves, rather
than the leaves. But it's not just any old fruit that catches my eye,
nor even the most gaudy one. After all, the one green apple that
hung on the lowest branch of the dwarf Prairie Spy tree this summer was certainly nothing to write home about. The pale green
edge of it was just barely visible behind a leaf, but the minute
I looked out the kitchen window this morning I noticed it was
missing. And so did Kate — "I've been growing that all summer!
I've had my eye on it the past five months. And now it's gone,
thanks to the deer!" I quickly went hunting for it in among the
hosta leaves below the tree, but it was Kate who found the precious
fruit a few minutes later. And it tasted so good to both of us — so
crisp, so tart — I wouldn't have missed it for all the world. Or so
I'd like to think.

THURSDAY *September 28*

On my way home from class today, I decided to walk by Wendy's place, to look at her flower garden. It runs the length of her deep corner lot, open for all to see, and there's always something worth seeing. Several weeks ago, Kate and I and Pip stopped by to admire her collection of seven- and eight-foot sunflowers, arching their heavy heads over all the others beneath them — black-eyed Susans, white coreopsis, purple coneflowers, and a full spectrum of zinnias. A blowzy array of things, still vividly in bloom, despite the drought and the heat. Today, the only flowers left were a little square of pink petunias and a clump of pink asters. Everything else was past its prime or killed by the freeze. A panoply of dead and browning plants. No wonder she saw the color at our place. Her eye had been sharpened by the loss of it. I too know something of that heightened sensation, having recently come to notice more cats in the neighborhood than I'd ever seen before — crouching in window sills, sunning on front steps, taking the night air by the edge of a lawn or the corner of a sidewalk. Recently, I've also noticed that I don't even need to lose something to pay it attention. Just the anticipation of loss will do the trick. The eggplants, peppers, tomatoes, pattypans, and zucchini now seem so much more precious than before the frost that yesterday morning I rushed into the house telling Kate I wanted to cook a ratatouille for dinner. But I settled instead for a tangy shrimp Creole she made from our fresh tomatoes, peppers, and onions, flavored with a sliced clove of garlic, a piece of hot red pepper, and a bouquet garni of our fresh bay, basil, parsley, and thyme. What more could one ask for?

Even without the benefit of fresh herbs and spices, teaching has also become so delicious an experience that I suddenly find myself unwilling to leave the table as soon I'd planned. Now every class seems more pungent than the last, everyone more alert and articulate than before, as if they and I alike had seen the trickling sand. And the same for their writing. How strange — that just a few weeks ago, I didn't even want to think about teaching after retirement, didn't want to face another batch of student writing, and now I've decided not to retire this June, but to continue teaching half-time for one more year. And then if possible teach a course every year or so after I retire. Maybe it won't always seem so alluring as it does right now, but the pleasure seems undiminished by my decision to stay on. Better the provocations of my students than the fate of a man I beheld the other day, a man who seemed to be about my age, walking the circuit of a local mall. Three times I crossed his path in the process of running my errands, and each time he looked ill at ease, as if he had lost his way.

FRIDAY *September 29*

The thought of that man pacing around the mall got me thinking about how I incessantly put myself through the paces of this daybook. Rising each day, not with a mind at ease, but with a head aching from the same set of questions day after day — "What will I write about today? And how will this day's piece connect to yesterday's or the days' before?" Tomorrow and tomorrow and tomorrow creeps in this petty pace from day to day. So incessant the demands of this daybook that yesterday Kate was talking about how it consumes our lives, turning them into material for the daily entry. No longer do I feel free just to live a day without considering how the circumstances of the moment — a walk by Wendy's, a remark by Kate, a visit by Rebecca, or a chat with Jim — will fit into the daybook. Nor do I feel free to live my day without making room for the two or three or four hours I need to write an entry. Couldn't possibly go to a movie tonight, because I still haven't drafted this piece, much less revised it. And every day it's the same. I garden to write, I eat to write, I think to write, I live to write — observing myself and everyone else to see what I can make of us each day. And to make matters worse, it's not enough just to tell what happened each day from start to finish. Oh no, I have to consider each moment and decide whether it might serve as the lead-in to a well-turned story or description or set of reflections.

Today, for example, the intensely yellow leaves of the Dolgo crabapple took me by surprise the minute I got out of bed, and I wondered why I hadn't noticed them before, and then I wondered if I might build a piece around them, especially when I went into the guest room and noticed that the Whitney crabapple tree in our neighbor's yard had also turned golden. The turning year made visible. Of course, the leaves hadn't turned as suddenly as I'd thought. It was just the overcast sky that heightened my awareness of them. But then I couldn't help thinking about the overcast sky and the rain we need so badly that I've been fretting about it in these entries all month long. Another possible subject for this piece. Yet the overcast sky also reminded me to transplant the endive seedlings before the impending rain, and the thought that those seedlings might be the last things I put into the garden this year made me wonder if they should be the focus. Bittersweet greens, and all that. Then the thunder and the downpour and the hyperventilating Pip had me thinking once again about the rain. The sweet sound of its falling, so rare these past two months. The sweet smell of its falling on newly fallen leaves. But how about the next three hours I spent writing a letter to support the promotion of my former graduate student Laura? Oh yes, the rain was still falling in the background, but wouldn't Laura's situation make a neat counterpart to the story of my own career? Especially since I'd paired our stories back in March? Or better still, how about the afternoon with my essay reading group, in the department conference room, the wall behind me covered with photographs of all my retired colleagues? How could I possibly forget the delicious moment when my graduate student Ned asked if I'd be the one to occupy the empty picture frame in the corner of the bottom row? But where would I go from there?

SATURDAY *September 30*

I've just come upstairs after mincing a bunch of ginger for a green tomato chutney that Kate's in the process of cooking right now. Grated green tomatoes and fresh ginger, combined with chili powder, minced garlic, sugar, salt, malt vinegar, and garam masala, that wondrous Indian blend of aromatic spices — cardamom, coriander, cinnamon, clove, cumin, caraway, and black pepper. The fragrance of it all was so alluring that I just went back downstairs, between the last sentence and this one, to smell the brew up close. But smelling wasn't enough, not after I caught a glimpse of the seven-quart pot itself, filled almost to the top with that dark, heady, aromatic soup. Kate warned me, "It'll take a while to cook down and thicken up." Still, I couldn't resist, and happily I didn't, for now that I'm back upstairs at the computer, I can report that even in its raw form this concoction not only looks like a quintessential Indian chutney, but it also tastes like one. The sweet and the sour and the spice and the heat and the fruit racing around my mouth, yearning only for a lamb curry to make the zing complete. But it sure didn't feel zingy at noon when this chutney escapade began.

I'd just finished washing up for lunch when Kate came in the back door with a grim look on her face. "One of your tomato poles is down, looks like it broke off at the ground. It's one of the Big Beef slicers, the one at the east end, the good-looking one you've been saving for a cover shot." My editor had called me a few weeks ago, thinking it might be a nice idea to have a tomato plant and me on the book jacket, and I was just waiting for a few more of the tomatoes to redden up. Then I would ask our neighbor Marybeth to take a few slide shots of me, hugging the colorful, fruit-laden pole. A passionate gardener and his vegetable love. But when I went out to look at it this morning, a cover shot was clearly out of the picture. The pole was lying aslant on the ground with big green tomatoes scattered all around it — a scene fit only for the cover of a Sherlock Holmes thriller, *The Mystery of the Green Tomato Killer.* And Kate, who just a few minutes earlier had been commiserating over the loss, was gently chiding me. "See where your vanity gets you?" Actually, it wasn't my vanity, so much as a rotten pole and an overnight wind. But it was time to make lunch, so I shoved the pole back in the rain-soaked ground, a dozen tomatoes still clinging to the vine, and we gathered up the other green ones, wondering what to do with them all. Kosher dill tomatoes, I thought, remembering the bowls of them from the delicatessens of my youth. But then Kate found the chutney recipe in my forty-year-old Indian cookbook by Savitri Chowdhary, and the problem was solved. I've just been downstairs to taste it once again — the flavor more intense, the brew thicker, and darker too, the bubbling pot of grated green tomatoes, minced garlic, and ginger so permeated by the rich and haunting colors of the malt vinegar, the chili powder, and the garam masala as to be perfect for the cover of a new cookbook, *The Art of Indian Preserves.*

OCTOBER

"Did you see that young man sitting next to me? He must've had four or five platefuls. Of everything." Kate's friend Glenda, fresh in from California, was sitting on the back terrace with us this afternoon, an hour or so after we'd all come home from "the Annual Fall Dinner" at "Goosetown's own St. Wenceslaus Church." The sun slanting through the maple tree, the yellow leaves drifting off the walnut trees. October glowing all around us, especially now that the grass is greening up. But the glow outside was nothing compared to the gleam in the eyes of all the folks who'd come to eat the midwestern, Bohemian harvest feast of roast turkey, giblet stuffing, mashed potatoes, gravy, green beans with bacon bits, sauerkraut, rolls, kolaches (apricot, cherry, poppyseed, and prune), and pie (apple and pumpkin). All of it made from scratch by the women's Altar and Rosary Society, whose members start preparing things on Wednesday evening in order to get up enough food for the fifteen hundred or so who usually troop through the church basement between noon and six on Sunday. Or until the food runs out — $6.50 a person for all you can eat, "family style." And the man sitting next to Glenda wasn't the only one refilling his plate from the heaping bowls and platters that the young men and women in white aprons kept bringing to the rectangular tables of eight, again and again. Was anyone really listening to the cocktail pianist playing in the background?

Only a fit of panic over my weight could have brought me to the point of abstaining from today's feast. But I can vouch for the sanctity of its aroma. For two hours, in fact, the heavenly odors of the roast turkey, the herb- and onion-flavored stuffing, the pickled and stewed sauerkraut wafted my way, like incense, as I sat behind a card table at the entry to the basement, right next to the quilt raffle, selling our new Goosetown T-shirt. A vivid image of the hundred-year-old brick church, its steeple rising directly through the *t* in *Goosetown,* its gothic windows aglow with golden light, a gaggle of six geese with golden beaks walking by its golden entry-way — all rampant on a bright red, Bohemian red, T-shirt. So striking, I thought we'd sell all twelve dozen that we had on hand. But the look of that T-shirt could hardly compete with the smell of the meal. Just a few minutes ago, a few minutes after six, I smelled those sacred odors once again, when I went back to the church to pick up Marybeth, who followed me at the table, and to bring home the unsold T-shirts. This time, the aromas drew me all the way to the back of the basement, by the tables with the unfinished bowls of turkey and stuffing, and the uneaten platters of kolaches, and the card tables full of pumpkin pie. The holy grail. Then out again to the car, so filled with regret that all I could taste was the folly of my restraint.

MONDAY *October 2*

"Stop by my office when you're free. I've got something you might like." My longtime colleague and collaborator, Miriam, had a sly look on her face when I saw her in the faculty library this morning. So I was eager to discover the mystery. But before I stopped in at her place, I finished eating the piece of moist brown cake I'd taken off the platter that was sitting by the coffee pot. So fraught with the sweetness of the season I almost reached for another piece, but yesterday's resolve kept me in check. Then down the hall to Miriam's office, and there she sat, beaming, as she offered me yet another piece of that cake I'd just finished eating in the library. "I'm sorry you couldn't make it for honey cake yesterday afternoon, but I saved a piece thinking you might want one. Or another." So how could I refuse? Especially since I was completely flustered about having forgotten Miriam's Honey Cake party, her annual celebration of the Jewish New Year. I tried to explain about the Goosetown T-shirts and all, but Miriam wouldn't even let me finish the sentence. "I didn't mean to make you feel guilty. But just think of all the T-shirts you could've sold at my place." Miriam, Miriam, ever my Jewish aunt, steeped in the knowledge of guilt — the gift that never stops giving.

What would she have thought had she let me finish my sentence, telling her that I sold those T-shirts at St. Wenceslaus Catholic Church? And that the shirts were emblazoned with the image of the church itself. Talk about guilt! Actually, all the time I was down there in the basement yesterday afternoon, I was feeling a bit strange, and not just because I was sitting amid the alien corn. But because I was remembering Succoth, the Jewish harvest festival that captivated me during my childhood — the ancient festival commemorating the booths in which the Israelites resided during their forty years in the wilderness. I guess it was the shocks of dried corn and the pumpkins standing in front of the trelliswork panel, just a few feet away from my table, that got me thinking about the Succoth — the shelter of branches and leaves and shocks of wheat — that miraculously appeared outside the temple in Cleveland, every year at this time. Every year my classmates and I walked single file into that rustic place, and there would be the rabbi, standing at the back of it, with a lulav and an ethrog in his hand. The lulav, the festive palm branch. And the ethrog, fruit of the citron tree, looking for all the world like the biggest lemon I'd ever seen in my life. And I remember how he would wave the lulav and the ethrog in the air, in celebration of the Israelites' endurance and of the harvest. And I remember too the big shiny red apple that he handed me on my way out, the apple that never tasted quite as good as it looked — too mushy, too sweet. But most of all, I remember how snug and secure and filled the succoth was with the bounty of the season — pumpkins, pears, grapes, nuts, and so many other things, I sometimes wished I could stay in there forever.

TUESDAY *October 3*

On a crisp, clear morning like this, I sometimes wish I could stay home forever. Just sitting on the back steps, taking it all in. The grass spangled with yellow walnut leaves. The yard framed with golden walnut trees. A shaft of sunlight angling through the open branches, suffusing the air and a piece of the big vegetable bed with its luminous beam. Yellow and green, yellow and green. With a few spots of pale brown among the pin oak leaves, and several specks of purple and pink among the pear leaves, and a few hints of orange amid the maple. So striking a leafscape, a landscape, I was momentarily transfixed by it.

But no sooner had I wished myself upon the back porch forever than I was back in the kitchen. Just to get the camera for a wide-angle shot of the vegetable garden with that shaft of light shining on it. Also a few zoom shots of the orange and yellow cosmos still blooming right in front of the dried-up corn patch. And a snapshot of the once grand sunflower, its head darkened, its neck bent, its leaves shriveled, its stalk withered. But the volunteer tobacco flowers below it were still white and sweetly redolent in the morning air. So fragrant and sweet an aroma that when I knelt down and put my nose up close to the long, milky white flowers, I momentarily imagined myself on the Big Island, sniffing plumeria blossoms.

But no sooner had I transported myself to that beguiling place than I was peeking under the row covers right next to the tobacco flowers. Just checking on the fall vegetables. Turnips and radishes still putting out leaves, not yet beginning to swell. But the first crop of green onions almost ready to pull. And the second crop of onions just beginning to show. And the broccoli, the cauliflower, the lettuces, and the bok choy all doubled in size since last week's feeding and rain, burgeoning at last under the influence of these balmy days. Days so mild and sunny, I imagined myself spending them forever in the gazebo, reading and eating my way from dawn to dusk.

But no sooner did I arrive in the gazebo than I came upon the flat of basil that I never transplanted and the surplus arugula, their soil visibly dry. So I went back to the garden for a watering can, then down to the lily pond for water, and back to the gazebo again. Just to give them all a little drink. No point in moving the basil to the garden, even under row covers, so I decided to plant up a big pot of it, enough to carry us through the winter. And a big pot of arugula too. But I couldn't do it this morning, not with a class to teach. But I did have time for a quick check of the summer vegetables. Eggplants still forming, peppers still ripening, and the fabled Brandywine looking like a show horse again.

And then down to class, wishing all the way down that I could just learn to sit still. Just once. Just long enough to take it all in.

WEDNESDAY *October 4*

"Good God! Those things are still making squash?" Kate had just come down for breakfast and seen the four large patty-pans I harvested early this morning. I'd arranged them on the white counter like a still life, a display of their cupcake shapes and their vivid colors — bright yellow with a green bull's-eye at the base — as a wake-up surprise. Also on the chance she might stuff them for supper tonight or tomorrow. I certainly didn't expect her to be all that amazed by their presence. But maybe she was appalled rather than amazed — at the prospect of having to deal with more squash, when she's been steeling herself to cope with three or four dozen red peppers. Still, I'd have to admit that when I looked under the row covers I too was surprised to find four large pattypans at this late date, on the remnant of that bush I almost destroyed back in August. Maybe my earlier conjecture was right — maybe my inadvertent pruning helped to invigorate the plant so much that it put out a new leader and is now producing on two separate branches. But when I peeked under the row covers to check on the zucchini plants, again I found more fruit than I imagined, without benefit of pruning by me, the borers, or the deer. I thought it might be the row covers, but when I looked behind me to check on last spring's broccoli plants, a whole row of them without covers, I found enough side shoots to make us another meal or two. A cool-weather crop, thriving in the open air, the chilled soil, and the suddenly abundant moisture in the ground. But how about the tropical okra, still blooming, still putting out fruit, even after the frost, without any benefit of covers? Even after I picked it clean on Monday for a spiky dish of stewed okra, onions, peppers, and tomatoes that Kate cooked up that evening, flavored with chopped anchovies and a few flakes of hot red peppers. I thought it was the last okra of the season, just as I thought the chard I cooked up the night of the frost was the last we'd have of it this fall. But now there's enough for yet another meal of it too. And yesterday, I even found three more cucumbers on the leprous cucumber vines that I planted back in June. So what's going on here? Everything putting out more than I'd expected, tropical and cool-weather plants alike, row-covered or open to the air. I thought about it all the while I was planting a patch of Egyptian onions that Kate asked me to start this fall. My initial impulse — always sentimental — was to celebrate the abundance of things, more bountiful than we imagine, especially in this season of harvest. But as I pushed those shallotlike onions into the soil — onions that not only multiply below ground, but also produce onions at the tip of their three-foot-tall greens, which in turn bend over to plant themselves in the ground — I suddenly felt the urgent need of things to perpetuate their kind. Making more fruit to make more seeds to make more plants to make more fruit to make more seeds. World without end.

THURSDAY *October 5*

L ast week, I thought the endive might be the last vegetable I'd plant outside this year. Now I think the Egyptian onions will be it. And what a way to end. Not only with a new beginning for next year, but also with a rare moment itself. A golden day so fit for planting — clear sky, crisp air, warm sun, gentle breeze — that I couldn't stop talking about it yesterday. And I wasn't the only one. The young man who mows our lawn, a laid-back character with a skinhead haircut, was so ecstatic that he stopped his mower, came over to where I was staking out the onion patch, and started to talk about it. Something he's never done before. "Can you believe it? Can you believe this day?" And Kate in the midst of calling her sister Martha, to commiserate about hurricane Opal, was also moved to talk about it. "Let me tell you what it's been like here today." Actually, it wasn't just the day that had me babbling. It was the moist earth in the spot I set aside for the Egyptian onion patch, and the richly textured feel of it after I added a wheelbarrow full of the century-old cow manure that Dan brought us back in May. By the time I tilled the patch with my one-wheel plow and raked in the rotted manure, I was able to pull my three-pronged claw through the rows as easy as pie. And I myself felt as good as the soil. Everything so harmoniously attuned, it seemed as if I was destined to plant those onions yesterday. I'm beginning to sound like a mystic, and it makes me uncomfortable. But no matter how much I've read about the biological and chemical processes that account for germination, there's still something deeply mysterious to me about what arises (or not) from the coming together of the seed and the soil, the bulb and the earth. Ignore the mystery, and you wind up with burned-out seedlings, as I did in mid-August. Or with a hyperflexed posterior cruciate ligament, as I discovered just an hour or so ago from my chiropractor, who told me that when I knelt down to plant those beet seeds back in September, I evidently put too much weight on the ligament. And the beets haven't done much better, despite the otherwise favorable circumstances. Once I'd stressed out my ligament, I should have given up on the planting. The manna was clearly not with me. But it sure was yesterday. And even today, gray and chilly and rainy as it's been, the manna was there when I finally got home, walked in the door, and smelled Kate's seventeen-bean soup cooking away on top of the stove. A pot of mysteries before my very eyes. There's no accounting for what arises from the coming together of those seventeen kinds of beans with her homemade turkey broth, fresh tomatoes, chopped green peppers, celery, leek, ham, and garlic, spiced with chili powder, lemon juice, and a California bay leaf, studded with a clove. Such a hearty brew, such a multitextured stew, it actually made me grateful for this otherwise gloomy day.

FRIDAY *October 6*

Soil too wet and air too chill to work in my own garden, so I decided to tend someone else's. Ideally, I'd have chosen to pull some more weeds on that hillside tropical garden in Kauai, overlooking the Pacific. But the best I could do today was a little spot at the University of Southern California, known as the Tele-Garden. A site on the Internet that I heard about back in July, but that I deliberately chose to save for a wet and chilly day like this. So, after lunching with Kate on her seventeen-bean soup, the clovy broth still zinging on my tongue, I hustled down to my office, booted up my machine, clicked on Netscape, pulled down my bookmarked list of web sites, clicked on the Tele-Garden, and up came its home page: "The Tele-Garden: A Tele-Robotic Installation on the WWW." For three months, I'd been waiting for this moment, and there it was at last. First, a drawing of the circular garden with a schematic image of the robotically controlled camera right in the center of it — the camera that can be used to view every bit of the garden, with zoom control, image enhancement, as well as special color, lighting, contrast, and depth effects. Also to select specific spots in the garden where one can plant seeds and water already existing plants. Real plants in a real garden. Not virtual plants in a virtual garden. Or as the home page declares, "This tele-robotic installation allows WWW users to view and interact with a remote garden filled with living plants. Members can plant, water, and monitor the progress of seedlings via the tender movements of an industrial robot arm." Nothing like "tender movements" for a fussy gardener like me. For a few minutes, I just stared at the drawing, transfixed by the image of such a wondrous idea, a wedding of art, nature, and technology. A small, circular garden in the center of a laboratory at the University of Southern California, illuminated eighteen hours a day by a grow-light, thriving in a constant Edenic temperature of seventy-two degrees, watered robotically by members around the world in doses of one tablespoon each. I could tell right off that I was in the right place, especially given the resonant quotation from Voltaire right below the drawing — "Il faut cultiver notre jardin." Better still, a garden including my favorite vegetables — cucumbers, egg-plants, lettuce, peppers, and tomatoes. Also a few beguiling plants and flowers — dianthus, flax, lobelia, petunia, phlox, and zinnia. What more could I ask for on a cold and rainy day like this? So I scrolled down to the next line on the page, where I expected to find a cue to enter the garden, and there in bold print was a special bulletin: "Due to increased usage in the past 3 weeks, the wires routed through the robot arm became frayed and fried our color CCD camera." I guess the robotic arm was more ten-der than anyone imagined. But it's good to know that all the plants are temporarily being watered by hand. There's nothing like real hands for cultivating a real garden.

SATURDAY *October 7*

"It wouldn't have been possible without the garden. Where else could I have gotten fresh arugula, French sorrel, lemon thyme, and Swiss chard?" Kate was giving me a rundown of the greens and herbs she harvested yesterday afternoon and minced along with garlic and bread crumbs for the stuffing she put in last night's rolled pork loin. The minute I tasted it, I knew what was missing in the Tele-Garden. Nothing else could have mois-tened the pork with such a distinct but delicate taste as those lemony herbs and spicy greens. Still, I couldn't stop thinking about the Tele-Garden, trying to figure out why it allured me even as it repelled me. At first, I thought my ambivalence arose from the difference between a real hand and a robotic arm — between the actual feel of a plant in the earth and the mechanical feel of my desktop mouse, pointing and clicking on the screen, in order to tend a plant I couldn't even see, except through an overhead cam-era. That real garden out in Southern California might just as well have been a virtual garden for all I could touch or taste of it. No herby stuffings from it, even if I had been able to plant a few herbs with the robotic arm. Yet I also have to admit that I was — and am — beguiled by the fact that with a click of my mouse I might soon be able to plant a seed or water a plant two thousand miles away. And watch it grow two thousand miles away. I can hardly wait for the robot to be fixed and the camera repaired. Gardening at such a long distance, in such a controlled setting, I can extend the season year-round, and never worry about the weather or the deer or the squash vine borers. So what if I can't touch the food or taste it? I'll still have a hand in it. But then I got to thinking that I won't be the only one tending this garden. Anyone on the Internet, anywhere in the world, can plant seeds and water plants. And hundreds, maybe thousands, have already done so. The ultimate threat to a fretful gardener like me. The loss of control. Worse still, I discovered from a news release about the project that "There is nothing to prevent one member of the cooperative from planting in the same space as another, from overwatering the plants or even crushing them with the robotic arm." Yet even that anarchic possibility didn't trouble me quite so much as one of the project's basic premises, that "The garden will be a living model of small-planet social interactions." It's not exactly that I have anything against "social interactions." I have them all the time, when I'm walking the dog or chatting with friends or teaching a class. Or having a stuffed pork tenderloin dinner with Kate. But when I'm out in my garden, I don't really want to "rub shoulders with strangers, raising questions of cooperation versus competition in the use of limited resources." All I want to do just then is cultivate my own garden. And that, as Voltaire well knew, is something one does alone.

SUNDAY *October 8*

The harvest moon, almost full. I saw it rising yesterday at dusk, just over Kate's right shoulder as she was biting into a lettuce-wrapped egg roll at the Mekong Restaurant and I was supping on a piece of Vietnamese lemon chicken, a hot-sweet-curried dish, suffused with aromatic spices and fresh lemon leaves, like the quintessence of Southeast Asia. A small-planet social interaction, especially given the lemon leaves flown in from Florida. An hour later, my mouth still fired by that radiant chicken, I saw the moon again as Pip and I were walking down the back yard, so bright it lit up the bok choy growing under the row covers. And lit up my mind with stir-fried greens to come. A few hours later when

I was up here in the attic finishing yesterday's report, there it was again, glowing on the window seat where Phoebe used to curl up. And this morning at dawn, I beheld it once again, setting behind the seventy-foot spruce trees in front of our house.

But it never quite looked like a harvest moon. Too bright, too white. "Not enough dust in the air," according to Kate. Not enough orange or yellow in the moon. But there is enough orange and yellow and pink and rose and red at the top of the maple tree outside my attic window to make up for the moon. Thirty years the tree has been standing there, ever since my longtime friend and former colleague Bob bought it from a local nursery and planted it the first year he owned this house. I remember stopping over for a glass of wine, just a few days after he'd put it in. We drank to the tree and the house and probably a few other things as well. Little did I know that five years later, he'd be on his way to Brown University and I'd be on my way to a lifelong love affair with that tree. It looked a bit scrawny back then from its years in a nursery field. And I knew so little about trees I hardly realized that in my own time here its head would grow to be fifty-five feet in diameter — I just went downstairs to step it off. And sixty feet tall — I just eyeballed it from the back of the yard. Now it casts so large a shadow that it cools the south side of our house and shades the terrace all summer long — all nine hundred square feet of it. And brings our faithful treeman Leon back every three years to thin it out, lest the tree suffocate itself with growth. And even so a few weeks from now it will fill the entire terrace with its newly fallen leaves. Some tree, some harvest! Enough to fill a six-bin composter with its shredded leaves.

No wonder Kate's been spending her time on the Heritage Trees project, conducting surveys, designing brochures, mapping tree walks, illustrating the leaves. And typing out postcards all afternoon, inviting people to a tree pruning workshop. If I hadn't spent almost half my life with that maple, and the pin oak we planted twenty-five years ago, and the spruces we planted twenty years ago, I don't think I'd ever have realized what it means to plant a tree — or to cut one down. Now at dusk on this suddenly overcast day, my eye is filled with the trees enclosing our yard, embracing our world, like the harvest of a lifetime.

MONDAY *October 9*

"See those yellowish-green ones over there? Those are ash or hackberry. You can tell them apart by their bark. The ashes have finely ridged, corrugated bark. They're a favorite of city foresters. Disease free. Long-lived. The hackberries have irregularly pebbled bark. Now, can you identify this one?" Kate and Pip and I were out for an afternoon stroll, down to the campus and back, and she was giving us a little refresher course on the trees. On the ones that are sometimes hard to tell apart. But the minute she made those distinctions, I had no trouble at all remembering the hackberry from my stint on last year's Heritage Trees survey. Scaly and warty bark, just like one of the tree books said. Probably my least favorite tree of all. And Pip seconded the motion by lifting his leg on one just a few seconds later. Then the maples — the red, the sugar, the black, and the Norway. The little-leafed reds already deep into their fall color, most of the others just getting underway, except for "those picture postcard sugar maples over there." And then a fascinating little account of how the oaks can sometimes cross-breed so well you can't really tell them apart. By the time we started walking back home, my tree pump was so well primed I was able to identify a Washington hawthorn the minute she asked me to, even without any prior instruction. I could've stopped off at the Botany Building, just a block away, for a twenty-minute quiz or done another tour of duty for the Heritage Trees survey. Pip, on the other hand, was pulling at his leash, more interested in the coed directly in front of us than the trees along the way. Probably because Kate just then was in the process of giving us a refresher course in the current styles of dress. "That's fashionable-casual. A sorority sort of look. You can tell by the oversize bright red sweatshirt, the black tights, the athletic shoes, the white socks, and the sunglasses propped on top of the hair." No problem with that variety. As familiar as all those greenish-yellow ashes along the parking. But I couldn't figure out the one that was coming toward us in an army surplus jacket over a plain white T-shirt, with a baggy pair of jeans, ripped across the knees. "That's coffee-house conscious. Fashionable grunge. You can tell by the

John Lennon sunglasses, the little wire-rimmed lenses, the intense squint, and the black ankle boots." No wonder I thought it looked a bit like the sixties. Like a countercultural nostalgia. As if the years had never passed, and I had never aged. Except, of course, for the pain in my back from the tug on the leash and the throb in my hyperflexed ligament. Still, it was a good walk, like the harvest of a lifetime. And by the time we got home, I felt better prepared to meet tomorrow's class than if I'd spent the whole afternoon reading and commenting on their most recent batch of writing. There's a time and a place for everything. And today was for looking at bark and leaves. Today was for looking at leaves.

TUESDAY *October 10*

Thirteen women in class and not a single one of them in an oversize sweatshirt, even on a crisp morning like this. I noticed it the minute I entered the seminar room and sat down at the table, fingers still chilly from my walk in. Sweaters, vests, blouses, and sport jackets. But no sweatshirts, oversize or otherwise. Apparently not the fashion for thirty- and forty-year-old graduate students. I wouldn't have bothered to mention it here, if it hadn't been for a question from Ellen, who was sitting across the table from me in a white T-shirt and a blue fleece V-neck pullover. "What's happening in your journal these days? What are you planning to write about today?" So many things on my mind just then — eggplants on the bush, leaves on the lawn, gardening on the Internet, and the essay for class discussion — it was all I could do just to tell her about yesterday's tree walk and Kate's running commentary on the coed in the oversize sweatshirt. "Oh my God," said Marilyn, who was sitting directly to my right in a green pleated blouse. "I almost wore one today. And tights too." And then on my left, Marie chimed in. "And me too." Suddenly, the oversize sweatshirt was a bigger deal than I'd thought. And then I remembered the Goosetown sweatshirts we've just started selling and Jim asking me to get him an XXL, and I recalled my own oversize sweatshirt from Hawaii with a yin-yang symbol on the front of it. Before I knew it, the oversize sweatshirt seemed like a humungous emblem of something, but I knew not what. Not even an inkling of it, until we started to talk about the essay for today, a piece by E. B. White called "The World of Tomorrow," an essay about his first encounter with the World's Fair of 1939 — a visit permeated by the cold outside and the cold in his head that were evidently afflicting White just then. "I realize that the World's Fair and myself actually both need the same thing — a nice warm day." A charming lead-in, I gradually came to realize, for White's satiric depiction of the fair as a coldly mechanical vision of the future: "You sit in a chair (wired for sound) or stand on a platform (movable, glass-embowered) and while sitting, standing, you are brought mysteriously and reverently into easy view of what you want to see." But everything's at a distance, "extremely impersonal," like "the trees of Tomorrow" that White beheld in a futuramic display, "each blooming under its own canopy of glass." Not exactly the Tele-Garden in Los Angeles, but close enough to give me a chilly feeling of kinship with White. The robotic arm, the overhead camera, the clicking mouse, the cool screen. No wonder everyone's trying to keep warm — with an oversize sweatshirt, or a blue fleece pullover, or whatever else will do the trick.

WEDNESDAY *October 11*

Today the weather's so warm I shed my sweatshirt by noon and put on a short-sleeved shirt. Crisp nights, warm days, sunny skies, gentle breezes, turning leaves. The golden time, and the harvest continues as if it were high summer rather than midfall. Monday, more yellow pattypans. Enough on hand for Kate to stuff a couple that night with couscous, corn, onions, and peppers, and freeze a few for the winter. Also more Big Beef slicers, enough for me to make a tomato sauce for the pattypans to bake in, with basil, parsley, garlic, and chili powder. A Mexican sort of concoction that Kate invented during the family reunion back in August — so rich and tasty now with the whole wheat couscous, we both agreed it's ready for a recipe contest. More slicers on the back porch, and more turning ripe on the vines. And more zucchini to go with the batch already in the crisper, enough for two or three dinners. And a bunch of eggplants hanging on the bush, even after I sliced a couple last night, dabbled them with olive oil, garlic, rosemary, thyme, and oregano, baked them on a tray, and dressed them with a little oil and vinegar. And a few dozen peppers still on the bush, even after Kate spent the better part of an afternoon freezing several dozen for the winter — some halved for stuffing, others roasted and puréed. And a bushel or two of Enchantments still on the vines, gradually changing color along with the changing leaves. And a twenty-foot row of fresh basil, hiding under the row covers.

And the maple tree so fiery in the late afternoon sun I could hardly keep my eyes upon these flat gray letters, this cool white page. So I went downstairs and walked out to the back of the yard, to view the maple from a distance. But the color wasn't visible. Not from that perspective. Not yet. The tree just turning at the top. But I did see the big walnut tree nearby, its golden leaves still hanging on, backlit by the sun. And I did feel the warm air, warmer than the breeze up here. And I picked a handful of red raspberries. So my tour of the yard was worth it, especially when I stopped to look at the asters in Kate's perennial bed, four big clumps of them, spaced out along the back, their pumpkin-colored centers and lavender petals fully open at last. Swaying in the breeze. Covered now with butterflies and bees. And on the way back in, I stopped to gaze at the pear tree, its fruit turning yellow on the branch. And the yellow marigolds, blooming again along the front of the big vegetable bed. And the orange coreopsis in the center. And the leaves on the grass. And the grass itself. So green again, even over Phoebe's spot, that I almost passed it by without a glance.

THURSDAY *October 12*

"Just look at all its colors through the trees — gray, silver, brown, blue." And green, I hastened to add, green way over there against the other shore. A few hours ago, Kate and Pip and I were sitting at a picnic table under a canopy of oak and hickory trees, beholding Lake MacBride, a nearby lake I've been going back to ever since the first early summer afternoon I fished it some thirty-three years ago. A day as warm and sunny and breezy as this. Actually, we were viewing the lake from a sloping little hillside, sitting under a canopy of oak and hickory trees, their red and brown and green and golden leaves illuminated by the sun, like stained-glass windows, as we lunched on our homemade sandwiches of charcoal broiled steak, grated jack cheese, sliced onions, alfalfa sprouts, salsa and lettuce on sourdough bread, along with some kosher dills, Calamata olives, and ale. Kate had put together the sandwiches while I was off teaching, and she layered them up just right, the sweet crisp Walla Walla onions in the center playing off against the meat and cheese on one side, the greens on the other. We also had a couple of red Bartlett pears, the color and sweetness of the season. A favorite of Pip's. But when Kate was talking about the color of the lake, we were still eating our sandwiches, still sipping our ale, still marveling about the leaves and the breeze and the sun glittering along the ripples in the water. And I was thinking just then, or perhaps I'd already said by then, that it didn't get any better than this. We hadn't yet walked along the shoreline, hadn't yet seen the sunfish schooling in the clear green water of a log-strewn cove, hadn't yet beheld the lunging Pip stopped short by water lapping at his paws. But nothing I foresaw just then could possibly exceed the vividness of that particular moment. Of Kate and Pip and the sky and the water and the trees and all. Maybe it was the food that made me think so. Or the ale. Or my sudden recollection of the sign along the road at Joensy's Bar, THE BIGGEST AND BEST TENDERLOIN IN IOWA. But just then, as if to prove me wrong, a big gust of wind whipped through the trees, the biggest and best of the day, and blew down a little branch of light brown oak leaves that landed with a *thuck,* right in the middle of our green and white checked tablecloth. A gift from on high. A centerpiece to grace our day. I'm looking at the branch right now — swamp white oak, according to Kate — sitting on the oak table a few inches from my computer, its leaves propped up against the dark brown base of my table lamp. And now, with the aid of my lamplight, I can see all the tiny veins in one of its leaves, running back and forth between the main ones, branching off in every lobe, an intricate network of life, suddenly cut short just then, though I didn't think about it until just now. And now I can see all its buds, perfectly formed, also cut short. But just a few hours ago, I thought it was the best thing that had happened all day.

FRIDAY *October 13*

After finishing yesterday's piece, I went downstairs and made one of the best Creole dishes I've ever had. So piquant a stew of squid — with okra, onion, green pepper, celery, tomatoes, basil, bay, garlic, hot red pepper, parsley, thyme, and gumbo filé — I almost forgot about that fallen oak branch and its perfectly formed buds. But this evening, as if to put things in their place, I completely forgot about that Creole squid when Kate and I were downtown sipping our cocktails, trying to choose between the sautéed tenderloin of venison in cranberry-raisin sauce and the broiled beef tenderloin in green peppercorn sauce. Maybe my kids are right when they tell me I'm always saying this or that dish was one of the best I've ever had. Actually, it wasn't just the food that rang my bell. It was the crowd-lined street of painted faces, fall costumes, oversize sweatshirts, and undersize children right outside the restaurant, waiting for the Homecoming parade to start. And the parade itself, suddenly about to begin, and out we ran, drinks in hand, just in time to behold the high-stepping drum major in his long white tails and his creased white pants and his bright gold sash, and to hear the razzle-dazzle beat of the alumni marching band, sashaying down the street in their flat black pants, and their glossy gold vests, and their jaunty straw boaters. *"Fight, fight, fight for Iowa!"* on everyone's lips in unison with the big brass tubas bringing up the rear, swaying back and forth, all the way down the street and around the block by the floodlit reviewing stand. And then back inside for the mixed green salad with the Dijon poppyseed dressing, while the green John Deere tractors passed by the window, pulling the floats — their papier-mâché mascots, their scarecrow players, their plywood fields, their jimcrack goalposts assuring us that Iowa would bowl over Indiana tomorrow. And the retinue of high school bands from Coralville and Dewitt and Camanche and Solon and Tipton and West Branch and Mount Vernon and Williamsburg and other burgs also assuring us that Iowa would carry the day. How could we fail with all those drums beating on our side? They certainly did sound good when we ran outside to hear them between the salad and the beef tenderloin. But how about the Iowa City chapter of the Harley Davidson Clubs of America — those black-leather–silver-studded guys and their smiling molls? And the bravura sign of the gay liberation group — *"Homo-coming!"* And the big black and gold *"Rose-Bowl Bound"* bus bringing up the rear, a caravan of dreams. And the steak and the oven-browned potatoes and the crisp green beans and the bordeaux. How about those? Better still, how about the thick-sliced Neapolitan mousse, surrounded by a bittersweet chocolate glaze, surrounded by a raspberry purée, with a dollop of whipped cream on each side? Best of all, how about that big, big Iowa marching band, in their gold-colored spats and their gold-striped pants and their gold-striped capes and their gold-trimmed caps drumbeating their way down the street, down Iowa Avenue, walk-dancing their way across campus and up the steps of the Old Capitol, the floodlights shining on the brass tubas as they swayed back and forth between the tall neoclassical columns, pumping out the sounds we all declared — *"Fight, fight, fight for Iowa!"*

SATURDAY *October 14*

"It's almost over." Not the words I expected to hear from Kate when we were out in the yard this afternoon, putting row covers over the bell pepper plants and eggplants. Not after the past two or three days of summery weather. Or perhaps, I should say they were not the words I wanted to hear just then. But once she made that chilly announcement, I could hardly deny the truth of it. Not with a harsh wind gusting in from the northwest and the temperature predicted to drop into the lower thirties this evening. And the row covers billowing so much, it was difficult to keep them in place. Kate already had her bout with the cold and the wind at an indoor/outdoor tree pruning workshop she'd organized this morning for the Heritage Trees project. I'd predicted a group of fifty or sixty people, like the turnout back in July for the cemetery tree tour, but the weather scared off all but fifteen tenacious tree-huggers. Even I didn't stay for the outdoor part, figuring I'd better get home and start bedding down the summer vegetables and herbs. But a call to the local TV weather channel put me temporarily at ease — until the predictions started to worsen this afternoon. Then the panic set in, the pressure to get everything covered before dinner and darkness, the compulsion to protect it all, even in the face of Kate's indisputable announcement. After helping me with the peppers and the eggplants, she was, I could see, not eager to go through the rigmarole with the tomatoes, not after this morning. And neither for that matter was I, but something inside me refused to give in. Perhaps it was my willfulness that produced her sad and wistful look just then, a look which seemed to suggest this frenzied plant-covering escapade was my own private journey, and I'd have to go the rest of it alone. She and Pip were going back inside to a warmer and saner place than the battle-scarred row of tomato plants I was hoping to bring through yet another bout of frost. One pole, holding a Big Beef slicer, had already broken off again in the wind, and was lying on the ground like a wounded soldier. Then the Brandywine slid down its pole when I tried to cover it with a plastic sheath. And the Enchantments looked as if the charm of their existence were forever past. But I couldn't stop until I'd covered them all with sheaths or sheets and tied them all with rags or string to protect them from the billowing wind. And now as I sit here remembering my predinner frenzy, I cannot help but wonder what drives me to it every year at this time. Why can't I just let go? Especially when it's always so easy once they're gone. Sometimes I think it's a reluctance to forgo all those summery vegetables without making the most of all they have to offer. Creole squid the other night. Curried lamb this evening with fresh onions, peppers, and tomatoes. But sometimes I think there's more to it than just the food. Not even the best curried lamb in the world, even with Kate's green tomato chutney, could arouse such a frenzy.

SUNDAY *October 15*

F rost on the grass — the first thing I look for out the attic window. And there it is, a thick covering, all the way from the terrace back to Kate's flower bed, from one side of the yard to the other. The mower's tracks turned white. And the windshield wipers' too. Heavier than I'd expected, especially given the TV weatherman's prediction of temperatures between thirty-two and thirty-four. Heavy enough to make me wonder if I've lost all the peppers and the eggplants and the tomatoes, for want of enough protection. But a half-hour later, after I've showered and shaved, the frost is completely gone. Only the dew remains, as if the frost had never come. And when I go outside to check on things, I'm amazed to see that nothing's been damaged, not even the patty-pan plant I'd mistakenly left uncovered. The big chill averted or delayed. Another mid-October cliffhanger happily resolved. So much for yesterday's frenzy. The sky is clear, the sun is bright, the maple's on fire, the temperature's on the rise, and I'm on my way to the co-op to get the Sunday paper and some smoked trout for a brunchy omelet with fresh parsley and chives. A celebratory meal. All the summer vegetables still alive for another week or two or more. And the Egyptian onions I planted last week beginning to show. And best of all, the fall vegetables thriving under their covers. The first crop of radishes and green onions ready to eat just a month after I planted them. As crisp and moist as the first ones of spring. And the lettuce almost ready for salads, and the bok choy for stir fries. The ground, I see, is beginning to dry out again, so I haul out the hose and water all the greens. And the air is beginning to warm up again, so the potted herb plants go back outside for another few days in the sun — the lemon grass, the rosemary, the tarragon, and the bay. Nothing can spoil this day, not even the continuing glitch somewhere in my computer or my word processing program that shows up once or twice a day with a vertical rectangle right in the middle of a w□rd, or a slash right / in the middle of a sentence, and sometimes a tab space and some-times a page break. Even the glitch fails to appear when my neigh-bor Ken, a computer specialist, comes over to observe it. And then as if to crown this glowing day, Rebecca shows up with a bottle of champagne and stories of her miraculous reprieve without any row covers at all. "All my herbs survived, even the basil, and I harvested three dozen more tomatoes, and there's more on the vines beginning to turn." Sitting in the kitchen just then, sipping champagne, munching pistachios, tasting Kate's improvisational concoction of Swiss chard, sorrel, arugula, shallots, bread crumbs, wine, and tomato juice, the possibilities of the moment seem almost limitless. Only the reappearance of that rectangle this evenⅡng reminds me that there's something, somewhere in the system, waiting to return.

MONDAY *October 16*

The glitch in my computer or the glitch in my knees? It's hard to decide which one is giving me more trouble, especially right now, when I've just switched to a different font from the one I regularly use, as Ken suggested last night, to see if the problem is "font-specific." A sensible solution, but I'm so tense with curiosity to see if the glitch will appear in this particular font that I'm sitting at my computer with my legs pulled back under my chair, the way my chiropractor Jean says I'm never supposed to do. Too much stress on my posterior cruciate ligament. So I stretch my feet out under the table in front of me, but then they start slipping forward on the hardwood floor. So I cross one ankle over the other, and then remember that a cardiologist once told me to avoid that position, because it impedes the circulation in one's feet. I wonder what I can do with my feet that won't be pain-specific or problem-specific. I also wonder what I'm going to do next if the glitch turns up in this font (New York) just as it has in my favorite (Palatino).

I'm also thinking about a conversation I had a few hours ago with Jim, when I asked him if he's ever had any trouble with his knees. "Trouble? It was so bad after a few hours in the duck blind this morning — my feet were curled under the seat — that I could hardly stand up. But it sure did feel good to stretch 'em out." Duck hunting already. Just then, our knees seemed less interesting than his morning endeavors. "We just got a couple. The air was too calm. The water like glass. Not a ripple." His arm stretched out in a smooth, unruffled arc. Perfect conditions, I thought, for fly-fishing or casting with any kind of surface lure, but evidently not for duck hunting. "They're smarter than you think. If they look at those decoys and don't see any ripples, they know they're not the real thing. It was too nice for duck hunting." It never occurred to me that such good October weather could be such a bad thing, like a glitch in the computer or a pain in the knee, but I've never been duck hunting. I guess it depends on your point of view.

But Jim did touch a chord in me when we were looking at the remains of his pole-staked tomatoes — four of them still covered with green fruit, but nothing else left in his garden. "It sure is hard letting go of all these things, almost like it was family they've been in so long. I could hardly pull up those pepper plants last week, and there wasn't even anything left on 'em anymore." Maybe that's why the sandwiches were so tasty that Kate and I had for lunch — a little sliced cheese and alfalfa sprouts with our own sliced tomatoes, onions, leaf lettuce, and the last cucumber of the season, on sourdough bread. And the first of our fall radishes and green onions. Six things fresh from the garden that rarely if ever converge. And kosher dill pickles to boot. So special a meal, it more than makes up for the gl□□tches that just recurred.

TUESDAY *October 17*

"Click with your mouse at any point within the circle and the robot will move to that point and return the image of the actual garden as viewed from that point." The glitch in my computer and the glitch in my knee made we wonder if there was still a glitch in the Tele-Garden's robot arm. So I clicked on the lower left quadrant of the circle and up came a circular image of greenery with a couple of petunias in the center of it. The robot's arm was working again, better than my knee, which was aching all the way down to campus this morning. So I clicked on the Tele-Garden Help file and printed a copy of it to study while I was microwaving the leftover chard-arugula-sorrel dish from my own garden. "Refer to the water overlay option within the options page to see areas that have been watered recently." And sure enough, I saw patches of blue where the robot had released "a short burst of water for about 3 seconds." The petunias didn't need water, but there were numerous spots of gray where the garden was evidently as parched as our place in mid-August. So I moved the robot arm to one of those spots, and up came three yellow marigolds, as vivid as the ones along the front of our big vegetable bed. Then I pressed the Water cube on the Menu Bar, and a bold-faced announcement suddenly appeared on the screen: *Activate the system info option to display your hit count.* My "hit count"? I hadn't realized I was out to hit anything, much less that anyone was keeping track. But when I activated the system info option, I discovered I'd already made thirty-three hits. Back to the Tele-Garden Help file, and I discovered that "You increase your hits by moving the robot, posting messages, watering, and by any other garden activities. After 100 hits you will be allocated one seed, after 500 hits another, and a final third seed at 1000 hits." So, it turns out, if I want to plant a seed, I have to be a good white rat. I have to visit the Tele-Garden, water the plants, post messages for other white rats, and in general modify my behavior to conform with the suggestions that appear on the screen each time I water something different. By watering the flax and the phlox and moving the robot arm to several other spots, I gradually worked my hit count up to forty-nine. But it took me an hour to do so. A long time, even for a white rat to work himself halfway toward planting a single seed, especially when I can plant one in my own garden without any hassle. Still, the process of accumulating those hits made me realize how incredibly active that robot's arm must be, what with thousands of tele-gardeners trying to get enough hits to plant a seed or two. No wonder it broke down two months after being put into operation. Now I understand what my chiropractor Jean was talking about this noon, when I asked her what had gone wrong with my knee. "It's not anything specific. It's just the normal wear and tear, the stress you've been putting on it your whole life. Especially when you kneel down like that in your garden. Look at it this way. You've been dying from the day you were born. And it's the same with your knee." Still, I'd rather have my own worn-out knee than a new robotic arm.

WEDNESDAY *October 18*

"Disable your extensions, and see if that helps." "Disable" was the last word I wanted to hear this morning, especially with my knee aching all the way downstairs. But after the glitch turned up again on the screen last night, I figured it was time to visit the chipheads at the university's computer center. And after a few explanations, I began to understand their lingo. "Just boot up the machine with the shift key depressed and that'll turn things off that might be producing some kind of static in your word processing program." So I've disabled my extensions, and I'm waiting to see if this crippling maneuver will get my computer up to snuff again.

But the real news of this morning is the batch of radishes I seeded in right after breakfast. I don't know what got into me. The mild air, the hazy sky, the warm sun. Or yesterday's frustrating episode in the Tele-Garden. Or Kate's question the other noon — "Do you think there might be any radishes left for Thanksgiving?" Or just a foolish desire to end my planting year, much as I'd begun it, by planting radishes again, somewhat out of season. Whatever was driving me just then, it was a pleasure from start to finish. Just to work the pointed hoe back and forth through the soil one last time, then to lie down on the grass with the sun on my back (no kneeling right now) and crumble the earth in my hand, and level it out, and draw my finger through it to make a light depression, and drop the pinkish seeds in one by one, spaced out enough so I won't have to thin them, and cover them all with compost, packing it down with the palm of my right hand. Not as remarkable, perhaps, as getting the robot three thousand miles away to "create a hole in the soil," to "suck up a seed" from the "seed dispensing unit," to "drop it into the hole," to "pack the soil over the seed," and to "dispense 3 seconds of water over the newly planted seed." But it felt better, I'm sure, a lot better. And it looked better too. Especially the part where I patted the compost down with the palm of my hand, then stood up, turned around, and beheld the maple tree glowing like a pumpkin in the morning sun. Also when I carried my yellow sprinkling can to the lily pond, filled it with fish water, walked back to the row, and slowly sprinkled it back and forth, watching it soak in and darken up the surface.

When I put the polyester cover back on and walked to the other end of the row, I noticed a cricket crawling over its pale white surface, like an emblem of endurance, and the shadows of the earlier radish leaves visible under its surface. Another batch ready for eating with our sandwiches this noon. Radishes in, radishes out, without a hitch. Words in, words out, without a glitch. Now all I have to do is figure out which one of the forty-four disabled extensions is the culprit. And I thought the Tele-Garden was a trick.

THURSDAY *October 19*

Now that I've compared my extensions folder at home with the one in my office computer, I see they contain only eight extensions in common. So, given the fact that neither machine has a virus, it must be one of those eight extensions that's causing the glitch. Nothing like mincing a large, tear-jerking shallot to clear one's head. Also a green pepper, a stalk of celery, and some fresh parsley. I was making a minced vegetable and bread crumb stuffing for a couple of fresh flounders last night when I first realized that the presence of the glitch on two different computers could help to solve the problem, if only by reducing the number of extensions to be checked. That flash of insight was so thrilling I could hardly keep my mind on the pan of minced vegetables I was sautéing just then. So I called up my neighbor Ken, to be sure my reasoning would hold up in the mysterious world of computers. "Makes sense to me. But don't start the process of elimination until you've spent another day or two with all the extensions disabled, to make sure you've isolated the general area of the problem." So I've still got all my extensions disabled, eagerly waiting for the moment when I can begin to track down the sole culprit. But already I feel like Sherlock Holmes, in search of a bizarre criminal. Even the laid-back chipheads at the computer center said, "We've never seen a problem like this before."

One thing I discovered last night for sure is that a little curry added to those sautéing vegetables produces a taste that delicately suffuses itself through the firm white flesh of the flounder. I also discovered that a very fine extra-virgin olive oil suffuses itself exquisitely through any dish to which it's added. Actually, I've always assumed that to be the case. How could it be otherwise? But until Kate and I received a bottle of Aprutium (Italian) olive oil from her friend Glenda, I don't think a supremely fine cold-pressed oil had ever found its way into our kitchen. Except perhaps for the Stutz (California) olive oil that Glenda sent us last May. Glenda's a sometime food critic, chef, and cooking teacher, who now owns a Mediterranean food store in Carmel, so she knows her way around the world of olive oil. I first uncorked the Aprutium a couple of nights ago to dress a platter of spaghettini before adding garlic, parsley, asiago, salt and pepper. Just the look of it, the pale green color of it caught my eye, lightly coating the pasta. And then the ethereal taste of it caught my tongue, like a heavenly nectar. But the spirit of scientific caution, inspired in me by my neighbor Ken, compelled me to test and retest the oil on a variety of foods, to validate my results. Last night, its delicacy highlighted a dish of the sliced Black Prince tomatoes with chopped basil. This evening it graced a romaine salad. Now its wondrous influence seems as certain to me as the salutary effect of disabling my extensions. Words in, words out again without a glitch.

FRIDAY *October 20*

" It's all over." This time I was hardly surprised by Kate's announcement. How could I be, especially with a raw northwest wind gusting through her hair, reddening her cheeks, as she stood on the front porch this morning, tying the long wooden swing to the side railing. Mid-seventies yesterday, mid-forties today, with a wind-chill factor in the mid-twenties. Now the glitch in my computer seems like a trivial matter compared to the rainy, blustery weather. So much for the quiet time I planned up here today. Instead, I've been tethered to the National Weather Service, the howling wind, and all the tender plants. Potted ones down to the outside cellarway. Outdoor ones encased with another set of row covers. An easy matter on the printed page — just a couple of sentences — but the whole rigmarole took me almost three hours, thanks to a thirty-mile wind. The worst of it came in the midst of trying to wrap the spun-bond polyester around the plastic-sheathed tomatoes — the wind whipping the cloth in and out of the swaying seven-foot poles, and I whipping myself with the absurdity of trying to carry them through another cold spell. Now those onetime show horses of mine don't even look like work horses anymore. More like terminally ill patients in the oxygen tents of yore. Only a piping hot bowl of Kate's chili could have fortified me for such an ordeal — the two-day-old concoction rich with the taste of diced beef, onions, bell peppers, and kidney beans in a brew of tomatoes, beef broth, salsa, chili powder, cumin, garlic, vinegar, salt, and pepper. The lingering taste of that well-aged stew convinced me, after all, that I wanted to keep those pepper and tomato plants alive for a few more days. Also the National Weather Service prediction of "more-seasonal" weather by Sunday. Also a reluctance to face the task of picking one or two bushels of green tomatoes, lugging them down to the basement, and laying them out on shelves to ripen in darkness.

But the real story of this day is coming to its climax now in late afternoon, as Kate is peeling, halving, coring, then poaching and canning our big old-fashioned yellow Bartlett pears in a syrup of fresh apple cider, cinnamon sticks, lemon juice, lemon zest, and brown sugar. She brought a sample up here an hour ago, and the heady confusion of all those tastes and smells is still on my tongue, still in my nose. But the thing I'm remembering now as I look out my window at the tree, its mahogany leaves rustling in the wind, is the stately progress of those pears from late April to late October, from the pale white blossoms to the greenish-yellow fruit, from the branch to the grass to the oak basket on the back porch to the poaching pot on the stove to the canning jars on Phoebe's old counter, layered with the pale halves in rich brown syrup. Kate assures me "They'll go well with some whipped cream in the center and some gingerbread on the side." And I'm sure she's right.

The only thing she didn't mention was a chilled glass of Spätlese wine to set them off.

Maybe it was the thought of those pears. Or the sight of the skewered red peppers and onions sitting on the kitchen counter at my colleague David's house last night. They caught my eye the minute Kate and I arrived. Whatever aroused it, a vegetarian ethic must've been stirring in me, right in the middle of dinner with David and his wife Rebecca and our mutual friends from Minnesota, Trish and Terry. We were sitting around his big oak table, speculating about the value that people of different cultures put upon their lives and the lives of others, a discussion occasioned by the continuing madness and misery in Bosnia, Croatia, and Serbia. And Trish had just taken pains to account for the peaceableness of the Czech and Slovak split-up, when suddenly I was wondering out loud whether our belief in the sanctity of life might be subverted by the ease with which we accept the growing and killing of animals for food. No sooner had those thoughts crossed my lips than Kate was reminding me that "Man is an omnivore." And reminding me too of the county fair, where I'd seen the farm children learning to part with their beloved animals at the sale barn. Then David, who grew up in rural Missouri, told a story he'd heard about a farm child mourning over her "Lamby" at a lamb dinner one evening, despite assurances from her parents that she was not dining on "Lamby." To which she evidently replied in tears, "But I wanted to eat Lamby." From Bosnia to Lamby in such a short time that Terry the Calm suddenly exclaimed upon the extraordinary arc of our conversation. So it was difficult to get much sympathy for my position, especially when I was feasting just then on a tasty fillet of salmon that David had grilled over charcoal. The love of animals is deep within me, I guess, and there's no point in trying to avoid it.

The love of college football is also deep within me, as I discovered today at the Iowa–Penn State game, thanks to Kate's cousin Mary and her husband Larry, who drove in from western Iowa with a ticket for me to join him at the game. Though I haven't been to a game in five or six years, there was a time during my college days that I couldn't imagine the possibility of missing a single one of Michigan's home games. But I'd come to believe I could live without it, much as I sometimes think I could live without meat. I thought about watching the game on television, given the overcast skies, blustery winds, and near freezing temperatures this morning. But Linda the Gruff set me straight, when she stopped over to check about gathering our walnuts. "If I had a ticket, I sure wouldn't miss the game. Just bundle up." And I did. Longjohns, oversize sweatshirt, a hooded parka and all. A half hour before game time, the skies cleared, the air warmed, the wind died down, and there we were on the forty-yard line, sitting amid a host of black and gold fanatics, looking down at the bright green grass and the chalk white lines and the yellow lettered end zones and the Iowa band going through its razzle-dazzle pregame warm-up, right down the center of the field. So what if I was sitting next to four porkers who couldn't stop swilling beer, so they couldn't stop going to the john, so they couldn't stop moving back and forth in front of me. So what if Iowa lost the game right after it got the lead midway through the fourth quarter. So what if our quarterback threw a game-breaking interception, just after completing one hundred straight passes this season. I can still see the others, spiraling through the air to our big tight end and our fleet-footed halfback. I can still hear the band at halftime, the beat of the drums, the sound of the brass. I can still feel the sun on my forehead. And I can still taste the rare beef tenderloin I had at our postgame dinner at the Lark Supper Club in Tiffin — the oldest and biggest and still the best steakhouse in Iowa.

SUNDAY *October 22*

The only problem with our postgame dinner is that it ended with Kate's eighty-one-year-old mother, Lib, sprawled on the ground outside her retirement home, moaning in pain, her frail bones injured, though we knew not which. Face down, her head just inches from the right front wheel of our car, there she lay in the freezing late night air, gasping for breath, with Kate hunched over her, propping her chest up, holding her head up lest she choke to death. Child and mother, mother and child. So quickly it happened, it was over in seconds, just a few quick takes from my angle of vision. I pull up to the sidewalk by her building and stop the car. Kate says, "I'll walk you to your apartment." Lib says as usual, "No need to bother. I can do it myself." Then Lib gets out of the passenger seat next to me, Kate gets out of the back seat behind her, and a misstep or two later Lib is falling, twisting headlong toward the car, Kate lunging helplessly behind her. A time-motion study that cannot be altered no matter how many times I might replay it. For when push comes to shove, as Lib would say, this is one of those times when she cannot do it herself, cannot do it for a lifetime of reasons — her aging, her breathing, her footing, her smoking. And Kate cannot reach her, no matter how hard she tries, for time and motion and intention have put Lib out of reach. I run to her apartment, call the retirement health center to solicit their aid, and run back with blankets to keep her warm. Fifteen minutes later the nurses arrive with oxygen, and Lib initially refuses it. "I can breathe on my own." Twenty minutes later I put the car in reverse, hoping it doesn't jump forward, when I give it the gas, to make room for the ambulance. Thirty minutes later I can hear the sirens and see the whirring lights of the county ambulance even before they turn into the drive, while the city fire department's emergency crew parks its long green engine out in the street. Three firemen, two paramedics, two nurses, two of us, and Lib, who can hardly breathe on her own, even with the help of oxygen. Three hours later, she's in a hospital bed, facing the decision of whether to be bedridden for the rest of her days or to risk a potentially fatal operation to pin her broken hip back together again. Ten hours later the frost-covered grass has completely thawed in the morning sun, but when I peek under the row covers, the dark brown leaves of the basil plants and the limp green leaves of the pepper plants and the blackened leaves of the eggplants tell me they're all beyond my reach. Bad omens. Twelve hours later, Lib's about to leave for the operating room, wishing she'd eaten the ripe tomato that Kate gave her a few days ago. And thirteen hours later, she's come through the operation, her forecast suddenly as bright and crisp as the day itself. Tomorrow, we're told, she'll be sitting up, two days from now she'll be starting to walk. Still, I'm thinking there are times when it's probably best to take someone's arm, even with a cane of one's own to lean on.

MONDAY *October 23*

"Just look at your tomato plants! Don't they remind you of Lib?" Kate and Pip and I were on the way to her flower border, after finishing a lunch of her homemade lentil soup, chock-full of celery, mushrooms, and our own fresh onions and peppers. I could still taste its rich brown lamb and tomato broth, zingily flavored with bay, clove, and garlic. And so, I'm sure, could Pip, having just finished licking my bowl clean. But when Kate made that surprising remark about the tomato plants, I suddenly forgot about the soup. Surprising, not because it seemed far-fetched, but because that's exactly what I too had been thinking yesterday when I looked at them after the frost. I didn't have the nerve to share my impression with Kate, not yesterday morning, not when we were chatting with Lib right before the operation. And then I completely forgot about it while we were waiting for the surgeon's report. But her remark called me back to that haunting resemblance — so gaunt, but still hanging on, a few green leaves still clinging to their vines, the rest all browned or shriveled up. Yet still enough fruit on the vines to make a few quarts of spaghetti sauce or tomato purée. If I didn't know any better, I'd be tempted to say those vines are as willful as Lib. But the truth of it is that I'm the willful one in this case, as I discovered this afternoon when I decided to leave them standing a little while longer, hoping to get a few more days of ripening on the vine. And why not? So mild and sunny all morning that I didn't even need a jacket when I went out in the back yard.

A little bit later, right after Kate went off to visit Lib, a blustery wind blew in from the south, so fierce the sky clouded over in a trice, and a driving rain slanted in. So fierce, it blew two of the Enchantments halfway toward the ground, twisting them out of their polyester covering. And all the while they were going down,

I was up here, looking out my window, looking at the storm, looking at the summer garden coming to an end before my very eyes. And no way of stopping it, not even if I had run out and reset those plants in the midst of a wind-driven rain. But then the storm blew out as fast as it had blown in. A sudden reprieve. So I went down to reset the leaning Enchantments, only to discover the damage was worse than I'd thought. Not even the surgeon who put Lib back together could have done anything to save them. One pole broken off at the ground, its tomatoes scattered over the surrounding straw. The other pole still intact, but its main stem cut off at the ground. So I harvested their tomatoes, reinforced the three Enchantments and three Big Beef slicers still standing in the row, and called it a day. Now as I sit here at midnight finishing this report, the wind is howling again, howling so loud I wonder if any of them will be standing tomorrow. And what for.

TUESDAY *October 24*

The minute I got up this morning, I could tell it was another downer. Six-thirty, and the wind still howling, the sky still gray, the cold still seeping through the window frames, and the maple tree outside our bedroom window almost completely leafless. Kate was asleep as I dressed for my morning class, but I had a fairly good idea of what she'd say when I called later on, and she didn't let me down. "It's here, and we might as well face up to it." She never did say what she meant by "it," but I could see it in the windblown tomato poles, and I sure could feel it walking down to campus, even inside my hooded parka and my wool shirt and my Hawaiian T-shirt with the palm trees waving in the tropical breeze. Not even the power of suggestion could keep me warm this morning. And it didn't get any better when I got to the office, picked up the *New York Times,* and started reading a weather piece, "Autumn's Winter Storms," or when I clicked on the Netscape, and called up a National Weather Service forecast for tonight. "Clear and cold. Low 25 to 30." A tomato-killing frost, unless they're bundled up inside two or three layers of polyester wrapping. Then as if I hadn't seen enough, I picked up the student newspaper, and there right in the center of the front page was a color picture of Clinton and Yeltsin, sitting next to each other in bentwood chairs, "overlooking the sunny splendor of the Hudson Valley." So many maple trees in fall color that the picture was a blur of reddish-orange and green.

I guess it was that balmy picture that finally drove me to the Tele-Garden in Los Angeles. I clicked the Info cube to get an update on my accumulated total of "hits" — seventy-six. Only twenty-four more to go, and I'd be allotted a seed for planting. Then I looked up the identity of the Current Seed — Eggplant — and that bit of news turned me on like a true white rat. Just two days ago, I'd harvested our last eggplant of the season, the plant itself a victim of the overnight frost. So it seemed only fitting I should get that current seed for myself. Twenty-five minutes before the start of my morning class, and twenty-four hits to go. Oh, how I clicked my way around the garden, moving the robot's arm from spot to spot, watering at each dry spot along the way — lobelia, petunia, marigold, and phlox. A hit for every click. Five minutes before class, and still three hits to go. Two minutes before class, and the seed was mine. "Be sure to plant your seed in an empty spot on the plant overlay." And I did — at M4 on the Robot Schematic. Suddenly the camera image of the garden reconfigured itself with my code name — CarlKlau — directly over the site of my newly planted seed. My own eggplant growing in the Tele-Garden. I swept off to class on a wave of pride in the speed of my achievement. Afterward, I clicked on the Info cube to get the specifications on my eggplant and discovered it would be ready for harvest in "120 to 150 days," but that I must "never let the soil dry out." So now it seems I've been trapped by the Tele-Garden. Unless I abandon my seed.

WEDNESDAY *October 25*

To water my seed or not to water it. That is the question I pondered late yesterday afternoon, as I bundled the tomato plants with two more layers of polyester wrapping. Whether 'tis nobler in the mind to tend the thing I started, suffering the prods and pointers of the Tele-Garden teleprompter — "The blue dots in the water overlay fade away to simulate drying" — or to take arms against behavioral modification and by opposing end it and my seedling too. Just then, Carol stopped by the garden on her way home to make dinner for Jim. She'd come over to pick up a few Goosetown T-shirts and sweatshirts for sale at their trophy shop, and I offered her a few red peppers into the bargain. Hard to keep my concentration on the question, especially when she was looking at the ghostly shapes of the covered tomato plants. "Jim harvested all his tomatoes a few days ago." To wrap or not to wrap. That is the question I was suddenly pondering in the clear, crisp air of the setting sun, the needles of the bald cypress glowing gold just a few feet away. Whether 'tis nobler in the mind to suffer the slings and arrows of outrageous weather, or to take cloth against a sea of troubles and by opposing block them, at least for another week or so. Balmy weather back in the forecast after tonight's cold snap. Not much time to ponder, so I went with my deepest instincts. Wrap for the night is coming wherein you cannot wrap. Then I hustled around, harvesting the last of the pepper crop and a few zucchini still blossoming and fruiting under four layers of cloth. On the way in, I picked out three bright red Enchantments from the table of green and pink tomatoes ripening on the back porch, covered the rest with some old bed sheets, and then set out to make something of all my summer vegetables. Something to go with the potatoes baking in the oven and the veal cutlets that Kate had set out on the kitchen counter.

By the time I came in, she'd finished reading yesterday's report, and as usual had a sensible solution to my seed-watering problem. "It's no big deal. Just water it. It'll give you something to do for the next five months." When I asked about the veal cutlets, about the possibility of doing something with onions, paprika, and sour cream, in the Hungarian manner, she had a similarly sensible solution. "Just keep it simple, in the French manner, like you usually do." So I sautéed the veal and braised it in a little beef broth, red wine, and herbs of Provence, the gravy heightened with a dash of lemon and a few chopped chives. Then I put together a plate of sliced tomatoes with a little olive oil, red wine vinegar, and fresh chopped basil from the plants sunning themselves in the dining room window. For a counterpoint, I sautéed a mix of sliced red peppers, zucchini, and onions, in olive oil, garlic, and basil. Nothing fancy. Just some bright summer dishes for a midfall day.

THURSDAY *October 26*

*B*ut the arrangements sure were fancy at the faculty lounge this morning — cranberry bread, croissants, sweet rolls, fresh fruit, orange juice, coffee, tea, milk, and specially mailed invitations to fête our long-retired chair, John, for the publication of his book about the first hundred years of the English department. A fine occasion, arranged by our current chair, Dee, hoping, I'm sure, to heal the wounds of last spring's thunderstorm. And there was John, signing copies of his book, surrounded by old colleagues and friends, beaming in the light of their affection, as if nothing had ever happened. I couldn't help wondering just then what thoughts might be passing through his mind, but then I remembered a bit of good advice he'd given me some twenty-five years ago, when I was considering a high-pressure administrative appointment in New York City. "If you can handle the defeats and disappointments and insults that inevitably come with such an appointment, and come back smiling the next morning, then I think you're just the right person for the job." Thanks to that advice I didn't take the job, else I'd probably not have been around to see John still smiling after all these years.

The weather the past two days has also had me smiling so much I've just been wafting around the yard again, peeking under the row covers, taking the breeze, gazing at the trees. Maybe that's why Kate was so upset with me last night after I came home from visiting Lib. "Do you realize all the things that have to be done in the next few weeks? Rake the leaves, turn the garden, winterize the car, put on the storms. And here we are going off to Chicago for a weekend. And we haven't even carved our pumpkins yet." The turning of the year, and everyone facing up to it but me. All the way down to campus this morning I was still in a daze. The balmy air, the blue sky, the glowing trees. Everything so captivating that even some of my favorite lines from Emily Dickinson, lines about this delusory season, still couldn't break the spell — "These are the days when skies resume the old, old sophistries of June, a blue and gold mistake." Not until Kate and I were finishing lunch at a downtown restaurant, and I couldn't find my blue and gold Visa card, did I begin to come to my senses. From then on, the omens got worse and worse. The minute we left the restaurant, Kate noticed the sky had clouded over while we were inside. A few minutes later, I found out that no one had turned in my credit card at the bank. Back at the office, when I clicked on Netscape to get a weather report for Chicago, my connection broke down, and I couldn't get it restored. So I couldn't get a report, and I couldn't water my eggplant seed. Then after dinner, our friend Lynda called from Chicago — "Ron will pick you up at the train station, and you better bring some warm clothes. It's turned cloudy and cold here."

FRIDAY *October 27*

So we're off to Chicago — sweaters and coats in hand. But before we go, the herb plants have to be moved to the outside cellarway, and the tomatoes on the back porch have to be redraped with sheets, and why not check the Thanksgiving radishes to see if they've germinated? And they have, so why not give them a drink of water, the ground feels so dry? And the leaves on the lily pond. Best clear them off, so the fish don't suffocate. And best stop fussing around, else we'll never make the train, fifty miles south of here in Mount Pleasant.

So we're off, and Kate's driving, dazzled by the blue and gold landscape. "I thought it was supposed to be cloudy and cold, but look over there." A field of corn stubble, lit by the sun. "Look over there." A new crop of winter wheat, greener than grass in the morning sun. "Look at all those oaks turning and the willows in front of them." So much to look at that before we know it, we're sitting in the red brick railroad station, with the brown marble floor, and the art nouveau radiators, and the mission-style benches, and the white walls tiled halfway up, and the white stucco walls to the ceiling, and the wood-framed windows with the dark green shades, and the wood-beamed ceiling, and the oak-framed ticket window. I'm looking closely at everything, because we're on our way to the Monet exhibit in Chicago, and I want to get in the habit of seeing all the touches, all the fine points. Like the American flag hanging over the hallway to the men's and women's rooms, and the fig tree in a yellow pot, and the rubber tree in a black pot. Kate puts it all in a nutshell — "It's done in arts-and-crafts style. I also think somebody's taken it in hand since the last time we were here. Remember how tacky it used to be?" And there's the train whistle, and there's the conductor calling us aboard.

So we're on our way, zipping by field after field of corn stubble, bean stubble. The glitter of grain, the color of wheat. The clatter of wheels. And suddenly it's time for lunch in the dining car, with the white tablecloth and napkins, and the red and white carnations in the slender metal flower holders, ours looking like it's been to San Francisco and back without a drink. And the friendly hostess — "We've got hamburgers and cheeseburgers and salad and minestrone soup, and I'm sorry the menu's so small, but we've been running behind, and we're trying to make up time." And the Mississippi right outside the window, and the ducks in the backwaters — maybe I should tell Jim they're here. And the friendly waiter who keeps bringing us more than we ordered, including a bouquet of carnations from all the surrounding tables that he puts together in front of Kate. "It's an old railroad tradition. The last lady in the car gets all the flowers." From then on central Illinois seems even flatter than before. But the beige of the fields, especially against the cream and gray of the lowering sky — no wonder Monet was captivated by those haystacks!

SATURDAY *October 28*

The minute we entered Lynda and Ron's house, I was captivated by the images on the wall. How could I resist a skull mask, just below a color engraving of a vulture, just a few feet away from a little nineteenth-century oil painting of a tree-sheltered lakeside scene, just across the hall from a World War I poster in red, white, and blue of a man, woman, and child standing against the backdrop of an American flag and an immigrant ship, urging me to *"Remember! The flag of liberty. Support it!"* In the world of our friends Lynda and Ron there's no telling what you might find on the walls, in the chairs, on the floors, and you don't have to view it through a mass of bobbing heads and moving bodies. It's right there for you to see, like the Mexican skeleton costume on the wall facing our bed, its arms and legs covered with painted wooden skulls.

The path to Monet was a bit less direct. It led the four of us and a few thousand others on a serpentine walk through the Chicago Art Institute's reconstructed interior of the Midwest Stock Exchange, then its corridor of Greek pottery and sculpture, its display of Renaissance jewelry, its collection of artifacts from the Prairie School — shades of the Mount Pleasant railroad station. And then nineteenth-century American painting, and the Hudson River school, and oh, what I'd have given just then to be standing in one of those serene landscapes. But my wishes changed the minute I saw Monet. Especially his life-size *Luncheon on the Grass,* with all the grapes and pears and apples and wine, along with a roast turkey, and an unidentifiable dish that could have been a pâté or a torte. Kate couldn't figure it out either, but it clearly didn't bother her. "Don't worry about the food. Just look at the picture." Hard to keep focused, though, with all the talk going on around me. "It's all in the brushstrokes." "Look at all those dahlias!" "It's all in the light." "Can you imagine him spending all that time on those haystacks?" But nothing could match the one that Kate overheard in the gallery displaying Monet's Oriental woodcut collection — "Oh! I didn't know he did Japanese woodcuts too!" But the talk died down when we got to the *Houses of Parliament* — at sunrise, at sunset, in sunlight, in fog, in haze. And a shuffling of shoes was all I could hear among the waterlilies. A lifetime obsession with time and change, from season to season, from month to month, from minute to minute in his garden, and we got through it in two hours. Not bad for a Saturday morning. We also got a catalogue of the exhibition, and a book called *Monet's Table,* so we can sample his recipes. We didn't get a Monet calendar, or a Monet kaleidoscope, or a Monet umbrella, or a Monet datebook.

But we did get lunch in Chinatown, at the Moon Palace, where the steamed greens were so fresh and vivid, I can hardly wait to try a few of my own bok choy when we get home. And the eggplant with garlic sauce — it sure made me wish our plants hadn't died. But I didn't mourn long, especially when we went to the Day of the Dead exhibit at the Mexican Fine Arts Center museum. So many skeletons and skulls in festive offerings to the dead, it made me think that Lynda and Ron didn't have enough for their own place. So I got them a sugar skull with bright green eyes. The only problem is that Ron started eating its chin off before we got home. But there the skulls were again when Ron and Lynda took us out for a splendid Mexican dinner at the Frontera Grill. Finally, I was beginning to understand how Monet might have become obsessed with his waterlilies. Maybe I could do a series of entries on the human skull.

SUNDAY *October 29*

Right over the toilet in Lynda and Ron's guest bathroom is a gold-framed reproduction of a two-page medieval illumination, hanging at eye level, so I could hardly ignore it every time I went in. A cautionary scene, showing the naked figure of Venus in the upper left-hand side, standing under a mammoth classical archway, with a flaming torch in her hand. Directly below her the nude figure of Cupid, blindfolded, standing on a big blue platform. A bit to the left of Cupid a spread of white horses, named Imprudence, Intemperance, and the like. The rest of the scene was filled with famous lovers gone wrong — Paris and Helen, Jason and Medea, Antony and Cleopatra, all arm in arm, some chained to each other, or roped to each other, except for a solitary figure in the lower right-hand corner, whom I didn't notice until this morning. Narcissus, looking at a pale gray image of himself in a little pool of water, just about the size of our lily pond. I used to wonder how Narcissus got stuck in that position, but not since I've been keeping this daybook.

Soon after looking at that picture, I was down in the breakfast room, gazing at the maple outside the window, most of its yellow leaves still hanging on, aglow in the morning sun. Chicago, I thought, must be a week or two behind us. But my real longing then was not for another two weeks of fall gardening. I had my eyes on Lynda and Ron's garden, a manageable little plot, without any vegetables or fruits to fuss over. Just specimen trees and shrubs, elegantly placed, and a wide brick walk, bounded by hostas, angling through the yard, leading one's eyes and feet to a couple of small lily ponds and water plants back in the corner of the lot. An irresistible garden! Nothing much to tend and nothing much to do but sit in a chair or feed the fish or look in one of the ponds to see if I could really catch my image in its glassy surface. My own pond's too close to the house for seeing one's reflection, so I've never tried after the first few times. But when I looked into Lynda and Ron's, and saw my image there, I could understand how it might have been with Narcissus or the cat in Mr. McGregor's garden. A few minutes later when I was back in the house, a neighbor's marmalade cat walked into the yard, but it never even went near the ponds.

If it hadn't been for a visit to the Lincoln Park Zoo, I'd probably have thought about that cat all day long. But it couldn't hold a candle to the mountain lion or the spotted leopard or the great gray owl, rotating its head back and forth, or the bald eagle, or the cedar waxwings that arrived just when we were gazing at the secretary birds. Or the elephants, doing some fancy footwork and trunkwork in return for a lunchtime feeding by their trainers. Or the orangutans. Or the gorilla that put its palm on the glass right on the other side of Lynda's palm. I wonder what it was feeling or thinking then. I'm especially curious right now as I look out the window of our coach car, moving through the darkened landscape, and see myself more clearly there than anything I can see outside.

MONDAY *October 30*

"Spring forward, fall back." A cheery little aid to memory that usually leaves me depressed whenever I hear it, especially in fall. One day of twenty-five hours in exchange for several months of late afternoon darkness. Not a fair exchange of values, no matter how you look at it. Especially when it signals the visible approach of winter in the drastic reduction of daylight. Yesterday was the day we fell back, and yesterday at least I hardly noticed. Maybe it was the bright, sunny day in Chicago, or the train ride back to Mount Pleasant in late afternoon. But today, the full force of the change bore in upon me when I woke to an overcast sky and dined after sunset. Not even Kate's spicy Swiss steak with a sauce made from our own onions, peppers, and tomatoes could distract me from the darkness. It probably didn't help that I'd just come back from visiting Lib in the hospital. Now so afflicted by her breathing that she can hardly eat without gagging, or even practice her walking, especially given the crack they discovered in her pelvis. If it isn't one thing, it's another.

And sometimes it's several things at once. Like this morning, when I went down to the office, just to check on the mail and water my eggplant seed, and discovered that it had already been watered eleven times in the six days since I planted it. Turns out the System Log, which I'd never checked on before, enables members to discover when and where a new seed has been planted, and by whom. So it's not surprising that others want to get their few drops in. The only problem, as Kate said at lunch, is that "They'll probably drown it in water." Then I called Nate, the computer specialist who fixed my Netscape connection, and learned that the glitch in my word processing program has probably infected everything on my hard drive, and the only way to cure it is through a complete removal, cleanup, and reintroduction of all the files. "Somewhat like a total bodily transfusion of blood." A precarious operation that gives me the creeps just thinking about it. Then I checked the National Weather Service and the Weather Channel, only to discover that the overcast skies and cool wet weather today will be hanging in all week until Friday when the first Arctic blast is to be coming our way. So my ghostly tomatoes are probably nearing the end of their viny existence.

In the midst of this gloomy weather, the pin oak and the pear stood out more vividly than before, now almost fully turned, competing with each other for the mahogany leaf award. And Rebecca stood out in her blue felt beret and her blue farming jacket planting a bank of blue squills under the big old spruce trees. If winter comes, can spring be far behind? Four and a half months behind, and maybe more.

TUESDAY *October 31*

Halloween, and our pumpkins were still sitting on the back porch this morning, still uncarved. A cold and rainy day, hardly promising a festive evening. But the age-old urge to get oneself up and go out pranking, or at least out masking, must have been at work in me again. Else why would I have stopped at the local toy store right after class to buy a couple of animal masks for Kate and me to wear this evening? A white-faced cat, with pinkish ears, pinkish snout, pinkish mouth, big black whisker-dots between the snout and the mouth, and glaring chartreuse eyes. Also a cream-faced sheep, with a large cream-colored nose, sagging sad-sack eyes, and a wide gap-toothed smile. A companionable pair, I thought, but when I took them to the hospital where Kate was visiting Lib this noon, she suggested that I trade the sheep in for something "with more bite to it — a fox or a wolf." And Lib herself was feeling so much better at lunch that she not only got a kick out of the masks, but also got down a piece of pork tenderloin without gagging. Just then, I thought about getting a pig mask. The power of suggestion, I guess. But I thought better of it when I went back to the store, and exchanged the sappy sheep mask for a glaring wolf with a two-toned face — light brown on top, white on its cheeks and chin — with a black-edged mouth, gray teeth, and menacing turquoise eyes. Pip didn't much like the glare on its face, especially when Kate put it on and gave him a snarling "Grrrrrrrrrr." But I could tell from her growl that the wolf clearly fit the bill, though its eyeholes were a little too far apart for her to see through. Then we did the pumpkin-carving ritual. Hers with upslanting oval eyes, round nose, and wide grinning mouth. Mine with pointy downslanting eyes, pointy down-slanting nose, and pointy downslanting mouth, three pointy teeth in the center of it. Pumpkins glowing on the porch, we were ready for the trick and treaters just on the verge of darkness. The only problem was the weather — still so cold and rainy that only six or seven groups made their way up the steps of our spookish-looking house on the hill. Some with smiling parents, some alone, one with a German shepherd, much to the consternation of Pip. All assuming they need only knock on the door and we'd appear with handouts. "Smile, get your treat, and go," as our friend Trudy put it when she called this evening. The trick, it seems, has gone out of Halloween. How else to explain the confused and surprised faces when they saw me in a wolf mask and Kate in a cat mask. If I had my druthers, I'd have been on the other side of the door with a piece of Ivory soap in my hand, just like I used to get from my aunt Ada, and I wouldn't be looking for treats either. I'd be out sneaking around, looking for windows to mark, cast iron mailboxes to clang, and neighbors to trick, especially the ones I don't like. Oh, to be a wolf again, rather than a sheep in wolf's clothing.

N O V E M B E R

"Remember me as I am." Rebecca was standing on the stone steps by our terrace, when she issued that command. Not exactly like a parapet in Denmark. Still, her words gave me a faint sense of how Hamlet might have felt when his father's ghost commanded him to "Remember me." Given such a solemn obligation, I hustled into the house right after she left and jotted down a few notes on what she was wearing. Brown knit beret, long white cotton pullover sweater, quilted grape-colored vest with white buttons, dark brown chinos, and green felt clogs. Nothing ghostly about Rebecca, especially given her year-round suntan and the wry little smile on her face just then. But her getup this rainy, sixty-degree day was something I might not be seeing for a while. Especially given the Arctic cold wave coming our way, according to a "special weather statement" I found on the Internet. "The gray and damp weather will be a fond memory by the weekend. A blast of cold air will settle across the upper Midwest by week's end. By Saturday night temperatures will tumble across the state. Overnight lows will bottom out in the teens across Iowa . . . The balance of this workweek will provide an excellent opportunity to do any last-minute gardening." The minute she finished reading that statement, Rebecca issued her command and hustled off to do some last-minute gardening at her place. And I went back to finishing some last-minute work of my own, deconstructing the few remaining tomato plants in the back vegetable bed. Now for the first time in five months, the poles are down and the fruit is completely harvested — twelve dozen Enchantments and four dozen Big Beef slicers sitting on the back porch, to be ripened on shelves in the basement. And now as I look out my window in late afternoon, all I can see in that once abundant spot is the pile of dead pepper plants and tomato plants waiting to be bagged up for refuse, and a ghostly white row cover along the front of the bed, protecting the radishes and green onions. But I can still remember how it looked in high summer — tomatoes, peppers, and egg-plants pendant on all the vines and bushes. Maybe that's why the first few minutes out there this morning were a bit harder than I'd expected. Hard to let go, especially after getting through a few October freezes. Also hard to let go of a northern gardener's dream — vine-ripened tomatoes for Thanksgiving. But after I'd unwrapped the plants and started pulling them down, my mind was beginning to focus on the challenge to come. To protect all the radishes and onions and lettuce and bok choy and broccoli and cauliflower and spinach with enough row covers to get through this bitter cold snap. The radishes were so crisp and mild I bagged up a couple for Lib, along with some sliced red pepper and an Enchantment tomato. The freshly picked salad at lunch was so tasty and vivid, I'll be piling on the covers tomorrow.

THURSDAY *November 2*

"You are approaching the winter." My colleague Jix sounded like a Greek oracle or a Chinese fortune cookie when our paths crossed in the hallway this morning. And he looked like a prophet or sage, his hands crossed behind him, his gray beard touching his chest, his eyes glittering as he uttered that strange locution. I was on my way home, so maybe he was just warning me about the weather outdoors. A bit above freezing, with a twenty-mile-an-hour wind blowing snow showers in from the northwest. A wind-chill of eleven. Weather for late December or early January, certainly not early November. Actually, I'd been approaching the winter ever since I woke up at five this morning, shivering, because the temperature dropped twenty degrees overnight and the thermostat was set too low for the furnace to kick in. I approached it again at eight this morning when I took the car in to be winterized, and the snow showers started on my walk down to class. On my way back home at eleven, I approached it yet again when I stopped at a paint store to get some caulking for the attic windows, and there on the Weather Channel playing above the counter I saw a prediction for single-digit temperatures tonight west of the Mississippi. And I didn't stop approaching it until I was eating our first bok choy from the garden, stir-fried with shiitake mushrooms, garlic, and sesame oil, to go with some jasmine rice, fresh red peppers, and broiled chicken basted with tamari, ginger, garlic, and oil. To keep us company at dinner, Kate brought in our two carved pumpkins, so the thought of winter was still close at hand. Especially when I realized the bok choy could be our last, if I didn't put on enough row covers this afternoon.

The wind was blowing so hard I couldn't have gotten them on alone, so I called up Jim and asked him for help. But even together it was sometimes difficult to keep the twenty-foot strips of cloth from whipping out of our hands, as we put them on or tried to fold them over for double protection. The minute we started, Jim was muttering about duck hunting tomorrow morning with his son Kevin. "We're gonna freeze our buns off. It's goin' way down overnight. But this is the kind of weather that'll bring 'em here for sure." So I decided to put six layers of covering over the vegetables and herbs, enough to give the plants about twenty-four degrees of protection. When I showed Jim the bok choy and lettuce plants, I could see he was having second thoughts about late fall gardening, so I gave him a head of bok choy to stir his appetite a bit more. Also some of the zucchini I harvested from the plants after removing their covers to put them over the endive and parsley. Triage in the garden. And a chilling thing it was for both of us to think about — choosing which plants to protect, given a limited supply of row covers. But nothing was quite so chilling as the thought of Jim and Kevin in their duck blind at quarter of six tomorrow morning.

FRIDAY *November 3*

J ust when the cold and overcast weather were about to get me down yesterday afternoon, the clouds started to blow out, and by midnight, when I finished yesterday's report, the sky was clear, with a three-quarter moon, bright enough to shed some light on Pip and me as we made our way around the block. But the wind was still so harsh and the air so cold, I couldn't help wondering about all the covered vegetables. So I checked on the radishes this noon — a test case — and there they were, bright red roots bulging above the ground, their leaves erect, looking and feeling a lot warmer than the outside air thanks to the six layers of cloth and the warming influence of the sun. Now all they have to do is weather a couple of more nights in the low twenties, and the worst will be past — until the next cold snap arrives. Strange how the snaps have been coming this year at almost regular weekly intervals, each a bit longer, each a bit more severe than the last. As if we were gradually but deliberately heading into a long, harsh winter, when the snaps are the rule and the intervals but a fond memory. Not a pleasant conjecture, except for the warming soups it suddenly calls forth from Kate. Today at noon, it was a souped-up soup, a frozen leek and potato purée she made several months ago, raised to the level of an intense and richly textured chowder by the addition of her homemade chicken broth, low-fat sour cream, as well as fresh chopped leeks and potatoes, sautéed and flavored with thyme, garlic, and white pepper. Not a single ingredient from the vegetable garden, but who needs the garden with a soup like that on his lips?

Besides, if I'm looking for things from the garden, all I need do is visit the basement, as I did this morning, just to see how things look on the wide brick steps of the outside cellarway. Filled with plants and herbs and vegetables and fruit, it looks like a picture of harvest waiting to be taken. Especially with the midmorning sun streaming through the Plexiglas door above it. The tall lemon grass plant on the lowest step, next to the big oak basket filled with ripening pears. One step up, another oak basket filled with red and green peppers and a couple of eggplants, flanked on each side by a rosemary plant . The next step up, some basil plants standing in a quart jar of water, side by side with another oak basket filled with Enchantment tomatoes. Above them an azalea and a bay plant, companions from last winter. Then our twenty-year-old cymbidium, a full stalk of little orchid buds already formed, flanked on each side by a pumpkin we didn't carve. Then the lemon verbena plant, its wings spread from one side of the step to the other. And lastly, a pot of tarragon, sitting next to a batch of arugula seedlings to be transplanted for winter salads. Maybe I should get a shot of those steps, vertically organized, to show all the things that are sitting there right now, before we start eating our way up the steps.

SATURDAY *November 4*

"The endive? I was planning on that for Thanksgiving." Kate was sitting at the breakfast table, when I told her about the freeze-bitten endive I'd discovered this morning. My stomach churned the minute I lifted up the end of the row cover and saw those discolored endives, not just because of Kate's Thanksgiving plans, but also because it probably meant the demise of all the other greens. I didn't have the nerve, or the time, to look any further just then — I was on my way to the co-op for some pancake and waffle mix. But when I got there and stopped at the meat counter to chat with Jim, the butcher, he gave me a grim weather report. "I couldn't believe it when I came in to work. Couldn't have been more than five or ten, it was so bad." Actually, the low was fourteen, according to a local news station. Worse than the National Weather Service predicted yesterday, but I couldn't believe it was low enough, given my twenty-four degrees of protection, to destroy all the endives or anything else. I checked things again in late morning and discovered that only the greens at the ends of each row had been hit by the freeze. All the plants in the middle were firm, green, and plucky, as if they'd never even been touched by the overnight drop. After checking the greens, I walked up the back yard to check on Jim, for a duck-hunting report. He wasn't home, but Carol was out airing the dogs, hands shoved in her winter jacket, and a smile crossed her face when I asked about the ducks. "Can you believe him and Kevin going out in that cold? They got four big ones and a couple of little ones, but I don't think they'll be able to keep going much longer, 'cause they're already having to chip ice away from the decoys."

The traumas and troubles of putting food on the table. I couldn't help thinking about it this afternoon, while Kate and I were witnessing the madcap calamity that besets Anne Bancroft, who plays a suffocating mother in the Thanksgiving movie *Home for the Holidays*. It's bad enough that Bancroft's spinster sister Gladys, played by Geraldine Chaplin, brings a key lime pie topped with M&Ms, as a gesture of unrequited love for Bancroft's obese husband. Worse still, Bancroft's yuppie daughter and son-in-law insist upon bringing their organic turkey to compete with her own. Two big turkeys at one small table of nine people — one at each end of the table. An emblem of the seriocomic troubles besetting that dysfunctional family. Not exactly a situation most people could identify with. Still, I couldn't help thinking about our Thanksgiving to come, featuring a twelve-pound organic turkey, for a guest list that's dwindled from twelve to eight — what with Lib in bed for several more weeks, Kate's brother John going from Denver to California to start a new job, and Glenda calling last night to report that she and her son can't make it from California. At this rate, a few frozen endives will be the least of our worries.

SUNDAY *November 5*

That movie we saw yesterday afternoon — I can't get it out of my mind. And not just because of the two roast turkeys, one of which went flying off the platter directly into the simpering face and prim green dress of Bancroft's yuppie daughter JoAnn. Nor even because of the sixty-four roast turkeys reportedly used in rehearsals to achieve that lofty effect. I could probably do it with a single bird, if need be. Every Thanksgiving, in fact, I've come close to launching one into the Lib's lap, when I'm trying to cut through the joint between its thighbone and back. No, it's something else that's been nagging at me — the remarkably swift changes that take place in the life of Bancroft's daughter Claudia, the heroine, played by Holly Hunter. On the Wednesday before Thanksgiving, when the movie begins, she suddenly and unpredictably loses her job at a Chicago art museum, and on the Friday morning right after Thanksgiving, when the movie ends, she's flying back to Chicago with a man she's met while visiting her parents in Boston. So in just two days she loses her job and finds a new love. Her life, it would seem, is completely transformed, yet in ways that seem plausible not only in the movie but also in actual life. Claudia's experience has been nagging at me, I guess, because recently things have been changing so swiftly and unpredictably all around me. I'm not just talking about the weather and the garden, though they're certainly part of the story, given the swift change from balmy to wintry conditions in a single day. I'm also thinking how Lib lost her footing, and nearly her life, in a few seconds. Then, how she could barely eat or breathe at the start of last week, and now she's back at her retirement home — in the infirmary, to be sure — but sitting up, eating heartily, and chatting like a magpie about all her visitors. I'm also thinking of how my own life suddenly changed one day this fall, when I decided to keep teaching another year, rather than retire at the end of this one. So just a few days ago, I found myself signing up to teach a couple of courses next year that I never imagined myself teaching before — on the writing of daybooks and journals. And now as I look out my attic window at the white row covers in the vegetable gardens and herb beds, I realize my gardening has suddenly been reduced to a minimalist activity. I peek under the covers to check on the life below, and I harvest a few things for dinner. So many changes in such a short time. But then I remember how the movie put Kate in mind of a three-act, swiftly paced comedy she wrote several years ago, called *The More Things Change,* the resolution of which suggests how much things stay the same. Then I realize how little, really, has changed in the rhythm of Lib's life, my life, or the garden. The one change, after all, that really makes a difference, is the one that Yitzhak Rabin suffered yesterday in Tel Aviv, that Phoebe went through this summer, the one that binds all creatures great and small.

MONDAY *November 6*

"**K**indly stay on the flagstone, if you will." The idiom was so antique it took me by surprise, as I had not been addressed that formally since I left Brunswick, Maine, some thirty-five years ago. The minute I heard Nancy's voice behind me, the voice of Kate's chief collaborator on the Heritage Trees project, I knew that I'd evidently stepped out of place. Nancy is a person of Lib's generation who grew up in Maine, so it's not surprising that she spoke to me in such a starchy fashion. But it took me a few seconds to figure out how or where I'd misstepped. Jim and Kate and I were carrying some twenty cartons of Heritage Trees brochures from our house to Nancy's, to store in her basement, and I was delighted just to be rid of them, having put up with them in our dining room and front entryway for the last month. So I wasn't paying much attention to where I was walking, as we carried the boxes around the side of Nancy's house and down toward the back entryway to her basement. Then on our first trip back up the hill toward Jim's truck, I heard the voice, heard the kindly request, looked around to see where I'd erred, and realized after a few embarrassed seconds of confusion, face to face with Nancy, side by side with Jim, that I'd stepped right in the middle of her Zen rock garden. And so had Jim. And so, I later discovered, had Kate. Jim and I caught her doing it two or three trips later. But at first, it seemed that I was the sole culprit, the only klutz, and my cheeks were hot with embarrassment. In my eagerness to be rid of the cartons, I must've mistaken her smoothly raked bed of varicolored little river rocks for common pea gravel. I still don't know how I could have overlooked the two jagged stones placed diagonally opposite each other in the pool of stone. Nancy, of course, deflected my apologies by assuring me she was only concerned for the safety of our footing. But the next trip down, when we were walking alone, Jim said in a whisper I could barely hear, "I guess we've had our hands slapped." He too understood how we'd misstepped, given the fussiness he lavishes on his own flower beds and borders. So it wasn't as if either of us thought Nancy out of order for fretting about her tranquil pool of stones. In fact, I can even remember asking folks not to step in my own garden when the soil's been freshly cultivated and raked after a spring rain. Talk about putting your foot in the wrong place! Just before we went over to Nancy's, I had an appointment with my chiropractor, Jean, who gave my anterior cruciate ligaments another treatment with her electrical muscle stimulator — "It reduces the swelling, reduces the muscle spasms, and increases the blood flow." The only problem is that I mistakenly lifted my foot up in the middle of the treatment — "Keep your foot down the next time" — and got a shocking spasm all the way down my leg. As painful a little jolt as I felt when I looked at my footprints in Nancy's Zen garden.

TUESDAY *November 7*

Yesterday's piece, I thought, would be expiation enough for having stepped in Nancy's garden, but all during class this morning I was thinking about it again. How could I avoid such thoughts when we were discussing a draft of Corinne's essay about stepping into someone else's garden? In this case a garden filled with daffodil and tulip beds planted by the ex-wife of the man she's currently living with. Beds that despite their lovely blooms — or perhaps because of them — remind her all too much of her predecessor. So Corinne imagines herself digging up those bulbs and planting them in a different spot, much as she has already mown paths through the uncut orchard grass — paths that lead to the barn, to the chicken coop, to the creek, and the granary. Corinne not only didn't want to step in someone else's garden — she evidently didn't even want to look at someone else's garden, or walk along paths that might lead her to that garden. The thought of her hunger to efface that other woman's garden and landscape suddenly brought me face to face with the full import of what I did yesterday when I stepped into Nancy's Zen garden. At the time, I was chiefly concerned that my carelessness had led me to mess up all those carefully raked stones, and that in doing so I'd spoiled the artfulness and tranquility of the spot. But this morning, I couldn't help thinking that what I'd really done was to trample on a deeply personal place, a place endowed with the spirit of its maker. Which is, of course, what any garden must be for the person who creates it and tends it. Why else would Nancy have been so emphatic about our staying on the flagstone? Why else would I get so upset sometimes when people just tromp into my garden without so much as a please or thank you?

Now I'm beginning to understand what's been bothering me about the Tele-Garden and all those people watering my eggplant seed. It's not just a matter of wanting to be alone in the garden, though that's certainly part of it. It's also a matter of wanting my garden, my sacred spot, to be left alone. Maybe that's why the deer and the groundhogs and the raccoons and the squirrels have bothered me so much that when I see their depredations I sometimes feel myself profoundly shaken, unsteady, as if the ground of my being were threatened. Well, I don't want to get too carried away by that sort of thinking. It's only a vegetable garden, after all, and right now I'm actually feeling grateful to the recent freeze for freeing me from any more worry about the tomatoes and the peppers and the eggplants. Still, it was annoying the other day when I came into the office and discovered that another member of the Tele-Garden had planted another eggplant seed right next to mine, and that people are now watering both of our spots incessantly, so they're both sure to drown. Now I know why I won't be visiting that place anymore. And why Nancy must have been wishing just then that Jim and I had never set foot on her place.

WEDNESDAY *November 8*

"I could've done without the blinking eye in the stag, but its oak leaf ears and real antlers were something else. Didn't you think so?" Actually, I could've done without the five buses of schoolchildren giggling their way through the outside doors of the Des Moines Botanical Center just when we arrived. Shades of the thousand chattering people at the Monet exhibit. But I did notice the life-size topiary stag the minute we walked into the special air-controlled geodesic dome, and not just because of the little orange light bulb blinking in its eye. For me, it was the live sphagnum moss covering its head and neck, like a pale green counterpart of actual fur, and the small single-petal yellow chrysanthemums growing all over its body and its legs. Like a stag in full bloom. A fanciful beast, standing in the midst of an even more fanciful landscape of the largest chrysanthemums I've ever seen. As big as my oversize hands. Anemones, incurves, pompons, quills, spiders, spoons, and thistles. Solid white, solid yellow, beige and brown, gold and scarlet, mauve and blush, lavender and purple, and more. A rising field of this beside a rolling field of that. Hundreds of flowers pinched and pruned and fed and trained and arranged — just so, just so — by two mainland Chinese horticulturists who spent a whole year in Des Moines creating the stag in the field. And the chrysanthemum-feathered peacocks, one pair trailing their daintily flowered tail feathers behind them, the other pair holding their flowery plumage up like fans, as they stroll beside a pool of live koi. And the bonsai chrysanthemums. And the long sprays of orange and yellow mums cascading over a stone wall, on each side of a splashing waterfall. And the undulating stream of purple-eyed blush-white chrysanthemums, flowing beside a curved wall, laden with potted orchids, right under the banana tree laden with clusters of green fruit. Or were the orchids under the papaya tree? Or the banyan tree? Or the coconut palm? So many tropical botanicals, I almost forgot about the chrysanthemums and the children and the turtles on the log in the pool beneath the waterfall and the old folks strolling and sitting in pairs amid the curving walkways and the doves flying amid the trees, right beneath the silver dome. "In Xanadu did Kubla Khan a stately pleasure-dome decree: where Alph, the sacred river, ran through caverns measureless to man, down to a sunless sea." No wonder we got up early this morning and drove two hours west through rolling fields of pale dried corn and lush green winter wheat, the Black Angus feeding on hillsides in the middle distance, the steely farm ponds nestled in below, the flocks of crows circling overhead in the bright blue sky, scattered with mauve and white clouds. The clouds and the crows and the ponds and the cattle and the corn were still there on the way home, and so were the hillsides of evergreens and the browning oaks and the red-berried hawthorns — but looking, it seemed just then, like fields of chrysanthemums. Maybe it was that we were heading east and the sun was at our back. Or that we were tired and the light was playing tricks with our eyes. But somehow I don't think so.

THURSDAY *November 9*

The light sure wasn't playing any tricks on me this morning, not when I went out before breakfast to check on our own chrysanthemums, a little stretch of scarlets with yellow centers just outside the gazebo where Kate planted them some ten years ago. Even in the best of times, vivid as they are in late October, they'd still have paled in comparison to their brethren in Des Moines. But now they're faded and bedraggled by the weather and my protective sheets — their petals ruffled, their heads hanging this way and that. Oh for a dome, a geodesic dome. And not just for the flowers, but the rest of us as well. All the way down to campus this morning, the harsh wind and the fierce cold had me thinking fondly of that dome, and all the way back at noon too. I could hardly believe the weather forecast of temperatures in the fifties and sixties. And neither could Kate. The only good thing about the bad weather was that it inspired her to cook up a big pot of black beans for supper tonight. Black beans and rice. And what a concoction it was — somewhere between a soup and a stew, made from her own chicken broth, flavored with tomato juice, lemon juice, chopped fresh tomato, and a battuto of garlic, cayenne, oregano, mustard powder, and salt, then filled not only with the beans, but also with chopped onion, green pepper, more garlic, celery, and a diced defatted smoked ham hock. Black beans nonpareil. A rich, hot, spicy dish, just right for the weather. Except that the weather turned so warm in midafternoon it was safe for me to lift up the covers on the lettuce and radishes, and harvest enough for several meals. And what a surprise they were. Some of the radishes almost the size of Ping-Pong balls — I saved the biggest one to give to Lib as a get-well radish. And all the lettuces almost as big around as my foot. Big enough, all of them, to have captivated those Chinese horticulturists — their light green, dark green, and reddish-green leaves ruffling out like flowers, their petals more expansive than even the largest of those spectacular chrysanthemums. And there they were growing under my own protective covers, all arrayed in a decorative double row, but no one to pay them any attention. No schoolchildren, no old folks. Just me, gawking at all my greens, all of them alive and growing, even in the frigid temperatures of the past week. I couldn't help wondering just then what kind of animal or landscape those horticulturists might have made of them. I settled for a crisp salad of arugula, buttercrunch, green leaf, and red oak leaf lettuce, lightly dressed with Glenda's delicate olive oil and Kate's homemade basil red wine vinegar, to go with the black beans and rice, the chilled crisp radishes, and some Jamaican beer. Also a few slices of sesame semolina bread from the co-op, just for dipping in the juices of that spiky stew. Black beans with all the fixings. So warm and comforting a meal, on so mild and comforting an evening, I momentarily imagined I could ignore the winter storm that's coming tomorrow.

FRIDAY *November 10*

"That's a hard one, and I don't know the answer for sure. I know from hunting that whenever it's cold and it starts to rain and my clothes get wet, it's a lot colder with all those wet clothes on. A lot colder. So I wouldn't want those lettuces getting wet with a hard freeze comin' on. It might freeze 'em stiff, just like that." Just when I thought my six layers of row covers were enough to protect things down to the low teens, last night's forecast had me fretting again today, especially given the overnight rain, the prediction of snow, of steadily falling temperatures, and Kate's Thanksgiving menu, which called for a fruit salad on top of mixed greens from the garden. Even if we hadn't reviewed the menu over lunch, the lettuce would have been on my mind. The salad last night and the sandwiches at lunch had both of us going on about the crispness and tastiness of fall lettuce. So the thirty-degree temperature drop this afternoon had me panicking, and I called Jim to ask his opinion about putting a layer or two of plastic over the row covers. "Then again, I wouldn't want to lock in all that cold water and those freezing temperatures with a plastic tarp. That'd just make it worse. It's a real hard one. But if it was me, I guess I'd stick with your covers, just as they are. Especially with three or four inches of snow comin' on. That's better insulation than plastic. Besides, it's not supposed to get any worse than eighteen or twenty this time, and you've already gotten through worse than that." That was also the opinion I got from Bill, a carpenter who grew up on a farm just a few miles west of here and knows his way around situations like this. Bill's immaculate finish work is visible all around me in the attic — in the bookcases, the cabinets and the trim he made during a winter and spring as cold as this one's shaping up to be. So I decided not to use the two plastic tarps I bought at the lumber yard this morning. And now in late evening as I sit up here finishing this piece, I can hear the wind howling, I can see the snow covering the entire back yard — three or four inches just as they predicted. And I can tell the harvest's probably going to end a bit sooner than usual, maybe just a few weeks from now. All my holding devices can only work for so long — the row covers outside, the pears and peppers in the cellarway, the tomatoes ripening under paper on the basement shelves, the basil up here in the attic. As if the weather weren't enough of a harbinger, Kate turned into a messenger when she got home from visiting Lib this afternoon, looked through the mail, and eagerly called up to me the most important news of the day — "The first spring gardening catalogue just arrived! From Thompson and Morgan." Like everything else, a month or two early.

SATURDAY *November 11*

I felt reasonably secure about weathering the storm when I finished yesterday's report. But a few minutes later when I went out with Kate and Pip for our first midnight snow walk of the season — a major ritual for both of them — I didn't feel secure at all, especially after Pip and I went to check on the lettuce rows and couldn't see or feel any sign of the humped-up row covers. All I could imagine just then was a row of lettuce plants buried alive under the weight of the snow. Just like last year's first winter storm in early December. Pip, of course, couldn't have cared less. The snow and the wind and the chill and the walk with both of us in tow were all that mattered to him just then. Ears flapping, head bobbing, he plowed his way through snowdrifts all around the block, more buoyant than he's been since he lost the companionship of Phoebe. And Kate herself was so invigorated by Pip that she didn't have any solace to offer either, especially since she thought I probably should've put on the plastic tarp just to provide a little more support for the weight of the snow. And that made me wonder if I should try to remove some of the snow. "Just leave it alone. It's in God's hands now. Besides, if you try to remove the snow, you'll probably rip a hole in the row covers." I didn't think she needed to bring God into the picture, but it was clearly out of my hands. This morning, though, at the first light of dawn, I ran up here to get a bird's-eye view of the garden, and there were the covered lettuce and bok choy rows more humped up than I'd imagined. And the radishes too. And the junipers shagged in white. And the yard filled with crows. And the trees casting shadows on the snow. And Kate with even more sage advice for the day. "Just don't try to peek under the covers. Don't even think about lifting the covers. It's like baking a soufflé. You never open the oven door, otherwise the whole thing will flop." I never imagined that my lettuces might be as touchy as a soufflé, but I caught the drift of her advice. Still, I've been looking out there with longing, especially while I've been up here writing this piece, and even when I haven't been looking out there my mind's been there, I think. Otherwise I wouldn't have sliced off the tip of my right thumb at noon when I was shredding the cabbage for a salad with red peppers, tuna, oil, and lemon. Actually, my mind's been somewhere else all day long. First it was in Cleveland, in those mammoth snows of my Lake Erie childhood, so I called my aunt Ada, her voice more crackly, her hearing more antic than ever before. Then it was in Evanston, Illinois, at the Iowa-Northwestern football game. Then it was in Berkeley, when my brother Marshall called from California, just to let me know that it's seventy out there, and I might want to note it in the daybook. And now it's in the emergency room at the nearby hospital, where I'm going right after I finish this sentence, to see if they can stop my thumb from oozing blood all over the keyboard.

SUNDAY *November 12*

"Do you make it with mayonnaise or vinegar?" The emergency room nurse, Georgene, routinely asked me how I cut off my fingertip, but the minute she discovered I was slicing cabbage, her eyes lit up and she wanted to know the ingredients I use for the dressing. Right then I began to feel I was in good hands, especially after I told her my preference for lemon and oil. "Plain or olive oil?" Food, oh food — the universal language. Before I knew it, she was telling me about some of her favorite restaurants in Chicago, and then about a cooking display she'd seen on TV just a few hours before, involving the largest piece of strudel dough she'd ever seen in her life. "But the most surprising thing of all was when the camera panned on the audience, and it turned out to be a room filled with professional chefs, all wearing their tall puffy white hats. Can you imagine what that looked like?" With chatter like that to distract me, and a few injections to block the nerves in my thumb, I was feeling no pain when she and the doctor, Merry Jayne, started cleaning up the wound and dressing it. An hour or so later, with my arm in a sling and Georgene's admonishment ringing in my ears — "Keep that thumb above your heart, otherwise it'll start bleeding and throbbing!" — I drove home with my right arm in a sling and my left hand on the wheel, like a one-armed bandit on a quick getaway. Actually, I was eager to get home to the chicken breast I was planning to broil for dinner, and the spaghettini to go along with it, and the last of the little green zucchini sautéed in olive oil with our own sliced onions and a few chopped Enchantments and some fresh basil from the basement cellarway. Remnants of summer for a wintry day. The only problem, of course, was the thumb above my heart. But Kate pulled herself away from the Advent wall hanging she's been making for Hannah and played sous-chef for a while, not only chopping all the stuff for the zucchini dish, but also concocting an improvisation of her own for the spaghettini — sliced mushrooms, sautéed in butter, olive oil, and garlic, then braised in dry marsala wine and a little lemon juice, then slightly reduced for a topping. Then, truly, I was feeling no pain, especially after a few ibuprofen and a few glasses of wine. And now as I sit up here on this overcast Sunday afternoon, looking out upon the snow-covered landscape again, I'm still feeling no pain. Even after having visited the covered lettuces this morning and noticing that the snow has weighed down the row more heavily than I imagined. The first thought that came to mind just then was that next year I should use a few more hoops to hold up the covers in a snow like this. Then it occurred to me that I was already gardening a year in advance. Maybe the Thompson and Morgan catalogue wasn't as early as I thought. But when I turned around and looked up at the pin oak tree, still covered with leaves, many of them still green, or greenish red, or reddish brown, then, then I was back here, right now, wishing the snow had never come.

MONDAY *November 13*

"It's too early for this. Much too early." I was sitting across the conference table from my colleague Susan, waiting to begin a thesis exam, when she looked out the window, a pained expression broke across her face, and those words came rushing out of her mouth. Like an echo of Rebecca a month ago, when we were starting to wrap the tomato plants. But an unusual remark for someone as restrained as Susan, especially someone not given to chatting about the weather or the garden. I could tell from the rest of our conversation that she wasn't just talking about the snow, but also about the continuing temperatures fifteen or twenty degrees below normal, as if winter were here to stay. I was feeling much the same when I nearly fell on the ice-covered back steps this morning on my way to the compost pile, and again just now when I overheard Kate warning someone at the front door to be careful on the steps. It's not just the ice on the steps, it's the birds at the feeders — sparrows, juncos, chickadees, nuthatches, goldfinches, redpolls, cardinals, grackles, cowbirds, crows, woodpeckers. From sunrise to sunset, pecking at seed to keep themselves warm. At this rate, I think it might be spring before I get to peek under those row covers again. Kate says I'm "behaving like a kid with a scab who can't stop picking at it," which is actually not too far from how I'm feeling about the bandage at the end of my thumb. But my thumb and the lettuce and the bok choy and the row covers are nothing compared to the unraked leaves and the unturned garden and the clutter of snow-covered furniture, tools, pots, and supplies strewn around the gazebo and the terrace and the yard, waiting to be packed away in the basement. Like the redheaded woodpecker with the whirlygig wings standing in front of the freeze-dried corn stalks at the back of the garden — a constant rebuke every time I go out to peruse the row-covered vegetables nearby. Still, there's so little that can be done outside until a thaw comes our way that I'm almost tempted to visit the Tele-Garden again. Especially since my editor just called, so fascinated by the Tele-Garden that she's interested in the possibility of an epilogue on my eggplant seed and the world of desktop gardening. To water my seed, or not to water it, that is the question.

Before I come to terms with that question, I need to start putting all my other seeds in order. So, I've been sorting through my two plastic cartons of CURRENT VEGETABLE SEEDS — A–O and P–Z. From Arugula to Zucchini, looking first for the sure keepers, the ones that did so well this year and before (if I've grown them before) that I plan to grow them again. Like standard arugula. Greencrop, Jade, and Rocdor beans. Green Comet broccoli. Cashmere cauliflower. Cross Country picklers. Ichiban eggplants. Très Fin endive. Buttercrunch, Simpson Elite, and purple oak leaf lettuce. Ace and Biscayne peppers. German Giant radishes. Sunburst pattypan. Space flat-leaf spinach. Ruby Swiss chard. Big Beef, Brandywine, and Enchantment tomatoes. Tokyo turnips. Burpee zucchini. Also though I didn't grow it this year, Ambrosia cantaloupe. For taste, abundance, hardiness, and beauty, those are the best I've seen. As for the rest, the sure losers and the possible keepers, it's time to consult with the Vegetable Review Committee. For in just a few months, the time will come to be ordering and starting seeds for the spring garden.

TUESDAY *November 14*

"Where's the Silver Queen? How could you possibly leave it off the list?" The minute Kate finished reading yesterday's report, she was already convening a session of the committee. I could have explained that Silver Queen is the long-

est-season sweet corn ever bred — ninety-four days from planting
the seed to harvesting a fully ripened ear. So it's often hobbled by
drought or smut or intense heat before it ever comes to fruition. In
fairness, though, I'd also have had to admit that Silver Queen is
unquestionably the tastiest and most beautiful white corn ever
bred, possibly even the best all-round sweet corn ever bred. Given
that admission, I could easily imagine an endless debate about the
relative merits of the risks versus the rewards of growing Silver
Queen. One of those irresolvable questions that makes for the
mystery and the challenge of gardening. Instead of debating the
question, I simply decided to give it another try next summer and
hope for the best. After all, it's been three years since I last grew it,
and perhaps next season will be a good one for Silver Queen.
Besides, gardening, like farming, is always something of a gamble,
especially given the vicissitudes of the weather in Iowa. Why not
gamble on something like Silver Queen, especially when I already
have so many sure things going elsewhere in the garden? Not only
the ones I mentioned yesterday, but also vegetables I forgot to put
on the list. Like Walla Walla sweet onions, and Dutch purple
onions, and Dutch hybrid Spanish sweet onions. And the Con-
queror leeks I've grown in seasons past. So many sure things I
wonder why I even bother to consider the losers and the possible
keepers. But then I'm reminded again of that parable about the
fruitless fig tree — that timeless story embodying not only the
Christian spirit of forgiveness and mercy, but also an ecological
wisdom about the vagaries of the weather and other circumstances
that beset all living things. The seed that performed badly or just
adequately or moderately well this year might produce splendidly
next summer. Surely the Early Wonder beets would have come to
something had I planted them in spring rather than in late summer at the height of the heat wave. Maybe those fingerling potatoes might have produced more sizable tubers had I planted them
earlier. And perhaps the Liberty pickling cucumbers might have
lasted as long as the Cross Country cukes had I dusted them with
copper fungicide. The more I consider such questionable varieties,
the more it seems as if the gardener himself is coming under
review. But just to balance the record, I don't think the slightly
loose heads of the Packman broccoli are ever likely to be as firm as
the Green Comet broccoli, given the optimum care and weather

they both received from start to finish. Some things, after all, are not in the gardener but in the seed, not in the nurture but in the nature of things.

WEDNESDAY *November 15*

The most nurturing thing I could imagine right now, at least for the garden, would be a big enough thaw to melt all the ice and snow on the row covers, but it's not in the cards for today. So I've been thinking instead about one of the most nurturing things of my childhood, a fabled dish my aunt Celia used to make during the years I was living with my uncle Manny, a dish that never failed to warm me up on snowy days like these. A German-Hungarian concoction of stewed tomatoes alternating with layers of sauerkraut, alternating with meatballs, brisket, and kosher hot dogs. I can still see Aunt Celia in her flowered apron and her long print dress and her black clodhopper shoes, her white hair pulled back in a bun, standing at the kitchen counter, carefully building up the layers in the long, blue and white spackled enamelware roaster with the cover on top. And I can still smell all those spicy things slowly commingling as they cooked in the oven from Friday evening to Saturday evening. All day long that intense aroma gradually increased until it suffused the entire second floor of the big brick building where Uncle Manny's medical offices took up one side of the hall and our high-ceilinged living quarters the other. No wonder he never allowed Aunt Celia to make it during the week, when he was holding office hours afternoons and evenings. Then again he never forbade her to make it on the weekends. I can still remember him slowly rocking back and forth at the end of the long hallway, in his big flat-armed wooden rocking chair, his vest unbuttoned over his portly chest, taking in the fumes all Sabbath long, until it was time to celebrate its end in German-Hungarian fashion with the sauerkraut and the meatballs and the brisket and the hot dogs and all those intense juices — don't forget the juices, for God's sake — ladled on top. Or on top of the mashed potatoes. Or on top of everything, please.

I guess it must have been the jar of sauerkraut sitting on the counter last night when I came home from work that got me thinking about Aunt Celia's sauerkraut and meatballs, as we used to call it for short. Next to the sauerkraut, a pair of thick boneless tenderloin pork chops, and a welcome from Kate inviting me to make something of them for dinner. How could I resist the old yearnings? Especially given our own canned tomatoes? And our own onions, sage, and thyme for a bread crumb stuffing of the pork chops? Aunt Celia, of course, wouldn't have approved of the meat, so the next time I'm planning to get some garlic hot dogs from the Czech meat market in Cedar Rapids. Then again, I can't believe she'd have frowned upon the vibrant juices that arose from browning those paprika-dusted chops in oil and butter, then deglazing the pot with white wine before I layered up the tomatoes and sauerkraut and browned pork chops. And though it roasted for only an hour, I think Uncle Manny might have rocked to the smell, even on a Tuesday evening.

THURSDAY *November 16*

"I thought I told you not to go snooping around under those covers." Before I headed off for school this morning, I couldn't resist a little peek at the radishes. The snow and ice were all melted off, the temperature slightly above freezing and headed for the forties, so there wasn't any danger in lifting up the cover just at the end of the row. If it were simply a matter of wanting a fresh radish, I certainly wouldn't have bothered, not right after breakfast. No, I was interested in getting a hint of what might be going on under the ice-bound, snow-covered lettuce rows, without having to break the seal. More than that, I was wondering if I'd have anything fresh from the garden for Thanksgiving dinner. Even the lowly radish would be enough to satisfy me on that score. But when I told Kate about my little investigation, she had me feeling a bit like the time when Aunt Celia caught me fingering the edge of her fresh-baked pumpkin pie. Well, not exactly, because Aunt Celia had those long black eyebrows that she could angle into a really forbidding frown. And Kate had a slight twinkle in her eyes, even before I told her the good news about the radishes, their leaves still plucky, their bright red root balls edging above ground, as firm as before the snow and the freeze. Come to think of it, I now remember they made it through an even worse freeze and heavier snow last December, and survived long enough to provide a bunch from the very same spot when Hannah, Monty, Ben, and Lizzie were with us for Christmas.

I'd probably not have been so curious about the radishes this morning had Kate not been so full of her plans and displays for the Thanksgiving hors d'oeuvres the past two days. Bloody Marys made with our own homemade tomato juice, to go with her salmon mousse from a poached Atlantic fillet, the organic olives from California (garlic-stuffed, pimiento-stuffed, and Italian-spiced greens), and pumpernickel rye from the Lithuanian bakery in Omaha. Aunt Celia and Uncle Manny would certainly approve of the pumpernickel. But without my fresh radishes, something would have been missing — the crisp texture, the pungent garden taste to pair up with the Bloody Marys and to play off against the rest. Without the radishes, those hors d'oeuvres wouldn't be quite as captivating a treat for Lib, who's still bedridden in the infirmary for a few more weeks, so we're planning to take her a special care package of the hors d'oeuvres, every one of which is a favorite of hers, especially the olives and radishes. So much depends on a red radish, glazed with wet soil, under the white row covers.

Actually, it contains very little food value, except for some vitamin C. And I can hardly eat one without remembering the daikon radishes I burped up right before my heart attack some ten years ago. But they do taste good. And they sure will look good on a plate, right next to a dab of the pale pink salmon mousse, a few green and purple olives, and a slice of dark brown pumpernickel. Still life with radishes.

FRIDAY *November 17*

"What were you doing out there in your bathrobe and pajamas? I saw you when you were coming around the corner of the gazebo with a shovel in your hands." Kate's tone this morning was completely different from yesterday. Not even a hint of reproof. Just mild curiosity. I could hardly blame her, given how strange I must've looked in my burgundy robe over my green plaid pajama bottoms over my brown rubber snow shoes. It all started last night when I called up my graduate student Dan, to see if he could help turn the garden this weekend, what with the temperature predicted to reach the fifties tomorrow and Sunday. The thaw I've been waiting for to clean up the yard and the gazebo and the terrace and put the garden to bed for the winter. So, when I got up this morning, picked the newspaper off the front porch, and noticed how mild it was outside, I couldn't resist a little check on the condition of the soil. Dan wondered how heavy it was with water, and so did I. A few turns of the shovel, and I could see it wasn't as heavy and mucky as I'd feared — midway between mucky and moist, as I confirmed by pulling up the row of broccoli plants from last spring and the freeze-dried basil plants from this fall. Hardly any soil clinging to their roots. By that point I was just a few feet from the row-covered endive plants and couldn't resist a peek at the snow-free end where I'd put in a few surplus oak leaf lettuce plants. And there they were, their lower leaves a vibrant reddish green, only their tip leaves frost-nipped from the low-lying covers. Surely the hoop-covered let-tuces would be fully intact, and they were, as I discovered a couple of hours later, when the sun melted enough snow that I could lift the covers and look at the Simpson green leaf, before going into the office. Such good news that I hustled up the back yard to share it with Jim. The only problem is that my route to Jim's took me directly by the dwarf sweet cherry tree I planted this spring, its branches freshly chewed off, its bark completely stripped two thirds of the way down. The second time this season it's been savaged by the deer. And this time completely done in. I was furious with the deer the minute I saw the damage. But Jim wasn't home to sympathize. Kate was furious with me — and rightly so — when I called at noon to tell her about it. "Surely we've had enough trouble with deer, especially with that tree, that you should've known by now to put a tall wire fence around it. You know how it is with young cherry bark. But no, you've been so preoccupied with the lettuce you completely forgot about the young fruit trees. Some gardener!" Sometimes I just want to dig the proverbial hole and pull myself in after it. But right now, I'm thinking I'd better go home and put some tall fencing, or maybe the plastic tomato sheaths, or both, around the young apple tree and the other young cherry tree. Right away.

SATURDAY *November 18*

Jim was wearing his one-piece camouflage suit when I tracked him down by his garage yesterday afternoon. All worked up over his duck-hunting fiasco. "We didn't get a one. Not one. Ice already too thick. Can you believe it?" But the minute he heard about my deer-bitten tree, his eyes narrowed and he headed off to see the victim. "It's probably a buck did it. A buck with a big rack. I seen him the other night in my side yard. He didn't eat it. He barked it with his rack, like this." Just then, Jim bent down on his hands and knees and started rubbing his head up and down against the trunk of the tree. "That's his way of marking your yard. They're in rut now, so he's saying 'This is my place' to any other buck that comes along. He's also marking it to attract the does. He's probably also peed around it." He bent down again to smell the grass. "Sure enough, you can smell it. They also excrete some- thing from their eyes all along the bark. I seen 'em doing it when I'm out in the woods. In spring it's something else. Then they're rubbing the velvet off their new antlers. If he hadn't gotten this tree, he'd've gotten some other. I seen 'em bark things as big around as your pear." Listening to Jim, I was beginning to feel less guilty about my neglect, as if I'd knowingly saved the old pear tree by sacrificing the young cherry. Kate had a different view of it. "I thought they bugled or something. Why couldn't he just trumpet his presence and be done with it?" There's no accounting for a deer, so Jim helped me put plastic sheaths around the other young cherry and the young apple. Also a few more hoops to support the row covers over the lettuce. And then I called it a day.

Strange how a calamity one day can seem like a mere curiosity the next or just a blip on the screen of one's existence. Maybe I was distracted from the tree by Kate asking me to get a few kolaches at the church bazaar this morning. Or the mess of yard work to be done. Or Dan showing up to turn the garden, an annual reminder of my doctor's order not to lift heavy loads of soil (or anything else) on chilly days — I did turn a few shovelfuls, though, just to feel the heft of it again. Or the day itself, cloudy and cool to begin with but gradually turning sunny and milder by noon. Or the big vegetable garden gradually being put to bed as Dan turned the soil and I pulled out the dried corn stalks and the dead cosmos, marigold, okra, and sunflower plants. The accumulated stuff of an entire season's growth, fruition, and decay so quickly cast away. A mess of rotten straw, dried-up cucumber vines, sodden leaves, and soggy squash plants gradually turned under, gradually exposing the rich dark soil itself, chiseled by the spade, moistened by the snow, glinting suddenly in the noonday sun. Just the dark soil and the white row covers. So striking a contrast, so striking a change, I almost forgot about the deer-barked cherry tree, until Kate and Marybeth walked up to see it and returned, exclaiming, "How brutal it looks."

SUNDAY *November 19*

"This is how you can tell it's winter." Kate was hanging up the wind chimes right above the double sink in the basement, when I came down the cellarway steps with a load of garden tools in hand. I'd seen her taking the chimes down from the gazebo a few minutes earlier, while Dan and I were raking up the last batch of leaves from the terrace. Now I could hear them chiming away, for the last time this year. It never occurred to me until then that the silencing of chimes might be the signal of winter's onset. Maybe because I was checking off my own signs all morning long: Dan turning over the eggplant-pepper-tomato bed, now marked just by the heaved-up clods and the long white cover on the Thanksgiving radishes and green onions; Kate cleaning out the dead plants from her annual bed in the neighborhood park; Rebecca cutting down the tall dried plant tops still on display in Kate's flower border — the black-headed rudbeckia, the gray-stalked Russian sage, the brown-tipped snow-on-the-mountain. The bed was now a display of low-level foliage — the golden leaves of the Siberian iris, glowing in the slant November sun. And

I was carrying clay pots, plastic sheaths, rubber hoses, wooden tables and chairs, and cast iron creatures to the basement. The frog and carp from the lily pond, the bootjack cricket from the gazebo, the falcon lantern from the pear tree, and the stone turtle from the birdbath. The terrace stripped to its stony floor, and the gazebo bare except for the big stoneware tool crock and the small hanging lantern that Kate intends to light on Christmas Eve.

Winter? The day so balmy, the people so bouncy, I could hardly believe we'd just gotten free of an Arctic cold snap. There was Rebecca, hopping around the flower bed in her jean jacket, blue jeans, green socks, and green clogs. Dan, digging his way through the garden in an unbuttoned flannel shirt and a lightweight T-shirt. Kate, bagging up plants in her tan farm jacket, turtleneck, and brown corduroys. And I, hustling up and down in my overalls and a lightweight flannel shirt. So I could hardly believe I might have to plug in the stock-tank heater this week to keep the lily pond from icing over the languid goldfish. Or that I needed to straw up the turnips against a hard December freeze. Or that I had to get everything put away and buttoned up today. But when Dan's wife Maura showed up, and I gave them a six-pack of basil, her face lit up as she thanked me for "the winter basil." And when I gave her the bird's nest I found this summer, along came Kate, telling her to put it in their Christmas tree for good luck. As if it were then rather than now, and this day were an illusion. Late this afternoon, though, when I went to harvest some lettuce for dinner, and I knelt down on my hands and knees, the soil under the row covers was so cold it sent a chill through my bare fingers and palms. Chillier by far than the chimes I heard this morning, or anything else I felt today. Except, perhaps, for the prickly head of the old sunflower, looking down upon the row-covered lettuces. Cold comfort in a wintry season.

MONDAY *November 20*

Eight o'clock this morning, and I was gazing out the back door at Kate's Halloween pumpkin, sitting on the corner of the terrace wall where I put it yesterday afternoon, its toothless grin backlit through its orange rind by the rising sun. Kate thought I should get a picture of it, but the camera was out of film. The intense orange glow of its rind had me fantasizing about the pumpkin pie or pumpkin torte that Marybeth is planning to make for our Thanksgiving dinner from the two uncarved pumpkins I gave her on Saturday. Just then my reverie was shattered by the telephone, ringing on the wall right next to me, and then a cheery voice on the other end of the line — "This is Kim calling from Dr. Bauer's office. Just want to make sure you don't forget your nine-o'clock tooth-cleaning appointment." So much for the pumpkin's grin and my reverie.

Actually, the pumpkin's grin was nothing compared to Kim's greeting, once she had me flat on my back, scraping away on the inside of a molar. "I saw your garden on TV. Just a few months ago. Do you remember when that was?" Why is it, I wonder, that they always ask questions when you can't possibly get a word out, or even a nod for that matter, without risking damage to your mouth or their fingers? "I saw your garden, but I didn't see you. That sure must've felt strange, to see your garden and not your-self." My very thoughts, but I didn't dare utter them. Maybe Kim was getting me ready for John's dental inspection, for when he popped in the room and confronted me with another gardening question, I was momentarily silent, even though my mouth was then completely free and clear. "What'd you say was the name of that stuff you use to keep the deer away?" How surprising that he should pick up on our conversation of several months ago as if it had happened just a few minutes before. But I shouldn't have been surprised, given that John's a fellow gardener, and he too spent a summer contending with the deer. "They got almost all my stuff, the lettuce, the peas, the beans, even the tomatoes. One night in June, my wife was talking about how she planned to pick the peas the next morning, and they were really beautiful. But we never got a single one. Can you believe it? The only thing they didn't get were the potatoes. They don't know how to dig for potatoes. That's a good one, isn't it? They don't know how to dig for potatoes." John's a humorist, who usually regales me with a slightly off-color joke, so I figured that was the lead-in. But then he stiffened up, his face turned red, he put out his right arm to shake my hand, and said, "This is goodbye." He seemed right then to be on the verge of tears, and so was I. "I'm going to be sixty-five in a few months, and I just decided it was time to let go, to do some other things while there's still time. It was hard at first, real hard. But now I'm really feeling good about it." Then the smile was back on his face, his hands up in the air, and I was telling him about Hinder, and how often to put it on, and he was taking notes, and I could see he was planning to spend more time in his garden. And I could easily see why. A sweeter place by far than my mouth.

TUESDAY *November 21*

K ate's jack-o'-lantern was glowing again this morning, when I was about to leave for class, and I was thinking again about my conversation with John, especially about doing things while there's still time to do them — about seizing the day. Actually, I was thinking about that all day yesterday when the temperature was dropping to the mid-thirties after the mid-sixties on Sunday. And again this morning — the wind gusting up to thirty miles an hour, the wind-chill hovering around zero, and I shuddering at the thought of what it would have been like to put the gardens and gazebo and terrace to bed on a day like this. Then I was wondering if I too should be doing some of those other things while there's still time to do them. But in class today, when we were talking about Ellen's piece, called "Promised Land," I couldn't imagine any place I'd rather be than right there in that room, talking about her flawed but fascinating essay with that lively group of students. I certainly didn't hunger for the garden, not on a day like this, not for another four or five months. And I could wait a month for the promised warmth of Hawaii.

I was just where I should be, it seemed, until I went home for lunch, and Kate greeted me with a display of her most recent Thanksgiving harvest. The organically raised turkey, the gray candles to go in the amber glass candle holders, the gray-blue lavender stalks to go with the rust and red and burgundy and white mums waiting in the outside cellarway. Thanksgiving — only two days away, and I'd been musing about a time almost two years away. Actually, I too have been giving thanks, and not just for the fresh lettuce to go under the apple, pear, and grape salad with celery seed dressing, but also for all the preparations that have been going on the past month. The cubing and drying of the three different kinds of bread (plain white, French white, and sourdough) for the sage-onion-giblet dressing. The simmering of the turkey backs, necks, and giblets with onions, celery, and carrots to produce the turkey broth for the dressing and gravy. The extensive research into northern and southern variations upon the theme of baked oysters before discovering a Creole concoction of green onions and parsley (from our garden) together with cracker crumbs, lemon juice, cream, paprika, cayenne, Worcestershire sauce, and oysters from Galveston Bay. The secretive hoarding of our best homegrown Dutch onions for the creamed onions with yogurt, Tabasco, cheddar, parmesan, and Swiss cheese. The diplomatic choice of petits pois as the green vegetable (too bad some guests don't care for Brussels sprouts). The systematic review of corn bread and corn muffin recipes before settling upon our own invention of corn muffins with minced bits of Amana ham. And don't forget my homemade cranberry sauce with fresh minced lime added at the peak of boiling. Talk about seizing the day? I could almost devour it.

WEDNESDAY *November 22*

I could also imbibe it. Starting with Kate's homemade tomato juice, the quintessence of summer. With or without Tanqueray's juniper berry juice. And the other sacred fluids — Tabasco, Worcestershire, lemon or lime, with a celery stick to blend them. Then a host of other fruity pressings. A Côtes du Ventoux rosé, "with the sun of Provence in it," according to Wally, our local wine merchant who runs the best little shop in the state out of a nearby grocery known as John's. Kate and I stopped off there on the way home from visiting Lib, to pick up the Thanksgiving wine, and Wally as usual was running his daily degustation. Plastic sipping cups and all. So we tried a chenin blanc from the Columbia Valley "with the rain of Washington in it," according to Kate. Sweet in front, dry in the back — Wally's choice "to complement both turkey with trimmings and the slight saltiness of ham." And a bit later, just to cover all palates, I picked out a Johannisberg Riesling from the same valley, "distinctly dryer than the chenin blanc," according to Wally. Also a half gallon of locally grown cider, with no preservatives added, an uncompromising juice, softer and a bit sweeter, perhaps, than the chenin blanc, but a fine harvest companion to every part of the meal, especially for the teetotalers. Also for experimental purposes, sparkling cranberry cider from the co-op. And last but not least, we hope, a cherry bounce distilled by our neighbor Ken.

Speaking of precious fluids, don't forget the Kona coffee from whole beans that Kate mail-ordered from Hawaii! And the pint of fresh cream, oozing with sweet butterfat, that she picked up first thing this morning from Moss's dairy, a nearby Golden Guernsey farm — whole cream for whipping (gently, lest it turn to butter) to accompany the pumpkin dessert that Marybeth is bringing. Will it be a pie? Or a torte? Or some other confection? Whatever it is, I hope she doesn't forget the sugar. One fall, when Lib was still reigning over Thanksgiving at the old family place in Lisbon, she must've gotten so distracted by all the guests and preparations, she forget to add the sugar, an oversight that produced the most memorable pumpkin pie in everyone's experience. "Do you remember the year when Lib forgot . . . ?" And all the heads nodded in unison. Maybe that's why Kate usually offers me a spoon of this and a taste of that. A few minutes ago, it was a tangy sauce for the creamed onions, and by the time I've finished this piece, there might also be a nip of the salmon mousse. But the thing I'm looking forward to right now is the mulligan stew I can smell wafting all the way up here — the traditional preholiday soup that she learned from Lib, with the homemade broth, and the canned tomatoes, and the beef, carrots, onions,. and potatoes. A whole meal in a pot, with enough left over for Amelia and Joseph when they arrive this evening from Wisconsin. I can hardly wait to imbibe it.

THURSDAY *November 23*

Thanksgiving. And I could hardly wait to preserve it, before I devoured and imbibed it. So there I stood in the soft early morning light, gazing at the dining room through the viewfinder of my Pentax IQZoom, focused reverently on the table and the heirloom linen tablecloth with the cutwork ecru embroidery, and the burgundy stoneware with the carefully pressed napkins folded on top to display the cutwork pattern, and the old Fostoria amber glass bowl in the center, waiting to be filled with mums. Like a stage set before the play begins. But when I pressed the shutter-release button, the built-in flash didn't flash, the stage didn't light up. Not the first time, not the second, not even after checking the battery, the owner's manual, and the mechanical know-how of Joseph. It wasn't any better when I tried the old Ricoh and discovered its auto-filmforward still out of line. And it only got worse when I put the wine out to chill on the back porch and noticed one of our two remaining goldfish, belly up at the surface of the lily pond. Some Thanksgiving. The pilgrims at least had a new land, a good harvest, and their Wampanoag friends. But then I remembered how good I felt yesterday afternoon when the temperature rose into the fifties, and I was kneeling on the newly cut lawn, harvesting the radishes, green onions, and lettuce. And better still how I felt when Amelia and Joseph showed up with a head of their homegrown garlic and a batch of Wisconsin cheeses to go with the hors d'oeuvres — an herb-flavored goat cheese, a pesto jack, and a dill-garlic Havarti. So many things to be thankful for I was almost on the verge of slobbering with a sense of gratitude, when Kate swept downstairs in her nightgown and robe, down to the basement, and back up with the mums. First in the kitchen, arranging a centerpiece for the dining room, a set piece for the living room. Then in the dining room, decking out the table with serving pieces at her end, carving set at mine. Back in the kitchen, making up a package of hors d'oeuvres for Lib, to be delivered by Amelia and Joseph. The final preparations clearly underway. Countdown and bird launch just a few hours away. Then on to the stuffing, and "Yes, you can help by chopping some onion and picking a bunch of fresh sage and thyme and chopping it fine." Such a virtuoso performance, I could hardly wait for my own moment on stage — stuffing, trussing, roasting, and basting the bird itself. The only problem was Public Radio's Thanksgiving special, featuring Calvin Trillin's repudiation of the Pilgrims and turkey in favor of spaghetti carbonara, and the conjecture of a specialist at the American Museum of Natural History that the Pilgrims probably had dried beans, corn, and wild berries for their first Thanksgiving. It sounded just then as if I were about to take part in a politically and historically incorrect Thanksgiving. But the feel and smell of the sage, the taste and texture of the stuffing, were so captivating they swept me up in the myth of the moment. And I never recovered my senses. How could I, as I watched the bird turn golden brown, and smelled the herb-flavored stuffing, and tasted my wine-flavored, cream-laced gravy, and beheld Rebecca walking up the drive in a red beret and a blue brushed mohair robe with two loaves of fresh baked kuta-squash bread in hand, and then Marybeth and Ken and their daughter Elizabeth, with a four-layer pumpkin torte and a bowl of homegrown red raspberries and a chilled bottle of Spätlese and a haunting little pumpkin-colored doll made by Marybeth, with oak leaves on its body, bittersweet on its head, a white goose in its arms, and "Jack Frost Visits Goosetown" inscribed on the back of its head? Even if I had recovered my senses, I'd have lost them for sure at the dinner itself, and not just over the food, but what the food contained. A harvest beyond my wildest imagination, starting with Rebecca's announcement — "Look what I found in my oyster!" — and then her display of a diminutive pearl. That crisp, brown, Creole-flavored dish, baked under the broiler, was clearly a jewel beyond compare. No doubt about it, especially after Elizabeth quietly reported yet another pearl — "I found one, too." And then Marybeth — "I think I'm chewing on one, but I can't tell for sure." So many pearls, it seemed hard to believe I too was chewing on one, and my disbelief was confirmed when I came up with three little pieces of shell in my mouth. Some harvest. And that episode reminded Kate of the time when she casually flicked a red hibiscus into a steaming caldera on the Big Island, to appease the goddess Pele, and I followed suit, only to have my offering blown back in my face. But by that point in the meal, I was hardly feeling any sense of rejection, for Ken and I were engaged in a systematic empirical study of the various wines, in and of themselves, and in combination with the food. Nothing, of course, could match the combination of Marybeth's pumpkin torte and Ken's 1983 vintage bottle of Spätlese, though Amelia's memory of Lib's sugarless pumpkin pie ran a close second, especially the part where she remembered sprinkling sugar on her piece and Joseph nodded in agreement. Just then, it occurred to me that all our dinners and all our harvests and all our gardens lead back — back to the stories that bind us to one another and nurture us more than we may imagine, whether they tell of wild turkeys or dried beans and corn, of pearls or oyster shells.

FRIDAY *November 24*

A bottle of Spanish champagne and a row of limp-leaved bok choy. Hardly the way I expected the season and my story to end. But there's no predicting what might happen when Rebecca turns up, as she did this afternoon, in a yellow beret, with two of my plastic tarps, her dog Murray, and a bottle of champagne in hand. On her way out the door last night, she promised to bring back my tarps, and I promised some Chinese greens in return. But she didn't say anything about the champagne, and I certainly didn't expect anything to be wrong with the bok choy, especially given the mid-forties temperature this afternoon when Rebecca and I lifted up the row covers. I had in mind a dinner of turkey fried rice with stir-fried greens and a few sliced tomatoes. But it wasn't in the cards, not at least for tonight, not with the hangdog look of all that bok choy. "Didn't you know it dropped down to nine last night?" No, I didn't. No wonder Murray was about to pee on it. But Rebecca shooed him away, and we agreed to try again on Sunday when the temperature's predicted to be in the fifties or sixties, and the bok choy probably turgid again, especially because it didn't show any signs of being frozen or even frostbitten. Just a bit shocked by the big drop. Enough of a drop, though, to convince even me that it's probably time to harvest most of the greens and put a period to things before another Arctic storm comes along and makes its own conclusion. I'm not looking to set any outdoor records, just to keep eating our homegrown stuff as long as we can. Like the arugula and basil now taking the sun up here right behind my chair. Maybe I'd feel differently, more inclined to keep everything going outside under the row covers if I hadn't lost all of last year's fall lettuce one night in early December, when the temperature suddenly and unpredictably dropped below zero. Maybe I'd feel differently if Rebecca hadn't stopped for a moment to look at the yard and said, "I think it's beautiful just like this, when everything's put to bed." And it is, especially now in late afternoon, with the sun casting shadows on the lawn and Kate calling upstairs to "Look out the south window. Canada geese flying over the spruces. In double vees." Maybe, after all, I'd be inclined to keep things going a little longer if I hadn't gone down to the basement at noon to get a tomato for turkey, lettuce, and tomato sandwiches, only to discover they're all ripening so fast that some of them are beginning to rot before we can get them eaten. Even after giving several to Rebecca, I'm still feeling the pressure of those tomatoes. And it wasn't only the tomatoes that were speaking to me just then. Standing down there in our old stone-walled basement, surrounded by all the tools and pots and hoses and garden furniture, and the cast iron garden creatures staring me in the face, and all the potted plants sitting on the steps of the Plexiglas-covered cellarway, I suddenly realized the season is virtually over. The earth has been turned. The gardens are tending themselves. The geese are flying over the spruces. In double vees. So, when Rebecca comes over this Sunday, I'm planning to break out that bottle of champagne and drink to the end of the growing season. By that time, I should have all my seeds put away in their new storage chest, safely housed until the coming of spring.